Workers'
Struggles,
Past and Present

WORKERS' STRUGGLES, Past and Present

A "Radical America" Reader

Edited by James Green

Temple University Press
Philadelphia

Temple University Press, Philadelphia 19122
© 1983 by *Radical America*. All rights reserved
Published 1983
Printed in the United States of America

Library of Congress Cataloging in Publication Data

Main entry under title:

Workers' struggles, past and present.

Articles published in the journal from 1967 to 1982.
Includes index.
1. Labor and laboring classes—United States—History
—20th century—Addresses, essays, lectures. 2. Trade-
unions—United States—History—20th century—Addresses,
essays, lectures. I. Green, James R., 1944–
II. Radical America.
HD8072.5.W67 1983 331.88'0973 83-4656
ISBN 0-87722-293-2
ISBN 0-87722-315-7 (pbk.)

TO
C. L. R. JAMES
AND
E. P. THOMPSON

Contents

Contents

Contents

Workers'
Struggles,
Past and Present

Introduction

by James Green

This reader contains a selection of articles about workers' struggles in the United States published in the journal *Radical America* during the fifteen years from 1967 to 1982. The topic headings correspond to some of the main political and historical concerns of the activists and historians who have written for the journal. These include the struggle for control at the point of production, the problem of organizing the unorganized, the relationship of rank-and-file militancy to union politics, and the quest for workers' control.

The writers who have contributed to this collection share certain perspectives on workers' struggles. First, these writers examine the unrecognized potential of mass struggles organized by rank-and-file workers themselves. In the past, labor historians concentrated largely on organizations and their leaders, and often ignored the struggles and aspirations of ordinary workers. Second, *Radical America* historians extended their inquiry beyond the traditional economic and political concerns to include social and cultural questions. As a result, *RA* never confused the history of unions and political parties with the larger story of working-class struggle. Indeed, the journal took a critical view of labor organizations for failing to represent the working class as a whole and for reducing the goals of workers' struggle to narrow economic and institutional demands. The struggles described in this reader involve much more than issues of wages and working conditions. They also center around issues of dignity, freedom, and control.

Introduction

Radical America emerged from the student and anti-war movements of
the late 1960s. This is a bit ironic since those movements spurned class
analysis and rejected the labor movement as an agency of radical change.
Paul Buhle founded *Radical America* in 1967, and for the first four years it
was published mainly by a group of radical graduate students at the University of Wisconsin in Madison. That campus had been swept by militant
actions against U.S. involvement in the Vietnam War and had spawned an
active chapter of the Students for a Democratic Society (SDS), a radical
organization that reached its peak in 1968.[1] Indeed, until 1970 *RA* called
itself "An SDS Journal of American Radicalism." Buhle and the other
editors wanted to explore past radical movements and draw lessons the New
Left could use in its own organizing efforts.

The New Left developed during the early 1960s in the political vacuum
left by the suppression of the Communist Party in the late 1940s and the
repressive McCarthy period that followed. The New Left, however, had
little in common with the old Communist Left. Young radicals did not
defend the Soviet Union as a socialist society. Indeed, the student movement was not explicitly socialist at first. For example, SDS's Port Huron
statement of 1962 adopted a vague moralistic stance attacking the Cold War
mentality and calling for a revival of democracy. Young radicals of the 1960s
shared a disgust with the cultural conformity, moral hypocrisy, and political
apathy that characterized the era.[2]

Inspired by the civil rights movement in the South, the New Left grew in
certain private colleges and a few leading state universities like Wisconsin,
Michigan, and California. SDS drew important lessons from the black
freedom movement, which seemed to embody the concept of "participatory
democracy," the notion that people could and should make "decisions that
affect their lives." The explosive "free speech" fight at the University of
California, Berkeley, in 1964 crystallized New Left opposition to the modern university as a bureaucracy serving the needs of the military-industrial
complex. In 1965 SDS sponsored a march on Washington protesting increased U.S. intervention in the Vietnamese civil war. In the next few years,
an anti-war movement spread across the nation's campuses, fueled by
anti-draft activity. Uprisings of urban blacks, which began in the Watts
section of Los Angeles in 1965, continued in the bloody encounters of 1967
and in the aftermath of Dr. Martin Luther King's assassination in 1968. At
the same time a black power movement led by revolutionaries challenged
the established leadership of the civil rights movement and the strategy of
gaining racial integration with non-violent tactics. The growing militancy of
the anti-war and black power movements led many New Leftists to adopt
revolutionary political views on racism, imperialism, and capitalism.

While many New Leftists turned increasingly toward Marxism and
Leninism, the movement continued to espouse cultural radicalism. Student
rebels not only embraced cultural revolution as it appeared in Cuba and

China and in the ideas of black nationalists; they also experimented with radical cultural activities at home. In the early sixties many students identified with folk culture as expressed by singers like Bob Dylan, but later on they turned to the more alienated forms of "acid rock" that celebrated youth culture and drug use. Young people also experimented with communal living and their own underground art forms. Though New Left cultural criticism attacked the traditional family, the movement and the counterculture were male-dominated. During the late 1960s radical women in the civil rights and student movements began to criticize male chauvinism in the movement and create their own cultural activities like consciousness-raising groups.[3] From these roots sprang the modern feminist movement, and a vital critique of hierarchical, authoritarian politics. *Radical America* was especially influenced by the New Left's cultural radicalism and by feminist ideas about culture and politics.

In 1969 and 1970 the New Left broke into factions, with one group maintaining the old Marxist-Leninist view about organizing a vanguard party to lead the working class and another faction holding to its support for black nationalism and youth rebellion. The anti-war movement had been the engine of radicalism in the late 1960s. It receded when massive protests against the U.S. invasion of Cambodia in 1970 failed to force a withdrawal of American troops. By the end of that year the New Left ceased to exist as a movement. Various forms of radicalism had taken on a life of their own. Black nationalism as represented by the Black Panther Party flourished briefly but suffered from severe police repression and internal dissension. The women's liberation movement charted its own course. While some feminists remained hostile to Marxism, others began to espouse a kind of socialist-feminism. Some of this thinking appeared in *Radical America* during the early 1970s. Those in the New Left who took youth rebellion to its extreme conclusion disappeared into the Weather Underground and suffered imprisonment or exile. Far more student radicals joined Marxist-Leninist groups, took jobs in factories and moved into working-class neighborhoods, and became active in local unions. In its own way *Radical America* took this turn toward the working class. Indeed, its attention to labor history had been there from the start. In 1970 labor historian David Montgomery, socialist and former union activist, issued this appeal: "American socialists cannot hope to develop a valid theoretical perspective for our times without an accurate assessment of the present aspirations of this country's industrial workers."[4]

In 1971 *Radical America* moved from Madison to Boston, a symbolic break with the journal's roots in the student movement. The editors were now former students who worked as teachers and in various "movement jobs." In the issue announcing the move editors Paul Buhle and Jim O'Brien evaluated the eclipse of the New Left and emphasized the narrow middle-class base of 1960s radicalism. The editors announced that *RA* would continue to be "largely concerned with the history, development and prospects of the American working class." And since American Marxist theory had been so limited, they would continue to look to the European left when it shed light on developments in the U.S. Paul Buhle bravely set out "39 Propositions" about Marxism in the U.S. and advocated a "new kind of political formation" in which cultural freedom and liberation from racism and sexism became an integral part of the struggle for working-class power.[5] In sum, *Radical America* had anticipated the New Left's turn toward working-class politics, but it did not welcome the return to the conventional Marxist-Leninist formulas for party building. Some *RA* writers drew upon more imaginative kinds of Marxism and followed the suggestions of George Rawick, whose 1969 article on "Working-Class Self-Activity" (Chapter 6) stressed the inherently radical nature of struggles workers organized for themselves.

Of course the New Left turn toward the working class resulted in part from renewed labor militancy, which was generated by the pro-business policies of the Nixon administration and by the recession that followed as the U.S. withdrew from Vietnam and decreased war-related production. In 1969 West Virginia coal miners launched their own political strike to force the passage of a black lung compensation law. Black autoworkers in Detroit who were disciplined after a wildcat strike formed the Dodge Revolutionary Union Movement. In France and Italy massive uprisings of workers and students in 1968 and 1969 took the official trade unions and left-wing parties by surprise and showed that young workers were open to New Left ideas and to autonomous forms of mass organization. In this country a young generation of factory workers rebelled against speed-up and authoritarianism, notably at the new General Motors assembly plant in Lordstown, Ohio. Moreover, rank-and-file union members openly opposed conservative union leaders, most dramatically in a 1970 national postal workers' wildcat strike and in Appalachia, where the formation of the Miners for Democracy followed the murder of union insurgent Jock Yablonski and his family. In 1972 Stan Weir, a socialist veteran of workplace struggles since the 1940s, outlined the new alignments of class forces in the seventies (Chapter 12) and emphasized the exciting possibilities for radical change, especially among younger workers affected by the anti-war movement and the 1960s counter-culture.

During the 1950s and 1960s the dominant school of labor history took a very limited view of what workers and their organizations could accomplish. Professor John R. Commons and his students founded this school of interpretation at the University of Wisconsin, where radical history students would publish *Radical America* many years later. The Commons School produced impressive institutional histories of trade unions which often justified narrow, conservative forms of organization on the grounds that workers demanded no more and conditions allowed for no more. Socialist ideas about class-conscious solidarity and worker control allegedly came from utopian intellectuals, not from hard-headed workers.

Early issues of *RA*, on the other hand, showed that workers had been agents of radical change. Mass strikes, like the ones described by Mike Davis (Chapter 3), showed how unskilled, non-union workers could challenge capitalist control. The activity of the Industrial Workers of the World (or Wobblies) demonstrated to *RA* historians the unrecognized radical potential of mass struggles organized by workers themselves and supported by revolutionaries who were willing to follow the workers' lead. The Wobblies believed in direct democracy versus bureaucracy, direct action versus electoral politics, equality versus hierarchy, and internationalism versus nationalism. These were values New Left radicals could readily embrace, all the more so because they were held by proletarians, not students.[6]

Marxist historians did construct an alternative to the Commons school's interpretation by emphasizing class struggle. For example, Philip Foner produced a series of important books detailing the disastrous effects of exclusionary business unionism on the labor movement. Rank-and-file workers, he suggested, would have taken a more class-conscious route if they had not been misled by Samuel Gompers and other conservative officials.[7]

New Left historians faulted this Old Left version of labor history on several grounds. In the mid-sixties, radical historians argued that Foner's class-struggle approach ignored the way in which the "corporate liberals" in business and government had co-opted the labor movement. Trade union leaders from Samuel Gompers of the AFL to Sidney Hillman of the CIO found accommodation more attractive than confrontation. James Weinstein also rejected the Old Left's criticism of Socialist Party reformism. The socialist movement provided a viable alternative to business unionism until it was suppressed during World War I and split apart by the new Communist movement in 1919.[8]

These new viewpoints appeared in *Studies on the Left*, a journal founded in 1959. A number of the editors and contributors studied at the University of Wisconsin with William Appleman Williams, the leading New Left historian. In *The Tragedy of American Diplomacy* and other works Williams explained U.S. expansion abroad as a result of capitalists' search for new markets. Big business and its political allies defended imperialism, but so did many leaders of farmers' and workers' organizations who also wanted foreign markets for the goods they produced. Williams's interpretation became important to New Left attacks on modern U.S. imperialism, especially in Vietnam.[9]

Other New Left intellectuals expressed more direct pessimism about workers' capacity for change. The radical sociologist C. Wright Mills described postwar labor leaders as "pro-capitalist" managers of discontent. In his well-known 1960 letter to the British New Left, Mills said he did not understand why some New Left writers "clung so mightily to 'the working class' of advanced capitalist countries as *the* agency of historic change, or even as the most important agency, in the face of the really impressive historic evidence that now stands against this expectation."[10] In 1963 philosopher Herbert Marcuse published his influential book *One Dimensional Man*, in which he analyzed the cultural and political bases of corporate domination in America. Marcuse saw workers alienated from work and from politics and escaping into consumerism.[11]

Radical America historians shared some of these critical perspectives but they rejected the pessimism of the early New Left theorists. They also criticized the historical work in *Studies on the Left*, which ceased publication in 1967, the same year *RA* was founded. Those historians who emphasized the hegemony of corporate liberalism concentrated largely on organizations and leaders without examining the activities of ordinary working people. They also read back the conservative status quo of the post-World War II years into earlier periods. In doing so they "virtually read class conflict out of American history."[12]

Radical America historians needed a theoretical approach that transcended the economic determinism and political elitism of the Old Left as well as the cultural pessimism of the early New Left. Since left theory in the U.S. tended to be one-dimensional, *RA* historians looked for a more imaginative Marxist approach to history and politics. They turned to the work of two activist historians from abroad, C. L. R. James and E. P. Thompson, to whom this book is dedicated.

C. L. R. James, born in Trinidad, became a leading Caribbean intellectual through his writings, which ranged from fiction to cricket reporting. He was best known for his powerful 1938 history of the San Domingo slave revolution, *The Black Jacobins*. During the 1930s James lived in England, where he joined the Trotskyist movement and helped form the pan-African nationalist movement. When James came to the U.S. in 1938 he joined the small Trotskyist movement and plunged into learning about American conditions. As a spokesman for an opposition group within the Workers' Party and later as the leader of his own little group in Detroit, James published a remarkable collection of philosophical and political writings before his deportation from the United States in 1953.[13]

James called for a return to Marxist fundamentals and to dialectics as outlined by Hegel and applied by Marx and Lenin. All historical development occurred through "self-movement, not organization or direction by external forces," he wrote. Applying dialectical Marxism to Russian history, James argued that the Communist Party bureaucracy had captured the Soviet Union and created what he called state capitalism. Alienation afflicted workers in the Soviet Union and Eastern Europe just as it did in the United States and Western Europe. The Hungarian Revolution of 1956 showed that working-class self-activity in Stalinist states could lead to outright rebellion. Nothing so dramatic touched the U.S., but the same contradictions existed. Socialist intellectuals should emphasize to workers their own power and bring out the "socialism that exists in the population, the resentment, the desire to overturn and get rid of the tremendous burdens by which capitalism is crushing people." Intellectuals should not lecture workers on correct political lines, James maintained, but they should make their views known "as a contribution to that democratic interchange and confrontation of opinion which is the very life-blood of socialist society."[14]

Radical America started publishing C. L. R. James's writings in 1968, and they appealed strongly to the New Left sensibility. James's revolutionary optimism contrasted favorably with the view of the modern worker as a one-dimensional economic man. His book *Facing Reality*, written in 1958, also seemed to one young reader to be "full of practical suggestions for socialist activity that were decidedly different than the shoddy manipulations many of us associated with 'vanguard' politics."[15]

Finally, James demonstrated the importance of cultural activity through his writing on black nationalism and Pan-Africanism. In *The Black Jacobins* he employed the notion of self-activity to show how African slaves used their own cultural traditions and the ideas of the French Revolution to create an autonomous national liberation movement that overthrew the master class as well as a succession of imperial armies and then founded the black republic of Haiti. The essays in this collection by Harold Baron, Manning Marable, and Ernest Allen share a similar perspective on the importance of independent black movements for the class struggle as a whole. Furthermore, as a James associate, George Rawick, showed, the concept of self-activity could be useful in understanding not only black liberation movements but workers' struggles of all kinds.[16] Rather than despairing over the lack of theory, the corruption of unions, or the absence of a strong Socialist Party, *RA* writers were inspired to examine actual workers' struggles, past and present, to see in what ways they prefigured the coming socialist society.

E. P. Thompson's historical and political work also shaped *RA*'s approach. After the Russian army suppressed the Hungarian Revolution in 1956, Edward Thompson left the Communist Party of Great Britain. He then became a leading activist in the peace movement and the British New Left. His hugely influential book *The Making of the English Working Class*, published in 1963, showed New Left historians that culture could not simply be reduced to "superstructure." Culture had a life of its own and influenced politics in ways previous Marxist historians had ignored. Thompson believed that class was a "historical relationship" that emerged in different ways at different times, and that class consciousness emerged in unpredictable ways depending on historical and cultural contexts. Rather than be governed by theories or laws of history, he studied the "peculiarities" of the English and emphasized the political importance of unique cultural traditions. These ideas proved liberating to radical historians in the U.S. who were laboring under the weight of the social science theory that America was an exceptional place, free from class conflict and class consciousness.[17]

By 1968 historians like Herbert Gutman, Jesse Lemisch, Staughton Lynd, and George Rawick had written about the serious resistance movements created in the U.S. by peasant immigrants, revolutionary sailors, colonial tenant farmers, and rebellious slaves.[18] These insurgents were not to be dismissed as "primitive rebels" but rather understood as conscious working people whose struggles generated serious social conflict and created important cultural forms and political ideas. Just as Thompson carefully and lovingly described the Romantic poets, village atheists, and utopian artisans who attacked the new capitalist order in Britain, radical historians of the 1960s described dissenters in this country. If historians stopped looking for some ideal form of proletarian socialism, the history of workers' struggles in this country looked very exciting, not exceptionally passive. Perhaps the New Left's cultural radicalism made it easier to identify with the romantic rebels of the preindustrial era who expressed their dissent in peculiarly American voices.[19]

In order to write what Jesse Lemisch called a "democratic history from the bottom up" *RA* historians adopted the methods and approaches Thompson and other social historians used to study ordinary people's lives. They also employed the oral history techniques first introduced by the Federal Writers' Project in the 1930s and popularized by Studs Terkel in the 1960s.[20] Staughton Lynd, fired from his teaching job at Yale for his "strident" protest against the Vietnam War, led the way in applying oral history to radical concerns. He helped to organize a workshop in Gary where steelworkers criticized the 1971 contract and wrote alternative provisions based on the demands of rank-and-file caucuses and insurgent locals. He also worked with Alice Lynd interviewing veteran union organizers who explained how the early militancy of the CIO had been deflected or suppressed. Lynd used some of these interviews in his historical essay (Chapter 9) on the rank-and-file steelworkers' movement of the early 1930s and why it failed to create a more militant, democratic national union.[21] Like James and Thompson, Staughton Lynd showed how an activist historian could work outside of the academic establishment and write sophisticated history that addressed present-day tasks of movement building.

In 1971 *RA* began a series on "Work in America" which featured subjective accounts of alienation and resistance on the job. Some of these reports examined the role of the informally organized work group as a locus of resistance and creative activity; this approach provided a useful alternative to studies focusing entirely on unions and other formal organizations. For example, one lively report on resistance and sabotage in an auto factory revealed what the author called "counter-planning on the shop floor." This, he argued, was a new social form that could succeed modern unions and provide the basis for a less bureaucratic, more democratic organization, like the workers' council. In "Their Time and Ours" a Chicago postal worker offered a surrealistic account of how people's "play time" allowed them to oppose a regimented labor process. In the capitalist labor process play seemed to be irrational or escapist because it represented the refusal "to submit to the brutal 'rationality' of work." In a worker-controlled post office, play would be a regular part of the work day. John Lippert's article on "shop-floor politics" in a Cadillac assembly plant (Chapter 18) also describes how play unified the vanguard group of workers who rejected the "wages for work exchange." In another article in the "Work in America" series a Detroit clerical worker discussed the "work community" and distinguished between the informal work process which brought workers together, often in cooperative efforts, and the "authority system" which workers often refused to take seriously.[22]

Other *RA* writers also employed the informal work-group concept, especially Stan Weir, a former seaman, dockhand, and autoworker. He argued that informal work groups acted as the cadre for organizing the CIO industrial unions in the 1930s and for the wildcat strikes against the wage freeze and the speed-up during World War II. He has criticized left organizing theory for focusing entirely on formal trade union and party structures without addressing workers' informal group life where militancy and creativity have often originated.[23] In his analysis of workers' struggles (Chapter 12), he insisted that in the 1970s the left would remain isolated from spontaneous and potentially radical outbursts of working-class militancy and political activity unless it developed a new theory and practice based on the reality of workers' daily lives.

The informal work group was clearly the center of the "work community" described by Susan Porter Benson explains in her revealing article on "the clerking sisterhood" (Section I). *RA* has yet to publish articles following Benson's suggestion that women workers' group life differed significantly from that of craftsmen. Indeed, the journal has not fully explained why some informal group activities, wildcat strikes for example, involve militant opposition to capital and the State while others may also involve the exclusion of minority and women workers. Furthermore, the emphasis on group activity and work culture has rarely extended beyond the capitalist workplace to the home, the family, the community, and other social settings. In recent years, feminists writing in *RA* have studied various working-class cultural activities like watching daytime television, organizing Tupperware parties, and joining family camping groups. They have also explored various cultural spaces used by women like beauty parlors, battered women's shelters, and self-help groups.[24] And they have explained how these seemingly "free spaces" are still affected by traditional cultural forms that inhibit liberation. It has been difficult, however, for historians to discover this dimension of working-class life in the past partly because sources are lacking. For example, Marxists and feminists intensely debated

11

the politics of housework in *RA* during the early 1970s, but the journal never published a historical article on women's work in the home or on the housewife's place in the working-class community. This gap in *RA*'s cultural approach to history is particularly unfortunate because the social historians who have studied workers' daily lives often romanticize traditional culture as a basis for resistance and exaggerate the freedom women enjoyed within their own sphere.[25]

Radical America, however, was influenced more by feminism than were any New Left or labor-oriented publications that continued into the seventies. Indeed, in 1970 the journal published a special issue on women's liberation and a year later featured a pathbreaking article by three women's historians who combined feminism and class analysis.[26] Another special issue on women's labor in 1973 aimed toward a synthesis of Marxism and feminism, but this merger would prove elusive. As *RA* editor Linda Gordon explained, Marxists had not provided a "good definition of what class is for women." The working-class experience had to be understood "not just in the shop but also the home, in bed, in ball parks and movie theatres."[27]

In other words, *RA*'s failure to move historical analysis beyond the workplace and the political group to include the family and the community could not be blamed simply on lack of sources or lack of imagination. There were conceptual and political reasons as well. From a feminist viewpoint, the journal still focused largely on wage-earners as economic and political beings, not as human beings in the fullest sense. This criticism, which came from within the editorial collective as well as from the outside, forced the editors to reexamine their approach.[28] A reconsideration seemed all the more necessary as the political situation changed. By 1979 it appeared that "cultural crises—the family, sex, religion, crime, abortion, homosexuality—easily compete[d] with economic ones for popular attention and anxiety." The New Right's appeal to working people centered almost entirely on cultural and sexual issues, and the Left had no serious or appealing cultural response.[29] The challenge *Radical America* carries into the eighties is to model its political and historical work on an original insight of the women's movement—that "the personal is political." In recent years the journal has expanded its definition of what is political in order to explore more fully the prospects for human liberation from the frightening world capitalism has made.

Since *Radical America* formulated historical questions through its understanding of contemporary struggles, the discouraging events of the seventies led to a reconsideration of the journal's approach to autonomous workers' movements. The rapid collapse of the League of Revolutionary Black Workers, discussed here by Ernest Allen (Chapter 14), showed how difficult it was for a militant group to oppose the recognized union and maintain shop-floor power in an industry. The disbanding of the Miners for Democracy followed the victory of a reform slate in the United Mine

Workers Union and indicated how easily independent movements could be incorporated into trade union structures. The founding of the Coalition of Labor Union Women in 1974 seemed to promise an autonomous arena in which socialist-feminists could make direct contact with women workers, but within a short time top labor union officials took firm control of CLUW and outflanked the left.[30]

In Europe the large New Left formations of workers and students did not survive long in the 1970s. The Italian extraparliamentary Left, which exerted a strong influence on *RA*'s politics, suffered from factionalism and repression. The largest group, Lotta Continua, experienced police harassment and false identification with Red Brigade terrorism. The New Left in Italy revealed the exciting possibilities of a radical movement autonomous of trade union and political party structures. Lotta Continua also developed an interesting body of post-Leninist theory in which the idea of "mass vanguards" replaced that of the self-appointed vanguard party. Even before its suppression, however, the Italian "autonomista" movement left many questions unanswered. Its militants had not clearly shown how to link up various autonomous struggles without the leadership of a union or party, and they had failed to integrate the kind of cultural or feminist analysis that emerged from the New Left.[31]

Of course all of these initiatives suffered from the impact of a worldwide economic slump. In the U.S. inflation and unemployment discouraged militancy, and the level of wildcat strike activity dropped off dramatically. Unofficial strikes still erupted and *RA* worker-writers confirmed the important role of informal work groups in these autonomous struggles. But shop-floor reports also indicated that these locally initiated insurgencies remained quite isolated.[32] Even the coal miners' strike of 1977–1978, which came closest to being a national struggle controlled by the rank and file, failed to break out of the legal and organizational nets that weighed so heavily on independent workers' movements (Chapter 17).

Of course socialists could celebrate victories in other parts of the world during the seventies, notably the triumph of Left-led national liberation movements in Vietnam, Angola, and Nicaragua. But *RA* had never adopted Third World political models as readily as had some segments of the New Left. The military strategies adopted by Marxist-Leninists abroad seemed of less relevance to workers' movements in industrialized countries than the Left-led movements that mobilized workers in countries like Chile, Portugal, and Poland. But of course the revolutionary workers' movements in these countries all met with crushing defeat.

These events led to a shift in discussion about workers' struggles. Initially, working-class self-activity and autonomous struggle were the main subjects of the journal's inquiry. During the 1970s these subjects became problems for debate and reconsideration. For example, in 1972 a special issue on working-class militancy during the Depression underlined the radical potential of self-organized workers' movements. In 1975 a similar issue on labor in the 1940s placed far more emphasis on the ways in which unions and the government joined employers to restrict rank-and-file militancy and to expel the organized Left from the labor movement.[33]

Some *RA* writers then returned to the Old Left's study of the objective conditions that inhibited or defeated class-conscious movements and to the early New Left's emphasis on the co-optive effects of state intervention and regulation. Contributors also followed Harry Braverman's *Labor and Monopoly Capital* in studying how capitalists used scientific management and technology to deskill workers and to fragment work groups.[34] The journal also concentrated more on the divisive role of racism and sexism in working-class struggles. Early articles on the Southern Tenant Farmers' Union and the CIO showed how black and white workers united and fought together, whereas later issues explained how racism had become the main obstacle to working-class unity.[35] Located in Boston, *RA* was strongly affected by the violent school-busing crisis of the mid-seventies when the struggle against racism seemed far more vital than any effort to manufacture unity among black and white workers.[36]

This turn toward a more structuralist analysis of the workplace emerged together with criticism of *RA*'s emphasis on spontaneity and its somewhat anarchist perspective on the need for autonomous struggle. After the New Left and black power movements disintegrated and the women's movement suffered from fragmentation and frustration, leftists who read and contributed to *Radical America* participated more in established organizations, notably local trade unions. The contributions to this book by worker-writers like Dorothy Fennell, John Lippert, and Dave Wagner discuss the possibilities and limitations of such activity. Labor historian David Montgomery, who first called upon the New Left to make an assessment of working-class struggles in 1970, questioned the view that unions always functioned as "agencies which deprived workers of the power to control their own destinies." Surely, union leaders, structures, and demands had been "successfully incorporated into American capitalism time and again," but this happened to all kinds of workers' struggles that stopped short of taking real power. Even workers' councils had been bureaucratized or absorbed by trade union structures.[37] Nonetheless, union organization could "unleash shop-floor struggles in the first place, rather than contain them." For Montgomery a dialectical relationship existed between spontaneity and organization, not a one-way line from militancy to bureaucracy. Socialism grew from "the work and living patterns of working people" and not just from the intervention of external vanguards. Like Edward Thompson and C. L. R. James, Montgomery maintained that socialism would take root in the "mutualism" that developed from workers' "daily struggle for control of the circumstances of their lives." This mutualism appeared in workers' "values, loyalties and thoughts" as well as in their daily actions, but such spontaneous activity could "only triumph by becoming increasingly conscious and articulate." As Montgomery reminds us in his concluding essay, "The struggle for workers' control advances only as it moves from the spontaneous to the deliberate, as workers consciously and jointly decide what they want and how to get it."[38]

As a result of this sort of discussion *Radical America* developed a more subtle approach to the relationship between spontaneity and organization. At the same time, feminist criticism deepened the journal's understanding of the relationship between culture and society and between personal and political life. Questions of strategy and tactics will continue to be debated within the pages of *Radical America*, and so will the political and historical questions about how best to understand workers' history. But the journal's approach will undoubtedly remain fixed on how workers themselves create new insights and new strategies in their ongoing struggle for power. Jeremy Brecher, a frequent contributor to the journal, clearly summarized this approach. "If socialism grows from the work and living patterns of working people," he wrote, then "we should look for its development in their working and living groups, not in the formal or radical organizations that, at least for the last 50 years, have been external to those groups." The class struggle itself creates the basis for socialist consciousness. Only through their own action can workers see evidence of their potential power. "It is only because workers stick together that their co-operative take-over of society is conceivable," Brecher concludes. "It is only because they plan and organize their actions themselves that the planned coordination of production by those who produce could be imagined."[39]

Political events in the seventies and early eighties did not obviously confirm this optimistic view of workers' struggles. But for a journal that rejected the conventional models of left politics and refused the accept the limits of existing organizations, it was necessary to take the long view of human liberation. For example, even in defeat, Poland's Solidarity confirmed some aspects of *RA*'s original approach to working-class movements. Solidarity reaffirmed the enormous resiliency and creativity of workers' oppositional activity. The movement's spectacular emergence in the Lenin Shipyard occupation at Gdansk in 1980 came after decades of workers' resistance to state-dominated party and trade union organization. Solidarity seemed to fulfill the expectations for a revolt against "state capitalism" in the East discussed by C. L. R. James in his writings about the Hungarian Revolution of 1956. The Polish workers' struggle showed how "new organization" began with "free creative activity" and how bureaucratic party organization had become "*the* obstacle, *the* opposite" of workers' liberation.[40]

Solidarity's origins in the Gdansk occupation reminded *RA* of the American auto and rubber workers' sitdowns of the 1930s, the Hungarian workers' councils of 1956, the French factory occupations of 1968, and the

Chilean *cordones* of 1972–1973. In each case, wrote *RA* editor Frank Brodhead, workers built "a community of struggle and self-government around great concentrations of capital and industry." And in each instance they resisted efforts to end direct, democratic control over the means of production. More specifically, Solidarity revealed the tactical value of organizing horizontally in various workplaces and communities so that "class-wide regional organizations" replaced vertical organizations based on industrial and professional distinctions.[41] In this collection, Staughton Lynd suggests such a horizontal approach in his description of the fight against plant closings in Youngstown, Ohio (Chapter 16). In that struggle to assert workers' control over investment decisions, the international union played a negative role, while the coalition-building effort within the community actually raised questions of socialism, questions that rarely arose in internal union fights.[42]

Solidarity relied a great deal on traditionalism and nationalism for its cultural appeal, forces which have a very different significance in U.S. workers' struggles. The movement's spontaneity and reliance on local autonomy also exposed it to counterattack by the state, though it is not clear that Solidarity could have accomplished as much as it did with a more tightly disciplined, centralized organization. In any case, for all its limitations, Solidarity indicated again how a self-organized workers' movement could break out of the bureaucratic limits imposed by the party, the unions, and the state, and, by making a strong cultural appeal, come to represent the whole society's desire for liberation.[43] It was this kind of movement whose precursors *Radical America* historians sought in studying workers' struggles, past and present.

NOTES

Acknowledgments. I would like to thank the *Radical America* editorial collective for its support in this project. Comments by Joe Interrante, Linda Gordon, Allen Hunter, and Ann Withorn were helpful. Paul Buhle also offered some very important suggestions. And Jim O'Brien made a major contribution, especially in criticizing early drafts of the Introduction.

1. For an interesting view of the Madison Left, see Paul Breines, "Germans, Journals and Jews/Men, Marxism and Mosse: A Tale of Jewish/Leftist Identity Confusion in America," *New German Critique*, no. 20 (1980), pp. 81–103. Also see editor's intro., "15 Years of *Radical America*: An Anthology," ed. Paul Buhle, *Radical America* (hereinafter cited as *RA*) 16, no. 3 (1982): 3–6.

2. This description of the New Left is based upon James O'Brien, "Beyond Reminiscence: The New Left in History," *Radical America* 6, no. 4 (1972): 11–49.

3. See Sara Evans, *Personal Politics: The Roots of Women's Liberation in the Civil Rights Movement and the New Left* (New York: Knopf, 1979).

4. David Montgomery, "What's Happening to the American Worker?" *Radical America Pamphlet* (Madison: *Radical America*, 1970), p. 1. Also see Jim

O'Brien, "American Leninism in the 1970's," *RA* 11, no. 6/12, no. 1 (1977–1978): 27–63.

5. Editors' Introduction, *RA* 5, no. 6 (1971): 1–3, and Paul Buhle, "Marxism in the U.S.: 39 Propositions," *RA* 5, no. 6 (1971): 88.

6. For specific reference to the student movement's affinity for IWW politics, see Melvyn Dubofsky, *We Shall Be All: A History of the IWW* (Chicago: Quadrangle, 1967), p. xii.

7. See, for example, Philip S. Foner, *History of the Labor Movement in the United States*, vol. 3 *The Policies and Practices of the American Federation of Labor, 1900–1909* (New York: International, 1964).

8. Ronald Radosh, "The Corporate Liberal Ideology of American Labor Leaders from Samuel Gompers to Sidney Hillman," in James Weinstein and David W. Eakins, eds., *For a New America: Essays in History and Politics from "Studies on the Left," 1959–1967* (New York: Vintage, 1970), pp. 125–151, esp. p. 126. Also see James Weinstein, *The Decline of Socialism in America, 1912–1925* (New York: Monthly Review Press, 1967).

9. William Appleman Williams, *The Tragedy of American Diplomacy* (Cleveland: World, 1959) and *The Roots of the Modern American Empire* (New York: Random House, 1969).

10. C. Wright Mills, *The New Men of Power* (New York: Harcourt, Brace, 1948) and "A Letter to the New Left," in Priscilla Long, ed., *The New Left* (Boston: Porter Sargent, 1969), p. 22.

11. Herbert Marcuse, *One-Dimensional Man* (Boston: Beacon Press, 1963).

12. "New Left Historians of the 1960's," *RA* 4, nos. 8–9 (1970): 104–105. The quote is from Roger Keeran's essay on labor history.

13. See Paul Buhle, ed., "C. L. R. James: His Life and Work," a special issue of *Urgent Tasks*, no. 12 (1981), especially the editor's introduction.

14. Quotes are found in excerpts from *Modern Politics* (1960), p. 10, *Facing Reality* (1958), pp. 34–35, *State Capitalism and World Revolution* (1949), pp. 19–27, the Introduction by Martin Glaberman, reprinted in a special issue, *RA* 4, no. 4 (1970), and Paul Berman, "*Facing Reality*," in Buhle, "C. L. R. James," pp. 105–107.

15. Ibid., p. 105.

16. C. L. R. James, *The Black Jacobins* (New York: Vintage, 1963), and "The Revolutionary Solution to the Negro Problem in the U.S.," *RA* 4, no. 4 (1970): 12–13; George Rawick, "Historical Roots of Black Liberation," *RA* 2, no. 4 (1968): 3–8.

17. See Alan Dawley, "E. P. Thompson and the Peculiarities of the Americans," *Radical History Review*, no. 19 (1978–1979), pp. 33–60.

18. "New Left Historians of the 1960's," pp. 85–91, and George Rawick, "Historical Roots" and *From Sundown to Sunup: The Making of the Black Community* (Westport: Greenwood, 1972).

19. Paul Faler, "Cultural Aspects of the Industrial Revolution: Lynn, Massachusetts, Shoemakers and Industrial Morality," *Labor History* 15, no. 3 (1974): 366–394, suggests this New Left affinity with artisans.

20. Jesse Lemisch, "New Left Elitism," *RA* 1, no. 2 (1967): 43–53. Oral histories focused in particular on acts of resistance and on organizing efforts. For example, see Dale Rosen and Theodore Rosengarten, "Shootout at Reeltown: The

Introduction

Narrative of Jess Hull," *RA* 6, no. 6, (1972): 65–74, and Nell Painter and Hosea Hudson, "A Negro Communist in the Deep South," *RA* 11, no. 4 (1977): 7–23. Both of these oral histories later appeared in book form as Theodore Rosengarten, *All God's Dangers: The Life of Nate Shaw* (New York: Alfred A. Knopf, 1974), and Nell Irvin Painter, *The Narrative of Hosea Hudson: His Life as a Negro Communist in the South* (Cambridge: Harvard University Press, 1979).

    21. Staughton Lynd, "Guerilla History in Gary," *Liberation*, Oct. 1969; "Two Steel Contracts," *RA* 5, no. 5 (1971): 41–46, and "Personal Histories of the Early C.I.O.," *RA* 5, no. 3 (1971): 49–76. Also see Alice and Staughton Lynd, *Rank and File: Personal Histories by Working-Class Organizers* (Boston: Beacon Press, 1973).

    22. Bill Watson, "Counter-Planning on the Shop Floor," *RA* 5, no. 3 (1971): 77–85; David Schanoes, "Their Time and Ours," *RA* 5, no. 5 (1971): 78; L. Valmeras, "The Work Community," *RA* 5, no. 4 (1971): 77–96. Also see M. Guttman, "The Informal Work Group," *RA* 6, no. 3 (1972): 78–86.

    23. Stan Weir, "American Labor on the Defensive: A 1940's Odyssey," *RA* 9, nos. 4–5 (1975): 163–186, and "Informal Work Groups: Invisible Power in the Workplace," *Against the Current* 1, no. 4 (1982): 46–48.

    24. Carol Lopate, "Daytime Television," *RA* 11, no. 1 (1977): 33–52; Elayne Rapping, "Tupperware and Women," *RA* 14, no. 6 (1980): 39–50; Phyllis Ewen and Margaret Cerullo, " 'Having a Good Time': The American Family Goes Camping," *RA* 16, Nos. 1-2 (1982): 13–44; Phyllis Ewen, "Beauty Parlor—A Women's Place," *RA* 11, no. 3 (1977): 47–58; Lois Ahrens, "Battered Women's Refuges: Feminist Cooperatives vs. Social Service Institutions," *RA* 14, no. 3 (1980): 41–47; and Ann Withorn, "Helping Ourselves: The Limits and Potential of Self-Help," *RA* 14, no. 3 (1980): 25–40.

    25. For a critique of liberal and populist notions about the potential for liberation within traditional culture, see Ewen and Cerullo, " 'Having a Good Time,' " pp. 13–44; Jim Green, "Culture, Politics and Workers' Response to Industrialization," *RA* 16, nos. 1–2 (1982): 101–130; and Marla Erlien, "A Future for Liberal Feminism?" *RA* 16, nos. 1–2 (1982): 163–167.

    26. Editors' Introduction, *RA* 4, no. 2 (1970): 1, and Mari Jo Buhle, Ann D. Gordon, and Nancy Schrom, "Women in American Society: An Historical Contribution," *RA* 5, no. 4 (1971): 3–66.

    27. "Women's Labor," *RA* 7, nos. 4–5 (1973): 7, quote from editors' introduction.

    28. For a critique of "economism" in labor history and an alternative approach, see Joanna Bornat, "Home and Work: A New Context for Trade Union History," *RA* 12, no. 5 (1978): 53–69.

    29. Linda Gordon and Allen Hunter, "Feminism, Leninism and the U.S.," *RA* 13, no. 5 (1979): 35. Also see Linda Gordon and Allen Hunter, "Sex, Family and the New Right: Anti-Feminism as a Political Force," *RA* 11 no. 2/12, no. 1 (1977–1978): 9–26.

    30. Annemarie Troger, "Coalition of Labor Union Women: Strategic Hope, Tactical Despair," and Susan Reverby, "Epilogue or Prologue to CLUW?" *RA* 9, no. 6 (1975): 85–115.

    31. See the essay by Lotta Continua theorist Adriano Sofri, "Organizing for Workers' Power," *RA* 7, no. 2 (1973): 33–46; Dan Georgakas, Introduction to "Italy: New Tactics and Organization," *RA* 5, no. 5 (1971): 7–9.

32. See John Lippert, "Fleetwood Wildcat: Anatomy of a Wildcat Strike," *RA* 11, no. 5 (1977): 7–38, and Frank Kashner, "A Rank-and-File Strike at G.E.," *RA* 12, no. 6 (1978): 43–60.

33. See James Green, "Working-Class Militancy in the Depression," *RA* 6, no. 6 (1972): 1–35, and "Fighting on Two Fronts: Working-Class Militancy in the 1940's," *RA* 9, nos. 4–5 (1975): 5–47. Nonetheless, the 1940s issue was criticized for exaggerating the political significance of wartime wildcat strikes and for ignoring racist "hate strikes." Even in studies which described American labor as being on the "defensive," *RA*'s emphasis on spontaneity and autonomy in workers' struggles remained strong. See Joshua Freeman, "Delivering the Goods: Industrial Unionism during World War II," *Labor History* 19, no. 4 (1978): 570–593. Also see the response to these criticisms by Mark McColloch, "Letter to the Editor," *Labor History* 20, no. 3 (1979): 470–474, which objects to the idea that *RA* historians saw workers just as "economic beings" concerned only with "shop-floor issues."

34. See Margery Davies, "Woman's Place Is at the Typewriter: The Feminization of the Clerical Labor Force," *RA* 8, no. 4 (1974): 1–29, and Ed Greer, "Racism at U.S. Steel, 1906–1970," *RA* 10, no. 5 (1976): 45–68. Also see Margery Davies and Frank Brodhead, a review of *Labor and Monopoly Capital* by Harry Braverman, *RA* 9, no. 3 (1975): 79–94.

35. Compare, for example, Mark Naison, "The Southern Tenant Farmers' Union and the CIO," *RA* 2, no. 5 (1968): 36–56, and Dave Wells and Jim Stodder, "A Short History of New Orleans Dock Workers," *RA* 10, no. 1 (1976): 43–70. For an analysis of racism as "the key element in the popular acceptance of capitalist rule," see Noel Ignatin, "Black Workers and White Workers," *RA* 8, no. 4 (1974): 41–60, and the editors' introduction noting disagreement over this theory of racism, *RA* 8, no. 4 (1974): 40.

36. Jim Green and Allen Hunter, "Racism and Busing in Boston," *RA* 8, no. 6 (1974): 1–17.

37. David Montgomery, "Spontaneity and Organization: Some Comments," *RA* 7, no. 6 (1976): 70–80. And for the critical discussion of workers' councils see Carl Boggs, "Marxism, Prefigurative Communism, and the Problem of Workers' Control," *RA* 11, no. 6/12, no. 1 (1977–1978): 99–122.

38. Montgomery, "Spontaneity and Organization," p. 77.

39. Jeremy Brecher, "Who Advocates Spontaneity?" *RA* 7, no. 6 (1976): 91–112, quotes on pp. 95 and 92.

40. C. L. R. James, *Notes on Dialectics* (1948), excerpt reprinted in *RA* 4, no. 4 (1970): ii.

41. Frank Brodhead, "Solidarity, Cold War and the Left," *RA* 16, nos. 1–2 (1982): 57–64, quotes from pp. 61–63.

42. Also see Staughton Lynd, "What Happened in Youngstown: An Outline," *RA* 15, no. 4 (1981): 37–48, and *The Fight Against Shutdowns* (San Pedro: Singlejack Books, 1982).

43. James Green, "Where's Labor's Solidarity?" *Boston Globe*, Oct. 5, 1981, p. 15, reprinted in *Labor Notes*, no. 34 (Nov. 23, 1981), p. 14. On Solidarity's ability to represent the interests of "the whole society," see "Understanding the Polish Revolt: An Interview with Daniel Singer and Marta Petrusewicz," *RA* 15, no. 3 (1981): 13.

PART ONE

The Struggle
for Control

The articles in this section address questions about power and authority in the capitalist workplace. How have industrialists and managers attempted to control the workforce in the twentieth century? How did they manipulate the labor market and foster divisions within the workforce? How did they try to dominate skilled workers who enjoyed some control over their work and how did they attempt to discipline new immigrant laborers? And, most important, how did workers respond? Did they assert their own demands for control?

Radical America writers examined the structure of capitalist control, but they also explored the workers' own culture of resistance. Only by discovering the hidden history of workplace struggles could historians understand the workers' search for power. Susan Porter Benson's article on the work culture of women department store clerks provides an excellent example of this approach. She studies management strategies and shows how workers exerted their own kind of control even though they were not formally unionized. Indeed, the existence of a vibrant "clerking sisterhood" indicated that workers created a life for themselves on the job. Benson also suggests through this case study that women workers' struggles differed significantly from those of skilled male workers whose crafts were being destroyed by modern management and new technology. In many areas women workers have been required to gain new skills, and in some cases they have been able to use the opportunity to gain increased power as well.

21

In "The Stop Watch and the Wooden Shoe," Mike Davis describes how industrialists used scientific management to gain greater control over workers around the turn of the century. The capitalist drive for efficiency and productivity produced a militant response not only from entrenched craft unions defending job control but also from unorganized immigrant workers resisting speed-up and management tyranny. The revolutionary Industrial Workers of the World intervened in many of the mass strikes of the early 1900s. The Wobblies urged workers to fight scientific management with sabotage or what they called the "conscious withdrawl of efficiency." The IWW also countered the capitalist drive for total control with a radical vision of worker-controlled industry.

Capitalist control over the international labor market gave industrialists decided advantages. They could tap the reserve army of the unemployed in boom times and fire the newcomers in hard times. They could also pit the white English-speaking workers against immigrants or Afro-Americans. *Radical America* historians tried to show, however, that in feeding their demand for cheap labor the capitalists often created unforeseen results. The unskilled East European workers who provided stability for the steel industry in the early 1900s became the backbone of the 1919 steel strike and the mass upsurge in industrial unionism during the mid-1930s. And as Harold M. Baron argues in his influential essay "The Demand for Black Labor," Afro-American workers came to bedevil the same employers who thought cheap black labor was an answer to their prayers.

In the once-segregated Southern textile industry, manufacturers have been forced to hire blacks, and in some plants these new workers are now predominant. Despite the racist practices of white trade unions, black textile workers are today the strongest supporters of unionism in the South. As Mary Frederickson indicates, civil rights struggles for political and social equality created a consciousness among Southern black workers that supported collective workplace action.

Like Old Left historians, the New Leftists who wrote for *Radical America* emphasized the potential militancy of the unskilled and unorganized workers, and highlighted examples of unity and solidarity that cut across divisions based on skill, race, nationality, and gender. Nonetheless, *RA* writers never underestimated the divisions created by racism, sexism, and nationalism or the degree to which trade unions exacerbated those divisions with exclusionary policies. Indeed, the black power and women's liberation movements of the late 1960s and early 1970s forced historians to recognize the importance of autonomous movements against racism and sexism, even if these struggles *seemed* to heighten disunity within the working class. As Harold Baron maintains, capitalists created a separate labor market for blacks which made unity with white workers exceedingly difficult. In fact, he argues, blacks caught in an "urban web of racism" experienced their oppression not just as workers but as a separate national minority. Therefore, black nationalism should not simply be dismissed as a divisive, separatist movement. Rather it should be viewed as an autonomous struggle to free the nation's most oppressed group of workers—a struggle with positive implications for the entire working class.

In her historical essay on sexual harassment, Mary Bularzik reveals how capitalists used sexism to maintain control over women workers. Just as white supremacy could be enforced by the constant threat of violence, patriarchy could be strengthened by creating fear of sexual assault. Like Baron, Bularzik shows that chauvinism is not simply the product of capitalist practices. White male workers have often engaged in racist and sexist violence or in the forms of intimidation related to it. Union women have gained little support from "union brothers" in opposing sexual harassment. Like black workers, they have looked outside the organized labor movement for strategies to combat harassment and intimidation on the job. Unfortunately unions have lost the spirit of the principle the Knights of Labor articulated a hundred years ago: "An Injury to One is an Injury to All."

The articles in this section suggest that a constant battle for control has been waged in the American workplace. Indeed, the struggle to resist capitalist control has been bitter and protracted, like a guerilla war in which the invading forces of capital have enormous scientific and technological advantages, but are unable to subdue the forces of resistance. The workers' struggle for control has generally been defensive and localized. In fact, as the articles in this section suggest, these struggles have been different for various groups of workers. To some extent they *reflect* existing social and cultural divisions. Localized resistance to capitalist control reveals that workers, even the unskilled and unorganized, have unrecognized resources to employ in their search for power. The essays in this section uncover ordinary workers' striking tenacity and creativity in the face of oppression. They constantly assert their humanity against capitalist rationality and the tyranny of market forces. But the historians also suggest that these qualities are difficult to apply to a larger movement for workers' control if they remain isolated in localized struggles. Unless white and black workers, citizens and non-citizens, men and women, see their specialized struggles as essentially similar, they will remain isolated and divided. Then of course capitalists will maintain the initiative in their drive for total control, and the workers' movement will remain largely defensive.

CHAPTER ONE

The Demand
for Black Labor:
Historical Notes
on the Political Economy
of Racism

by Harold M. Baron

The economic base of racism would have to be subjected to intensive analysis in order to get at the heart of the oppression of black people in modern America. If we employ the language of nineteenth-century science, we can state that the economic deployment of black people has been conditioned by the operation of two sets of historical laws: the laws of capitalist development, and the laws of national liberation. These laws were operative in the slave era as well as at present. Today the characteristic forms of economic control and exploitation of black people take place within the institutional structure of a mature state capitalist system and within the demographic frame of the metropolitan centers. The economic activities of blacks are essentially those of wage (or salary) workers for the large corporate and bureaucratic structures that dominate a mature capitalist society. Thus today racial dynamics can be particularized as the working out of the laws of the maintenance of mature state capitalism and the laws of black liberation with the metropolitan enclaves (rather than a consolidated territorial area) as a base.

This essay places major emphasis on capitalist development. While attention will be paid to aspects of national liberation, it would be a very different essay if that were the main point of concentration. Further, in order to make the inquiry manageable, it concentrates on the key relationship of the demand for black labor.

Reprinted from Vol. 5, No. 2 (March-April 1971).

A backward glance at certain factors in the evolution of racism will help establish the cogency of the major categories that we employ in the analysis of the present day. Historically, the great press for black labor as the workforce for plantation slavery simultaneously supplied the momentum for the formation of institutional racism and set the framework for the creation of the black community in the United States. The strength of this demand for black slaves, in regard to both the vast numbers of persons involved and its duration over centuries, was based on the dialectics of the relationship between slavery in the New World and the development of capitalism in Europe: Each provided necessary conditions for the other's growth.

A large-scale accumulation of capital was a prerequisite for the emergence of capitalism as the dominant system in Europe. Otherwise capitalism was doomed to remain basically a mercantile operation in the interstices of a primarily manorial economy. From the sixteenth century on, the strength of developing nation-states and their ability to extend their tentacles of power beyond the limits of Europe greatly accelerated the process that Marx called "the primitive accumulation of capital."

> The discovery of gold and silver in America, the extirpation, enslavement, and entombment in the mines of the aboriginal population, the beginning of the conquest and looting of the East Indies, the turning of Africa into a warren for the hunting of black skins, signalized the rosy dawn of the era of capitalist production. These idyllic proceedings are the chief momenta of primitive accumulation. This phase of the accumulation process was accomplished not only by domestic exploitation, but also by the looting of traditional stores of non-European peoples and the fostering of a new system of slavery to exploit their labor.[1]

In a sense European capitalism created, as one of the preconditions for its flourishing, a set of productive relations that was antithetical to the free-market, wage-labor system which characterized capitalist production in the metropolitan countries. English capitalism at home was nurturing itself on a proletariat created through the dispossession of the peasantry from the land, while at the same time accumulating much of the capital necessary to command the labor of this proletariat through the fixing of African deportees into a servile status in the colonies. "In fact, the veiled slavery of the wage-earners of Europe needed for its pedestal slavery pure and simple in the New World."[2]

Slaves from Africa, at first in the mines and then on the plantations of the New World, produced goods that enlarged the magnitude of the circulation of commodities in international trade—a process that was essential to the mercantilist phase of capitalist history.[3] Although this slavery was not capitalist in the form of production itself, that it was not based on the purchase of alienated wage labor[4], the plantation system of the New World composed an integral part of the international market relations of the growing capitalist system. The demand for slaves was subject to mercantile calculations regarding production costs and market prices:

> Long before the trans-Atlantic trade began, both the Spanish and the Portuguese were well aware that Africa could be made to yield up its human treasure. But in the early part of the Sixteenth Century the cost of transporting large numbers of slaves across the Atlantic was excessive in relation to the profits that could be extracted from their labor. This situation changed radically when, toward the middle of the century . . . sugar plantings were begun in Brazil . . . and by the end of the Sixteenth Century sugar had become the most valuable of the agricultural commodities in international trade. Importation of Negroes from Africa now became economically feasible.[5]

Once in the world market, a commodity lost all the markings of its origin. No distinction could be made as to whether it was produced by free or slave labor. It became just a good to be bought and sold.

Production from the slave plantations greatly increased the volume of commodities in circulation through trade, but the social relations of slavery and racism rendered the black producers so distinctly apart that it was possible to appropriate a greater proportion of their product as surplus than it was through any other established mechanism that defined lowly social status. Two sets of conditions combined to make the exploitation of the New World slaves particularly harsh. First, the production of plantation goods for the impersonal needs of the rapidly expanding international market removed many of the restraints and reciprocities that had inhered in patriarchal forms of slavery in which production was essentially for home use. Second, since West Africa was outside of Christendom or Mediterranean civilization, there were few existing European cultural or political limitations that applied to the treatment of black chattels.

The economics of slavery could not have existed over an extended period as just a set of shrewd market-oriented operations. Elaboration of a whole *culture of control*—with political, social, and ideological formulations—was necessary to hold dominance over the black slaves and to keep the non-slave-holding whites in line. Given that the white Europeans were subjugating the black Africans, the culture of control became largely structured around a color-oriented racialism. "Slavery could survive *only* if the Negro were a man set apart; he simply had to be different if slavery were to exist at all."[6] The development of a rationale regarding the degradation of *all* blacks and the formation of conforming institutional practices were necessary to maintain a social order based on enslavement of *some* blacks. Accordingly, this culture of racial control rapidly diffused throughout the whole of North Atlantic civilization and all the American colonies of its various nations. In the United States, racism—that is, subjugation based on blackness rather than on servitude alone—was more sharply defined than in most other places in the Americas.

When the European powers extended their influence down the African coast, they did not have sufficient military and economic advantage to establish sovereignty over the lands. They could only set up trading outposts. However first on islands off the coast of Africa and then on the islands and coastal lowlands of the Americas, the Europeans were able to gain control of the land, often exterminating the indigenous population. In such distant territories black workers from Africa could be driven in the mines and plantations free from any constraints that could be imposed by the states, tribes, and traditions of Africa. Set apart by their servitude and their blackness, they were also removed from any rights that low-status groups within the metropolitan country might have had. Laboring on the American plantations came to embody the worst features of ancient slavery and the cash nexus.

Black chattel slavery, with the concomitant elaboration of institutional and ideological racism as its sociopolitical corollary, became a new type of societal formation. True, as David Brion Davis has pointed out, the institutions of New World slavery grew out of the forms of the late Middle Ages' Mediterranean slavery.[7] Regarding racism, Winthrop Jordan has shown that the preexisting derogatory imagery of darkness, barbarism, and heathenism was adapted to formulate the psychology and doctrines of modern racism.[8] While the adaptation of these available institutional and ideological materials provided the original forms for New World slavery, as a whole the system was something distinctly novel. This novelty was chiefly conditioned by the developing capitalist relations that provided the seemingly insatiable demand for plantation products. Accordingly, the demand for black labor under circumstances like these had to be different from any slavery that was indigenous to West Africa or had operated earlier in Europe.

Capitalism's stamp on New World slavery was sharply revealed via the slave trade that supplied the demand for black labor. Alongside the marketing of the output of slave labor, the trade in the bodies which produced these goods became a major form of merchant capitalistic enterprise in itself. Down into the nineteenth century the purchase of black slaves frequently was a constant cost of production. This held in extreme for parts of Brazil where it was considered more economical to work slaves to death within five to ten years and replace them with fresh purchases than to allow enough sustenance and opportunity for family living so that the slave force could be maintained by natural reproduction.[9] The latest and most careful estimate of the total deportation of black slaves to the Americas is between 9,000,000 and 10,000,000. Up to 1810 about 7,500,000 Africans were imported—or about three times the number of Europeans immigrating in the same period.[10]

Slave trade and slave production brought wealth and power to the bourgeois merchants of Western Europe. As C. L. R. James has summed up the situation for France: "Nearly all the industries which developed in

France during the Eighteenth Century had their origin in goods or commodities destined for either the coast of Guinea or America. The capital from the slave trade fertilized them. Though the bourgeois traded in other things than slaves, upon the success or failure of the (slave) traffic everything else depends."[11] In the case of England, Eric Williams, in *Capitalism and Slavery*, has detailed in terms of manufacturing, shipping, and capital accumulation how the economic development of the mother land was rooted in New World slavery.[12] But it is more dramatic to let a contemporary eighteenth century economist speak for himself:

> The most-approved judges of the commercial interest of these kingdoms have ever been of the opinion that our West Indian and African trades are the most nationally-beneficial of any carried on. It is also allowed on all hands that the trade to Africa is the branch which renders our American colonies and plantations so advantageous to Great Britain; that traffic only affording our planters a constant supply of Negro servants for the culture of their lands in the produce of sugar, tobacco, rice, rum, cotton, pimento, and all plantation produce; so that the extensive employment of our shipping into and from our American colonies, the great brook of seamen consequent thereupon, and the daily bread of the most-considerable part of our British manufacturers, are owing primarily to the labor of Negroes. . . .[13]

WITHIN THE BOUNDARIES OF THE UNITED STATES

In the colonial period of the United States the commercial basis of all the colonies rested largely on the Atlantic trade in slave-produced commodities. The Southern colonies directly used a slave population to raise tobacco and rice for export. While the Northern colonies all had slave populations, their major links were auxiliaries to the Atlantic trade—growing provisions for the Caribbean plantations, developing a merchant marine to carry slaves to the islands and sugar to Europe. In the territory of the United States, the elaboration of plantation slavery had some distinctive features that are worthy of attention for the light that they shed on the present. For one thing the slave system here tended to become a self-contained operation in which the demand for new slaves was met by natural increase, with the slave deficit areas of the Lower South importing black bondsmen from the Upper South. Self-containment was also defined in that there were few possibilities that a black man could achieve any other status than that of slave—involuntary servitude and blackness were almost congruent. Plantations operating under conditions of high prices for manufactured goods and easy access to their own land holdings for whites, had been forced to train black slaves as artisans and craftsmen. As one scholar concluded:

> Indeed, it is hard to see how the Eighteenth Century plantation could ever have survived if the Negro slave had not made his important contribution as an artisan in the building and other trades calling for skill in transforming

raw materials into manufactured articles. The self-sufficiency of the Southern colonies necessitated by the Revolution was more successful than it
could have been if the Negro slave artisan had not been developing for
generations before.[14]

But skills only exceptionally led to freedom. Even the relatively small
number of what John Hope Franklin calls "quasi-free Negroes" tended to
lose rights, both in the North and in the South, after the adoption of the
Constitution. By way of contrast, in Latin America an extensive free black
population existed alongside a large number of freshly imported slaves.

The position of the "quasi-free Negro" is one of the most important
keys to understanding later developments. Sheer economic conditions operated to prevent him from developing a secure social status. The flourishing
of the cotton culture sustained a high demand for slaves at the same time that
state and federal illegalization of the slave trade reduced the importation of
Africans. Therefore limitations on both the numbers and prerogatives of
non-slave blacks functioned to maintain the size of the slave labor force.

The completeness with which race and slavery became merged in the
United States is revealed by a review of the status of blacks on the eve of the
Civil War. About 89 percent of the national black population was slave,
while in the Southern states the slave proportion was 94 percent.[15] The status
of the small number of quasi-free Negroes was ascribed from that of the
mass of their brothers in bondage. Nowhere did this group gain a secure
economic position; only a few of them acquired enough property to be well
off. In the countryside, by dint of hard work, a few acquired adequate farms.
Most, however, survived on patches of poor soil or as rural laborers. Free
blacks fared the best in Southern cities, many of them being employed as
skilled artisans or tradesmen. The ability of free blacks to maintain a
position in the skilled trades was dependent on the deployment of a larger
number of slaves in these crafts and industrial jobs. Slave-owners provided a
defense against a color bar as they protected their investment in urban
slaves. However, the rivalry from a growing urban white population between 1830 and 1860 forced blacks out of many of the better jobs, and in
some cases out of the cities altogether. "As the black population dropped,
white newcomers moved in and took over craft after craft. Occasionally to
the accompaniment of violence and usually with official sanction, slave and
free colored workers were shunted into the most menial and routine
chores."[16]

Basic racial definitions of the slave system also gained recognition in the
North, through the development of a special servile status for blacks.
During the colonial era, Northern colonies imported slaves as one means of
coping with a chronic labor shortage. While most blacks were employed in
menial work, many were trained in skilled trades. "So long as the pecuniary

interests of a slave-holding class stood back of these artisans, the protests of white mechanics had little effect. . . ." With emancipation in the North, matters changed. As Du Bois further noted concerning Philadelphia, during the first third of the nineteenth century, the blacks, who had composed a major portion of all artisans, were excluded from most of the skilled trades.[17] Immigrants from Europe soon found out that, although greatly exploited themselves, they could still turn racism to their advantage. The badge of whiteness permitted even the lowly to use prejudice, violence, and local political influence to push blacks down into the lowest occupations. In 1850, 75 percent of the black workers in New York were employed in menial or unskilled positions. Within five years the situation had deteriorated to the point at which 87.5 percent were in these categories.[18] Northern states did not compete with slave states for black workers, even when labor shortages forced them to encourage the immigration of millions of Europeans. Through enforcement of fugitive slave laws and discouragement of free black immigration, through both legal and informal means, the North reinforced slavery's practical monopoly over blacks.

For the pre-Civil War period, then, we can conclude that there was no significant demand for black labor outside the slave system. The great demand for black workers came from the slave plantations. No effective counterweight to plantation slavery was presented by urban and industrial employment. As a matter of fact, in both North and South the position of the urban skilled black worker deteriorated during the generation prior to the Civil War. In the South the magnitude of cities and industries was limited by the political and cultural imperatives inherent in hegemony of the planter class. Whatever demand there was for black labor in Southern cities and industries was met essentially by adapting the forms of slavery to these conditions, not by creating an independent pressure for free blacks to work in these positions.

To a large extent the more heightened form of racism in the United States grew out of the very fact that the U.S.A. was such a thoroughgoing bourgeois society, with more bourgeois equalitarianism than any other nation around. Aside from temporary indenture, which was important only through the Revolutionary era, there were no well-institutionalized formal or legal mechanisms for fixing of status among whites. Up to the Civil War the ideal of an equalitarian-yeoman society was a major sociopolitical factor in shaping political conditions. Therefore if the manumitted slave were not marked off by derogation of his blackness, there was no alternative but to admit him to the status of a free-born enfranchised citizen (depending on property qualifications) prior to the 1830s.[19]

Under these circumstances the planter class made race as well as slavery a designation of condition. A large free black population that had full citizens' rights would have been a threat to their system. They therefore legislated limitations on the procedures for manumission and placed severe restrictions on the rights of free blacks. Low-status whites who did have citizens' rights were encouraged by the plantocracy to identify as whites and to emphasize racial distinctions so as to mark themselves off from both slaves and free blacks precisely because this white group did have a legitimate place in the political process. Fear of competition from blacks, either directly or indirectly through the power of large planters, also gave the large class of non-slave-holding whites a real stake in protecting racial distinctions. In Latin America, by contrast, the remnants of feudal traditions regarding the gradations of social ranks already provided well-established lowly positions into which free Negroes or half-castes could step without posing a threat to the functional hegemony of the slave-master class. Further, given the small number of Europeans and the great labor shortage, ex-slaves provided ancillary functions, such as clearing the frontier or raising food crops, that were necessary for the overall operation of the slave system.[20]

This absoluteness of racial designation, so intimately related to the character of bourgeois order in this nation, meant that racism became intertwined in the entire state system of rule. That is to say that not only were the procedures of slave control and racial derogation of the blacks embodied in the Constitution and other fundamental features of state action, but these mechanisms soon interpenetrated the general state operations for the control of certain classes of whites over other whites. Therefore, while racism was as American as apple pie, and was subscribed to in some form even by most white abolitionists, it also became a special weapon in the regional arsenal of the Southern plantocracy in their contention for a dominant position in determination of national policy. The planters' employment of racist appeals proved effective on a national basis, especially in the generation prior to the Civil War, only because an underlying acceptance of their assumptions existed in all regions. Domestically within the South, racism operated to cement the solidarity of all whites under the hegemony of the planter class—even though slavery provided the power base from which the plantocracy were able to subordinate the white yeomanry. This strategy met with success, for the intensification of racist propaganda during the antebellum period was accompanied by a slackening of attacks on the plantation system. In return for the security granted to the base of their power, the planters had to make some concessions to the poor whites regarding formal rights of citizenship such as extension of the franchise and legislative reapportionment; but alterations in form did not change the fundamental power relations. The racialist culture of control merged into both the political apparatus and the social forms of hegemony by which white class rule was sustained. White rule was not identical with, but did mediate, the rule of the plantocracy over all of Southern society.

THE TRANSITION ERA, FIRST PHASE:
1860 TO WORLD WAR I

So far we have been establishing a comprehension of some of the underlying contradictions that frame the control of black labor by examining their origins in the slave era. Before we turn to the present period there is another set of relationships that will provide further conceptual illumination: the conditions that underlay the abolition of slavery. One set of factors lay in the world development of capitalism itself. The bourgeoisie's seizure of power in the French Revolution destabilized that nation's colonial regime and undermined the slave system by promulgating the doctrine of the rights of man as a universal dictum. In England, the expansion of its capitalist might into Asia gave rise to a powerful political interest counter to that of the West Indian planters; plus, the success of the industrial revolution created the material base for envisioning a liberal bourgeois order with thorough formal equality. In the United States, the demise of slavery occurred in the midst of a war that established the further course of capitalist development—whether it would proceed on a "Prussian model," with the planters playing the role of the Junkers, or the industrialists and little men on the make would independently establish their hegemony through an entrepreneurially oriented state.

The other source of abolition lay in the role of the black people in the Americas. Denied the right to reconstruct their African societies, they strove to survive and reconstitute themselves as a people. Amidst the plantations and the black quarters of the cities, a new community was formed.[21] At crucial points these black communities transcended the need for survival and struck out for liberation. While sabotage, escapes, and uprisings were consistent themes of New World slavery, the key move was the successful revolt of the black Jacobins in Haiti under the leadership of Toussaint L'Ouverture, which set an example for black and other oppressed people from that time on. By winning their freedom and defeating the most powerful armies in the world, these revolutionaries not only forced changes in the relative relations of the forces in Europe, but also undermined much essential confidence in the continuing viability of the slave system as a whole. It was little accident that both the British and the U.S. abolition of the slave trade followed shortly on the heels of the Haitian revolution.

In the United States, where a large white population was always close at hand, there were few important slave revolts, and even those were invariably put down before they could become well established. Black self-determination took the form of day-to-day slave resistance, and the development of an independent political line within the abolitionist movement. Most important, the role of black people in the Civil War converted it into a struggle for their own freedom. As Du Bois cogently summarizes:

> Freedom for the slave was a logical result of a crazy attempt to wage war in the midst of four million black slaves, trying the while sublimely to ignore the interests of those slaves in the outcome of the fighting. Yet these slaves had enormous power in their hands. Simply by stopping work, they could threaten the Confederacy with starvation. By walking into the Federal camps, they showed to doubting Northerners the easy possibility of using them as workers and as servants, as spies, as farmers, and finally as fighting soldiers. And not only using them thus, but by the same gesture depriving their enemies of their use in just these fields. It was the fugitive slave who made the slaveholders face the alternative of surrendering to the North or to the Negroes.[22]

The Civil War destroyed the Southern plantocracy as a major contender for the control of national power. For a decade during Reconstruction, the freedmen struggled to establish themselves as an independent yeomanry on the lands they had worked for generations. However, both South and North agreed that blacks were to be subservient workers—held in that role now by the workings of "natural" economic and social laws rather than the laws of slavery. The Compromise of 1877 was the final political blow to black Reconstruction, remanding to the dominant white Southerners the regulation of the black labor force.[23]

Abolition of slavery did not mean substantive freedom to the black worker. He was basically confined to a racially defined agrarian labor status in which he was more exploited than any class of whites, even the landless poor. White landowners extracted an economic surplus from the labor of blacks through a variety of arrangements, including peonage, wage labor, sharecropping, and rent tenancy. Even the black owners of land were often dependent on white patronage for access to the small plots of inferior soil to which they usually held title. Profits predicated on low wages or onerous share arrangements were often augmented by long-term indebtedness at usurious rates of interest for advances of provisions and supplies. Many a sharecropper and laborer would not realize any appreciable money income for years on end.

The methods of labor control over the black peasantry did not greatly raise net labor costs over those of the slavery era. In both eras the black masses received only enough to survive and reproduce. Pressure on profits came from falling commodity prices rather than from rising labor costs. "The keynote of the Black Belt is debt. . . ," wrote W. E. B. Du Bois at the turn of the century. "Not commercial credit, but debt in the sense of continued inability of the mass of the population to make income cover expenses." Of conditions in Dougherty County, Georgia he wrote:

> In the year of low-priced cotton, 1898, of 300 tenant families 175 ended their year's work in debt to the extent of $14,000; 50 cleared nothing; and the remaining 75 made a total profit of $1600. . . . In more-prosperous years the situation is far better—but on the average the majority of tenants end the year even or in debt, which means they work for board and clothes.[24]

34

From the obverse side white planters in racist language gave their supporting testimony to this extra economic exploitation of the black peasants. One
Alabama landlord declared: "White labor is totally unsuited to our
methods, our manners, and our accommodations. No other laborers (than
the Negro) of whom I have any knowledge would be so cheerful or so
contented on four pounds of meat and a peck of meal a week, in a little log
cabin 14 by 16 feet, with cracks in it large enough to afford free passage to a
large-size-cat." From Mississippi a planter spoke to the same theme: "Give
me the nigger every time. The nigger will never 'strike' as long as you give
him plenty to eat and half clothe him: He will live on less and do more hard
work, when properly managed, than any other class or race of people."[25]

Black agriculturists were important to the economic development of the
South and the nation. Raw cotton production tripled between 1870 and
1910. Consumption of cotton by domestic manufacturers increased six-fold
from 800,000 bales in 1870 to 4,800,000 bales in 1910. Cotton continued to
be the United States' leading export commodity in global trade, still
accounting for a quarter of the value of all merchandise exports on the eve of
World War I—in spite of the fact that prices had decreased greatly through
international competition as the European powers encouraged cotton production in the overseas areas in which they were augmenting their imperial
power. Such rapid growth of cotton production (and that of other farm
commodities) implied a great demand for black workers in the fields.
Characteristically blacks were engaged on the cotton plantations, especially
those with richer lands. The form of engagement was roughly divided
between sharecropping, wage labor, and rental tenancy. Between 1890 and
1910 the number of black men in agriculture increased by over half a million,
or 31 percent. During this entire period three out of five black men were
employed in agriculture.

Maintaining the semiservile status of the black labor force required the
augmentation of color-caste distinctions. Southern slavery, after all, had
been more than just an economic arrangement: it was a cultural system that
provided a wide range of norms congruent with plantation discipline. Slave
status had served as a line of demarcation throughout the society. Therefore
emancipation not only changed the economic form of planter control, but
also left gaps in the social superstructure that reinforced it. Under these
conditions the strengthening of racialism per se in all cultural arrangements
became an imperative for any hope of continuance of the planters' hegemony over Southern society. Since racism had pervaded all major facets of
social and political control, much of the further elaboration of color-caste
distinctions arose in the course of the Southern ruling class's struggles to
keep the rest of the whites in line.

The road to the establishment of this new system of order in the South
was by no means a smooth one. Abrogation of the slave system had made
possible some new types of mobility among both blacks and whites, bringing

about changes in the forms of interracial conflict and class conflict. Blacks were now able to move geographically, even in the face of continued legal and extralegal restraints. The migration that took place was mainly a westerly one within the South. Inside the black community class mobility developed through the emergence of a small middle class. At the same time, there now opened up to poorer whites areas that had formerly been the preserve of slavery. During the pre-Civil War era no white would compete with a slave for his position on the plantation. Albeit when planters and slaveless small farmers did contend for land, as frequently occurred, the black slave was indirectly involved. With emancipation, racial rivalry for the soil became overt. Freedmen struggled to gain land, sometimes as owners but more frequently as indebted tenants. At the same time, many white smallholders, forced out from infertile and worn soil, sought many of the same lands. After the Civil War the white farmers increased in numbers at a greater rate than the blacks. By 1900, even as tenants, the whites were in the majority. Blacks moved from non-competitive status in slavery (or perhaps better "concealed competition between the bond and the free"), as Rupert Vance has pointed out, to a condition of overt interracial competition. "As slaves Negroes were objects of race prejudice; as a new competitive group struggling for status and a place on the land Negroes found themselves potential objects of mass pressure and group conflict."[26]

Transformations also took place within the Southern ruling class. Ownership of land tended to shift out of the hands of the old planter class into those of merchants, lawyers, and in some cases Northern interests, removing many of the impediments to landowners' making their decisions more nakedly, on the basis of pure entrepreneurial calculations. This partial unfreezing of labor and capital resources provided some important preconditions for the industrialization of the South. Nevertheless, the ideal for black labor in the eyes of dominant white groups was that of a contented agrarian peasantry. Paternalistic members of the Southern elite spoke of satisfied workers controlled by fair but rigidly enforced rules. "Let the Negro become identified with and attached to the soil upon which he lives, and he himself, the land-owner, and the country alike will be advanced by his labor."[27]

In the social and political realms the conflicts inherent in the black peasantry's subjugation became intertwined with the conflicts inherent in the subordination of any potential political power in the hands of the white smallholders and the landless. As things turned out, blacks were to suffer both from the control of the propertied and from the competition of the poor. The political process provided a major means by which this was carried out. "It is one of the paradoxes of Southern history," writes C. Vann Woodward, "that political democracy for the white man and racial discrimination for the black were often products of the same dynamics." The imperatives of preserving class rule supplied the basis of the paradox: "It took a lot of ritual and Jim Crow to bolster the rule of white supremacy in the bosom of a white man working for a black man's wage."[28] Functionally the poorer whites were permitted to influence the formal political process only under conditions that would not undermine the essential power and economic control of the ruling class. The execution of this strategy was completed during the defeat of the Populist movement in the 1890s by excluding the black people from politics and by heightening the color-caste distinctions through an extension of Jim Crow laws and customs. Since the black people had already been defeated through Redemption 20 years before, the moves to disfranchise black people at the turn of the century had as "the real question . . . *which whites* would be supreme." Ruling circles channeled disfranchisement to their own ends "as they saw in it an opportunity to establish in power 'the intelligence and wealth of the South' which could of course 'govern in the interests of all classes.' "[29] Many whites as well as blacks were denied the ballot, and the substantive differences expressed in the political process were delimited to a narrower range. Interclass conflicts among whites were much displaced by interracial conflicts, and the hegemony of larger property interests was secured.

The agrarian designation of the black masses was still reinforced by the lack of competition for their labor from other sectors of the economy. The Southern demand for factory help, except for unskilled work, was essentially a demand for white labor. The textile industry, the primary industry of the New South, was marked off as a preserve of the white worker. The mythology that black workers were incapable of measuring up to the conditions in the textile mills was reinforced by the rationale that the domestic peace required that white poor have some kind of economic preserve, free from competition.[30]

> Thus when the industrialization of the South began about 1880 and attained remarkable proportions by the outbreak of the [First] World War, it had comparatively little significance for the Negro agricultural workers. . . . The poor whites took the cotton mills as their own; and with the exception of sweeping, scrubbing, and the like in cotton factories, there was virtually no work for the Negroes in the plants. They were, therefore, compelled to labor on the farms, the only other work that was available.[31]

The rather considerable increase in industrial employment of blacks between 1890 and 1910 was concentrated in railroading, lumbering, and coal mining—that is, in non-factory-type operations with these three industries often located in rural areas. Lumbering and allied industries could almost have been considered an extension of agriculture, as the workers shifted back and forth from one to the other.

Outside of agriculture the vast bulk of black workers were to be found either in domestic and personal service or in unskilled menial fields that were known in the South as "Negro jobs." In the cities the growth occupations were chiefly porters, draymen, laundresses, seamstresses. However, non-propertied whites did begin to crowd into many skilled positions that had been the black man's preserve under slavery. Black mechanics and artisans, who had vastly outnumbered Southern whites as late as 1865, fought a losing battle for these jobs down to 1890, when they were able to stabilize a precarious minority position in some of the construction trades.[32]

Exclusion of black workers from industry was not based on rational calculation regarding the characteristics of the labor supply. Contrary to all the racist rationales about incapacity and lack of training, most industrial firms considered blacks good workers. When the employers were questioned specifically about the comparative quality of black and white workers in their plants, the majority held that they were equally satisfactory. *The Chattanooga Tradesman* in 1889 and 1891, on its own, and again in 1901 in cooperation with the Atlanta University Sociology Department, made surveys of firms employing skilled and semiskilled blacks. The *Tradesman*'s editor concluded from the results that "the Negro, as a free laborer, as a medium skilled and common worker, is by no means a 'failure' . . . he is a remarkable success." In the 1901 survey over 60 percent of the employers held that their black workers were as good as or better than their white workers.[33]

Northern ruling classes were quick to accept those conditions in the South that stabilized the national political system and provided the raw commodities for their mills and markets. Therefore they supported the establishment of a subservient black peasantry, the regional rule of the Southern propertied interests, and the racial oppression that made both of these things possible. The dominant Northern interests shared the ideal of the smooth kind of racial subjugation projected by the paternalistic Southern elite, but they went along with what proved necessary. "Cotton brokers of New York and Philadelphia, and cotton manufacturers of New England . . . knew full well the importance of bringing discipline to the Southern labor force. When theories of Negro equality resulted in race conflict, and conflict in higher prices of raw cotton, manufacturers were inclined to accept the point of view of the Southern planter rather than that of the New England zealot."[34] Northern businessmen who supported black education in the South had in mind a system that would encourage the students to stay in rural areas and would train them for hard work and menial positions.[35]

Thus, through a process that Harvard's Paul Buck approvingly called *The Road to Reunion* and Howard's Rayford Logan scathingly labeled *The Betrayal of the Negro*, national political, business, and intellectual elites came to define race as a Southern question for which they would not assume any leadership. By 1900, Southern sympathizer and Northern anti-slavery man alike agreed on the rightfulness of the subjugation of the black man. It was accepted as a necessary condition for order in the American state. And order was most essential to the extraordinary expansion of the industrial system. Beyond that point the black man was ignored and considered a "nothing," especially on Northern ground. Reasons of state and racism had combined to legitimize the new form of agrarian thralldom.

In the North itself during this period there was minimal work for blacks, even though the Northern economy was labor-starved to the extent that it promoted and absorbed a European immigration of over 15,000,000 persons. Blacks were not only shut off from the new jobs, but lost many of the jobs they had traditionally held. The Irish largely displaced them in street paving, the Slavs displaced them in brickyards, and all groups moved in on the once-black stronghold of dining-room waiting.[36]

The reasons for this displacement of black workers in the North are complex. Northern capital engaged Southern workers, both black and white, by exporting capital to the South rather than by encouraging any great migration, thus enabling itself to exploit the low wage structure of the economically backward South while avoiding any disturbance in its precarious political or economic balance. Sometimes racism would operate directly, as when the National Cash Register Company (Dayton, Ohio) laid off 300 black janitors because the management wanted to have white farm boys start at the bottom and work their way up.[37] In addition, job competition often led white workers to see blacks, rather than employers, as the enemy. At least 50 strikes, North and South, in which white workers protested the employment of blacks have been recorded for the years 1881 to 1900.[38] There was a minor countertheme of class solidarity which existed to a certain extent in the Knights of Labor and was reaffirmed by the Industrial Workers of the World, but as the job-conscious American Federation of Labor gained dominance over the union movement, racial exclusion became the operative practice, with the only major exception occurring among the United Mine Workers.[39] (It was actually more common in the South than in the North for black workers to hold a position so strong in particular industries that unions had to take them into account; in these instances they were generally organized in separate locals.) Episodes in which blacks were used as strikebreakers contributed to the unions' hostility toward blacks, but it should be added that racism seriously distorted the perceptions of white workers. Whites were used as scabs more frequently and in larger numbers, but the saliency of racial categories was able to make the minority role of blacks stand out more sharply, so that in many white workers' minds the terms "scab" and "Negro" were synonymous.[40]

The course of national development of black people was set within the framework of their concentration in the Southern countryside. During Reconstruction a truly heroic effort was made by the black masses to establish a self-sufficient yeomanry on the land. Smashing of this movement set back the progression of independent black militancy more than a generation. New forms of embryonic nationalism emerged or reemerged. Exodus groups tried with a certain success to establish themselves on the land in

Kansas, Oklahoma, and Indiana. Pan-Africanism appeared once again with interest in colonization. But the major expression took place in a muted form through the role of Booker T. Washington, who had his base in the black people's desire for racial solidarity, their struggle for land and for the preservation of crafts, and the aspirations of a rising bourgeoisie in the cities which derived its livelihood from the black masses.[41] Washington's social and political accommodations allowed the movement to exist and even gain support from Northern and Southern ruling circles. At the same time Washington's withdrawal from sociopolitical struggle reflected the weak post-Reconstruction position of black people in the agrarian South. Militant forms of black national liberation would not reemerge until a black proletariat had developed in the urban centers.

THE TRANSITION ERA, SECOND PHASE: WORLD WAR I TO WORLD WAR II

The new equilibrium of racial regulation that had stabilized around tenancy agriculture as the dominant force of black exploitation received its first major disturbance from the impact of World War I. A certain irony inheres in the condition that imperialism's cataclysm should begin the break-up of agrarian thralldom within the United States. The War's effect on black people took place through the mediation of the marketplace, rather than through any shake-up of political relations. Hostilities in Europe placed limitations on American industry's usual labor supply by shutting off the flow of immigration at the very time the demand for labor was increasing sharply due to a war boom and military mobilization. Competition with the Southern plantation system for black labor became one of the major means of resolving this crisis of labor demand.

The black labor reserve in the countryside that had existed essentially as a *potential* source of the industrial proletariat now became a very *active* source. Whereas in the past this industrial reserve had not been tapped in any important way except by rural-based operations such as lumbering, with the advent of the War the industrial system as a whole began drawing on it. This new demand for black workers was to set in motion three key developments: first, the dispersion of black people out of the South into Northern urban centers; second, the formation of a distinct black proletariat in the urban centers at the very heart of the corporate-capitalist process of production; third, the break-up of tenancy agriculture in the South. World War II was to repeat the process in a magnified form and to place the stamp of irreversibility upon it.

Migration out of the countryside started in 1915 and swept up to a human tide by 1917. The major movement was to Northern cities, so that between 1910 and 1920 the black population increased in Chicago from 44,000 to 109,000; in New York from 92,000 to 152,000; in Detroit from 6,000 to 41,000; and in Philadelphia from 84,000 to 134,000. That decade there was a net increase of 322,000 in the number of Southern-born blacks living in the North, exceeding the aggregate increase of the preceding 40 years. A secondary movement took place to Southern cities, especially those with shipbuilding and heavy industry.

Labor demand in such industries as steel, meat-packing, and autos was the key stimulant to black migration. The total number of wage-earners in manufacturing went from 7,000,000 in 1914 to around 9,000,000 in 1919—an increase twice that of any preceding five-year period. A survey of the experience of the major employers of black labor in Chicago reported that "inability to obtain competent white workers was the reason given in practically every instance for the large number of Negroes employed since 1914."[42] The profit-maximization imperatives of Northern capitalist firms for the first time outweighed the sociopolitical reasons for leaving the Southern planters' control over black labor undisturbed and without any serious competition.

Labor agents sent South by railroad and steel companies initiated the migration by telling of high wages and offering transportation subsidy. In some cases whole trainloads of workers were shipped North. Though American firms had employed labor recruiters for work among the European peasantries for decades, this was the first time they went forth in any strength to bring black peasants to the city. Many Southern localities tried to protect their labor stocks by legislating proscriptions on labor agents and charging them prohibitive license fees, but on the whole recruiters played only a secondary role.[43] A more important impetus to migration came from the Northern-based black press, most notably the *Chicago Defender*, and above all from the letters and the reports of blacks who had already moved north. Successful employment served as its own advertisement, and better wages outside the South proved very attractive. During the summer of 1917 male wage-earners in the North were making $2.00 to $2.50 a day while the money wages on Mississippi farms ranged from 75¢ to $1.25.[44] Early migrations to Northern cities had been from the Upper South. Now blacks came in from all over, with the Deep South having the heaviest representation. In many cotton areas boll-weevil invasions destroyed the crop, acting as a push off the land at the same time Northern industry was providing a pull.

There was a temporary slackening of the demand for black labor when postwar demobilization caused heavy unemployment. In Chicago, where as many as 10,000 black laborers were out of work, the local Association of Commerce wired to Southern chambers of commerce: "Are you in need of Negro labor? Large surplus here, both returned soldiers and civilian Negroes ready to go to work."[45] In Detroit in 1921, black unemployment rates were five times as great as those of native white workers, and twice as great as those of the foreign-born.[46] But a strong economic recovery at the very time that restrictive immigration laws went into effect brought a second great migration out of the South in the years 1922 to 1924. The magnitude of this second movement has been estimated at slightly under a half-million persons, and may have been greater than that of the wartime movement.[47] The employers who already had a black sector in their workforce were able to tap this supply with much less trouble and cost than had been incurred a few years before. As William Graves, personal assistant to Julius Rosenwald, told the Chicago Union League Club: "The Negro permanency in industry was no longer debatable."[48]

The tremendous social dislocations created by the mobilization and the wartime economic boom heightened interracial tensions and laid the groundwork for over 20 race riots that occurred on both sides of the Mason-Dixon Line. Careful studies of the two major race riots in Northern industrial centers (East Saint Louis in 1917 and Chicago in 1919) reveal the tremendous friction that had developed between white and black workers.[49] These hostilities were not simply an outgrowth of race prejudice, for in both cases employers had fostered competition for jobs, especially by employing blacks as strikebreakers. Conflict between working-class whites and working-class blacks was analogous in a way to the racial competition among tenants and smallholders for land in the South. When the conflict erupted into mass violence, the dominant whites sat back and resolved the crises in a manner that assured their continued control over both groups.

The first feature of the program that Northern industry developed in relation to the interracial conflicts that the riots evidenced was that the permanency of black workers in the North was conclusively established. Management accepted its interest in guaranteeing minimal survival conditions of housing, education, et cetera to perpetuate this labor force. Even during slack times business had to maintain a certain continuity of employment, especially in those jobs that functionally became "Negro jobs." Economically, even in a recession, long-run costs are reduced if something of a permanent workforce is retained, for when good times return the recruitment and training of an entirely new labor force can require a great monetary outlay.[50] Thus, as the 1920s wore on, while there was a virtual cessation of articles regarding the employment of blacks in business-oriented and welfare publications, the fact that blacks *would* be employed was now accepted. The shifting of racial stereotypes to fit the new situation was indicated by a business spokesman who reported that the black man "has lost his slovenliness, lazy habits, gambling, and liquor-drinking propensities." He noted that plant superintendents in heavy industry had come to consider black workers especially tractable. "They found Negroes on the whole far more adjustable than the foreign-born. They used a common language, were loyal in times of stress, and were more co-operative in matters such as stock purchases, buying insurance, et cetera."[51]

At the same time, it has to be understood that black workers were employed on management's own terms. Sometimes these terms would involve the deliberate use of blacks to divide the work force. As a case in point, International Harvester integrated the hiring of blacks into its open-shop policies. Part of its strategy was to keep any nationality group from becoming too numerous in any one plant lest they become cohesive in labor conflicts. The decision on hiring was left up to the individual plant superintendents, some keeping their shops lily-white, others hiring large numbers of black workers. Harvester's management was caught up in a contradiction between its need for black workers, especially in the disagreeable twine mill and foundry, and its desire to keep them below 20 percent at any one plant.[52]

A somewhat different approach was taken by Ford Motor Company. In the 1921 depression Henry Ford decided to maintain the black workforce at the gigantic River Rouge plant in the same proportion as blacks in the total population of the Detroit area. The great majority of blacks at the River Rouge plant were employed in hot, heavy jobs in the rolling mills and foundry, but it was company policy to place a few in every major production unit and even allow a certain amount of upgrading to skilled positions. At the other Ford plants, as at the other major auto companies, black workers were confined to hard unskilled jobs. But the job concessions at Rouge became a mechanism by which Ford was able to gain considerable influence over Detroit's black community. Hiring was channeled through some preferred black ministers who agreed with Henry Ford on politics and industrial relations. Company black personnel officials were active in Republican politics and in anti-union campaigns. Ford had learned early a racial tactic that is widely employed today—that of trading concessions, relaxing economic subordination in order to increase political subordination.[53]

In industry generally the black worker was almost always deployed in job categories that effectively became designated as "Negro jobs." This classification, openly avowed in the South, was often claimed in the North to be merely the way things worked out through application of uniform standards. The superintendent of a Kentucky plough factory expressed the Southern view:

> Negroes do work white men won't do, such as common labor; heavy, hot, and dirty work; pouring crucibles; work in the grinding room; and so on. Negroes are employed because they are cheaper. . . . The Negro does a different grade of work and makes about 10¢ an hour less.[54]

There was not a lot of contrast in the words of coke works foremen at a Pennsylvania steel mill: "They are well fitted for this hot work, and we keep them because we appreciate this ability in them." "The door machines and the jam cutting are the most undesirable; it is hard to get white men to do this kind of work."[55] The placement of workers in separate job categories along racial lines was so marked in Detroit that in response to a survey many employers stated that they could not make a comparison between the wages of whites and blacks because they were not working on the same jobs.[56] In the North there was some blurring of racial distinctions, but they remained strong enough to set the black labor force off quite clearly. While the pay for the same job in the same plant was usually equivalent, when blacks came to predominate in a specific job classification, the rate on it would tend to lag. White and black workers were often hired in at the same low job classification; however, for the whites advancement was often possible, while the blacks soon bumped into a job ceiling. In terms of day-to-day work, white labor was given a systematic advantage over black labor and a stake in the racist practices.

In the South, where four-fifths of the nation's black population still lived at the end of the 1920s, the situation of black labor was to all appearances essentially unchanged. The number of black men engaged in Southern industry grew during this decade only 45 percent as fast as the number of whites. Black workers were concentrated in stagnant or declining plants, such as sawmills, coal mines, and cigar and tobacco factories. The increased hiring of blacks in such places was chiefly a reflection of the fact that the jobs had no future and the employers were not able to attract white workers. Black employment in textiles was severely limited, as in South Carolina, where state law forbade blacks to work in the same room, use the same stairway, or even share the same factory window as white textile workers.[57] Industry in the South, as far as black workers were concerned, still offered little competition to the dominance of agrarian tenancy.

Beneath the surface, however, significant changes were taking place in the rural South. While as late as the mid-1930s Charles S. Johnson could write of a cotton county in Alabama that "the plantation technique on the side of administration was most effective in respect to discipline and policing, and this technique has survived more or less despite the formal abolition of slavery,"[58] this state of affairs was then being undermined. Cotton cultivation was moving westward, leaving many blacks in the Southeast without a market crop. Out in the new cotton lands in Texas and Oklahoma whites provided a much larger proportion of the tenants and sharecroppers. By 1930 a slight decrease was seen in the number of black farm operators and laborers. Later, the great depression of the 1930s accelerated this trend as the primary market for agricultural commodities collapsed and the acreage in cotton was halved. Black tenants were pushed off land in far greater proportions than whites. New Deal agricultural programs were very important in displacing sharecroppers and tenants, since they subsidized reductions in acreage. In the early government-support programs landlords tended to monopolize subsidy payments, diverting much of them out of tenants' pockets. When the regulations were changed in the tenants' favor, the landowner had an incentive to convert the tenants to wage laborers or dismiss them altogether so as to get the whole subsidy.[59] The great depression marked the first drastic decline in the demand for black peasants since their status had been established after the Civil War.

In 1940 there were 650,000 fewer black farm operators and laborers than there had been a decade earlier—representing a one-third drop in the total. The push out of the countryside helped maintain a small net rate of migration to the North. More significantly, however, during the depression decade a high rate of black movement to the city kept on while the rate of white urbanization slackened greatly.

Although the great majority of black people remained in the rural South, we have dealt primarily with the character of the demand for black workers in the course of their becoming established directly in the urban industrial economy. This initial process was to form the matrix into which the ever-increasing numbers of black workers were to be fitted.[60] As the size of the black population in big cities grew, "Negro jobs" became roughly institutionalized into an identifiable black sublabor market within the larger metropolitan labor market. The culture of control that was embodied in the regulative systems which managed the black ghettos, moreover, provided an effective, although less rigid, variation of the Jim Crow segregation that continued with hardly any change in the South. Although the economic base of black tenancy was collapsing, its reciprocal superstructure of political and social controls remained the most powerful force shaping the place of blacks in society. The propertied and other groups that had a vested interest in the special exploitation of the black peasantry were still strong enough to maintain their hegemony over matters concerning race. At the same time, the variation of Jim Crow that existed in the North was more than simply a carry-over from the agrarian South. These ghetto controls served the class function for industrial society of politically and socially setting off that section of the proletariat that was consigned to the least desirable employment. This racial walling off not only was accomplished by direct ruling-class actions, but also was mediated through an escalating reciprocal process in which the hostility and competition of the white working class was stimulated by the growth of the black proletariat and in return operated as an agent in shaping the new racial controls.

The prolonged depression of the 1930s that threw millions out of work severely tested the position of blacks in the industrial economy. Two somewhat contradictory results stood out for this period. First, whites were accorded racial preference as a greatly disproportionate share of unemployment was placed on black workers. Second, despite erosion due to the unemployment differential, the black subsectors of the urban labor markets remained intact.

In the first years of the slump, black unemployment rates ran about two-thirds greater than white unemployment rates. As the depression wore on, the relative position of the black labor force declined so that by the end of the decade it had proportionately twice as many on relief or unemployed in the Mid-Atlantic States, and two and a half times as many in the North Central States. In the Northern cities only half the black men had regular full-time employment. In the larger cities, for every four black men in full-time regular employment there was one engaged in government-sponsored emergency relief. The differential in the South was not as great, for much of the unemployment there was disguised by marginal occupations on the farms.

The rationing out of unemployment operated in such a way as to reinforce the demarcation of "Negro jobs." Blacks were dismissed in higher proportions from the better positions. In Chicago they were displaced from professional and managerial occupations at a rate five times that of whites. The displacement rate from clerical, skilled, and semiskilled jobs was three times larger, while from unskilled and service jobs it was down to twice that of whites. As a result the total percentage of skilled and white-collar workers in the black labor force declined to half its former proportion, and the servant and personal service sector expanded again. Nationally, blacks lost a third of the jobs they had held in industry, declining from 7.3 percent to 5.1 percent of the total manufacturing employment. In the South the continuous unemployment even made white workers bid for those jobs in the tobacco industry that for generations had been recognized as "Negro jobs." An example from Northern industry: International Harvester no longer had a dire need for black workers, and the company let them slip off from 28 percent to 19 percent in the twine mill, and 18 percent to 10 percent at the McCormick Works.[61]

The limited openings available to black job-seekers were in precisely those fields that were defined as "Negro jobs." Therefore, in the urban areas, young white workers with less than a seventh-grade education had a higher rate of unemployment than blacks. With grade-school and high-school diplomas, however, the whites' chances for jobs increased markedly while blacks' chances actually declined. In general increased age and experience did not improve the black worker's position in the labor market.

On the eve of World War II, when defense production really began to stimulate the economy, the number of jobs increased rapidly. At first, however, it was almost as if the black unemployed had to stand aside while the whites went to work. In April 1940, 22 percent of the blacks (about 1,250,000 persons) were unemployed, as were 17.7 percent of the white labor force. By October, employment had increased by 2,000,000 jobs, and white unemployment had declined to 13 percent, while black unemployment remained at the same level. Firms with tremendous labor shortages still abided by their racial definitions of jobs and refused to take on available black workers. In September 1941 a U.S. Government survey found that of almost 300,000 job openings, over half were restricted to whites. In Indiana, Ohio, and Illinois, 80 percent of the openings were thus restricted.[62]

Military mobilization of much of the existing labor force and an almost 20 percent growth in non-farm employment from 32,000,000 in 1940 to 40,000,000 in 1942 were the preconditions necessary to enlarge the demand for black labor. While the President's creation of the Fair Employment

Practice Committee (FEPC) under pressure from black organizations helped open up some doors, it was the logic of the labor market that shook the racial status quo. By 1942, management-oriented publications were dealing with the question of employing black workers—a topic they had not considered since the mid-1920s.

The American Management Association told its members: "As some shortages develop for which there is no adequate supply of labor from the usual sources, management is forced to look elsewhere. It is then that the Negro looms large as a reservoir of motive power—a source which management has hitherto given only a few furtive, experimental pokes with a long pole." Once more surveys were conducted which showed that most employers consider black workers as efficient as whites. Management reiterated statements about non-discrimination when production conditions forced them to change their racial hiring practices. *Fortune* magazine consoled its executive readers that their personal racism need not be violated: "Theoretically, management should have fewer objections to hiring colored labor than any other part of the industrial team. The employer seldom has social contact with his workers anyway, and his primary concern is production efficiency and satisfactory investment return."[63]

Nationally, the demand for black labor was tremendous. In the spring of 1942 it composed 2.5 percent to 3 percent of the war-production work force, and by the fall of 1944 this proportion had risen to 8.3 percent. These million and a half black war workers were concentrated in the areas of the most stringent labor shortage. Fourteen industrial centers accounted for almost half of these war workers, and of these centers only one was located in the South and only two were border cities. In areas of acute labor shortage, the absence of any white reserve of labor gave blacks much greater access to war work than in labor surplus areas. Black migration was a necessary condition for this employment, and the movement of the families out of the Southern countryside and small towns was accelerated.

The vast demand for labor in general, that had to turn itself into a demand for black labor, could only be accomplished by way of a great expansion of the black sectors of metropolitan labor markets. Training programs for upgrading to skilled and semiskilled jobs were opened up, at first in the North and later in the South. By 1943–1944, 35 percent of preemployment trainees in shipbuilding courses and 29 percent in aircraft were blacks. World War I had established a space for black laborers as unskilled workers in heavy industry. During World War II this space was enlarged to include a number of semiskilled and single-skilled jobs in many industries.[64]

World War II marked the most dramatic improvement in economic status of black people that has ever taken place in the urban industrial economy. The income of black workers increased twice as fast as that of whites. Occupationally, blacks bettered their positions in all of the preferred occupations. The biggest improvement was brought about by the migration from South to North (a net migration of 1,600,000 blacks between 1940 and 1950). However, within both sections the relative proportion of blacks within skilled and semiskilled occupations grew. In clerical and lower-level professional work, labor shortages in the government bureaucracies created a necessity for a tremendous black upgrading into posts hitherto lily-white.

During the era between the two World Wars the national aspirations of blacks worked themselves out on the base of their new material conditions— that is, those of their becoming an urban people whose masses were proletarians. Conflicting tendencies beset this movement at every stage. The dominant white society usually followed the strategy of denying the very existence of its peoplehood. The black community was considered a pathological form rather than something valid in itself. Whenever the black community did thrust itself forward, the tactics of management shifted to a balance of naked repression with co-optive channeling. Within the community there was a constant contention as to which of the class forces would dominate—the black bourgeoisie, that sector of the black working class operating under the dominance of white trade-union organizations, or a nationally based black working class.

The greatest organized expression of black nationalism occurred in the Garvey Back-to-Africa Movement after 1920. As Harry Haywood has so-trenchantly characterized this broad mass development, it was conditioned by the convergence of two class developments:

> On the one hand it was the trend of the recent migrants from the peasant South. . . . The membership of these organizations by and large was composed of the new, as yet non-integrated Negro proletarians; recent migrants from the cotton fields, who had not yet shaken the dust of the plantation from their heels and remained largely peasants in outlook. Embittered and disillusioned by post-war terror and unemployment, they saw in the Garvey scheme of a Negro nation in Africa a way out to the realization of their deep-grounded yearnings for land and freedom. . . . On the other hand, Garveyism reflected the ideology of the Negro petty bourgeoisie, their abortive attempt at hegemony in the Negro movement. It was the trend of the small property-holder: the shopkeepers, pushed to the wall, ruined or threatened with ruin by the ravages of the crisis; the frustrated and unemployed Negro professionals—doctors and lawyers with impoverished clientele, storefront preachers, poverty-stricken students— in sum those elements of the middle class closest to the Negro laboring people and hence affected most keenly by deterioration of their conditions.[65]

When the migration of black peasants to the Northern cities dropped off in the mid-1920s, the Garvey movement began to lose out, and the U.S. Government was able to move in with prosecutions to break it up.

The more successful entrepreneurial types, such as the bankers, insurance executives, and newspaper publishers, were able now to seize the lead in the cities. They generated an optimism about the future of black capitalism that has never been recaptured. This group, which provided services chiefly to a black clientele, lost out when the depression brought wholesale bankruptcy, and this experience smashed illusions about the future of black business.[66]

Proletarian leadership now reemerged on a firmer foundation of having assimilated its new conditions of existence. From the masses themselves there was a surge of battles in the cities for emergency relief and against housing evictions. This intervention of the working class and unemployed inserted a new vigor into the "Don't Buy Where You Can't Work" campaigns that bourgeois leadership had initiated to win jobs from white firms operating in the ghetto. In 1935 a riot broke out in Harlem, and for the first time blacks moved from a defensive posture in such a situation and employed violence on a retaliatory basis against the white store-owners. As concessions were gained, part of the energy was channeled into the New Deal relief bureaucracy and Democratic Party politics, where patronage and paternalism took the edge off much independent thrust. Nevertheless, important struggles for jobs, government-supported housing, and more territory for living space helped consolidate an institutional infrastructure for the black community and gave an urban definition to its national consciousness, or race pride, as it was called in those days.

The trade-union organizing drives of the CIO which actively sought out black workers in heavy and mass-production industry provided a new focus. From 1937 to World War II the CIO conducted the most massive working-class campaign that has ever taken place in America. Its dynamism was so great that it reset the direction of the political activity of the working class, the black community, and the Left. Even the bourgeois-led organizations, like the NAACP, came to accept the decisive leadership role of the CIO. While black workers played an integral part in this organizing campaign, with over 200,000 members in the CIO ranks by 1940, the black working class did not develop an independent program or organization that dealt with the national oppression of their people.[67]

Only after the outbreak of World War II, when blacks were still being excluded from much of the rapidly expanding economy, did a black movement set out independently from the New Deal–labor coalition and take the initiative in defining a race position on the national level. In January 1941 A. Philip Randolph, president of the Brotherhood of Sleeping Car Porters, an all-black AFL union, issued a call for a massive march on Washington to demand of the Government a greater share in the defense effort. The March on Washington Movement expressed the mood of the black community and received an upswelling of support sufficient to force President Roosevelt to establish a Fair Employment Practice Committee in return for the calling off of the projected march. Although this movement was not able to establish a firmly organized working-class base or sustain itself for long, it foreshadowed a new stage of development for a self-conscious black working class with the appeal that "an oppressed people must accept the responsibility and take the initiative to free themselves."[68]

CURRENT CONDITIONS OF DEMAND:
AN OUTLINE

(A full examination of the present-day political economic conditions regarding the demand for black labor requires a whole separate essay. We are limited here to indicating some of the most essential features.)

The changes that took place in the economic deployment of black labor in World War II were clearly an acceleration of developments that had been under way since World War I. In a process of transition, at a certain point the quantity of change becomes so great that the whole set of relationships assume an entirely different character. Such a nodal point took place during World War II, and there resulted a transformation in the characteristic relations of institutional racism from agrarian thralldom to a metropolitan ghetto system.

Within a generation, few of the concrete economic or demographic forms of the old base remained. In 1940, over three-fourths of all blacks lived in the South, close to two-thirds lived in rural areas there, and just under half were still engaged in agriculture. By 1969, almost as many blacks lived outside the South as still resided in that region, and only 4 percent of the black laborers remained in agriculture, as they had left the farms at a much more rapid rate than whites. Today, only about a fifth of the total black population live in the rural areas and small towns of the South.

The United States, during the twentieth century, has become a distinctively urban nation—or, more accurately, a metropolitan nation with its population centered in the large cities and their surrounding configurations. The first three decades of this century witnessed the rapid urbanization of whites; the next three decades saw an even more rapid urbanization of blacks. In 1940 the proportion of the country's black population living in urban areas (49 percent) was the same as that proportion of whites had been in 1910. Within 20 years, almost three fourths of all blacks were urban dwellers, a higher proportion than the corresponding one for whites. More specifically, the black population has been relocated into the central cities of the metropolitan areas—in 1940, 34 percent of all blacks resided in central cities; in 1969, 55 percent. The larger cities were the points of greatest growth. In 1950 black people constituted one out of every eight persons in the central cities of the metropolitan areas of every size classification, and one out of every twenty in the suburbs. By 1969, black people constituted one out of every four in the central city populations of the large metropolitan areas (1,000,000 plus), and about one out of six in the medium-size metropolitan areas (250,000 to 1,000,000), while in the smaller-size metropolitan areas (below 250,000) and the suburbs the proportions remained constant. Today black communities form major cities in themselves, two with populations over 1,000,000, four between 500,000 and 1,000,000, and eight between 200,000 and 500,000.[69] Newark and Washington D.C. already have black majorities, and several other major cities will most likely join their ranks in the next ten years.

The displacement of blacks from Southern agriculture was only partially due to the pull of labor demand in wartime. Technological innovation, being a necessary condition of production, acted as an independent force to drive the tenants out of the cotton fields. The push off the land occurred in two phases. Initially, right after the war, the introduction of tractors and herbicides displaced the cotton hands from full-time to seasonal work at summer weeding and harvest. The now part-time workers moved from the farms to hamlets and small towns. During the 1950s mechanization of the harvest eliminated most of the black peasantry from agricultural employment and forced them to move to the larger cities for economic survival.[70]

Elimination of the Southern black peasantry was decisive in changing the forms of racism throughout the entire region, for it meant the disappearance of the economic foundation on which the elaborate superstructure of legal Jim Crow and segregation had originally been erected. Not only did this exploited agrarian group almost vanish, but the power of the large landholders who expropriated the surplus it had produced diminished in relation to the growing urban and industrial interests. While the civil-rights movement and the heroic efforts associated with it were necessary to break the official legality of segregation, it should be recognized that in a sense this particular form of racism was already obsolete, as its base in an exploitative system of production had drastically changed. The nature of the concessions made both by the ruling class nationally and by the newer power groups of the South can be understood only in terms of this fuller view of history.[71]

For the United States as a whole, the most important domestic development was the further elaboration and deepening of monopoly state capitalism. As the political economy has matured, technological and management innovation have become capital-saving as well as labor-saving. Capital accumulation declines as a proportion of the gross national product, and a mature capitalist economy enters into a post-accumulation phase of development. Under these conditions the disposal of the economic surplus becomes almost as great a problem as the accumulation of it. Corporations promote consumerism through increased sales effort, planned obsolescence, and advertising. The State meets the problem by increasing its own expenditures, especially in non-consumable military items, by providing monetary support to consumption through subsidies to the well-off, and by spending a certain amount on welfare for the working class and the poor.

Markedly lower incomes would add to the surplus disposal problems and would create economic stagnation as well as risking the most disruptive forms of class struggle.

Working-class incomes have two basic minimum levels, or floors. One is that which can be considered the level of the good trade-union contract which has to be met even by non-union firms that bid in this section of the labor market. State intervention is usually indirect in the setting of these incomes, but has grown noticeably in the last few years. The other income floor is set by direct government action via minimum-wage and welfare legislation. In the Northern industrial states where trade unions are stronger, both these income floors tend to be higher than in rural and Southern states.

Although in the mature capitalist society both economic and political imperatives exist for a certain limiting of the exploitation of the working class as a whole, each corporation still has to operate on the basis of maximizing its profits. The fostering of a section of the working class that will have to work at the jobs that are paid at rates between those of the two income floors works to meet the needs of profit maximization. Other jobs that fall into this category are those that might pay at the collective bargaining contract level but are subject to considerable seasonal and cyclical unemployment, and those from which a high rate of production is squeezed under hard or hazardous conditions. In all the developed Western capitalist states, there exists a group of workers to fill the jobs that the more politically established sectors of the working class shun. These marginal workers generally are set apart in some way so that they lack the social or the political means of defending their interests. In Western Europe usually they are noncitizens coming from either Southern Europe or Northern Africa. In England they are colored peoples coming from various parts of the Empire.[72] In the urban centers of the United States race serves to mark black and brown workers for filling in the undesirable slots.

Further, in the distribution of government transfer payments each class and status group strives to maximize its receipts. Therefore the powerless tend to receive a smaller proportion of these funds, and those that are delivered to them come in a manner which stigmatizes and bolsters political controls.

Specifically, in the metropolitan centers in America, there is a racial dual labor-market structure.[73] Side by side with the primary metropolitan job market in which firms recruit white workers and white workers seek employment, there exists a smaller secondary market in which firms recruit black workers and black workers seek jobs. In the largest metropolitan areas this secondary black market ranges from one-tenth to one-quarter of the size of the white market. For both the white and black sectors there are distinct demand and supply forces determining earnings and occupational distribution, as well as separate institutions and procedures for recruitment, hiring, training, and promotion of workers.

The dual labor market operates to create an urban-based industrial labor reserve that provides a ready supply of workers in a period of labor shortage and can be politically isolated in times of relatively high unemployment. In a tight labor market the undesirable jobs that whites leave are filled out of this labor reserve so that in time more job categories are added to the black sector of the labor market. If the various forms of disguised unemployment and subemployment are all taken into account, black unemployment rates can run as high as three or four times those of whites in specific labor markets in recession periods. The welfare and police costs of maintaining this labor reserve are high, but they are borne by the State as a whole and therefore do not enter into the profit calculations of individual firms.

This special exploitation of the black labor force also leads to direct economic gains for the various employers. Methodologically it is very difficult to measure exactly the extra surplus extracted due to wage discrimination, although in Chicago it has been estimated that unskilled black workers earn about 17 percent less on similar jobs than unskilled white workers of comparable quality.[74] While in a historical sense the entire differential of wage income between blacks and whites can be attributed to discrimination, the employer realizes only that which takes place in the present in terms of either lesser wage payments or greater work output. Estimates of this realized special exploitation range on the order of 10 percent to 20 percent of the total black wage and salary income.[75]

The subordinate status of the black labor market does not exist in isolation, but rather is a major part of a whole complex of institutional controls that constitute the web of urban racism.[76] This distinctive modern form of racism conforms to the 300-year-old traditions of the culture of control for the oppression of black people, but now most of the controls are located within the major metropolitan institutional networks—such as the labor market, the housing market, the political system. As the black population grew in the urban centers a distinctive new formation developed in each of these institutional areas. A black ghetto and housing market, a black labor market, a black school system, a black political system, and a black welfare system came into being—not as parts of a self-determining community, but as institutions to be controlled, manipulated, and exploited. When the black population did not serve the needs of dominant institutions by providing a wartime labor reserve, they were isolated so that they could be regulated and incapacitated.

This model of urban racism has had three major components with regard to institutional structures: (1) Within the major institutional networks that operate in the city there have developed definable black subsectors which operated on a subordinated basis, subject to the advantage, control, and priorities of the dominant system. (2) A pattern of mutual reinforcement takes place between the barriers that define the various black subsectors. (3) The controls over the lives of black men are so pervasive that they form a system analogous to colonial forms of rule.

The history of the demand for black labor in the postwar period showed the continued importance of wartime labor scarcities. The new job categories gained during World War II essentially were transferred into the black sectors of the labor market. Some war industries, like shipbuilding, of course, dropped off considerably. In reconversion and the brief 1948–1949 recession blacks lost out disproportionately on the better jobs. However the Korean War again created an intense labor shortage, making black workers once more in demand, at least until the fighting stopped. The period of slow economic growth from 1955 to the early 1960s saw a deterioration in the relative position of blacks as they experienced very high rates of unemployment and their incomes grew at a slower rate than those of whites. The civil-rights protests had generated little in the way of new demand. Only the coincidence of the rebellions of Watts, Newark, and Detroit with the escalation of the Vietnam War brought about a sharp growth in demand for black labor.

All the available evidence indicates that there has been no structural change of any significance in the deployment of black workers, most especially in private industry. Certain absolute standards of exclusion in professional, management, and sales occupations have now been removed, but the total growth in these areas has been slight except where a black clientele is serviced, as in the education and health fields. The one significant new demand in the North has been that for women clerical workers. This arises from a shortage of this particular kind of labor in the central business districts, which, being surrounded by the black community, are increasingly geographically removed from white supplies of these workers. About 90 percent of Chicago's black female white-collar workers work either in their own communities or in the central business districts, and are not employed in the rapidly growing outlying offices. In the South the whole pattern of racial regulation in the major cities is shifting over to a Northern model, so that the basic situation of black workers in Atlanta or Memphis is approaching that of the North about a decade ago.

Until the uprisings in the mid-1960s, management of racial affairs was carried out either by the unvarnished maintenance of the status quo (except when black workers were needed) or by an elaborate ritual of fair practices and equal employment opportunity. The latter strategy operated as a sort of sophisticated social Darwinism to make the rules of competition for the survival of the fittest more equitable. Actually it blurred institutional realities, channeling energies and perceptions into individualized findings of fact. The black protest movement finally forced a switch to a policy of affirmative action that is supported by legal encouragement. In either case no basic structures have actually been transformed. As a review of studies on the current racial status in several industries finds: "Over the long haul, however, it is apparent that the laws of supply and demand have exercised a greater influence on the quantitative employment patterns of blacks than have the laws of the land."[77]

In the Cold War era the trade-union movement lost its innovative dynamism and became narrowly wage-oriented. Overwhelmingly, the net racial effect of the collective-bargaining agreements was to accept the given conditions in a plant. Only a very few unions, usually from the CIO, conducted any fights for the upgrading of black workers. More usual was the practice of neglecting shop grievances. Within union life itself the black officials who arose as representatives of their race were converted into justifiers of the union administration to the black workers.[78] On the legislative and judicial fronts—that is, away from their day-to-day base of operations—national unions supported the programs of civil-rights organizations and the fair-employment symbolism. In fact by the early 1960s the racial strategies of national trade unions and those of the most-sophisticated corporate leadership had converged.

The actions of the black community itself were destined to become the decisive political initiator, not only in its own liberation struggles but on the domestic scene in general. From World War II through the Korean War the urban black communities were engaged in digesting the improvements brought about by the end of the depression and by the wartime job gains. Both bourgeois and trade-union leadership followed the forms of the New Deal-labor coalition, but the original substance of mass struggle was no longer present.

The destabilization of the whole agrarian society in the South created the conditions for new initiatives. The Montgomery bus boycott was to reintroduce mass political action into the Cold War era. The boldness of the civil-rights movement, plus the success of national liberation movements in the Third World, galvanized the black communities in the major cities. At first the forms of the Southern struggle were to predominate in pro-integration civil-rights actions. Then youth and workers were swept into the movement and redefined its direction toward black self-determination. The mass spontaneity in the ghetto rebellions revealed the tremendous potential of this orientation.

The ghetto systems and the dual labor markets had organized a mass black proletariat, and had concentrated it in certain key industries and plants. In the decade after World War II the most important strategic concentration of black workers was in the Chicago packing houses, where they became the majority group. United Packinghouse Workers District I was bold in battles over conditions in the plants and supplied the basic leadership for militant protest on the South Side. Even though the UPW was the most advanced of all big national unions on the race question, a coalition of black officials and shop stewards had to wage a struggle against the leadership for substantive black control. This incipient nationalist faction was defeated in the union, and the big meat packers moved out of the city; but before it disappeared the movement indicated the potential of black-oriented working-class leadership. The Packinghouse Workers' concrete struggles contrasted sharply with the strategy of A. Philip Randolph, who set up the form of an all-black Negro American Labor Council and then subordinated its mass support to maneuvers at the top level of the AFL-CIO.[79]

After the ghetto uprisings workers were to reassert themselves at the point of production. Black caucuses and Concerned Workers' Committees sprang up across the country in plants and installations with large numbers of blacks.[80] By this time the auto industry had created the largest concentration of black workers in the nation on its back-breaking production lines in Detroit. Driven by the peculiarities of the black labor market, the "big three" auto companies had developed the preconditions for the organization of the Dodge Revolutionary Union Movement (DRUM) and the League of Revolutionary Black Workers. The insertion onto this scene of a cadre that was both black-conscious and class-conscious, with a program of revolutionary struggle, forged an instrument for the militant working-class leadership of the Black Liberation Movement. The League also provides an exemplary model for proletarians among other oppressed groups, and might even be able to stimulate sections of the white working class to emerge from their narrow economistic orientation.[81]

The ruling class is caught in its own contradictions. It needs black workers, yet the conditions of satisfying this need compel it to bring together the potential forces for the most effective opposition to its policies, and even for a threat to its very existence. Amelioration of once absolute exclusionary barriers does not eliminate the black work force that the whole web of urban racism defines. Even if the capitalists were willing to forego their economic and status gains from racial oppression, they could not do so without shaking up all of the intricate concessions and consensual arrangements through which the State now exercises legitimate authority. Since the ghetto institutions are deeply intertwined with the major urban systems, the American Government does not even have the option of decolonializing by ceding nominal sovereignty that the British and French empires have both exercised. The racist structures cannot be abolished without an earthquake in the heartland. Indeed, for that sophisticated gentleman, the American capitalist, the demand for black labor has become a veritable devil in the flesh.

NOTES

1. Karl Marx, *Capital* (Chicago, 1906), vol. 1, p. 823.
2. Ibid., p. 833.

3. "As is well known, commodity production preceded [capitalist] commodity production, and constitutes one of the conditions (but not the sole condition) of the rise of the latter." V. I. Lenin, *Development of Capitalism in Russia* (Moscow, 1956), p. 606.

4. Eugene D. Genovese, *The Political Economy of Slavery* (New York, 1967), contends that the plantation slave system was the base of a social order in the American South that essentially was precapitalist and quasi-aristocrat.

5. Marvin Harris, *Patterns of Race in the Americas* (New York, 1964), p. 13.

6. Winthrop Jordan, *White Over Black* (Chapel Hill, 1968), p. 184.

7. David Brion Davis, *The Problem of Slavery in Western Culture* (Ithaca, 1966), pp. 41–46.

8. Winthrop Jordan, *White Over Black*, pp. 3–43.

9. Carl N. Degler, "Slavery in the United States and Brazil: An Essay in Comparative History," *American Historical Review*, April 1970, pp. 1019–1021; Davis, *The Problem of Slavery*, pp. 232–233.

10. Philip Curtin, *The Atlantic Slave Trade* (Madison, 1969), p. 269; A. M. Carr Saunders, *World Population* (Oxford, 1936), p. 47.

11. C. L. R. James, *The Black Jacobins* (New York, 1963), p. 48. See also Gaston Martin, *Nantes au XVIII Siecle: L'Ere des Negriers* (Paris, 1931), pp. 422–433.

12. Eric Williams, *Capitalism and Slavery* (Chapel Hill, 1944), pp. 50–84.

13. Malachi Postlethwayt, *The Advantage of the African Trade* (1772), quoted in Abram L. Harris, *The Negro as Capitalist* (Philadelphia, 1936), pp. 2–3.

14. Marcus Wilson Jernegan, *Laboring and Dependent Classes in Colonial America, 1607–1763* (Chicago, 1931), p. 23.

15. By this time free blacks constituted between 40 percent and 60 percent of the black population in Brazil and 35 percent in Cuba. Herbert S. Klein, "The Colored Freedmen in Brazil," *Journal of Social History*, Fall 1969, pp. 30–54.

16. Richard Wade, *Slavery in the Cities* (New York, 1964), p. 275.

17. W. E. B. Du Bois, *The Philadelphia Negro* (New York, 1967), p. 33. See also Herman Bloch, *The Circle of Discrimination* (New York, 1969), pp. 21–26.

18. Robert Ernst, "The Economic Status of New York Negroes, 1850–1863," reprinted in August Meier and Elliot Rudwick, eds., *The Making of Black America* (New York, 1969), vol. 1, pp. 250–261.

19. This statement is not meant to imply that there were not some important class distinctions or inequalities in income or wealth, but it does claim that the social and political means of defining status along these lines were not as clear-cut as they were in Europe or in Latin America.

20. Harris, *Patterns of Race*, chap. 7.

21. C. L. R. James, "The Atlantic Slave Trade and Slavery," *Amistad I* (New York, 1970), pp. 133–134.

22. W. E. B. Du Bois, *Black Reconstruction in America, 1860–1880* (Cleveland, 1962), p. 121.

23. "The Compromise of 1877 did not restore the old order in the South, nor did it restore the South to parity with other sections. It did assure the dominant whites political autonomy and non-intervention in matters of race policy, and promised them a share in the blessings of the new economic order. In return the South became . . . a satellite of the dominant region. . . . Under the regime of the Redeemers the

South became a bulwark instead of a menace to the new order." C. Vann Woodward, *Reunion and Reaction* (2nd ed.; New York, 1956), pp. 266–267.

24. W. E. B. Du Bois, *The Souls of Black Folk* (Chicago, 1903), chap. 8.

25. Quoted in Woodward, *Origins of the New South* (Baton Rouge, 1951), p. 208.

26. Rupert Vance, "Racial Competition for Land," in Edgar T. Thompson, ed., *Race Relations and the Race Problem* (Durham, 1939), pp. 100–104.

27. J. B. Killebrew, *Southern States Farm Magazine*, 1898, pp. 490–491, cited in Claude H. Nolen, *The Negro's Image in the South* (Lexington, Ky., 1968), p. 170. For a concrete explication of this approach, see Alfred Holt Stone, *Studies in the American Race Problem* (New York, 1909), chap. 4.

28. Woodward, *Origins of the New South*, p. 211.

29. Ibid., pp. 328–330.

30. Charles H. Wesley, *Negro Labor in the United States, 1850–1925* (New York, 1927), pp. 238–239; Nolen, *The Negro's Image in the South*, p. 190.

31. Lorenzo J. Greene and Carter G. Woodson, *The Negro Wage Earner* (Washington, D.C., 1930), pp. 49–50.

32. Wesley, *Negro Labor*, p. 142; W. E. B. Du Bois, *The Negro Artisan* (Atlanta, 1902), pp. 115–120.

33. Du Bois, *The Negro Artisan*, pp. 180–185. However, when the *Manufacturer's Record of Baltimore* conducted its own survey in 1893, the majority of manufacturers held that blacks were unfitted for most employment, but admitted that with training they could be used—an opinion they also held of the "primitive white man." One big difference in this latter survey was the inclusion of the cotton mills, a line that had already been declared a "white man's industry." Cited in Wesley, *Negro Labor*, pp. 244–248.

34. Paul H. Buck, *The Road to Reunion* (Boston, 1937), pp. 154–155.

35. Carter G. Woodson, "Story of the Fund," chap. 2, typescript, Julius Rosenwald Papers, University of Chicago Library; Louis Harland, *Separate and Unequal* (Chapel Hill, 1958), p. 77.

36. Leon F. Litwack, *North of Slavery* (Chicago, 1961).

37. Frank U. Quillan, *The Color Line in Ohio* (Ann Arbor, 1913), p. 138.

38. W. E. B. Du Bois, *The Negro Artisan*, pp. 173–175.

39. Sterling D. Spero and Abram L. Harris, *The Black Worker* (New York, 1931), is still essential on this. Also see Bernard Mandel, "Samuel Gompers and the Negro Workers, 1886–1914," *Journal of Negro History*, Jan. 1955, pp. 34–60; Herbert G. Gutman, "The Negro and the United Mine Workers of America," in Julius Jacobson, ed., *The Negro and the American Labor Movement* (New York, 1968), pp. 49–127; and the entire issue of *Labor History*, Summer 1969.

40. William M. Tuttle Jr., "Labor Conflict and Racial Violence: The Black Worker in Chicago, 1894–1919," *Labor History*, Summer 1969, pp. 406–432; Spero and Harris, *The Black Worker*, pp. 131–134.

41. August Meier, *Negro Thought in America, 1880–1915* (Ann Arbor, 1963).

42. Chicago Commission on Race Relations, *The Negro in Chicago* (Chicago, 1922), pp. 362–363.

43. Ibid., pp. 22–23, 27–33, 118–122; Allan H. Spear, *Black Chicago* (Chicago, 1967), pp. 33–38.

44. Wesley, *Negro Labor*, pp. 293–294; U.S. Labor Department, *Negro Migration in 1916–17* (Washington, D.C., 1919), pp. 125–126.

45. William M. Tuttle Jr., *Race Riot: Chicago in the Red Summer of 1919* (New York, 1970), pp. 130–132.

46. Herman Feldman, *Racial Factors in American Industry* (New York and London, 1931), pp. 42–43.

47. Louise V. Kennedy, *The Negro Peasant Moves Cityward* (New York, 1930), pp. 35–36.

48. William C. Graves, "Memorandum of Address Made June 17th Before the Inter-racial Committee of the Union League Club," Julius Rosenwald Papers, University of Chicago Library.

49. Elliot M. Rudwick, *Race Riot at East Saint Louis, July 2, 1917* (Carbondale, 1964); Tuttle, *Race Riot*.

50. Spero and Harris, *The Black Worker*, pp. 167–168.

51. Graves, "Memorandum of Speech Made June 17th."

52. Robert Ozanne, *A Century of Labor-Management Relations at McCormick and International Harvester* (Madison, 1967), pp. 183–187.

53. Lloyd H. Bailer: "The Negro Automobile Worker," *Journal of Political Economy* 51 (Oct. 1953): 416–419; Herbert Northrup, *Organized Labor and the Negro* (New York, 1944), pp. 189–195.

54. Spero and Harris, *The Black Worker*, p. 169.

55. Horace Cayton and George S. Mitchell, *The Black Workers and the New Unions* (Chapel Hill, 1939), p. 31.

56. Kennedy, *The Negro Peasant Moves Cityward*, p. 98; Feldman, *Racial Factors in American Industry*, pp. 57–58.

57. Erwin D. Hoffman, "The Genesis of the Modern Movement for Equal Rights in South Carolina, 1930–1939," *Journal of Negro History*, Oct. 1959, p. 347.

58. Charles S. Johnson, *The Shadow of the Plantation* (Chicago, 1934), p. 210. For a good review of the situation of blacks in the rural South during this period, see E. Franklin Frazier, *The Negro in the United States* (New York, 1949), chap. 10.

59. Gunnar Myrdal, *An American Dilemma* (2 vols.; New York, 1964), vol. 1, pp. 256–269.

60. One indication that the current pattern was established by 1930 is given by Herman Feldman's *Racial Factors in American Industry*, published the following year. Feldman was able to prescribe and to concretely illustrate a set of industrial-relations practices that sound amazingly similar to what today are called equal-opportunity programs. The major difference is that in 1930 the firms did not have to take into account the political strength of the black community.

61. St. Clair Drake and Horace Cayton, *Black Metropolis* (New York, 1945), vol. 1, pp. 215–217 and 226–227; Richard Sterner, *The Negro's Share* (New York, 1934), pp. 36–46 and 219–291, providing a useful compilation of material used in this and the following paragraph; Ozanne, *A Century of Labor Management Relations*, p. 187; Charles S. Johnson, "The Conflict of Caste and Class in an American Industry," *American Journal of Sociology*, July 1936, pp. 55–65.

62. "The Negro's War," *Fortune*, June 1942, pp. 76–80.

63. Ibid.; American Management Association, *The Negro Worker* (Research Report No. 1, 1942), pp. 3–4 and 27–28; Nicholas S. Falcone, *The Negro Integrated* (New York, 1945).

64. Robert Weaver, *Negro Labor: A National Problem* (New York, 1946), pp. 78–93.

65. Harry Haywood, *Negro Liberation* (New York, 1948), pp. 198–199.

66. A few years after the collapse of 1929 Abram Harris surveyed this flourishing of black capitalism and concluded that the limits of a separate economy were precariously narrow within the confines of the present industrial system. The independent black economy—whether it develops on the basis of private profit or on the basis of cooperation—cannot be the means of achieving the Negro's economic salvation (Harris, *The Negro as Capitalist*, p. x).

67. Cayton and Mitchell, *Black Workers and the New Unions*; Drake and Cayton, *Black Metropolis*, vol. 1, pp. 312–341; James Olsen, "Organized Black Leadership and Industrial Unionism: The Racial Response, 1939–1945," *Labor History*, Summer 1969, pp. 475–486.

68. The standard work on the MOW movement is Herbert Garfinkel, *When Negroes March* (Glencoe, 1959). The MOW movement actually presaged two forms of future tactics. In its appeal to the masses for a black-defined program of struggle it summarized all of the decade's action for jobs on a local level and impelled them forward on a national basis. On the other hand, in that the movement failed to develop an organized working-class constituency, it foretold tactics of maneuver without mass struggle—of legislative lobbying, judicial procedures, and jockeying within the Democratic Party—which were to be pursued by the bourgeois and trade-union organizations until demonstrations and civil disobedience finally arose from below out of the civil-rights movement.

69. These estimates are as of 1969. Data from the 1970 census were not available at the time of writing.

70. Richard H. Day, "The Economics of Technological Change and the Demise of the Sharecropper," *American Economic Review*, June 1967, pp. 427–449; Seymour Melman, "An Industrial Revolution in the Cotton South," *Economic History Review*, 2nd ser. (1949), pp. 59–72.

71. Analysis of the relation of economic and class shifts in the South to the civil-rights movement and the nature of its limited victories from 1954 to 1965 has been seriously neglected. Anyone undertaking such a study should keep in mind V. I. Lenin's fundamental law of revolution: "It is not enough for revolution that the exploited and oppressed masses should understand the impossibility of living in the old way and demand changes, it is essential for revolution that the exploiters should not be able to live and rule in the same way." Stated in *Left Wing Communism*.

72. David J. Smyth and Peter D. Lowe, "The Vestibule to the Occupational Ladder and Unemployment: Some Econometric Evidence on United Kingdom Structural Unemployment," *Industrial and Labor Relations Review*, July 1970, pp. 561–565.

73. This and following paragraphs on the dual labor market are basically a summary of Harold M. Baron and Bennett Hymer, "The Negro Worker in the Chicago Labor Market," in Julius Jacobson, ed., *The Negro and the American Labor Movement* (New York, 1968), pp. 232–285.

74. D. Taylor, "Discrimination and Occupational Wage Differences in the Market for Unskilled Labor," *Industrial and Labor Relations Review*, April 1968, pp. 375–390.

75. For a recent estimate see Lester Thurow, *The Economy of Poverty and Discrimination* (Washington, D.C., 1969). He finds the gains due to wage discrimination were $4,600,000,000 in 1960. Advantages to white workers due to higher employment rates were $6,500,000,000.

76. For an extended treatment of the institutionalization of racism in the metropolis see Harold Baron, "The Web of Urban Racism," in Louis Knowles and Kenneth Prewitt, eds., *Institutional Racism in America* (New York, 1969), pp. 134–176.

77. Vernon M. Briggs Jr., "The Negro in American Industry: A Review of Seven Studies," *Journal of Human Resources*, Summer 1970, pp. 371–381.

78. William Kornhauser, "The Negro Union Official: A Study of Sponsorship and Control," *American Journal of Sociology*, March 1952, pp. 443–452; Scott Greer, "Situational Pressures and Functional Role of the Ethnic Labor Leader," *Social Forces*, Oct. 1953, pp. 41–45.

79. The writer has the records of the Chicago chapter of the NALC in his possession. See also Chapter 10, below.

80. For a description of some of these organizations see Herbert Hill, "Black Protest and Struggle for Union Democracy," *Issues in Industrial Society*, 1969, pp. 19–24 and 48.

81. See Chapter 14, below.

CHAPTER TWO

Four Decades of Change: Black Workers in Southern Textiles, 1941–1981

by Mary Frederickson

Black workers in the Southern textile industry have experienced rapidly changing patterns of employment during the last forty years. Before 1940 fewer than one Southern textile worker in ten was black and 80 percent of black workers toiled as "mill laborers" in non-production jobs. By 1978 one of every five workers was black, and black workers held one-fourth of all operative positions. At present, black workers represent the largest group of recently recruited workers within the industry, and in many Southern mills they are a majority of the work force. The political importance of black workers' entry into and mobility within the textile industry can be measured in terms of their role in ongoing organizing efforts within the textile industry. The solidarity of black textile workers in local Southern communities and their role in grassroots organizing for social, political, and economic freedom in the decades after World War II laid the groundwork for the contemporary political action of this group of workers who hold hard-won positions within the region's industrial workforce.[1]

The patterns of black employment in the South began to change during World War II as a labor shortage due to high levels of wartime employment and wage competition from war industries increased the opportunities for black workers in the mills. In the postwar period, after an initial decrease in jobs for black workers in the early 1950s, the traditional structure of produc-

This essay appeared in slightly different form in Vol. 16, No. 6 (November-December 1982).

tion in Southern textile manufacturing gave way to competition within a more diversified industrial base, resulting in an increasing need for black workers. These changes, combined with the impetus of federal civil rights legislation and pressure from locally organized blacks, have resulted in an industrywide occupational breakdown in which black workers hold a large proportion of the positions within a broad range of job classifications.

The employment shift which has occurred in the Southern textile industry in the last four decades followed a period of sixty years in which black workers in the South faced restricted opportunities in a regional manufacturing system which rigidly segregated workers on the basis of race and sex. The argument will be made here that despite the overt exclusion of black workers from textile manufacturing between 1880 and 1965, black men and women have always played a critical role in the growth and development of the industry in the South.

First, behind the statistics which indicate small percentages of black employees in the South's most important industry were thousands of workers for whom the title "mill laborer" masked work which ranged from the least skilled to the most skilled of any performed in the mills. Secondly, black workers comprised a reserve labor pool which management could and did tap whenever necessary. Although black workers were only occasionally used as strikebreakers, their mere presence in proximity to Southern mill communities functioned as a potential threat to white job security and served to keep the demands of white operatives to a minimum. Mill-owners continually considered hiring greater numbers of black workers and did so whenever a shortage of white labor appeared imminent. For example, during both World War I and World War II the percentage of black workers in the mills increased slightly. But not until the 1960s did the long-waited severe shortage of white employees finally transpire and result in the hiring of black workers in significant numbers. After 1965, black men and women were actively recruited for production jobs for the first time.

THE HISTORY OF BLACK PARTICIPATION
IN SOUTHERN TEXTILES

The long history of black participation in the Southern textile industry began before the Civil War when slave labor was responsible for spinning and weaving in the home production of cloth. Slave women on Southern plantations often returned from a day of hard field work to "spin, weave, and sew well into the night." In the Southeast the transition from home to factory production was made by bondswomen and men who were either owned by industrial entrepreneurs or hired out by their owners to work in the small antebellum mills which dotted the streams and rivers of the Piedmont. Prior to 1860, no one questioned the ability of black workers in handling industrial work. To the contrary, industrialists praised the virtues of black labor over white, and slave labor over free.[2]

After freedom, Southern workers faced a reorganization of the region's occupational structure and a redefinition of the occupational status of the black worker. In plantation areas the transition from slavery to share-tenancy resulted in black workers attaining virtually the same economic rank as non-land-owning whites. Changes in the occupational alignment of black and white workers in cities and small industrial towns, however, resulted in the loss of skilled and semiskilled positions for blacks. In urban mill communities and industrial villages this meant that black workers who had been textile operatives before 1865 began to be replaced by white workers. The number of mills in the South increased two-and-one-half-fold between 1880 and 1900, and as new mills were built, jobs as spinners and weavers went to white workers, predominantly women and children who left small farms to work in textiles. Thus, the operative workforce which had been largely black before the Civil War became predominantly white before the turn of the century.[3]

By 1900 the number of black workers in textiles had declined to less than 2 percent of the total labor force. Industrialists had bargained with white Southerners and granted them limited amnesty from direct competition with black workers for positions as operatives. Moreover, racial lines were drawn within the mills which reflected new twentieth-century patterns of racial segregation throughout the South. As part of the extreme racism of these years an ideology developed regarding blacks and industrial work which simultaneously mirrored and then reinforced the occupational segregation of black workers in textiles. As Herbert Lahne wrote in 1944: "There appeared to be no limit to the supposed justifications of the exclusion of the Negro from the work of operatives—Negroes were said to be temperamentally, morally, physically, etc., etc., unfit to be anything but laborers. All these reasons were, of course, beside the point. . . ."[4]

The reorganized labor system in Southern industry was intact by 1915; in textiles, the region's most rapidly expanding industry, the new occupational codes which virtually excluded black workers from operative positions were given legal expression in South Carolina. In that state a law passed by the State General Assembly in 1915 and not rescinded until 1960 established conditions which necessitated separate weave and spinning rooms for black and white employees. In this way black workers were banned from the primary work areas of the mills. The ruling read in part:

> Be it enacted by the General Assembly of the State of South Carolina, That it shall be unlawful for any person, firm or corporation engaged in the business of cotton textile manufacturing in this State to allow or permit operatives, help and labor of different races to labor and work together within the same room. . . .

The act had a second clause, however, which excluded its application to firemen as subordinates in boiler rooms, truckmen, or to floor scrubbers and those persons employed in keeping in proper condition lavatories and toilets, and carpenters, mechanics and others engaged in the repair or erection of buildings.[5]

There is evidence that mill-owners violated this law whenever convenient or necessary, although the second clause of the ruling left considerable leeway for hiring black employees in a variety of positions. Textile entrepreneurs across the South clearly wanted the flexibility to hire whomever they pleased, but as concessions to white Southerners they gave white employees priority, hired black workers as needed, segregated the workforces within the mill, and liberally interpreted the title "mill laborer."

MILL LABORERS AND INDUSTRIAL OBSERVERS

It was as "mill laborers" that black workers in Southern textiles performed tasks which ranged from cleaning floors to installing electrical wiring to repairing looms to constructing mill buildings and mill housing. In the years after black workers were segregated out of operative positions thousands of black employees continued to perform essential functions within Southern mills. The work of black men and women included the most arduous tasks of lifting and loading bales of raw cotton and rolls of finished goods, as well as assignments in the opening and carding rooms, the sections of the mill with the highest concentrations of cotton dust. In addition to doing the most disagreeable jobs, black workers made the lowest wages paid in the textile industry, a result of both the fact that blacks were restricted to the lower-paying textile jobs and wage discrimination on the basis of race. Sex provided a third discriminatory factor for white men made more than white women, and black men earned more than black women. Race was the predominant wage determinant, however, for black men were paid less than white women. For example, in Georgia, in 1938, black men made 65 percent of the wages paid to white men; black women earned only 56 percent of the wages paid to white women; and black men were paid 78 percent of the wages paid to white women.[6]

Clearly black workers received lower wages than their white counterparts, within identical job classifications, but it is of greater long-range significance that the 80 percent of black workers categorized as "mill laborers" actually held a wide range of jobs within the mills. As early as 1900 an Atlanta cotton manufacturer testified before the United States Industrial Commission that he never attempted to work black and white labor together "except when the white help goes out to get a can of snuff the colored sweepers run the loom." A 1922 study of 2,750 women in ten textile firms (840 of the women were black) reported that black women were found in all of the twelve occupations in which white women were employed, although the black women also worked at cleaning and feeding, two jobs not performed by the white women. A sample of 115 black employees who worked in textiles in LaGrange, Georgia, for 25 consecutive years (between 1925 and 1969) listed 38 job classifications, and included master plumbers, skilled carpenters, card strippers, card tenders, picker tenders, mechanics, machine fixers, landscapers, a woman who stenciled flower designs, and, in 1969, a man who retired as a loom fixer. A survey of seventy textile mills in Virginia, North Carolina, and South Carolina in 1951 reported that black workers were employed as painters, plumbers, carpenters, and electricians, as well as truck drivers, sweepers, and janitors. Finally, in the late 1960s Richard Rowan reported in his study of black workers in Southern textiles that "close scrutiny of the jobs in the laborer category would probably result in some of them being reclassified as semiskilled. . . . the nomenclature remains basically the same that it has been since the early 1900's."[7]

The positions which black workers held in textile mills were more varied and required greater skill than Southern industrial lore has recorded. Moreover, mechanics, teamsters, painters, carpenters, and sweepers had considerable mobility within the mill. Unlike white operatives who could not leave their spindles or looms, black workers had the freedom to move from one section of the mill to another. As roving workers black employees observed industrial work and learned about the overall operation of the mill. When blacks worked as mechanics and loom cleaners they became familiar with industrial machinery, and as carpenters, electricians, and painters they were among the few workers in textiles who labored as craftsmen within an industrial setting. Thus, black workers employed in textiles prior to 1965 became "industrial observers," knowledgeable about the organization of the industry and the hierarchy of the workforce, and accustomed to the pace and environmental conditions of industrial work. Hired in significant numbers in many mills, these workers formed a substantial cohort of minority textile employees, forerunners of the thousands of black workers who moved into operative positions after 1965.

The work histories of two Georgia textile workers illustrate the role of the "industrial observer" in more concrete terms. Both Julian West and Minnie Brown grew up in Westpoint, Georgia, where their fathers worked in the mill. When West turned 18 in 1932 he entered the mill as a full-time worker. Brown got a mill job in 1942, when she was 28 years old, after having worked for over a decade as a domestic worker. Both West and Brown retired after 1975, and their worklives spanned four decades of change for black workers in the industry. Their own careful descriptions of their work delineate the parameters of their industrial experience and demonstrate the subtle distinctions which have to be made when correlating job descriptions with job classifications.[8]

Julian West's family moved to Westpoint in 1920 when he was six years old, after his father got a job as a sweeper in the mill. When teenagers, Julian and his two brothers went down to the mill with their father to help out in the cloth room for a few hours a day, and by the time West was 18 he had a full-time job cleaning and "chucking cloth." West left the mill in 1943, went to Michigan for several months, and when he returned asked for a job in the carding department. Hired immediately, West stayed in the carding department until he retired in 1978, and it was in the card room that West became an "industrial observer." Familiar with the mill since he was a child, knowledgeable about the cloth room where he had worked with his father and two brothers, West entered the card room as a sweeper in 1943. Promoted to lap racker in 1948, West became a card tender in 1965. But West knew how to tend cards long before he got promoted to a card tender's position. As he explained:

> Well, you see, when I was a lap racker I'd put up a bolt of cotton on this card machine. Well maybe now the end of that card has stopped. I mean the cotton has broke out and the card has stopped or either kept running and run over. Well, I would go over there. Now the card tender, he'd possibly be way down the line somewhere, and he got a card up here that's overrunning. Well, I would stop and pick that cotton up and put it back in there and start it back to running, although that wasn't my job. But I'd do it see, and that's the way it'd run.

For seasoned "industrial observers" like Julian West, transition to a production job did not involve additional training. By allowing West to "learn cards" and help the white card tender, management had ensured his training, and when the time came that West was needed as a card tender he was well prepared:

> They wouldn't bother you, you see it was allright if the racker would help the card tender keep his job up. I had to be around the machine anyway because I had to service the machine. What I mean by that is that I had to keep enough cotton up here for the card tender to run. I couldn't let the cotton go out of the machine. And at the same time, when I got through supplying the machine, putting enough cotton on the machine then see I had to sweep around it and keep the floor clean and all that kind of thing. So every chance I got to get up an end, as we call it, and start that machine back running, well then it was a help to that card tender, and finally, a long time before they gave me a job running them, I'd learned how to do it. One day the boss came out there and he asked me, "Julian, you reckon you could run a set of those cards?" I told him "yes, sir." And the next morning he gave me a job on them.

Unlike Julian West who changed positions three or four times during his worklife in the mill, Minnie Brown worked for 34 years in the same job. Hired in 1942 as a "cleaner," she retired in 1976 in the same position. As a child Brown "had been used to going to the mill carrying my daddy's dinner," and years later when one of the few jobs available to black women opened up she was eager to earn the money paid in the mill, wages much higher than those she could make as a domestic worker. Brown's job as a cleaner took her "all through the mill from one end to the other." But Brown did not just clean. Through her "white friends" in the weave shed and spinning room she learned how to weave, decided against spinning ("I'd seen how it was done all right, but I didn't fool with it"), and settled on work filling batteries:

> I'd be caught up with my job, you know, and I'd go down there and they'd let me fill batteries. Just every night I'd go on back down there to the weave shed. I'd get down there and they'd say "start up there." And I'd throw that spool in and whip it around there and like that. And I began to like it. They had so many to do. I didn't charge nothing 'cause I was just learning. They'd say "when you get ready just come on down here," and I'd say "all right."

The testimony of workers like West and Brown confirms the existence of an informal work structure within the mills which differed from the formal job and wage classifications used by management. While classified in "non-production" jobs both West and Brown performed tasks which directly affected production. Moreover, within "segregated" mills West and Brown worked side by side with the white workers who trained them. White employees expressed appreciation for the help they received and, according to West, would reciprocate with cash payment or favors. Thus, everyone benefited in some way from the operation of this informal system. White production workers received much-needed assistance, black workers got industrial training and some extra pay, and management gained from increased production without additional wage costs. In the long-run the industry benefited most from the existence of a well-trained reserve workforce of black men and women eager to move permanently into higher-paying jobs as production workers.

FARM TO FACTORY MIGRATION AMONG BLACK TEXTILE WORKERS

The historical and political significance of this group of "industrial observers" is two-fold. First, the experience of black textile employees hired in non-operative positions in the decades between 1900 and 1940 was that of Southern urban/industrial workers, not isolated subsistence farmers or sharecroppers. Like their white counterparts, these first-generation black textile workers came from agricultural backgrounds to take jobs within the mills. But the movement of black workers into industrial work in textiles was a three-step process involving three generations of employees. The initial stage involved migration from farms to Southern urban/industrial communities and non-production jobs in the mills. The second step, taken by another generation, involved the children of black textile workers who had been employed as sweepers and cleaners obtaining jobs at the level of picker tender and lap racker. The final step, by the third generation, included the large-scale movement of black Southerners into operative positions beginning in the mid-1960s.

Secondly, within the context of local Southern communities these individuals formed a small but important group of workers whose ability to earn regular cash wages augmented their standing within the black community and their power within the white community. For example, among the 115 long-term black workers in the LaGrange, Georgia, mills at least 40 percent owned their homes and many had credit at local furniture and clothing stores. It was the norm for the children of these workers to finish high school and many sons and daughters of this black community graduated from college. Active in church work, a majority of the LaGrange sample served as officers, deacons, or lay preachers within local black congregations.

The experience of black textile workers in LaGrange was not unique. In Westpoint, Georgia, in the "relatively progressive community" in which Julian West grew up and then raised his own children, the prevailing philosophy of life was based on the adage "if you work hard you can make it." Black families coming into town from nearby farms sought to buy a plot of land, build a house, and send their children to school. Parents worked extra hard to keep their children out of the mills. Mattie Ivey, whose grandfather was a slave and whose father worked on the railroad, worked the 6 P.M. to 2 A.M. shift as a cleaner in an Alabama mill, and held two additional domestic cleaning jobs to send her four children through college. She and her husband, a mill elevator operator, "survived and succeeded through hard labor." They labored in the mill for over thirty years, "did not drink, smoke or party," and used what little money they had so their sons and daughters could "follow what they learned." The children of Southern black mill communities were taught to work hard and maintain their allegiance to church and school.[9]

Firmly grounded in well-established black communities, the backgrounds of many Southern black workers who entered the mills in the 1960s and 1970s were substantially different from those of white operatives who migrated from farm to factory between 1900 and 1940. Numerous black workers who became textile operatives after 1965 did not come from the agricultural sector. Rather, their families were already a part of a Southern urban/industrial workforce, and they were second- or third-generation city dwellers and often second-generation mill workers. But unlike Southern white textile workers, black workers had experienced little mobility within the mill, and had made their homes in segregated communities shut off from equal access to full political, economic, or social participation even in the larger community of textile workers. The combination of these two factors, familiarity with industrial work and industrial skills on the one hand, and the denial of equal participation on the other, made Southern black textile workers more predisposed to both collective action and union organizing than the white workers who had preceded them into the mills.

For example, when Jim Thomas's grandson became a textile operative in the mid-1960s, his knowledge of industrial work was based in part on his grandfather's experience in the card, picker, and opener rooms of the Unity Spinning Plant in LaGrange from 1929 to 1954. Young Thomas's familiarity with factory-town living came from his father's position in the Elm City Weave Room in the 1950s and his own childhood spent in LaGrange. For Julian West, who grew up in the black community in Westpoint, Georgia, and whose father had retired from the mill, a job in textiles meant continuing his father's fight for civil rights within the workplace. Inside the mill working for equality meant fighting for the union, and West's allegiance was second nature. In the plant West worked for the union, and at home he fought to send his children to college, and not into the mill.[10]

Both Jim Thomas's grandson and Julian West worked in tandem with previous generations of black textile workers. The sons of men who believed that "if you were going to survive in this society you had to be able to hold a job" struggled to provide their children with the opportunities for work which they had been denied. Taught by their fathers to "go ahead but be careful" black workers in the period between 1940 and 1980 used their positions within the community and the plant to fight for the right to fill jobs they could already perform, to have access to better jobs and to earn wages equal to those of white employees.

RURAL INDUSTRIALIZATION

Another version of the multi-step migration pattern by black workers who have become textile operatives occurred in eastern North Carolina and in low country South Carolina where mills were built and still operate in small rural communities. In these areas the children of black sharecroppers have quit farming and come into the mills in a way which initially appears to duplicate the farm-to-factory migration of white workers in the years between 1900 and 1940. But the lives of black workers migrating to the mills in the 1960s and 1970s have been influenced as much or more by their experience off the land as by the fact that their parents were sharecroppers. For example, when James Boone, a black North Carolinian in his early twenties, took a job as a doffer in 1971, he came into the mill after already having worked for several months in textiles, and as a store clerk in Washington, D.C. Boone had grown up in the country outside Roanoke Rapids, but he had come into town to attend high school, and unlike the white tenant children who had migrated to textile communities in the 1920s, he was familiar with the local J. P. Stevens plants. His father had worked for many years in a paper mill and was a proud member of the International Woodworkers Union of America. When the textile workers union came to

Boone's plant in 1974, he was "raring' to go," saying that "blacks and some whites, too, are gonna make some changes here."[11]

In more rural areas, many workers still live with family members who farm, and they have depended on the land when work was irregular in the mills, and vice versa. One advantage of this dual farm/factory worklife by families had been that as black workers organized in the mills they had resources and options rarely available to earlier generations of white workers who lived in company-owned housing. For example, in a study of mill workers in a rural North Carolina community, Dale Newman reported that two black workers involved in collective action to improve working conditions in the plant expressed "sensitivity to the possibility their actions might result in losing their jobs but as they were both landowners, they and their wives were willing to take the chance."[12]

CHANGING PATTERNS OF EMPLOYMENT

The number of black workers in the textile industry has changed dramatically within the last forty years. Between 1940 and 1978, the participation of black textile employees multiplied six-fold (from 24,764 in 1940 to 152,458 in 1978). The greatest increase in black employment occurred between 1966 and 1968 when in North Carolina, South Carolina, and Georgia the proportion of black workers rose from 10 to 15 percent. In South Carolina and Georgia, the Southern textile producing states with the highest black populations, the percentage of black workers within the industry traditionally has been higher than the regional average. For example, in South Carolina in 1920, black workers comprised 10 percent of the state's textile workers, at a time when the industry average was 2.6 percent. The representation of black workers has been consistently highest in Georgia, where between 1966 and 1968, the percentage of black employees increased from 14 to 18 percent with black men comprising 22.5 percent of all male textile employees in the state in 1968. The gains made in black employment in the textile industry in the 1960s continued and were consolidated in the 1970s. By 1978 black workers in Georgia held 28 percent of all available jobs within the industry, and 58 percent of all black employees worked as operatives. Looking at Georgia and the Carolinas combined, in 1978 black workers held 26 percent of all positions, and 31 percent of all operative jobs.[13]

The pivotal point at which textile employment in the South opened to black workers occurred in the mid-1960s, a period which black workers refer to as "the change," and which Richard Rowan described as "a virtual revolution in employment in the southern textile plants." But the ground work for this transformation was laid in the 1940s and 1950s. In the forties with the growth of wartime industries and the subsequent diversification of local manufacturing within the South, textile firms began losing employees. As one Macon, Georgia, manufacturer lamented:

71

About World War II on, things started getting kind of rough. A lot of other industries came to this area and your skilled people, such as loom fixers, were the first ones they would hire away from you. They would move in here with the same wage scales they had up East, which was way above what we were paying down here.

The hiring of black workers increased during the 1940s. In the LaGrange sample of 115 long-term employees, 55 workers or 48 percent began work between 1940 and 1944. Nevertheless, few black Southerners entered the mill as operatives, even during World War II. During that period, however, workers classified as "laborers" were moved into "picker tender," "opener tender," and "lap racker" positions. Some workers retained these positions after the war, but many others were demoted after 1945.[14]

In addition to the diversification of Southern manufacturing, the post-World War II period brought significant changes within the black communities of Southern towns and cities. Black veterans returning from the military saw their hometowns and local industries in a different light after periods of travel throughout the United States and overseas. As John Foster, a black man employed in textiles from 1949 to the present, described:

It wasn't a whole lot better after we came back from the military, but we had been exposed to things a little different and not so much of trying to change the system as to get the opportunity to participate a little bit more from the standpoint of things like voting, and registering to vote. They gave veterans the opportunity to do those things. A lot of us were determined to fight the system to see if we could do it.

Fighting the system in the late 1940s focused on battling for equal political participation. Gaining the right to vote was the first step, as John Foster explained:

We felt that as long as we didn't try to participate in the political side of this society there was not a whole lot we could do. The guys who came back from World War II, we started opening up these little voter leagues you hear them talking about. We felt that if we could get involved in voter registration then we could get others involved. The only thing you had to do was to get enough black people together to make a politician realize that they could make a difference.[15]

Gradually, with constant pressure from black veterans and others, rigid segregation within Southern political, economic, and social systems began to give way. Within the textile industry changes also came slowly, at first. By 1954, John Foster, still actively working to register his people to vote, played baseball for the mill on an integrated team. After 1958, turnover among white male textile workers increased rapidly as they found higher-paying jobs in other industries. At the same time, Southern white women, the workers on whom the textile industry had grown dependent for many jobs, were also leaving the mills, specifically for jobs in the clerical sector. Meanwhile, local black leaders in Southern textile communities were waiting. Floyd Harris, a black man now in a management position within the industry recalled:

> I was active in the social revolution that went on from the fifties, through the sixties and early seventies, so I was aware of what the black leaders were talking about. We wrote the laws and they passed the Civil Rights bill, and I knew that if the federal government made it a law it'd have to be followed. Our management here is smart, and they knew it too. Besides, that was the only way they could survive.

By 1964, with the passage of the Civil Rights Act, both black workers and management moved cautiously. Black workers already employed in textiles, many of whom were World War II veterans, wanted to "integrate things ourselves so there wouldn't be trouble." As Floyd Harris remembered:

> Management would screen workers real carefully at central employment. You had to know somebody to get on. They would put a black here and a black there and this sort of thing.

Thus, when "the change" occurred it was both carefully planned and swiftly implemented, as Floyd Harris described:

> We didn't have such a difficult time in as much as the President of the Company when the bill was passed had employment meetings, group meetings and everyone was told in no uncertain terms that discrimination would not be practiced in this plant. Anybody caught doing this of course would be separated. Segregation was elemenated and everybody had the right to the job they were capable of doing. Management, top management, made it clear that there wasn't going to be any trouble so the transition wasn't bad because it came from the top.[16]

The relative ease with which Southern employers, generally a group intransigent in the face of federal mandates, responded to the regulations of the Equal Employment Opportunity Commission (EEOC) and the Office of Federal Contract Compliance reflected the industry's need for new workers and a growing reliance on black labor. Although a few supervisors had to be replaced, by 1969, the transition was over and management in most Southern textile communities feverishly sought to hire black workers, literally to keep the mills running. In 1970, with very low unemployment throughout the Southeast, Floyd Harris was promoted to a position recruiting black workers for the industry. Harris had a difficult time getting people to apply for the available jobs, and finally he set up recruiting stations in country stores within a fifty-mile radius to try to attract local black men and women to work in the mills.

LIVING IN TWO WORLDS

Southern textile communities have undergone innumerable changes, both obvious and subtle since the transition years of the 1960s. Exploration of the evolving relationships between black and white Southern workers within the mills and within the larger community reveals that integration within the workplace began the process of integration in textile-dominated towns and cities with long traditions of racial segregation. And most agree that once the mills integrated, the effects spilled over into the larger community. As Julian West remembered:

> The better it got down there at the mill, the better it got out here in the black community. Just about everybody, other than merchants, worked down there in those cotton mills. Where it started, where it began to get better was on the job.

Integration in the mills forced many white employees to recognize and come to terms with the abilities of black workers. John Foster argued that:

> Any close contact between individuals in any specific area made it possible for people to do a better job of evaluating abilities. The people in the mills had an opportunity to compare white skills against black skills and they found out that blacks did have skills, did have intelligence.

Foster, and others, agreed that one of the main things that black workers had to overcome was "the idea that Negroes were not intelligent enough to work with modern technology." Foster felt that:

> In each of the areas where Negroes had a chance to come together and work side by side with whites they were able to more and more disprove some of those theories. Eventually it just got to the point where they accepted the fact that there were blacks who could do this work, and blacks who could not, just like in any other ethnic group.[17]

But although integration within the mills made white workers more aware of the skills and abilities of black workers, few employees totally forgot the past. For example, Floyd Harris, a mill porter until 1965, delivered the mail to a plant where the receptionist, a white woman who sat in the front office, always called him "boy." Harris, then a man in his mid-thirties, repeatedly tried to get the woman to address him by his first name. In 1970, Harris, newly elected as one of the two black members of the local City Council, became assistant personnel manager in the mill where this receptionist still worked. No words were exchanged as the two adjusted to a new hierarchy which placed Harris in a supervisory role, but as Harris recalled, "I hadn't forgotten, and I'm certain she hadn't either."[18]

Nevertheless, once black workers could not be denied jobs in the production areas of the mills, Julian West emphasized that "the atmosphere changed. They changed and I changed. We got closer together in every way." The opening of production jobs to black workers in Southern mills affected the ways in which black and white employees interacted in the workplace, and the higher wages earned by black workers new to operative positions brought material improvements to homes and businesses within the black community. Integration of the schools in most Southern towns and cities followed closely behind integration of the workplace. But a man like Floyd Harris will tell you that despite integration in the workplace and the schools, the mill community he lives in "remains segregated, like it was." John Foster agrees that "segregation is still a part of this society," and adds that:

> You still have the same basic feeling being a minority, and you know that in everything you do, you will succeed or fail through how you respond to the majority.[19]

Tangible differences between the totally segregated society of the past and the partially integrated communities of the South today include the fact that black children no longer have to leave the region to become successful, that a decent education in an integrated public school is attainable for both black and white, and that black workers are not denied industrial jobs on the basis of their race. John Foster agrees that:

> There is a marked difference now, and people who couldn't get away from here fast enough are coming back comfortably.

Foster grew up in Alabama in the 1930s, served in a segregated unit in World War II, headed the mill-run recreation program for black workers while fighting for civil rights on the grassroots level in the 1950s and 1960s, and today he is an employment manager for a major Southern textile company. Reflecting on the changes he has experienced he concluded:

> I consider myself now as living in two worlds, the one I remember and the one that I'm involved in now. Now the younger black doesn't have the hesitancies that I have in a lot of situations because of the changes in the local area and in the southern region since he's been growing up. I find myself cautioning him about my experiences and about his relationship to the white majority.[20]

Black workers like Foster and Harris, who are among the few blacks who have been promoted to white-collar jobs in textiles, see themselves as blacks first and textile managers second. Their allegiance is to their people, and in their capacity as employee counselors and grievance arbitrators, they argue that they can play the role of the union in their company's unorganized plants. But these men are uncertain of what will happen next. They are concerned that black workers have not moved into management jobs as rapidly as they did into operative positions, and they noted that the affirmative action program, "the tool that has helped us get into these areas," is under fire both on the federal and local levels. It is arguable that the impetus for continued black equality in hiring, wages, promotion, and seniority cannot come from within the textile industry itself, but must be promoted by unionized workers on a regional and national basis.[21]

TEXTILE UNIONS

Beginning in the days of the CIO, textile workers in the South came to symbolize both the hope of equality and the promise of justice under the law. In the 1950s and 1960s a black man like Julian West found himself fighting for the union in battles that were waged once or twice a year. In his plant in southwest Georgia, votes for and against the union consistently divided along racial lines:

> I was for it. If we could have got it in there everybody felt like they would have bettered themselves. Where we didn't have a union and didn't succeed in getting it, well then we just had to put up with what we did have. White voted it down. It meant equal rights. The white voted it down to keep me down. If the white had voted the way the black voted then the union would have gotten in, would have taken over control. Then that would have made me get just as much as they get. They just didn't want it, it was a matter of keeping it segregated.[22]

West viewed the refusal of white workers to vote for a union as a political act executed to maintain the status quo both within the plant and within the community.

Since the 1960s, just as the textile industry has relied on black labor to run the mills, so have the unions organizing in Southern textiles depended on black Southerners to organize, to win elections, and to fight decertifications. The effects of black participation on efforts to organize in textiles are evident in recent union elections across the South. For example, the favorable vote at the Roanoke Rapids Stevens' plants in 1974 was ascribed to a 70 percent black vote. Neither the Amalgamated Clothing and Textile Workers Union (ACTWU) or the International Ladies Garment Workers Union (ILGWU) record the race of their members in the South, but unofficial tallies indicate a black majority. It has been argued that the unionization of textiles depends on black workers looking for the "promise of the civil rights movement." In fact, the most active black leaders in the textile unions grew up in Southern urban/industrial areas, learned their organizing skills in the civil-rights movement, lived outside the region in New York, Chicago, or Detroit, and then returned south. These activists, together with local union leaders from both urban and rural backgrounds, have formed a strong new core of Southern textile unionists.[23]

This new cohort of Southern textile leaders faces many of the same problems which always have plagued those trying to unionize Southern workers. Most importantly, the long-held anti-union stance of Southern industrialists remains unshaken. Today local Southern Chambers of Commerce try to entice Northern industry south with promises of low taxes, inexpensive energy sources, and cheap, non-union labor which duplicate almost word for word those issued in the 1920s. The companies which come south, and those long entrenched in the region, literally invest in the belief and hope that workers of the South will remain unorganized. Among the most successful in fighting unions are the large textile chains, J. P. Stevens, Burlington Industries, and Cone Mills; in the last decade these companies have expanded their operations, and with the elimination of the 1968 ban on mergers within the textile industry, more mergers and industry consolidation can be expected. For workers this means that union drives will become more difficult as an increasing percentage of employees work for major firms which can easily close plants or shift production schedules to fight organizing efforts within a local community.[24]

Although many similarities exist between the difficulties faced by union organizers in the Southern textile industry today and those which frustrated union drives among primarily white workers in the period before World War II, there are also many differences. Most significantly, the paternalistic vise within which Southern mill-owners kept their workers has been loosened. The mill villages have been sold, or torn down, and the majority of workers live miles away from the mill in which they work. Few, if any, young black workers have experienced life in a company town, and their willingness to respond collectively to their work situation underscores the different heritage they have brought into the mill. At present many black workers in Southern textiles come from backgrounds, both urban and rural, in which racially cohesive institutions—churches, agricultural and educational improvement associations—have provided the means for collective action to solve common problems faced by black communities. The values and attitudes shaped by generations of working together have been brought to the mill.[25]

After black workers entered the mills in the larger numbers in the mid-1960s, their initial response to unionization was so overwhelmingly positive that the unions tended to take that firm commitment for granted. As one organizer explained, "Back in the late 1960's, whenever you went into one plant the first thing you looked to was how many blacks are there working in here. And if there were forty blacks you could count on forty votes."[26] But after a decade, the relationship between black workers and management has begun to change. Managers have worked hard to break the racial solidarity of black employees by promoting black leaders and hiring some workers to spy against others.

Thus far Southern black workers have continued to respond collectively, but decades spent within the mill with individual production demands, pressure on individuals from foremen and supervisors, and the rigidity of time schedules which curtail communication between workers have made it difficult to sustain the cooperative values with which most black employees entered the industry. For example, in a Macon, Georgia, organizing drive in 1979–1980 black workers voted solidly for the union and remained united until management withheld wage increases for two years. Finally, some of the black workers broke rank and participated in a successful decertification election. A year later one of the black women leaders of the union campaign emphasized the necessity of continued efforts "to make our people understand" the ramifications of the tactics used by management.[27]

In many Southern mills the workers most responsive to seeking cooperative solutions to work situations have been black women. Long excluded from production jobs, black women now hold over 50 percent of the operative positions in many Southern plants. Many black women have entered textiles after having worked in domestic service; unlike their fathers and brothers they have come into the mill without previous industrial experience, and usually without having worked outside the region. For them the transition from home work to factory work is most analogous to the farm-to-factory transition experienced by workers who entered the mills between 1900 and 1940. As a Roanoke Rapids woman who went to work for Stevens in 1971 recounted, "To tell you the truth, when I first went in there, I thought I had stepped into hell. I thought I knew what hard work was, but until I went in there, I didn't."[28]

Black women who began to work in Southern textile mills after 1965 often came from Southern rural/industrial areas, where families both retain their ties to the land and work in the mill. This rural pattern of industrialization, so common in the South, involves a complicated set of interactions between those family members who farm and those who work in the mill. In these families black women are the steady textile employees, those who go to work in the mill at eighteen and stay (with maternity leaves) throughout their childbearing years and even longer. Their fathers, brothers, or husbands are often seasonal textile workers who farm, do pulpwood work, and labor in the mill in the winter when bad weather prohibits outdoor work. Women can get regular work in the mills more easily than men. There are still more jobs designated as "female jobs" than there are "male jobs," and a continually expressed demand for the "nimble fingers" of women workers.[29]

But although many Southern black women came to textiles from non-industrial backgrounds, they have brought with them to the mills a firm commitment to improving their lives by working together, the way their mothers worked within the church. The two women who became leaders of the organizing drive in Macon, Georgia, "prayed for those yeses to come" as the NLRB official counted the ballots at the Bibb Company's Bellvue Plant in the spring of 1980. For one woman, an inspector in the mill for three years before the election, working for the union was "working for God by working for humanity."[30] This continued dedication on the part of individual workers willing to work together for the common good is critical for the eventual success of textile unions in the South.

CONCLUSION

In the last four decades Southern black textile workers, once considered marginal, invisible mill laborers, have become the region's most prominent group of industrial employees. But even in 1940, black workers in fact formed a significant part of the workforce in most Southern mills, held a variety of essential positions, and also observed and performed production jobs whenever possible. In the post-World War II period, black textile workers became a well-trained reserve workforce ready to replace those white workers leaving the mills for jobs in a newly diversified Southern economy. Knowledgeable, long-term workers, and important local leaders within well-established black mill communities, many black textile workers fought for unionization within the mills and civil-rights legislation within the larger community.

But while black workers have brought about substantial changes within the textile industry, they have also inherited many of the traditional problems characteristic of this labor-intensive, low-wage industry with predominantly unskilled or semiskilled jobs. Textile workers today, as in the first decades of the twentieth century, are among the nation's lowest-paid industrial workers. In the fall of 1980 the average wage for cotton textile workers within the region was $5.21 per hour, compared to a national average manufacturing wage of over $8.00 per hour. Black operatives, as generations of white operatives before them, are exposed to the crippling effects of byssinosis from exposure to cotton dust. Moreover, in the early 1970s, many Southern mills faced with labor shortages and government pressure to reduce cotton dust levels within the mills, began to invest in new equipment, automated machinery which simultaneously increased production and reduced the size of the workforce. As a result, the number of U.S. textile workers, at over one million through the 1950s, and slightly below a million in the 1960s, declined to 779,620 workers in 1966, and 754,296 workers in 1978. The industry has never regained the employment levels which existed before the recession of 1974–1975. In the Southeast (with three-fourths of the workers) 95,000 jobs have been permanently lost, 19,000 between 1979 and 1980. Figures on the 1981–1982 recession are beginning to appear and indicate that the effects may be worse than 1974.[31]

At present unionized workers in textiles across the Southeast are being pressed for concessions on a model patterned after General Motors and Ford, but in plants where operatives make one-fourth of the wage of automobile workers. Textile employees from North Carolina to Alabama are on short-time, and in South Carolina twelve mills closed in the last six months of 1981, and 18,000 out of the state's 133,000 textile workers are out of work.[32] As the most recently hired workers black employees are bearing the burden of much of the current downturn in textiles. The rapid movement of black workers into the industry in the 1960s and 1970s transformed the industry and altered the interaction between management and labor; but now the problems of plant closings and unemployment, anti-union wage battles, and decertifications have replaced industrial segregation as the problems faced by black textile workers in the South. The solutions will be hard-won. Today, as black workers lead efforts to organize the Southern textile industry, their long and complex experience as Southern industrial workers enriches and informs that work, just as their participation in the civil-rights movement of the 1960s serves as a model for achieving the right to bargain collectively in the 1980s. The struggle to earn wages that equal the national average industrial wage, to participate in industry decisions about automation and health and safety, and, finally, to gain union representation will demand all the strength and courage of the men and women now running the looms of the South.

NOTES

This is a revised version of a paper presented at the Conference on Recent Black American History at Boston College, February 27, 1982. I would like to thank Jim Green and Herbert Hill for their helpful comments at the Conference and Judy Smith, Ann Withorn, Susan Benson, and Hal Benenson for their critiques of the manuscript.

1. U.S. Equal Employment Opportunity Commission, *Minorities and Women in Private Industry* (1978), vol. I, p. 19.

2. Eugene D. Genovese, *Roll, Jordan, Roll: The World the Slaves Made* (New York, 1972), p. 495; Robert S. Starobin, *Industrial Slavery in the Old South* (New York, 1970), pp. 13, 167.

3. C. Vann Woodward, *Origins of the New South, 1877–1913* (Baton Rouge, 1951, 1971), pp. 132, 222, 361; Jonathan M. Wiener, *Social Origins of the New South: Alabama, 1860–1885* (Baton Rouge, 1978), pp. 193–194; Paul B. Worthman and James R. Green, "Black Workers in the New South, 1865–1915," in *Key Issues in the Afro-American Experience*, vol. 2, ed. Nathan Higgins, Martin Kilson, and Daniel M. Fox (New York, 1971), pp. 47–69.

4. Herbert J. Lahne, *The Cotton Mill Worker* (New York, 1944); p. 81.

5. Ibid., p. 82.

6. State of Georgia, Department of Labor, *Second Annual Report* (1938), p. 24.

7. Lahne, *Cotton Mill Worker*, p. 289; Phillip S. Foner and Ronald L. Lewis, eds., *The Black Worker*, vol. 4 (Philadelphia, 1979), p. 315; U.S. Department of Labor, Women's Bureau, "Negro Women in Industry in 15 States," *Bulletin of the Women's Bureau* 20 (1922): 32; life and work history data of 115 Georgia workers obtained from the *Callaway Beacon*, vols. 1–18, (1949–1969), LaGrange, Georgia, hereafter cited as "LaGrange Work Data;" Donald Dewey, "Negro Employment in Seventy Textile Mills, Oct. 1950–Aug. 1951," in National Planning Association Committee of the South, *Selected Studies of Negro Employment in the South* (Washington, D.C., 1955), p. 184; Richard Rowan, "The Negro in the Textile

Industry," in *Negro Employment in Southern Industry*, ed. H. R. Northrup, R. L. Rowan, D. T. Barnum, and J. C. Howard (Philadelphia, 1970), p. 84.

8. The information and quotations which follow are from interviews with Julian West and Minnie Brown in Westpoint, Ga., on April 20, 1982. The name of each individual interviewed has been changed to protect their privacy. All interviews conducted by the author.

9. Interview with Mattie Ivey, Fairfax, Ala., April 21, 1982.

10. Data about the Thomas family from *Callaway Beacon*, vol. 6, no. 35 (Sept. 6, 1954); West interview.

11. Quoted in Mimi Conway, *Rise Gonna Rise: A Portrait of Southern Textile Workers* (Garden City, 1979), pp. 122–124.

12. Dale Newman, "Work and Community Life in a Southern Town," *Labor History* 19 (1980): 222.

13. Rowan, "The Negro in the Textile Industry," pp. 54, 98–99, 141; EEOC, *Minorities and Women in Private Industry* (1978), 1: 19. In Georgia 43 percent of white textile workers held operative positions; a higher percentage of white workers performed craft jobs (16% vs. 9%) and office work (10% vs. 2%).

14. West interview; Brown interview; Rowan, "The Negro in the Textile Industry," p. 85; interview with Finley Wickham, Macon, Ga., Sept. 1981; "La-Grange Work Data."

15. Interview with John Foster, Shawmut, Ala., April 20–21, 1982.

16. Interview with Floyd Harris, Westpoint, Ga., April 20, 1982.

17. West and Foster interviews.

18. Harris interview.

19. Interviews with West, Harris, and Foster.

20. Foster interview.

21. Interviews with Foster and Harris.

22. West interview.

23. F. Ray Marshall and Virgil L. Christian, eds., *Employment of Blacks in the South: A Perspective on the 1960's* (Austin, 1978), pp. 143–146; Frank Guillory, "N.C. Textile Firm Finally Unionized," *Washington Post*, Sept. 2, 1974; Bruce Raynor "Unionism in the Southern Textile Industry," in *Essays in Southern Labor History*, ed. Gary M. Fink and Merl E. Reed (Westport, Conn., 1977), p. 89.

24. Chip Hughes, "A New Twist for Textiles," in *Working Lives: The Southern Exposure History of Labor in the South*, ed. Marc S. Miller (New York, 1980), pp. 350–351; Doug McInnis, "A New Chill on Organizing Efforts," *New York Times*, May 30, 1982, 4F–5F.

25. Newman, "Work and Community Life in a Southern Town," pp. 220–222.

26. Quoted in Carolyn Ashbaugh and Dan McCurry, "On the Line at Oneita," in Miller, ed., *Working Lives*, p. 210.

27. Debbie Newby, "Long Campaign Worth It, Say Those Who Worked for Union," *Macon Telegraph*, March 21, 1980, 1B, 8B; interview with Laura Curry, Macon, Ga., Sept. 1981.

28. Quoted in Conway, *Rise Gonna Rise*, p. 91.

29. Interviews with Harris, Brown, and Ivey.

30. Newby, "Long Campaign," 1B.

31. U.S. Department of Labor, Bureau of Labor Statistics, Atlanta, Ga., "Southeastern Textile Mills Employment Monthly Reports," Oct. 1980; EEOC,

Minorities and Women in Private Industry, 1966:C-8, 1978:I-19; U.S. Department of Labor, Southeastern Regional Office, Bureau of Labor Statistics, "Textile Products Industry Employment in the Southeast, 1947–1979."

32. "South's Textile Mill Closings Continue from '74 Recession," *New York Times*, Feb. 17, 1982.

CHAPTER THREE

The Stop Watch
and the Wooden Shoe:
Scientific Management
and the Industrial Workers
of the World

by Mike Davis

According to the founding father of modern industrial management, the "conscious restriction of output" or "soldiering" has always been the original sin of the working class. "The natural laziness of men is serious," Frederick W. Taylor wrote, "but by far the greatest evil from which both workmen and employers are suffering is the systematic soldiering which is almost universal."[1] Taylor's lifelong crusade against the "autonomous and inefficient" worker was the crystallization of his personal experiences as a foreman at the Midvale Steel Company in Philadelphia. For three years he waged a relentless campaign against the machinists and laborers whom he accused of collectively restricting plant output. He was finally able to break up the group cohesion of the workers and reduce "soldiering" only after a ruthless dose of fines and dismissals. This pyrrhic victory took "three years of the hardest, meanest, most contemptible work of any man's life . . . in trying to drive my friends to do a decent day's work." It convinced Taylor that repression alone was an inadequate foundation for management control over the conditions of production.[2]

After further years of experimentation in the steel industry and in tool-and-die shops, and with the occasional backing of key corporate leaders from Bethlehem Steel and other large companies, Taylor systematized his theories in a series of books. Of his several works, however, his bluntly

Reprinted from Vol. 9, No. 1 (January–February 1975).

written *Principles of Scientific Management* popularized his ideas most effectively. Eventually, after being translated into a dozen languages, this book became a bible to "efficiency men" all over the world. Here Taylor proposed effective solutions to the problems of reduced output and "soldiering."

The traditional basis of soldiering, he explained, was the degree of job control exercised by skilled workers through their mastery of the production process. Craft exclusivism, maintained by control over entry into workforce and the monopolization of skills almost as an artisanal form of property, blocked the operation of free-market forces upon both the wage scale and employment.[3]

Taylor, moreover, recognized that the submission of the workforce to the new discipline of the assembly line would not automatically resolve these problems as long as even a minority of the personnel preserved the right to define a "fair day's work." He emphasized that the crucial precondition of complete management power was the appropriation from the skilled workers of the totality of their craft secrets and traditions. The techniques of time and motion study developed by Taylor (and later perfected by others) were precise methods for analyzing the content of craft skills involved in the production process. These "scientific" studies conducted by the newfangled production engineers and acolytes of Taylorism became the basis for undermining the autonomy of craft labor. Knowledge of the production process would be monopolized by management, while craft skills were simultaneously decomposed into simpler, constituent activities.

Skilled workers immediately perceived the twin menace of scientific management: the loss of craft control and the radical polarization of mental and manual labor. In 1916 a leader of the Molders' Union incisively analyzed the deteriorating position of American craftsmen as a whole:

> The one great asset of the wage worker has been his craftsmanship. . . . The greatest blow that could be delivered against unionism and the organized workers would be the separation of craft knowledge from craft skill. Of late this separation of craft knowledge and craft skill has actually taken place in an ever widening area and with an ever increasing acceleration. Its process is shown in the introduction of machinery and the standardization of tools, materials, products, and processes, which makes production possible on a large scale. . . . THE SECOND FORM, MORE INSIDIOUS AND MORE DANGEROUS THAN THE fIRST, is the gathering up of all this scattered craft knowledge, systematizing and concentrating it in the hands of the employer and then doling it out again only in the form of minute instructions, giving to each worker only the knowledge needed for the mechanical performance of a particular relatively minute task. This process, it is evident, separates skill and knowledge even in their narrow relationship. When it is completed, the worker is no longer a craftsman in any sense, but is an animated tool of the management. [My emphasis][4]

While scientific management demanded the progressive "dequalification" of labor's craft aristocracy, it also signaled a new slavery for unskilled workers. As Taylor recognized, even gangs of common laborers, unorganized and lacking a property right in a craft, frequently were able to convert the solidarity of their work group into an effective brake on increased output. Management, he argued, had to aim at destroying the solidarity of all functional work groups, skilled or unskilled.

Managers have always known that even in the absence of trade-union recognition the primary work group (defined by common tasks, skills, or departments) is a natural counterpole to management authority and the basis for collective counteraction. The daily work group constitutes a social unit for the individual worker almost as intimate and primal as the family. It is the atom of class organization and the seed from which great cooperative actions of the working class have always developed.[5] Before Taylor, however, there was no practical strategy for preventing the crystallization of primary work groups in which wage earners grew to depend on each other and to cooperate in resisting management authority. In order to prevent the work groups from evolving into "counter-organizations," Taylor proposed a judicious combination of the carrot and the stick. First, the most militant workers—the organic leadership—were fired or severely fined for the slightest infraction of the new rules. Then jobs were diluted, redesigned and "individualized" (that is, fragmented and serialized) to the greatest extent technically feasible. Finally, differential piece or time rates were introduced to promote competition and to sponsor the emergence of a new pseudo-aristocracy of "first-rate men" working from 200 percent to 400 percent above the new norms.[6] And so, out of the old mixture of skilled and unskilled labor, Taylorism helped precipitate the archetypal worker of the future: the machine tender, the semiskilled operative with the discipline of a robot. Taylor loved to argue that workers should be selected on the same "sensible" basis on which draft animals were discriminatingly chosen for separate tasks. The working class was divided by nature into groups of weak mules, ordinary drays, and superstrong work horses.[7]

Cooperation, Taylor explained, meant that future workers "do what they are told to do promptly and without asking questions or making any suggestions."[8] The interdependency of workers—previously expressed through their teamwork of conscious cooperation—would be replaced by a set of detailed task instructions prepared by management to orchestrate the workforce without requiring any initiative from the bottom up. Taylor also advised bosses to reduce the on-the-job socializing of workers through vigilant supervision and frequent rotation. In principle, the only tolerable relationships within a Taylorized plant would be the chains of command subordinating the workers to the will of the management.

The real message of scientific management, therefore, is not about efficiency; it is about power. Like many other aspects of the Progressive Era, it was a counterrevolutionary blow at the potential power of the working class to organize itself and transform society. The fundamentals of scientific management had been introduced into the basic manufacturing core of U.S. industry by the eve of American entry into World War I. Corporate capitalists were determined to install the reign of the "iron heel" within their plants, mills, and mines. Taylorism offered coherent principles and an ideological framework to corporate managers searching for a strategy to deal with labor relations at a time when higher and higher targets of productivity were being demanded by the capitalists. Scientific management gave U.S. industry an inestimable advantage in the world market. American production was generally recognized as the most intense in the world, with speed-up and working conditions which frequently scandalized observers from the European labor movement.[9] As Antonio Gramsci reflected in one of his *Prison Notebooks*, scientific management in the U.S. represented "the biggest collective effort to date to create with unprecedented speed and with a consciousness of purpose unmatched in history a new type of worker and man. . . . Taylor is in fact expressing with brutal cynicism the purpose of American society."[10]

REVOLUTION IN THE LABOR MOVEMENT

A good deal has been written about the American Federation of Labor's response to scientific management, from its initial strong opposition to its eventual conciliation (or capitulation).[11] However, the response to Taylorism among unskilled or immigrant workers has been explored only recently. And very little is known about the reaction of the radical Industrial Workers of the World. Although the Wobblies have received much attention in the last decade, they have not been taken as seriously as they should. In contrast to the AFL's narrow defense of endangered craft privileges, the Wobblies attempted to develop a rank-and-file rebellion against the rationality of Taylor and the speed-up. In fact, they were virtually unique among American labor organizations, in their time or any other, in their advocacy of a concrete plan for workers' control.

Nothing illustrates the specificity of IWW industrial unionism better than the IWW's role in the wave of mass strikes initiated by Eastern industrial workers from the first detonation at McKees Rocks, Pennsylvania, in 1909 through the Detroit auto strikes of 1913. Historians have yet to put these strikes in their proper perspective. Even Jeremy Brecher, searching in his recent *Strike!* for the central role of mass spontaneity in American labor history, virtually ignores this whole period of class conflict which included major strikes at McKees Rocks, East Hammond, New Castle, Lawrence, Passaic, Paterson, Akron, and Detroit. In all these strikes the IWW played a crucial role. Together with the concurrent mobilization of socialist-led garment workers in New York and elsewhere, these struggles marked the entry of the "submerged" majority of industrial workers into open class conflict. "Common labor" had long been considered unorganizable because of the ethnic divisions and racism, the hostility of skilled native labor, the inexhaustible reserve army of new immigrants, and corporate management's unprecedented apparatus of spies, cops, and finks. Therefore, the sudden and dramatic awakening of semiskilled factory workers, despised and ignored by the craft unions, constituted, in the words of William English Walling, "nothing less than a revolution in the labor movement."[12]

It is particularly significant that the storm centers of these strikes were located in the industries being rationalized by scientific management and the introduction of new mass-assembly technologies. A survey of conditions and complaints in the struck plants vividly reveals how the tactics of scientific management (time study, task setting, efficiency payments, etc.) had invariably resulted in extreme job dilution, speed-up, and a lowering of wages.

At McKees Rocks, for instance, where nearly a worker a day was killed in an industrial accident, the steel trust's Pressed Car Company had pioneered the techniques of work rationalization and ruthless efficiency:

> Before he reduced wage rates in 1907, President Frank Hoffstot had also introduced a new assembly line production method which accelerated the pace of work through a piece-rate system. At the same time he devised a technique for pooling wages which penalized all members of a labor pool for time and production lost by any single slow worker. This new production system also penalized workers for delays caused by company failure to repair machinery, and for breakdowns caused by vague instructions issued by plant superintendents. Although compelled to work at a feverish pace in order to satisfy the pool's production target, the men on the assembly line never knew what their actual piece rates would be and, in fact, usually found their weekly earnings well below expectation.[13]

Summarizing the conditions which led to the great strike of 1909, John Ingham's study of McKees Rocks concludes that "it was this rigorous but logical extension of the ideas of scientific management which led directly to the McKees Rocks Strike of 1909."[14]

Similarly, the Lawrence strike was precipitated by a premium system that enforced speed-up and by a wage cutback following the passage of the 54-hour work week for women and children. At Paterson, the silkworkers were driven to desperate rebellion by the introduction of the multiple-loom system, an especially fatiguing variety of speed-up which made weavers responsible for twice as many looms as before. In the Akron rubber industry, Philip Foner's analysis of the 1913 uprising shows that "the conditions the workers found made an eventual outburst inevitable. The speed-up system prevailed throughout the industry. A Taylor-trained man with a stop watch selected the speediest workers in a department for tests, and thereafter wages for the whole department were determined by the production of the fastest workers." Later in testimony before the Senate committee investigating the strike, "strikers told of the inhuman Taylor speed-up system in the plants, and even the employers, in their testimony, boasted that as a result of the speed-up system 'we got 40% more production with the same number of men.' "[15]

As for the auto industry, by 1913 it was becoming the last word in industrial efficiency; firms operating on a craft basis (one car completely assembled at a time) were rapidly being driven out of business; and Henry Ford was busy integrating Taylor's ideas into an even more ambitious model of the scientific exploitation of labor. At his plants and those of Studebaker, pioneering IWW organizers confronted "the Brave New World" being created by the most advanced capitalist manufacturers. As Foner notes:

> The steady mechanization of the industry reduced the skilled workers to a small fraction of the total number in the industry. The majority of the auto workers became mere machine operators with a job that could be picked up in a few hours. In no other industry was the process of production more subdivided and specialized or speed-up more prevalent. Pace setters under the direction of 'speed kings,' as they were called by the workers, with stop watches in hand, timed the men on every operation. A standard was thus obtained by which every job was to be done. If a worker failed to meet the standard, he was discharged.[16]

Two years before the IWW became involved in the auto strikes, the *Industrial Worker* printed a representative plea for help from "Only a Muff" working in a plant of 7,500 where time-and-motion men had just increased the mandatory output from 150 to 225 units a day. This unknown auto worker told the *I.W.* readership how the men in his department were planning to restrict output and to refuse to compete against one another for efficiency payments. He added, however: "Of course we can't fight alone. If they insist upon this new system, it will be a case of either eat crow or quit. Let some of those free speech fighters come here and get on the job!"[17]

Scientific management did not—as Taylor liked to claim—ensure that workers "look upon their employers as the best friends they have in the world[!]"[18] Rather, it sowed class conflict on an epic scale. In the particular circumstances of 1909–1914, moreover, when the Depression of 1907 led to a quickening in the economy's rhythm of explosive growth and sudden slump, scientific management posed an especially clear threat to the working class. Upon the basis of sharp economic fluctuations and chaotic disruptions in the labor market, Taylorization helped ensure that rising productivity could be realized without restoring wages to pre-1907 levels. It also retarded the recovery of employment from depression levels.[19]

AFL craft unions of course suffered a stunning debacle during this period in their remaining strongholds (especially steel) within basic industry. But for the mass of semiskilled workers, whom the AFL did not represent in any sense, the craft unions' fate was largely irrelevant. Undetected by AFL leaders and other observers, who were misled by chauvinist stereotypes of the "new immigrants," a rank-and-file leadership was shaping up among the semiskilled workers.

The immigrant factory proletariat could be united as well as divided by the diversity of its component cultures. Native traditions of revolution and struggle were brought to American soil along with the restricting consciousnesses of the *shtetl* or ancestral village. The high rates of immigration and internal job turnover made organization difficult, but these trends also produced an unprecedented circulation of ideas and experiences in the American labor movement.[20] The unique degree of back-and-forth movement of foreign workers in the immediate prewar period, at a time of worldwide labor upheaval, temporarily opened America to the diffusion of diverse ideas and experiences drawn from the breadth of European revolutionary movements. There were not many immigrant workers with the activist background of a Singer employee named James Connolly, recently arrived from Ireland, or the unnamed steel worker whom William Trautman talks about who had led in the Moscow uprising during the 1905 Revolution, but they were not unique.

The IWW had a particular attraction for the most advanced immigrant workers, and their combined experiences constituted an important reservoir of ideas and tactics for the organization. The IWW's very slow growth before late 1909 disguises the fact that the Wobblies already had semiorganized groups at Lawrence and Paterson which were helping to build a foundation of militancy. At Paterson there was an eight-year history of Wobbly agitation before the great strike of 1913. The Lawrence IWW local had initiated a series of slowdowns and wildcat walkouts against speed-up in the summer of 1911.[21]

At McKees Rocks the existence of a revolutionary nucleus among the car builders was revealed by the formation of the "Unknown Committee" of immigrants, including three Wobblies, which took over the leadership of the 1909 strike from the "Big Six," who were exclusively native skilled workers. This "committee from the base" contained veteran fighters with backgrounds in the struggles of at least nine countries, including the 1905 Russian Revolution. According to Foner:

> This committee quietly took charge of the strike, planned the tactics of the battle, and put into operation methods of strike strategy which, though used often in Europe, were new to the American labor movement and were to influence the conduct of strikes among the foreign-born workers for many years to come. Among the McKees Rocks strikers, the committee was known as the "Kerntruppen," a term derived from the military system of Germany where it referred to a "choice group of fearless and trained men who may be trusted on any occasion."[22]

The IWW supported these small industrial cadres with the skills of experienced, full-time organizers, including Italians like Arturo Giovannitti and Joseph Ettor, the young Irish Republican James Connolly, as well as noted Americans like "Big Bill" Haywood and Elizabeth Gurley Flynn. Well-versed in U.S. labor history, but unafraid to borrow from the international repertoire of the syndicalists and other militants, the Wobblies were particularly adept at turning the weaknesses of immigrant strikers into sources of strength. Ethnic cohesiveness, traditionally so divisive, became a wellspring of unity when strikes were organized on a radically democratic basis with strictly representative committees that could be recalled. Leaflets, speeches, and songs were presented in every language, while in each strike every conceivable parallel was found with the historic struggles of various European nationalities.

While the solidarity and internationalism which the Wobblies strove to create within each strike was very important, the IWW members also functioned as a transmission belt between strike movements. The big uprisings in steel and textiles seemed particularly important in providing a basis for organizing mass industrial unions. McKees Rocks, for instance, catalyzed strikes throughout the entire railroad-car construction industry, and the IWW was able to establish short-lived locals in every major center of the industry (Hammond, Woods Run, Pullman, Hegewisch, and Lyndera). A little later the Lawrence and Paterson strikes transformed the IWW's affiliate Industrial Union of Textile Workers into a movement of many thousand workers.[23]

The shock waves of these big struggles reverberated throughout Eastern industry and found resonance in the dozens of smaller strikes influenced by the IWW in the same period. "Fishing in troubled waters" during his 1913 organizing tour of Pennsylvania and Ohio, General Organizer George Speed found the electricity of class struggle everywhere. In a few whirlwind months during the Akron rubber strike, he chartered new locals or contacted strikers across the entire spectrum of the working class: steel workers, railroaders, electrical equipment makers, barbers, construction laborers, department-store employees, sugar refiners, safe makers, shoemakers, tailors, furniture makers, wire workers, match workers, and railroad car repairers.[24] The IWW membership statistics presented at the 1911 and 1913 conventions provide a dramatic measure of the organization's growing implementation in the major Eastern industrial centers.[25]

As is well known, the IWW failed to consolidate large numbers of Eastern industrial workers into its ranks. Between April and August of 1911, for example, even as 70 new locals were being organized, the disbanding of 48 old locals for reasons such as "lack of interest" was registered. But it has to be remembered that the AFL was also in deep crisis. It endured the crushing of the Amalgamated by the steel trust and did little or nothing to aid the epic two-year struggle of railroad shopmen who organized on industrial lines to resist the introduction of scientific management on the Harriman lines. Given the troubles of the labor movement in general, it is wrong to view the period as one in which the IWW demonstrated an inherent inability to build durable union organizations. The insurgency of 1909–1913 shaped a rank-and-file vanguard for the next, even more intense period of struggle in 1916–1922.

IWW members recognized that the industrial working class would not be organized in one single leap forward. Instead, the Wobblies saw the need for the forging of a "culture" of struggle among immigrant workers and the creation of a laboratory to test the tactics of class struggle. These years saw a vigorous debate on industrial strategy both within the IWW and between its partisans and the rest of the American left. Having traced some of the origins of the prewar strike wave to the impact of scientific management, it is time to consider the famous, somewhat enigmatic controversy over "sabotage" and its relationship to IWW practice in the Taylorized mills and plants.

THE IWW TURNS TO GUERRILLA WARFARE

In his exhaustive 1904 investigation of the *Regulation and Restriction of Output* for the Secretary of Labor, John Commons observed that "nowhere does restriction of output as a substitute strike policy exist in the United States."[26] Eight years later, however, the *Industrial Worker* weekly regaled its readers with examples of successful "sabotage," and the Socialist Party recalled IWW leader Big Bill Haywood from its Executive Committee for advocating sabotage. ("Sabotage," by the way, was probably first adopted as an appropriate French translation of Ca' Canny in an 1897 report by Pouget and Delassle to the CGT convention at Toulouse. It is derived from "coup de sabots," an idiomatic expression for clumsiness, and not, as often believed, from the mythic act of throwing the sabot [wooden shoe] into the gears.)

Haywood's "cause celebre" arose from a speech he gave before a huge crowd at New York's Copper Union in 1911, where he declared, "I don't know of anything that can be applied that will bring as much satisfaction to you, as much anger to the boss as a little sabotage in the right place at the right time. Find out what it means. It won't hurt you and it will cripple the boss."[27] His unrestrained oratory prompted the adoption of an anti-sabotage clause in the party constitution, the famous Article II, Section 6, which forced the exodus of Haywood and several thousand left-wing socialists from the party and completed the polarization of the radical labor movement into bitterly hostile right and left wings.

The sabotage controversy, therefore, demarcated a real turning point in the history of both the socialist and labor movements. The actual political content of the dispute remains elusive. Historians have tended to agree that "sabotage" was an indelible mark of IWW infatuation with European syndicalism. Philip Foner, an "Old Left" historian whose volume on the IWW remains the most carefully crafted account of the Wobblies' "heroic period," is firmly convinced that sabotage is the "one doctrine which the IWW borrowed directly from the French syndicalists."[28] Melvyn Dubofsky also traces its Parisian origin and argues that it acquired a special appeal for American workers enmired in what he calls (apropos Oscar Lewis) "the culture of poverty."[29] Even Fred Thompson, the crusty "house historian" of the IWW, discounts the application of sabotage in Wobbly struggles, arguing instead that it was only an exotic oratorical device employed on skidrow or Union Square soapboxes:

> Soapboxers found that talk of sabotage gave their audiences a thrill, and since the dispensers of the above publications (the Cleveland I.W.W. Publishing Bureau) were happy to send them for sale on commission to all who would handle them, there was nothing to stop spielers, whether they were I.W.W. members or not, from procuring these booklets, mounting a box, talking about the I.W.W., taking up a collection, and selling the literature.[30]

The problem with the traditional explanation of IWW advocacy of sabotage is that it does not explain why the sabotage debate split the Socialist Party or why the Wobblies persisted in making sabotage a central slogan in the period from the end of the McKees Rocks strike through the auto walkouts in 1913. ("Sabotage" made its first published appearance in a 1910 article in the *Industrial Worker* and appeared with increasing frequency until it became the theme of a serialized weekly discussion.) Unless the IWW spokesmen are dismissed as irresponsible and flippant rabble rousers, it remains to be shown why this organization, temporarily inserted into the leadership of a massive upheaval of unorganized workers, gave such priority to its "flirtation" with a foreign-made notion which it supposedly never implemented on any serious scale.

Much of the confusion about what the Wobblies really meant by "sabotage" stems from the fact that revolutionaries, especially in the pre-Leninist period, were forced to borrow old concepts or to employ only vaguely approximate analogies of practice in order to express the very different connotations of a new or transformed arena of struggle. A careful reading of the IWW literature concerning sabotage in this period reveals the striking mixture of old ideas and new which can be analytically reduced in each case to three fundamental and differing meanings of "sabotage." These three dimensions of "sabotage," in turn, correspond to different, historically specific tactics of the labor movement.

First, there is the meaning frequently assigned by Bill Haywood that sabotage was only the frank, open advocacy of the same "universal soldiering" practiced by most workers. In this sense, "the conscious withdrawal of the workers' industrial efficiency" boils down to the familiar and inherently conservative tactic which had been one of the main bases of craft unionism. Moreover, it was precisely this traditional form of job control through conscious self-regulation of the pace which, as we have seen, Taylorism and speed-up were dissolving through the transfer of total control over working conditions to management. It was in Europe, where industry was less rationalized, that the old conservative application of soldiering was still a ubiquitous safeguard of traditional worker prerogatives.

Second, "sabotage" sometimes carried that inflammatory connotation which so terrified right-wing socialists like Victor Berger—who thought he saw the ghost of anarchist bomber Johann Most in the IWW. The retaliatory destruction of capitalist property (and occasionally persons) was an unspoken but familiar tactic in American labor struggles. Undoubtedly the IWW had some first-hand knowledge of the efficacy of the match or fuse in Western labor struggles involving brutally terrorized miners, agricultural laborers, or lumberjacks. Workers in these industries had a long international tradition—"Captain Swing," "Molly Maguires," Asturian and Bolivian "Dynameteros," etc.—of using "sabotage" as a last resort against the daily experience of employer violence. In contrast, the Wobblies, while far from being pacifists, channeled the rebellion of Western workers into industrial unionism and new, essentially non-violent forms of struggle like the free-speech campaigns. These tactics helped break down the isolation of the casual laborer from workers in the towns and turned the migrant into a sophisticated and self-sufficient political agitator.

In urban, industrial strikes, moreover, the IWW used violence or property destruction far less often than the AFL because of its greater reliance on passive resistance and mass action. It is truly a remarkable fact that the Commission on Industrial Relations could attribute only $25 property damage to the Paterson IWW strikers during the whole course of that bitter struggle.[31] In fact, the principal reason for continued agitation around the idea of the workers' right to employ retaliatory property destruction as a tactic, whether actually used or not, was to demystify the sanctity of property and teach workers the methods of protracted struggle. There are many examples where the mere threat of sabotage (in this sense) taught an invaluable lesson in political economy and actually strengthened the strikers' position. According to the IWW's *Industrial Worker*:

> In Lawrence one of the reasons for the settlement of the strike on terms favorable to the strikers was the fact that the employers feared that the cloth might not be produced in the best of conditions by workers who were entirely dissatisfied. This knowledge, shared by the strikers, gave to the toilers the feeling that they were a necessary portion of the social mechanism and brought them that much nearer the time when the workers as a class shall feel capable of managing industry in their own interests.[32]

Another example is provided by Melvyn Dubofsky:

During the important I.W.W.-led New York Waiters Strike of 1913, Joe Ettor electrified the hotel and restaurant owners with his straightforward advice to beleaguered strikers: "If you are compelled to go back to work under conditions that are not satisfactory, go back with the determination to stick together and with your minds made up that it is the unsafest proposition in the world for the capitalists to eat food prepared by members of your union."[!][33]

It appears that the Wobblies rarely went ahead and actually brought the "fire next time," in the form of retaliatory destruction, down upon the heads of the bosses. Their typical emphasis in discussing sabotage was on a third meaning of the word, as a mass tactic requiring some form of continuing, although clandestine, mass organization in the plant or mill. Sabotage is clearly defined as a flexible family of different tactics which effectively reduce output and efficiency. Old-fashioned soldiering or the retaliatory destruction of capitalist property are merely potential applications, under specific conditions, of a much more diverse strategy which also included the "open mouth strike" (purposeful disruption by observing every rule to the letter) and (above all) the hit-and-run slowdown. The essence of the Wobbly advocacy of sabotage was to encourage the creativity of the workers in the discovery of different tactics. When moulded to the particularities of specific industries, these tactics could be applied directly on the job with maximum effect (whether or not union organization was recognized) and with a minimum danger of company retaliation against individual workers. Although little is really known about the history of unofficial job actions, there is good reason to believe that the IWW focused especially on systematic sabotage through repeated slowdowns and short, sporadic strikes. The relationship of these tactics to the overall Wobbly strategy is forcefully summed up by Elizabeth Gurley Flynn: "Sabotage is to the class struggle what guerrilla warfare is to the battle. The strike is the open battle of the class struggle, sabotage is the guerrilla warfare, the day-to-day warfare between two opposing classes."[34]

Furthermore, the IWW press offers abundant proof that this industrial "guerrilla warfare" was a direct response to scientific management and that sabotage in fact provided the only soundly based alternative to workers in the most rationalized industries. In addition to regular articles about scientific management, the *Industrial Worker* repeatedly editorialized the need to counteract the stop watch with prudent use of the wooden shoe:

> Many who condemn sabotage will be found to be unconscious advocates of it. Think of the absurd position of the "Craft Union Socialists" who decry sabotage and in almost the same breath condemn the various efficiency systems of the employers. By opposing "scientific management" they are doing to potential profits what the saboteurs are doing to actual profits. The one prevents efficiency, the other withdraws it. Incidentally, it might be said that sabotage is the only effective method of warding off the deteriora-

tion of the worker that is sure to follow the performance of the same monotonous task minute after minute, day in and day out. . . . Sabotage also offers the best method to combat the evil known as "speeding up." None but the workers know how great this evil is.[35]

The *Industrial Worker* also unhesitantly advised direct action to deal with the problem of the worker who, bribed by efficiency payments or promised promotion, broke group solidarity and became a "speeder." After comparing the function of the "speeder" to the "favorite" steer trained to lead his fellow creatures into the killing pen, it was suggested that ". . . in the steel mills this speeding up process has become so distressing to the average worker that still greater steps are taken for self-protection. In fact in speaking of these class traitors, it is often remarked that it is something dropped on their feet that often affects their brain."[36]

The close correlation between the introduction of scientific management and the appearance of the famous black cat of sabotage was widely appreciated by contemporary observers, whether friend or foe of the IWW. For instance there is the testimony of P. J. Conlon, international vice-president of the International Association of Machinists, before the Commission on Industrial Relations:

> . . . we believe that it (scientific management) builds up in the industrial world the principle of sabotage, syndicalism, passive resistance, based on economic determinism. We did not hear of any of these things until we heard of scientific management and new methods of production. . . . We find that when men can not help themselves, nor can they get any redress of grievances, and are forced to accept that which is thrust upon them, that they are going to find within themselves a means of redress than can find expression in no other way than passive resistance or in syndicalism.[37]

Conlon's perception is amplified by William English Walling in his widely read *Progressivism and After*. Walling, in this period a leading spokesman of the Socialist left, possessed a rich understanding of the IWW's actual practice and the trajectory of its strategic thought. After discussing the false identification of sabotage with violence Walling explains:

> But many representatives of the labouring masses, including well-known I.W.W. members, either attach little importance to such extreme methods or positively oppose them. To withdraw the "efficiency from the work," that is, to do either slower or poorer work than one is capable of doing, is also a mere continuation and systematization of a world-wide practice which has long been a fixed policy of the unions of the aristocracy of labor. But its object in their hands was merely to enable the workers to take things easy, to increase the number of employed, and so to strengthen the monopoly of skilled craftsmen.[38]

Having carefully distinguished these two traditional forms of sabotage, Walling goes on to say:

But what I want to emphasize at this point is that, in proportion as the scientific methods of increasing efficiency are applied in industry, one of the laborers' best and most natural weapons is the scientific development of methods of interfering with efficiency, which methods, it seems, are likely to be lumped together with entirely different and often contradictory practices under the common name of sabotage.[39]

SOLIDARITY FOREVER

Despite the occasional rhetorical extravagances of a few IWW spokesmen like Arturo Giovannitti—who loved to talk about sabotage as the "secret weapon" of the working class—it was never seen as an isolated panacea. The Wobblies were less fetishistic about their methods than any other labor organization in American history. "Tactics are revolutionary only as they are in accord with revolutionary ends," said the IWW paper. No exact formula can be set down as the proper tactics to pursue, for precisely the same action may be revolutionary in one case and reactionary in another."[40] In a 1912 *Industrial Worker* article, Louis Levine pointed to the real essence of the Wobblies' direct-action tactics: "Sabotage is not considered by the apostles of direct action as the only efficacious or even the most appropriate means of struggle. IT IS THE SOLIDARITY OF THE WORKERS THAT IS OF DECISIVE IMPORTANCE."[41]

The larger conception of revolutionary industrial unionism in which sabotage appeared as a tactic was vigorously discussed and debated in the pages of the *Industrial Worker* during the 1909–1914 period. Fellow Worker Will Fisher provided a succinct definition:

First . . . . Avoid labor contracts.
Second . . . . Don't give long notices to the employer what you intend to do.
Third . . . . Avoid premature moves and moves at the wrong time.
Fourth . . . . Avoid as far as possible the use of violence.
Fifth . . . . Use force of public education and agitation; the union is an agitational and educational force for the workers.
Sixth . . . . Boycott.
Seventh . . . . Passive strikes and sabotage, irritant strikes.
Eighth . . . . Political strikes.
Ninth . . . . General strikes.
Tenth . . . . Where possible seizure of warehouses and stores to supply strikers or locked out men.[42]

It is important to remember that at this time the formal labor contract and time agreement was one of the methods by which craft unions had preserved their control over the work place. The Wobblies pointed out that ". . . the time agreement under which the workers of each craft union are given a closed shop is often as bad for the workers as a whole as an open shop, because, under its terms, contracting craftsmen are bound to scab on the other workers."[43] At McKees Rocks, New Castle, Akron, and Paterson, the immigrant workers had seen their struggles broken by the native, skilled workers who signed independent agreements with the bosses and used them as legal cover to break strikes.[44]

In contrast to the maintenance of the closed shop by legal agreement and external compulsion, the IWW proposed an entirely different concept of shop control based on voluntary self-organization and shop-floor direct action (sabotage) to resolve grievances and preserve conditions won in previous strikes. During the Brooklyn Shoe Strike of 1911 the Wobblies introduced the "shop committee." "The IWW shop organization developed technical knowledge in the working class and prepared it to take over technical management."[45] Furthermore, the IWW local union, borrowing and extending the European precedent of the *Maison Du Peuple*, functioned as a high-energy agitational and educational force: "not only a union hall but an educational and social center."[46] Finally, by building entirely upon a basis of voluntary membership and rank-and-file activism, with a minimal full-time staff, the Wobblies told astonished questioners that they were ". . . doing away with the professional labor leader."[47]

This model of shop organization pivoted around sabotage, intermittent slowdowns, one-day wildcats, and walkouts was, in turn, a prototype of industrial unionism as a "culture of struggle":

> . . . we have the partial strike, the passive strike, the irritant strike, and the general strike—one continual series of skirmishes with the enemy, while in the meantime we are collecting and drilling our forces and learning how to fight the bosses.[48]

> The short strike is not only to pester the employer; it is like army drill, to become the school of practice in preparation for the coming general or universal strike.[49]

Sabotage was thus conceived as both a means of achieving some degree of shop control in scientifically managed factories, and also as an integral part of the "greviculture" (strike culture) preparing the American working class for the Social Revolution. Unfortunately we know very little about the actual development of job-action tactics and sabotage within the concrete context of individual factories. The daily building of collective organization on a plant level and the ceaseless guerrilla warfare against management's despotism constitute a "terra incognita" for historians. Staughton Lynd's ground-breaking interviews with rank-and-file steel workers, which challenge so many accepted theories of the CIO, demonstrate how vital this dimension of labor history is for a real understanding of the struggle to build industrial unionism.[50]

Judging the importance or "marginality" of the IWW in the Progressive Era by the Wobblies' failure to actually construct the One Big Union or to found permanent locals ignores the fact that the mass strikes of 1909–1913 transmitted a valuable arsenal of new tactics and organizational weapons to the industrial working class. Though the IWW failed to reach many workers struggling against scientific management within the AFL, the Wobblies' dual unionism allowed them to take a new course in developing direct-action strategies that would be used in later industrial struggles. Without romanticizing the IWW, we should take it seriously as the only major labor organization in the U.S. which seriously and consistently challenged the capitalist organization of production. In our own time, when "virtually all manufacturing operations in the industrial world are based on an application of scientific management rules"[51] and when workers are actually struggling to break those rules and to challenge the managers who make them, the old confrontation between the stop watch and the wooden shoe still has living significance.

NOTES

The author thanks Paul Worthman and James Green for their help on this article.

1. Frederick W. Taylor, *Principles of Scientific Management* (New York, 1911), p. 13.

2. Taylor before the Commission on Industrial Relations, April 13, 1914, *Report and Testimony*, vol. 1 (Washington, D.C., 1916), p. 782. For a description of Taylor's aberrant personality, including his habit of chaining himself at night to "a harness of straps and wooden points," see Samuel Haber, *Efficiency and Uplift: Scientific Management in the Progressive Era, 1890–1920* (Chicago, 1964).

3. For a provocative description of the degree of job control exercised by skilled workers before the advent of rationalization, see Katherine Stone, "Origin of Job Structures in the Steel Industry," *Radical America* 7 (Nov.-Dec. 1973).

4. John P. Frey, "Modern Industry and Craft Skills," *American Federationist* (May 1916), pp. 365–66. Cf. Andre Gorz's summary: "As a whole, the history of capitalist technology can be read as the history of the dequalification of the direct procedures." Andre Gorz, "The Tyranny of the Factory," *Telos*, Summer 1973, pp. 61–68.

5. For a sample of contemporary analysis of the primary work group by industrial psychologists see Leonard Sayles and George Strauss, *Human Behavior in Organizations* (New York, 1966). For another view see M. Guttman, "Primary Work Groups," *Radical America* 6 (May-June 1972).

6. At Bethlehem Steel output was almost doubled after adoption of a variation of the bonus payment, but the "shop employed 700 men and paid on the 'bonus' plan only 80 workers out of the 700." Louis Fraina, "The Call of the Steel Worker," *International Socialist Review*, July 1913, p. 83.

7. Taylor, *Report and Testimony*, pp. 765–810.

8. Taylor, "Why Manufacturers Dislike College Graduates," quoted in Haber, *Efficiency and Uplift*, p. 24.

9. See Paul Devinat, *Scientific Management in Europe* (Geneva, 1927).

10. Antonio Gramsci, "Americanism and Fordism," in *Prison Notebooks* (London, 1971), p. 302.

11. Haber, *Efficiency and Uplift*; Milton Nadworny, *Scientific Management and the Unions* (Cambridge, 1955); and Jean McKelvey, *AFL Attitudes Toward Production* (Ithaca, 1952).

12. William English Walling, "Industrialism or Revolutionary Unionism?" *The New Review*, Jan. 18, 1913, p. 88.

13. Melvyn Dubofsky, *We Shall Be All: A History of the I.W.W.* (Chicago, 1969), pp. 200–201.

14. John N. Ingham, "A Strike in the Progressive Period," *The Pennsylvania Magazine of History and Biography*, July 1966, p. 356.

15. Philip Foner, *The Industrial Workers of the World 1905–1917* (New York, 1965), pp. 374, 382.

16. Ibid., pp. 383–384.

17. Letter from "Only a Muff," *Industrial Worker*, Dec. 22, 1911.

18. Commission on Industrial Relations, *Report and Testimony*, vol. 1, p. 772.

19. Ibid., pp. 132, 141–143. Unemployment was 11.6 percent in 1910, 13 percent in 1911, 9 percent in 1912, 8.2 percent in 1913, and 14.7 percent in 1914. See Stanley Lebergott, *Manpower in Economic Growth* (New York, 1964), p. 512.

20. "The immigrant laborer, furthermore, had one standard remedy for disgust with his job: he quit. . . . Annual turnover rates ranging from 100–250% of the original labor force were found to be commonplace. Ford Motor Company hired 54,000 men between October 1912 and October 1913 to maintain an average workforce of 13,000." David Montgomery, "Immigrant Workers and Scientific Management," unpublished paper, 1973.

21. Foner, *Industrial Workers of the World*, p. 353, and Dubofsky, *We Shall Be All*, p. 234.

22. Foner, *Industrial Workers of the World*, pp. 287–288. Also see Ingham, "A Strike in the Progressive Period," pp. 363–377.

23. See Report of General Organizer George Speed in the *Stenographic Report of the Eighth Annual Convention of the I.W.W.*, 1913.

24. Ibid., p. 28.

25. At the 1911 convention there were 21 voting locals plus the national textile union, and 14 of these were either Western or based in mining districts. By the 1913 convention the number of voting locals had grown to 89 plus the textile union, and 38 of the locals (including four of the five largest according to the number of proxy votes) were Eastern. Report of General Secretary-Treasurer Vincent St. John, *Stenographic Report of the Sixth Convention of the I.W.W.*, 1911, and the *Eighth Convention*, 1913.

26. *Regulation and Restriction of Output*, 11th Special Report of the Commissioner of Labor, ed. John Commons (Washington, D.C., 1904), p. 28. The enduring complaint by manufacturers about employee soldiering and sabotage is reflected in Stanley Mathewson, *Restriction of Output Among Unorganized Workers* (New York, 1931), and "Blue Collar Blues," *Fortune*, July 1970.

27. "Haywood's Cooper Union Speech," *International Socialist Review* (Feb. 1912), pp. 469–470.

28. Foner, *Industrial Workers of the World*, p. 160.

29. Dubofsky, *We Shall Be All*, p. 163.

30. Fred Thompson, *The I.W.W.: Its First Fifty Years* (Chicago, 1955), p. 86.

31. Commission on Industrial Relations, *Report and Testimony*, vol. 1, p. 55.

32. *Industrial Worker*, May 16, 1912.

33. Melvyn Dubofsky, *When Workers Organize: New York City in the Progressive Era* (Amherst, 1968), p. 124.

34. Elizabeth Gurley Flynn, *Sabotage* (Chicago, n.d.), p. 4.

35. *Industrial Worker*, Feb. 6, 1913. See also Editorial, Dec. 28, 1911, and the articles by Covington Hall, Nov. 16, 1911, and B. E. Nilsson, April 24, 1913.

36. Editorial in *Industrial Worker*, Feb. 6, 1913.

37. Commission on Industrial Relations, *Report and Testimony*, vol. 1, pp. 874–877.

38. William English Walling, *Progressivism and After* (New York, 1914), pp. 301–302.

39. Ibid.

40. *Industrial Worker*, May 12, 1912.

41. Louis Levine, "Direct Action," *Industrial Worker*, June 20, 1912.

42. Will Fisher, "Industrial Unionism, Tactics and Principles," *Industrial Worker*, March 12, 1910.

43. Fisher in *Industrial Worker*, March 19, 1910.

44. "The more I see of the old unions the more I am convinced that we must fight them as bitterly as we fight the bosses; in fact, I believe they are a worse enemy of the One Big Union than the bosses, because they are able to fight us with weapons not possessed by the bosses." E. F. Doree, "Shop Control and the Contract: How They Affect the I.W.W.," reported in the *Stenographic Minutes of the Tenth Convention*, 1916.

Doree's sectarianism must be seen in the light of the innumerable instances of strikebreaking by AFL unions; the second walkout at McKees Rocks, for instance, was broken by armed native workers affiliated to the Amalgamated. (See Ingham, "A Strike in the Progressive Period.") Editor's note: On the IWW's opposition to the trade agreement, see Bruno Ramirez, *When Workers Fight* (Westport, Conn., 1978), ch. 11.

45. Justus Ebert, *The I.W.W. in Theory and Practice* (5th rev. ed.; Chicago, 1937), pp. 126–127.

46. Fisher, "Industrial Unionism."

47. Joe Ettor, Commission on Industrial Relations, *Report and Testimony*, vol. 2, p. 1555.

48. *Industrial Worker*, Feb. 5, 1910.

49. James Brooks, *American Syndicalism: The I.W.W.* (New York, 1913), p. 135.

50. Staughton Lynd, ed., "Personal Histories of the Early C.I.O.," *Radical America*, May-June 1972.

51. George Friedmann, *The Anatomy of Work* (New York, 1961).

CHAPTER FOUR

"The Clerking Sisterhood": Rationalization and the Work Culture of Saleswomen in American Department Stores, 1890–1960

by Susan Porter Benson

The work of recent historians has made it clear that work culture is an important key to understanding the lives of past generations of workers. By work culture I mean the ideology and practice with which workers stake out a relatively autonomous sphere of action on the job, a realm of informal, customary values and rules which mediates the formal authority structure of the workplace and distances workers from its impact. David Montgomery and Harry Braverman, in particular, have shown us the power and importance of the work culture that united conception and execution in the hands of skilled male workers in the nineteenth century. The tales they tell, however, are those of decline, despite Montgomery's vivid evocation of workers' struggles to preserve their traditional control over production. In the end, the effect of scientific management on these workers was decisive: skill was undermined, the work degraded, the control of the informal work group over the work process and the social relations of the workplace inexorably eroded.[1]

The history of women's paid labor and of the work culture growing out of it is somewhat different. My research on the work of saleswomen in American department stores from 1890 to 1960 suggests that, at least in this major women's occupation, the effect of changes in management practice over the twentieth century was, ironically, to increase the level of workers'

Reprinted from Vol. 12, No. 2 (March-April 1978).

skill and thus inadvertently to permit the development of a powerful and enduring work culture. There are critical differences between women's work and the men's craft work which are the central concern of Montgomery and Braverman. First, for most women in the paid labor force at the turn of the century, work was so poorly paid and so brutally demanding of mind and body that it would be difficult to conceive of its further degradation. This is as true of women's white-collar work as of women's factory work; women were never career clerks like Bartleby the Scrivener or fledgling entrepreneurs like R. H. Macy, but entered office and sales work only as they were becoming proletarianized. In the case of women's occupations, therefore, the story is not one of unrelieved degradation of the work process. Second, the study of women's work shows that craft skill was not the only basis of an effective work culture. The informal work group which thrived among saleswomen was grounded in the social relations of the selling floor. It was, in fact, exactly because new management practices in the department store industry altered these social relations only minimally that they failed to undermine the position of the informal work group and the strong influence of work culture over worker behavior.

As defined by the Census Bureau, a department store must sell a wide assortment of home furnishings as well as clothing and related items, but for my purposes this definition is too narrow. I include in the category "department store" those stores which saw themselves as part of the department store industry and which behaved like true department stores in their internal organization and policies. My arguments would therefore apply to specialty stores which carried only apparel, such as Filene's in Boston, as well as to chains such as Sears, Roebuck, which are outgrowths of mail order houses. Even by the Census Bureau's limited definition, however, the department store has had since 1929, when figures were first compiled, a larger share of total retail sales than any other detailed classification except grocery stores, auto dealers, and gasoline dealers.

Department stores have historically been major employers of women; since 1900, the job of saleswoman has ranked among the top ten women's occupations. The proportion of women in the department store workforce seems to have stayed fairly stable at around two-thirds since the early twentieth century. Most of these women have been in selling positions, with clerks making up from just under half to 90 percent of the total store force, depending on the level of extra services provided by the store. The experience of the non-selling workers had far more in common with production workers in manufacturing industries than with clerks, and so I have omitted it here. Saleswomen have not only been important numerically, but have played a central economic role as well. As Braverman notes, a key aspect of management is marketing, or the production of customers; in this process, salespeople are basic production workers, and the only ones who have close and frequent contact with the customers.[2]

Work culture is constrained but not determined by management practices; the two are constantly in struggle and cannot be understood separately. I focus below on some large continuities in the department store industry's development, minimizing short-term changes and fluctuations in order to suggest an overall conceptual framework. Probably the single most important factor in understanding large-scale retailing both as an industry and as an employer is the split consciousness of retail managers. On the one hand, they have been businessmen pure and simple, seeking to maximize profits by reducing costs. On the other, they have thought of themselves as purveyors of a service, managers of social institutions which sold not just merchandise but also style, respectability, and urbanity—things not strictly accountable in dollar terms, but which were of course expected to pay off in a general way.

In the early twentieth century, department store managers improved their physical plant, ameliorated basic working conditions, and centralized control in much the same way as the factory managers described by Daniel Nelson in his admirable book *Managers and Workers*.[3] What he calls "the new factory system" appeared in the factory between 1880 and 1920, and about a decade later in the large store. The department store management strategies which emerged during these years would be elaborated and spread more widely in the next thirty years, but not fundamentally changed.

First of all, department stores grew impressively. By 1898, for example, Macy's had 3,000 employees, making it comparable in size to such manufacturing giants as the Merrimack cotton mills in Lowell, the Waltham Watch Company, and Carnegie Steel's J. Edgar Thompson Plant, as well as larger than the towns in which 60 percent of Americans then lived. Although most stores were far smaller, the change in scale from the early nineteenth century's typical small, highly specialized shop to the department store was enormous. Retailers preceded factory managers in coping with the problems of scale; as early as 1905, for instance, department stores had widely adopted a functional structure which major manufacturing firms were only beginning to adopt by the 1920s.[4] This four-part functional organization consisting of merchandise, service or store management, publicity, and control or accounting divisions was the rule in department stores until after World War II.

Selling work in the turn-of-the-century department store had much in common with both sweated and machine-tending modes of manufacturing. Elements of the sweatshop in the department store included squalid surroundings, minimal sanitary facilities, unlimited hours, and mandatory unpaid overtime. From another point of view, clerks in most large stores were taught to regard their counters as machines to be tended but not controlled; they were expected to wait passively for customers, politely give them what they asked for, and send the merchandise to the wrapper and the payment to the cashier. Their work was defined negatively: they should not violate store rules or commit blunders of etiquette.

Department store sales work changed not just as part of a general change in business climate and in accepted managerial wisdom, but also as a response to two problems specific to department stores. First was the bad publicity given to department store working conditions by the Consumers' Leagues after 1890. Department stores were peculiarly vulnerable to public observation of their labor policies. The contrast between the work lives of their employees and the atmosphere of gentility and even luxury which they tried to convey to their customers was telling indeed. Worst of all, the reformers came from the same upper-income strata as the stores' most valued customers. As one magazine writer put it, "The public resents the worn out, famished type of clerk and its feelings are hurt by seeing women faint behind the counter."[5]

The second factor was the lagging productivity of the distribution sector of the economy compared to the production sector. While the output per person-hour in production increased two and a half times between 1899 and 1929, output per person-hour in distribution increased only one and a half times in the same period. Within a given store, the figures were sometimes even more discouraging to managers: for example, at Macy's the average yearly sales per employee doubled between 1870 and 1938, while the average weekly salary quadrupled.

Department store managers met the challenge of public relations and productivity with the full range of measures used by their counterparts in manufacturing, but with somewhat different results. Nelson has classified the elements of the new factory system into "three interrelated dynamics—the technological, the managerial, and the personnel;" of these, the technological was by far the least important in the department store. Basic urban technology such as electric lighting, elevators, and improved ventilation helped to make the store a cleaner and more pleasant workplace, but did not affect the sales transaction. Well-designed display cases and clothes racks, when substituted for the old practice of storing goods in huge piles, made it easier for the salesperson to show goods to the customer, but left the social interaction of the sale unchanged.

The managerial dynamic in the department store took much the same form as it did in the factory. After the depression of the early 1920s, the merchandise division, traditionally the foremost among the store's four divisions, found its territory invaded and colonized by the other divisions, in large policy matters as well as in day-to-day operations. The controller, armed with sophisticated new accounting procedures, exerted a degree of financial surveillance over the merchandise division which had earlier been impossible. Second, with the development of advertising and the consumption economy of the twenties, retailers redefined their economic role: it was now "to act as purchasing agent for the consumer, rather than as sales agent for the manufacturer."[6] In this new atmosphere, the merchandising division's traditional close relationships with manufacturers and wholesalers took a back seat to the judgment of the publicity division and its prophet, the fashion stylist. Third, this new active type of selling demanded salespeople who were more carefully selected and trained, functions which were assigned to newly created personnel departments.

From the perspective of the individual selling departments, these changes meant the diminution of the power of the buyers and floorwalkers, whose jobs changed in much the same way as that of the factory foreman. Buyers had traditionally been prima donnas, running their departments with intuition and high-handedness; the new buyer was hedged in on all sides by financial, style, and personnel requirements imposed by the other three divisions. Similarly the new floorwalker was no longer the suave host to the customer and the tyrannical disciplinarian of the sales force; at best, his job was downgraded, and at worst his tasks were split up among lesser employees. The net effect of these changes in the authority structure of the selling floor was to limit broad discretion on the part of the salesperson's immediate supervisors; authority moved up the hierarchy.

Finally, the personnel dynamic led to the gradual centralization and standardization of hiring, training, and employee service functions under the aegis of a single department. Beginning around 1890, department stores undertook extensive employee welfare activities, frequently outdoing factories in providing lavish dining, recreation, and health facilities, elaborate social programs, and even vacation retreats. By the twenties, the welfare departments were being transformed into personnel departments which took over the old programs and combined them with the newest techniques of employee recruiting, testing, and training.

These innovations, whether technological, managerial, or personnel, failed to change fundamentally the basic tasks of the salesperson, as they did the work of most factory employees. In 1960 as in 1910, sales work was made up of the same combination of waiting on customers and attending to stock. In fact, while most manufacturers wanted to dilute skills and to produce a new category of "semi-skilled" workers, retailers strove to upgrade an unskilled workforce into a skilled one. They sought to inculcate not the skill of the nineteenth-century machinist, or of the hand craftsman, but rather a new twentieth-century form of skill: skill in complex social interaction, skill in manipulating people rather than objects, a skill which would be taught by management rather than one that grew out of the workers' own grasp of the work process. An insistence on the centrality of selling skill is the dominant theme of retail management literature from the time of World War I to 1960.

The emphasis on selling skill grew partly out of retailers' ideal of service to the public, and partly out of the resistance of retailing to standardization and control in two major ways. First was the fluctuation of volume in the store's work pace; the flow of customers varied from department to department, season to season, day to day, hour to hour. Equally unpredictable were customers as individuals: their wants, moods, and personalities varied in infinite combinations and made each transaction a unique situation.

Management's best efforts to standardize conditions on the selling floor availed little, and it remained a highly unpredictable and largely uncontrollable environment in which the salesperson was expected to make the most of every opportunity to sell.

Department store managers resisted the alternatives to skilled selling which other branches of retailing devised; they were never wholly satisfied with allowing customers to be presold by advertising or to sell themselves in self-service departments. These methods were part of the department store arsenal of selling tactics, but only preliminary steps in a strategy of skilled selling. On the one hand, personal selling (as it came to be called) differentiated department stores from their crasser competitors, giving customers a reason to shop at Gimbel's rather than at J. C. Penney's; on the other hand, the department store's high proportion of fixed costs for such expensive services as parcel delivery meant that the payoff for sales efforts to boost the size of each transaction was high. In one department, for example, an 80 percent increase in the size of a sales transaction meant a 600 percent increase in the net profit.

Everything, then, converged on selling skill: the nature of the work, the managers' image of themselves, and the financial structure of the business. It was, however, difficult to define and transmit this skill. Was selling an art? A science? Was it inborn? Learned? Managers' definitions of it varied as much as conditions on the selling floor, in large part because of the contradictions surrounding the work of selling in store life.

The first contradiction in fostering selling skill was the contrast of bosses' high verbal valuation of sales work with their own avoidance of the selling floor and the low social status of the work. The retail literature constantly urged executives to spend more time on the selling floor, teaching by example and proving that management regarded selling with respect, yet department store managers were notorious for fleeing to their offices. Their behavior reflected not only their own sense of store hierarchy but also the generally bad image of sales work. Most saleswomen could console themselves only with their marginal prestige as white-collar workers and some minimal reflected prestige from their association with wealthy customers and luxurious goods, for the physical strains, psychological demands, hours, and pay of their work did not compare very favorably with factory and clerical work. Moreover, sales work had a number of similarities with domestic service, an increasingly unpopular occupation. John Wanamaker's classic statement that the customer was always right subjected generations of saleswomen to the idea of unquestioning obedience to customers' whims. Dress codes set uniform-like limits on what saleswomen might wear. And, finally, saleswomen found distasteful the personal services, such as helping customers try on clothes, which they had to perform.

The second major contradiction in skilled selling was between store managers' belief that they should and must teach it to their workers, and their actual unwillingness or inability to do so. When training became a formal store activity with the establishment of Filene's training department in 1902, it was negative, remedial, and mechanical, focusing on eliminating errors in paperwork and procedure. Conceptions of training subsequently broadened to include sales techniques, merchandise and fashion information, and general education, but the 1942 lament of a saleswoman was sadly true: "The average salesperson does not respect her job because management too often doesn't seem to care as long as her book [sales tally] is passable and she doesn't make too many errors in her transactions."[7]

The problem was that selling skill was learned not in the store classroom but rather in experience with merchandise and customers on the selling floor. Managers recognized this, and a Macy's program to collect and codify salespeople's "selling secrets" into a booklet entitled "20,000 Years in Macy's" was typical of their efforts to take over shop-floor knowledge. It should be emphasized that training difficulties were not due to resistance by salespeople; one survey showed them eager for substantive training (in merchandise training and techniques of selling and display) but uninterested in classes on trivia such as personal grooming. Sometimes, salespeople did balk at training, but small wonder when they were required to chant in unison "Personal service means showing interest" when an instructor held up a cutout of "a cheerful smile."[8]

The final contradiction in the upgrading of selling grew out of the fact that any but the most perfunctory sales transaction depended for its success on rapport between people of different classes. In most large department stores, the counter was a social as well as a physical barrier. On the selling side were women of the working classes; middle-class women with a choice shunned the low-status and difficult conditions of store work. On the buying side were women of the middle and upper classes; as late as 1950, the department store clientele included twice as high a proportion of upper income people as the population as a whole. One observer sympathetically reported on the resulting tensions:

> "It seems," a salesgirl said to me, "as though all the women who have servants they dare not speak to, or a husband who abuses them, take special delight in asserting their independence when they come to buy from us girls, who must say 'Yes ma'am' and 'Thank you' in the sweetest possible way."
>
> Often, within the hearing of sales people, a woman will make to the friend accompanying her some such remark as this: "I wouldn't buy that if I were you; only the shop girls are wearing them."
>
> It is common for customers to show, at least by their manner, that they consider the sales people beneath them.[9]

Managers persistently tried to ease this conflict by giving their employees a veneer of bourgeois culture; most of their efforts were absurd and superficial, such as requiring saleswomen to memorize a few French words and the names of chic Parisian streets, but a few spoke hopefully of remaking saleswomen's "inner consciousness" with "a cultural background which would enable [them] to talk easily, informedly, about the qualities of [their] merchandise . . . in such a way as to express its esthetic values as well as its use values."[10] Such programs generally backfired; saleswomen bungled (often, I suspect, intentionally) the minutiae, snubbed and therefore offended customers if they took the training too seriously, and for the most part simply continued to judge their customers' needs and means by their own class values.

THE DEVELOPMENT OF A WORK CULTURE

While managers, caught in these contradictions, were unable to control skilled selling behavior, the saleswomen themselves were developing a strong work culture and durable informal work groups. Conditions on the selling floor encouraged worker autonomy. Saleswomen spent only a small part of their time—some estimated as little as one-third—with customers and so had many opportunities to socialize with one another, enhanced by their relative freedom to move about their departments. Moreover, it was difficult to supervise a salesclerk closely. A supervisor who meddled during a sale risked annoying both clerk and customer and thus sabotaging the sale. The saleswomen's duties while not actually serving customers were often indistinguishable from the activities of the informal work group; a gathering of clerks might be discussing new stock, but then again they might simply be gossiping, and the lines between the two were never clear. Finally, unlike production workers who could only play production off against the bosses, saleswomen could play a complex three-way game, manipulating managers, customers, and merchandise to their own advantage.

Despite wide variations in time, place, and type of store, the basic features of the work culture of selling are clear. Sources discussing highly diverse situations from very different points of view reveal quite similar practices and standards. I do not mean to suggest that all saleswomen everywhere shared an identical work culture, but rather that the situation on the selling floor evoked analogous reactions among workers in different departments. What I am outlining is the range of variation of the work group's rules and tactics; every department devised its own individual subculture within the parameters of the work culture of selling in general.

The foundation of the informal work group was some degree of departmental solidarity. Departments were not only the administrative and accounting units of the store, but were social units as well. The selling departments of a large store were far more independent from one another than the production departments of factories, and were unlinked by any sequential processes. Moreover, personnel managers staffed departments selectively: young, attractive women were hired for the first-floor departments, motherly types for the children's clothing departments, glamorous women to sell high-fashion clothing, heavy women to fit their half-size sisters. There was an unofficial hierarchy of departments in the store, and solidarity frequently developed around a given department's place in it. The custodians of the fine linens regarded their stock, and therefore themselves, as a cut above the rest of the store in elegance; the women in one chaotic bargain basement refused transfers to upstairs departments because they preferred the liveliness and bustle of the basement. The physical and functional differences between departments, therefore, became social barriers as well, contributing to the power of the informal work group by emphasizing the uniqueness of the department.

Social interaction on the selling floor was friendly and supportive. The tendency of saleswomen to "huddle" or "congregate" on the floor was the aspect of their behavior most frequently remarked by managers and customers alike. Bosses constantly complained of high spirits and boisterous sociability in the departments, and did their unsuccessful best to stamp out loud laughing, talking, singing, and horseplay. Saleswomen in the more unified departments shared stockwork and paperwork even when it was assigned to individuals, and reinforced day-to-day contact with parties, both on the job and after hours. They integrated the rituals of women's culture into their work culture; showers and parties to commemorate engagements, marriages, and births (women in Boston stores who left to be married were sent off with a shower of confetti) are reported in employee newspapers by the score. Not all departments were this close, this intensely friendly, but it is significant that even when managers note that a department is quarrelsome and divided, they almost always marvel that it still unites in self-defense against outside threats.

The practices of the informal work group continually reinforced departmental solidarity. Work culture provided, first of all, an initiation process whereby new members were received, taught the ropes, and kept in line until they showed themselves willing to go along with the group. The initiation was not always a friendly one; new, part-time, and temporary clerks complained long and loud about mistreatment by regulars. Second, work culture supplied a common language with which saleswomen could discuss their world. Clerks had terms for types of selling behavior as well as for varieties of customers. A "crepe-hanger," for instance, was a salesperson who ruined a sale by talking a customer out of something she had resolved to buy; a saleswoman who called "Oh, Henrietta," while waiting on a customer was alerting her co-workers to the fact that the customer was a "hen," or a difficult type. Third, work culture imposed sanctions on those who violated the group rules: penalties included messing up a transgressor's assigned section of stock, bumping into an offender or banging her shins with drawers, public ridicule and humiliation, and complete ostracism, which sometimes drove people to leave the department. If the informal work group demanded loyalty, it repaid it with protection: it insulated the individual worker from the demands of bosses and customers alike.

Saleswomen had an ingenious variety of tactics for manipulating managers, customers, and merchandise to their own advantage. The first element, management, was well aware that saleswomen's highjinks were not just a way to blow off steam, but were evidence of an underlying unity. Bosses understood that the selling floor was the turf of the clerks, that it had its own elaborate rules and social system which were distinct from and often in conflict with the store's formal structure. They tried sporadically to suppress the more disruptive outbursts of the informal work group but in general they treated it with a wary respect and at least partially yielded control of the floor to it. They relied on the "clerking sisterhood" to maintain good order and high morale; they cautioned new workers to tread lightly until they learned the customs of the department; they even tried to co-opt and institutionalize the informal initiation process by designating one saleswoman an official sponsor of new clerks. Saleswomen were astute observers of their superiors, punishing the bad and rewarding the good. A boss who gave offense received the cold shoulder or petty harassment in return; the ultimate penalty was to embarass a buyer or floor manager in front of his or her superiors. A boss deemed worthy of respect could count on the saleswomen's backing when it counted, particularly against upper management.

Management directives frequently emerged from the crucible of work culture in quite altered form. Saleswomen reorganized cumbersome paperwork routines to fit their own convenience, and sometimes completely thwarted their purposes: in one department, they effectively short-circuited a management scheme for subtracting returned purchases from individuals' sales totals. Clerks refused to take on extra duties which would eat into their "spare time," and when they felt threatened by new practices, such as self-service, they fought back by doing sloppy or eccentric stock work on the new displays. Concerted action could bend rules quite sharply: the eight women in one especially well-unified women's shoe department unilaterally lengthened the lunch hour from 45 minutes to a full hour and compounded the insult by wearing huge hoop earrings forbidden by the store's dress code. A helpless management acquiesced. The informal work group also covered up for a certain amount of theft of merchandise and materials; managers warned one another worriedly that a department infected with the virus of thievery was a serious threat indeed.

The most important and effective way in which work culture worked against the interests of the bosses, however, was in restricting output and limiting intradepartmental competition. Each department had a concept of the total sales that constituted a good day's work. Saleswomen used various tactics to keep their "books" (sales tallies) within acceptable limits: running unusually low books would imperil a worker's status with management just as extraordinarily high books would put her in the bad graces of her peers. Individual clerks would avoid customers late in the day when their books were running high, or call other clerks to help them. Saleswomen managed to approximate the informal quota with impressive regularity, ironing out the fluctuations in customers' buying habits in ways the managers had never dreamed of. They adjusted the number of transactions they completed to compensate for the size of the purchases; if they made a few large sales early in the day, they might then retire to do stockwork. During the slow summer season or during inclement weather, they were more aggressive with the smaller volume of customers; at peak seasons, they ignored customers who might put them over their quota.

Department store managers attacked the workers' stint with a bewildering variety of commission, commission-plus-salary, and quota-bonus payment schemes beginning in the years just before World War I, but monetary incentives to break worker solidarity were no more effective with saleswomen than with skilled craftsmen. The definitive industry study of these plans concluded, not surprisingly, that no pay scheme could increase sales output, but that sales levels were linked to the overall atmosphere of the workplace. Bosses reported similar failure with competitive devices such as sales contests, even when they offered cash prizes, although they occasionally reported successes with group, as opposed to individual, incentive schemes. As universally as managers complained about restriction of output, nowhere did a boss testify to the successful elimination of the practice, even in the most insecure days of the depression.

The strongest epithet in the saleswoman's vocabulary—"grabber"— applied to those unwary clerks who ran excessively high books. The grabber seized on customers out of turn, sometimes two and three at a time; she shirked stockwork and paperwork; she gave the department a bad name for offensive overselling. The fear of grabbing accounts in large part for the rigors of the departmental initiation process. Ignorant of the amount of the informal quota, and perhaps even of its very existence, outsiders—new, part-time, or temporary clerks—required stern socialization. In some departments, newcomers were effectively prohibited from making any sales at all for the first few days; part-time and temporary clerks were exiled to the dullest corners of the department. The retaliatory power of the informal work group was amply demonstrated in one children's wear department when the management made the mistake of firing a popular though unproductive saleswoman and immediately replacing her with a new employee. The new clerk, experienced in the ways of saleswomen's work culture and sensible of the hazards of her position, tried eagerly to learn how the department defined a "good book," but her co-workers kept the information from her and thus excluded her from the work group.

Customers were the most strainful and least constant factors in saleswomen's work lives, barraging them with a kaleidoscopic succession of demands, moods, and quirks and constantly coming in for special treatment by the informal work group. While management ingenuously maintained the fiction that all customers could expect equal service, saleswomen picked and chose among their customers and served them with widely varying degrees of interest and efficiency. As one clerk, clearly near the end of her rope, put it, "All customers are crackpots!"; her co-worker, more relaxed but still wary, grimly affirmed, "I like a counter between me and the customer."[11] The customer was not an unambiguous enemy, for under the right conditions she might become the saleswomen's ally against management, but she was always a potential threat.

A theme that appears in management literature almost as frequently as "huddling" is that saleswomen, even those on commission, used a variety of tactics to avoid waiting on customers. Methods ranged from the subtle (pretending not to notice customers while engaged in stockwork or in conversations with fellow workers) to the blatant (disappearing on sudden errands) to the outright rude (explicit refusals to show merchandise). The work culture allocated customers among saleswomen in ways that included rough rotation as well as reserving certain types of customers for certain clerks; to violate this order was to risk being labeled a grabber. But there was a larger message to management and to the public in this behavior: the saleswoman was taking her clients on her terms and not theirs; while they might have a superior class position, she had the upper hand through her control of the merchandise. Hence, two important subthemes in management's laments about clerks' indifference to customers: first, they displayed goods reluctantly and usually only on direct request; second, they often addressed customers with unbecoming familiarity—the term that made bosses especially apoplectic was "dearie."

A customer whose only sin was to appear in the department when saleswomen were not prepared to greet her met with indifference, but far worse awaited the customer who committed a more active offense against the "clerking sisterhood." If a customer appeared to a saleswoman's practiced eye to be a looker, she might be harassed or treated rudely; if she asked for something that was out of stock, she might be told scathingly that no one wanted *those* anymore; if she was too slow in making up her mind, she might find a number of clerks ganging up on her to force a choice. Saleswomen discussed the worst customers loudly within earshot of other customers, an unsubtle warning to those who might dare to cross them.

Customers could be allies, however. A saleswoman who took a liking to a customer and sincerely tried to please her might be genuinely upset if she failed. In order to smooth rough transactions, saleswomen had a number of tactics with which they could secure the good will of the customer, often causing store management extra trouble and expense in the process. Clerks could suggest the delivery of small parcels to close a sale quickly, or suggest that a tediously undecided customer send home a selection of merchandise to reflect on at leisure. Dry goods clerks generously overmeasured yardage while their pleased customers looked on. To quiet customers' doubts, saleswomen would make wild guarantees or outrightly misrepresent merchandise; they also encouraged customers to place costly special orders instead of trying to talk them into something in stock.

Saleswomen often built up clienteles of frequent customers, keeping files of their addresses and purchases with their employer's encouragement. On the one hand, close clerk-customer relations could encourage extra purchases, but on the other saleswomen gave their clientele special treatment that was contrary to managers' interests—for example, they withheld items from display until markdowns could be taken on them, and then alerted favorite customers. Moreover, it was not uncommon for saleswomen to concentrate so exclusively on "their" customers that they completely ignored new or unknown customers.

Just as saleswomen would not wait on all customers equally, so they would not sell all goods with equal energy. Saleswomen developed legendary instincts for good sellers; as one retailer put it, they could "spot a lemon quicker than a Mediterranean fruit fly."[12] It was an unwritten rule that buyers should heed their judgments, a rule which saleswomen enforced ruthlessly. In one toy department saleswomen refused to sell stuffed toys that they had pronounced too low in quality, labeling them "drug-store Easter bunnies."[13] Frequently, saleswomen took a real proprietary interest in their merchandise, occupying themselves with stockwork and displays to the practical exclusion of selling. They eagerly showed fresh and interesting goods, consigning older or worn items to bottom drawers where they awaited profit-eating markdowns. Managers were sometimes able to introduce new items only with great difficulty. Domestics saleswomen were so impressed with the virtues of all-wool and Irish linen goods that they strongly resisted the introduction of synthetic fibers after World War II; buyers reported that clerks undid the advertising efforts of stores and manufacturers with their "silent scorn" for the new materials.[14]

Investigators who were dismayed at this lack of interest with which saleswomen presented goods and the noncommital or even inaccurate answers which they gave to questions were even more appalled when they discovered that these same saleswomen were extremely knowledgeable about their wares. One notably silent saleswoman, for example, was so intrigued to know more about her stock that she eavesdropped on a manufacturer's representative. There was no doubt that the training in merchandise information was conveying the message to the clerk; the problem was in convincing her to pass it on to the customer. In general, clerks persisted in selling what they themselves preferred, if they made special efforts to sell anything at all. A woman who tried to buy service-weight stockings from a clerk enamored with sheer silk hose would be treated insultingly; a customer contemplating a purchase, such as expensive silverware, which a saleswoman considered extravagant would be strongly discouraged.

Saleswomen not only policed the merchandise offered by the department, but also keenly observed the selling skill displayed by co-workers. A sociologist doing field work in a women's dress department observed the saleswomen "Playing Customer." They watched in total absorption as two among them acted out a sale, recreating familiar types from both sides of the counter. The skits were social glue, shared rituals in which the saleswomen reemphasized their group solidarity against the perennial threat of the customer. They also constituted an oral tradition, passing along and elaborating the wisdom learned on the selling floor. Finally, they reinforced the department pecking order by the ways in which different members were caricatured. Other departments had other forms of selling drama; frequently, saleswomen would demonstrate their selling skills to their co-workers by lavishing attention on "lookers" on slow days.

This recognition of selling skill suggests that the informal work group could tolerate a certain limited amount of amiable competition as long as it did not threaten the relationship of the whole group to managers and customers. Clerks could compete over favored customers, preferred selling locations, or rights to certain kinds of merchandise. Sometimes, these competitive aspects could erupt into outright conflict; more often, however, it appears that the relative flexibility of the selling floor allowed individuals to stake out special roles which were then tacitly recognized by the group. Hierarchies of age, experience, ethnicity, and skills played some part in assigning these roles, but there was ample room for simple personal inclination. In one department, the turf was elaborately allocated by the informal work group, despite bosses' persistent efforts to change the arrangement; the group functioned peacefully because everyone knew her place and kept to it. The clerking sisterhood was not invariably one big happy family, although it often was; but whatever the internal discord, it was clearly saleswomen's work culture and not managers' conceptions of selling skill which determined their conduct.

CONCLUSION

The outline of the development of the work of American department store saleswomen from 1890 to 1960 suggests some factors which we should bear in mind in studying the history of women's work. We must, first of all, rethink our definitions of skill. Whether in store, office, or factory, most women's work has been regarded as unskilled, but we should find new ways to conceptualize work which reflect its real nature and are not bound by traditional male-oriented notions of skill. Second, we should be alert to the fact that a linear degradation of work was not the invariable fate of the woman worker. It is critical to understand the impact of the whole process of rationalization: the limits of the application of scientific management, its differential effects on men and women, and the importance of other types of management reform, particularly personnel work and human relations. In many occupations, the impact of a more wholesome work environment may have been greater than that of Taylorism, and in some occupations managers actually sought, at least for a time, to upgrade employees' skills. Finally, we must investigate the ways in which work culture and the informal work group limited management's freedom of action and provided a measure of workplace autonomy for workers. The work culture of women workers is particularly ill-understood, but sales work provides an example of an enduring work group in the face of rapid turnover, a high incidence of part-time and temporary work, and women's supposed primary identification with home and family rather than with paid work. The prospects for the future are mixed; innovations in data processing and the pressure of discount-store competition may well have undermined the conditions favoring the work culture of saleswomen, and increasing numbers of workers are seeking the formal protections of a union in addition to those of the informal work group, but the practices which I have described here are hardly a thing of the past.

NOTES

I wish to thank Edward Benson, Ann Bookman, Roslyn Feldberg, Maurine Greenwald, Barbara Melosh, and Susan Reverby for helpful and supportive criticisms on earlier versions of this paper.

The phrase, "the clerking sisterhood" comes from Zelie Leigh, "Shopping Round," *Atlantic Monthly* 138 (Aug. 1926): 205.

1. David Montgomery, "Workers' Control of Machine Production in the 19th Century," *Labor History* 17, no. 4 (Fall 1976): 485–509; Harry Braverman, *Labor and Monopoly Capital: The Degradation of Work in the Twentieth Century* (New York, 1974).

2. Braverman, *Labor and Monopoly Capital*, pp. 265–266.

3. Daniel Nelson, *Managers and Workers: Origins of the New Factory System in the United States, 1880–1920* (Madison, 1975).

4. See Alfred D. Chandler, Jr., *Strategy and Structure: Chapters in the History of the American Industrial Enterprise* (Cambridge, 1962).

5. Anne O'Hagan, "Behind the Scenes in the Big Stores," *Munsey's Magazine* 22 (Jan. 1900): 535.

6. Beatrice Judelle, "The Changing Customer, 1910–1916," *Stores* 42, no. 10 (Nov. 1960): 14.

7. "A Saleswoman Speaks to Management," *Bulletin of the National Retail Dry Goods Association* 24, no. 12 (Dec. 1942): 18.

8. "How Bloomingdale's Trains for Better Customer Service," *Stores* 46, no. 11 (Dec. 1964): 24–25.

9. W. H. Leffingwell, "Sizing Up Customers From Behind the Counter," *The American Magazine* 94 (July 1922): 150.

10. "Expose Employees to Knowledge," *Department Store Economist* 1, no. 14 (Aug. 10, 1938): 35.

11. George F. F. Lombard, *Executive Policies and Employee Satisfactions: A Study of a Small Department in a Large Metropolitan Store*, D.C.S. thesis, Graduate School of Business Administration, Harvard University, 1941, pp. 348, 355.

12. Lawrence Bitner of Filene's, quoted in C. E. Eerkes, "The Employee—A Preferred Customer," in *Joint Management Proceedings, National Retail Dry Goods Association* (New York, 1934), p. 78.

13. Mildred Farquhar, "An Analysis of a Toy Department in a Department Store," M.A. thesis, University of Pittsburgh, 1933, p. 14.

14. "Training for Better Sales," *Stores* 35, no. 9 (Sept. 1953): 28.

CHAPTER FIVE

Sexual Harassment at the Workplace: Historical Notes

by Mary Bularzik

INTRODUCTION: WHAT IS SEXUAL HARASSMENT?

In 1908 *Harper's Bazaar* printed a series of letters in which working women wrote of their experiences of city life.[1] A typical experience was reported by G. E. D., a New York stenographer:

> I purchased several papers, and plodded faithfully through their multitude of "ads." I took the addresses of some I intended to call upon. . . . The first "ad" I answered the second day was that of a doctor who desired a stenographer at once, good wages paid. It sounded rather well, I thought, and I felt that this time I would meet a gentleman. The doctor was very kind and seemed to like my appearance and references; as to salary, he offered me $15 a week, with a speedy prospect of more. As I was leaving his office, feeling that at last I was launched safely upon the road to a good living, he said casually, "I have an auto; and as my wife doesn't care for that sort of thing, I shall expect you to accompany me frequently on pleasure trips." That settled the doctor; I never appeared. After that experience I was ill for two weeks; a result of my hard work, suffering and discouragement.[2]

The incident illustrates a common occupational hazard of women in the labor force: sexual harassment. Sexual harassment, defined as any unwanted pressure for sexual activity, includes verbal innuendos and suggestive comments, leering, gestures, unwanted physical contact (touching,

Reprinted from Vol. 12, No. 4 (July-August 1978).

pinching, etc.), rape, and attempted rape. It is a form of harassment mainly perpetrated by men against women. As in many other forms of violence against women, the assertion of power and dominance is often more important than the sexual interaction. Sexual demands in the workplace, especially between boss and employee, become even more coercive because a woman's economic livelihood may be at stake.

Sexual harassment of women in the workplace is one manifestation of the wider issue of the oppression of women. Violence is central to that oppression, an essential part of establishing and maintaining the patriarchal family.

Until recently violence has only been studied psychologically, as an aberration, not as a norm. When violence occurs in the nuclear family, it is treated as the occasional act of a deviant rather than a prevalent and socially sanctioned way of enforcing the status quo. Statistical evidence shows violence to be pervasive, yet this is ignored. Rape, for example, despite repeated studies showing it is extremely common in many social settings, is still often described as the isolated act of a stranger. Wife-beating was treated as a similar infrequent (though regrettable) event.

Sexual harassment at the workplace is, I would argue, an analogous problem. It is consistent, systematic, and pervasive, not a set of random isolated acts. The license to harass women workers, which many men feel they have, stems from notions that there is a "woman's place" which women in the labor force have left, thus leaving behind their personal integrity.

I would like to propose a model which sees violence, and more specifically the threat of violence, as a mechanism of social control. It is used to control women's access to certain jobs; to limit job success and mobility; and to compensate men for powerlessness in their own lives. It functions on two levels: the group control of women by men, and personal control of individual workers by bosses and co-workers. Violence is used to support and preserve the institutions which guarantee the dominance of one group over others. Sexual harassment is one form. The threat of lynching hanging over blacks in the South at the turn of the century was another such instance of the use of violence. So is rape. In neither case are the perpetrators of the "crime" totally condemned by society; though there are laws on the books against such behavior, it is clear to the victims that it may be dangerous to bring charges; and the victim is "marked" by the crime (or dead) while the attacker is considered "normal." Both "crimes" serve as warnings to certain groups not to walk the streets alone at night.

Words, gestures, comments can be used as threats of violence and to express dominance. Harassment often depends on this underlying violence—violence is implied as the ultimate response. Harassment is "little rape," an invasion of a person, by suggestion, by intimidation, by confronting a woman with her helplessness. It is an interaction in which one person purposefully seeks to discomfort another person. This discomfort serves to remind women of their helplessness in the face of male violence. To offer such a model is to suggest that it is not simply an individual interaction but a social one; not an act of deviance but a societally condoned mode of behavior that functions to preserve male dominance in the world of work.

The economic aspect of sexual harassment in the workplace differentiates it from other forms of violence against women. A rationalized capitalist economic order tended to separate spheres of sexual power (in the family) and economic power (in the workplace). Sexual coercion in the workplace reasserts the connection between the two. While the women involved did not see sexual favors as a right of their employers and male co-workers, their fear of losing jobs often stifled effective protest.

This essay will consider the historical conditions of sexual harassment and focus on white urban working women, primarily in Northern cities, and primarily in working-class jobs. Most of the evidence concerns single women, who predominated in the female labor force before the 1940s. (The entrance of many more married women into the labor force during and after World War II added another dimension to the problem which will not be considered here.)

Sexual harassment was a problem faced by paid women workers in the United States from colonial days. Violence and sexual coercion did not originate with industrialization. However, the dynamics of these issues were different in a paid labor force than in a preindustrial economy. The family setting of work in colonial days makes the incidents of sexual violence part of the history of violence in the family. In a capitalist industrial society, sexual harassment often became an interaction between strangers, not relatives or neighbors, which changed the psychological framework of the sexual violence.

There are scattered instances of women in colonial times protesting violence by male employers against women workers. In the January 28, 1734, issue of the *N.Y. Weekly Journal*, a group of women servants published a notice saying, ". . . we think it reasonable we should not be beat by our Mistresses Husband[s], they being too strong and perhaps may do tender women mischief."[3] Court records reveal many instances of servants being seduced by their employers. Since the status of domestic servants is complicated and little historical research has been done on their working conditions, I am not further considering them in this essay.

Much male public opinion didn't distinguish between women workers, prostitutes, the destitute, and the criminal classes in the industrializing stages of the economy. This was due to a complex of factors such as the necessity for women from poor families to be in the labor force, the unusualness of women working outside the family, the analogy between the prostitute and the paid women worker, both in some sense "escaping" from male control, and both "unprotected" and thus fair game for male lust. More thoughtful observers saw that low wages and poor working conditions in factories might make the temptations of the better-paying job of prostitute too much for some working girls to resist (or a logical choice from an economic point of view). As early as 1829, Matthew Carey offered a prize for the best essay on "the inadequacy of the wages generally paid to seamstresses, spoolers, spinners, shoe binders, etc., to procure food, raiment, and lodging; on the effects of that inadequacy upon the happiness and morals of those females and their families, when they have any; and on the probability that those low wages frequently forced poor women to the choice between dishonor and absolute want of common necessaries."[4] Thus from the early nineteenth century on, we have a series of studies and investigations of the connections between low wages and vice, culminating in the "Purity Crusade" of the Progressive era. The concern for the working girl shown by the middle-class reformers who conducted these studies was double-edged; working women often saw it as condescension, and resented the implication that they were morally weak.[5]

The experience of the women workers in the Lowell mills is an example of the assumed connection between the working woman who sold her labor power and the prostitute who sold herself. The idea that factory girls had loose morals was a commonplace in England, and this concept was also prevalent in the United States.[6] Current work on the Lowell mills emphasizes the "protection" offered by the boarding-house system, and implies a concern for the moral welfare of their employees by the owners. However, some contemporary accounts indicate public concern about the behavior of the women in the mills. Newspapers carried accounts by physicians and other prominent citizens of immoral activities:

> There used to be in Lowell an association of young men called the "Old Line" who had an understanding with a great many of the factory girls and who used to introduce young men of their acquaintance, visitors to the place, to the girls for immoral purposes. Balls were held at various places attended mostly by these young men and girls, with some others who did not know the object of the association, and after the dancing was over the girls were taken to infamous places of resort in Lowell and the vicinity, and were not returned to their homes until daylight.[7]

While these stories often were not verifiable (and were attacked by the women as lies), they do indicate an identification of the single working woman with the prostitute, and a refusal on the part of some men to distinguish the woman willing to sell her labor power with the woman willing to sell herself.

Other material shows evidence of sexual exploitation by supervisors. An article in the *Voice of Industry* told of a factory girl rumored to have saved $3,000 from her work who purchased a farm for herself and son (a favorite Cinderella theme of the management). The women's paper declared not only that the worker in question had less than half the sum, but that half of this "it was strongly suspected, was obtained as hush money of a prominent factory man who had been intimate with her and was the father of the boy now living in the country."[8]

Contrary to the view of the mill-owners as concerned for the morality of the decent girls they hired, the reality may be that they "consciously fostered the idea that the operatives were 'bad' women. Their advertisements carried special pleas for 'respectable young women.'" In fact, so prevalent did this idea become that the girls themselves issued a statement (which included) "we beseech them not to asperse our characters or stigmatise us as disorderly persons!"[9]

A theme in the study of sexual harassment begins to emerge here. The nineteenth-century ideal of True Womanhood required women to be the guardians of purity; if a sexual episode occurred, it was the woman's fault, and she was "ruined for life." In practical terms, this meant she might be thrown out of her job and house. "Ladies" were not to know even of the existence of sexual passion. To admit that sexual contact, even conversation, occurred, was to be blamed for it. Thus the double bind—while women workers were often at the mercy of male supervisors, the repercussions of admitting incidents happened were often as bad as the original event. This conflict between the "lady" or "good girl" who is above sexuality, and the "bad girl" or "whore" who is involved with it, is a major theme in the history of sexual harassment.[10]

Another dilemma for working women was the conflict between labor force participation and the pressure to stay in the home. The way in which industry was organized required a source of cheap labor; in many cases this was furnished by women workers. But traditional masculine control in the family was threatened by waged women; thus the social pressure for women to stay in the home intensified along with early industrialization. The social pressure to stay home was strongest for middle-class women as the ideology of the Home emerged as a companion ideology to True Womanhood in the mid-nineteenth century. The economic pressure to work, on the other hand, was strongest for working-class women, and of this group, for single, divorced, widowed women (i.e., those not tied in marriage to an individual man). Women were conflicted about being in the labor force; however, for working-class women, this conflict was not simply competing "attitudes" about their place, but in many situations a "choice" between starvation if unemployed and attempted rape on the job.

Sexual harassment served to reinforce those attitudes pushing women out of the labor force. Yet this was an untenable goal in an industrializing economy. A secondary effect of sexual harassment, then, was to reinforce women's feelings of powerlessness at work.

Again, if sexual harassment was completely effective at driving women out of the workforce, it would work against the interests of management and capitalists as a whole; for an industrialized economy needs women as a source of cheap labor. According to this line of reasoning, one would expect to find some support by management for measures to reduce sexual harassment by supervisors against working women if it threatens the efficiency of the labor force. The individual benefits accruing to males from sexual harassment (personal power) are thus not identical with, and at times contradict, benefits to the capitalist class (of controlling the workforce). At other times these benefits reinforce each other, as it may be cheaper for companies to allow executives the "free" benefit of harassing their secretaries than to give them a raise.

In the late nineteenth and early twentieth century, the increasing participation of women in the labor force went along with a pattern of segregation into low-paying jobs. If, as previously argued, women's occupational mobility was checked by sexual harassment, one would expect to find many instances of sexual harassment in this period. And indeed we do.

The most common description of the harassment victim at that time was—young, single, immigrant, uneducated, and unskilled.[11] This is of course also the description of the typical woman worker. Thus it suggests only that *most* women were harassed, not any particular type of women.

Furthermore, harassment victims could be found in a wide range of occupations. Not only waitresses and domestic servants, but also elevated railway cashiers, union organizers, garment workers, white-goods workers, home workers, doctors, dressmakers, shopgirls, laundry workers, models, office workers, cotton mill workers, cannery workers, broom factory workers, assistant foremen (sic), stenographers and typists, soap factory workers, hop-pickers, shoeshine girls, barmaids, legal secretaries, actresses, sales demonstrators, art students, and would-be workers at employment interviews.

The severity of abuse ranged from verbal suggestions, threats, and insults to staring, touching, attempted rape, and rape. Women were propositioned; promised money, jobs and automobiles(!); and then threatened with loss of jobs and blacklisting.

Harassment certainly crossed ethnic lines. Jewish, Italian, WASP, Southern white and black women were all harassed. Black women, however, often interpreted sexual harassment as racism, not sexism. Two Atlanta women talked about their experience in the 1930s:

> Isabel: Some of the girls wanted to work downtown as waitresses, you know, and I asked my daddy if I could—to earn extra money. Daddy said, "You will never work downtown. Not the way white men think about black women."
>
> Eva: Yes, a black woman was fair prey, you know.
>
> Isabel: You see, a white man that might not dare accost a white girl is safe in his advances on a black girl. Why? Because in court her papa or brothers or any black man—even a black lawyer—wouldn't dare stand up against one white man.
>
> Eva: The answer to all that was to protect us from it ever happening.

While this is both a middle-class and male-identified solution, the message is clear. As Eva pointed out, "the idea was that if you were a black girl outside your area, and a white man decided to insult you . . . nothing could be done."[12]

The reactions of women to the workplace hazard of sexual harassment can be divided into individual and group responses. There are several components of this problem. Women may have seen sexual harassment primarily as a social problem, or primarily an individual problem (i.e., one's personal bad luck to have a lecherous boss). Seeing it as a social problem led to group responses (unions, protective associations, settlement house organizations), and was a motivation for organizing. Another possible response was legal action. The joining of the group response with the attempt to achieve legal protection in the drive for protective legislation had as one motivating factor the protection of women from sexual harassment.

The initial move for protective legislation came before the Civil War. However, these laws were overturned, and a second wave of agitation for protective legislation for women began in the 1870s. Not until the *Muller v. Oregon* decision of 1908, though, was the principle of legislative limitation of women's hours upheld by the Supreme Court.

What were the motivations of those pushing this legislation? The weakness of the woman worker was the main reason often given—weaker in terms of physical strength, in terms of bargaining power, because of having other drains on their energy (housework), and having more to fear from factory employment.

Threats to morals were prominent among these "dangers" of employment to women. The general opinion was that women workers were subject to harassment of supervisors, and thus should be prohibited from certain occupations, and night work, for their own protection. Smuts, in *Women and Work in America*, writes:

> Disrespect for the working girl sometimes led to sexual advances by supervisors or male workers. Girls complained of stolen embraces, pinches and vulgar remarks. It was widely believed that many prostitutes were former working girls, first corrupted by supervisors who had threatened to fire or promised to promote them.[13]

Current studies found it an issue of concern for Jewish garment workers and Italian cannery workers.[14]

Many of the "participant-observer" investigations of working women, as well as early sociological analyses, reached the same conclusion. Maud Nathan writes of salesclerks:

> Floor-walkers in the old days were veritable tsars; they often ruled with a rod of iron. Only the girls who were "free-and-easy" with them, who consented to lunch or dine with them, who permitted certain liberties, were allowed any freedom of action or felt secure in their positions.[15]

Individual reactions of victims of sexual harassment encompassed a wide range of emotions. Many women felt guilt. S.H., a clerk in a store in Los Angeles wrote of this:

> I don't think there was one evening during that time when I worked in that store that I went home unmolested. I have walked block after block through the business part of the city with a man at my side questioning me as to where I lived, and if I would not like to go to dinner, how I was going to spend the evening, etc. I never answered, except to threaten to speak to the police. That I was ashamed to do, thinking it must be my own fault in some way, and that I ought to possess dignity enough to make men understand they were mistaken.[16]

And some women who had "made it" blamed those who didn't. M.C.P., a government worker in Washington, D.C., who made $1,200 a year in 1908, commented:

> Referring to the moral dangers of city life, of course there are many dangers, but it largely depends on the girl, in my opinion, whether she is led into temptation or not.[17]

Fear was another dominant reaction. Elizabeth Hasanovitch was so afraid of her boss after he attempted to rape her, that she never returned to collect her pay.

> I felt what that glance in his eyes meant. It was quiet in the shop, everybody had left, even the foreman. There in the office I sat on a chair, the boss stood near me with my pay in his hand, speaking to me in a velvety, soft voice. Alas! Nobody around. I sat trembling with fear.

But looking for a new job was agony for her:

> The thought of a new job made me so uneasy that I could hardly sleep. My bitter experience with my last shop pictured me all the bosses as vulgar and rude as the one from whom I ran away on Saturday.[18]

Rose Cohen was too stunned at thirteen to respond effectively to her boss' proposition:

> After a moment or so he said quite abruptly, "Come, Ruth, sit down here." He motioned to his knee. I felt my face flush. I backed away towards the door and stood staring at him.[19]

A Russian Jewish shopgirl wrote to the *Jewish Daily Forward* in 1907 after she had lost her job because she refused the foreman's "vulgar advances":

> The girls in the shop were very upset over the foreman's vulgarity but they didn't want him to throw them out, so they are afraid to be witnesses against him. What can be done about this?[20]

Sometimes their fear was replaced by anger. Elizabeth Hasanovitch expressed her rage:

If only I could discredit that man so that he would never dare to insult a working girl again! If only I could complain of him in court![21]

But more often the major reaction was confusion: guilt, anger, fear, and a feeling that attention paid to one as a sexual being was supposed to be appreciated, all intermingled. Even organizers were torn in their reactions. When her supervisor talked to her and asked her to be his girl, a young organizer in a garment shop laughed at him. But he persisted:

He went on "You know it's a rule not to pay the girls the first week, but I like you, and I'm going to pay you the first week." When I came home from work I told my sister about it and said, "I don't know if I should feel flattered or insulted."[22]

A Cleveland manicurist reported an experience comparable to a nineteenth-century potboiler. Alone in the city and propositioned by a friend of a friend to whom she has applied for a job, she was totally traumatized:

How I ever got out of the building I do not know, I was so blinded with confusion and shame. I did not take the elevator, but reached the street somehow by the long stairways, with the last words of this man ringing in my ears: "You will be glad to take up with my offer, after you have searched elsewhere."

Her subsequent failure to get work led her to plan suicide. On her way to drown herself in the harbor a young man whom she met at a restaurant offered her aid, lent her $5, and encouraged, she went back to the city and found a job.

Later I married the young man who gave me a helping hand.[23]

While most reactions were not as melodramatic as this (and marriage as an escape from sexual harassment may be questionable), the problem of sexual harassment was a serious threat to the health and well-being of women workers. Power and domination outweighed the sensual or sexual aspect of these incidents in women's working lives.

Sexual harassment was addressed in *Life and Labor*, the publication of the National Women's Trade Union League. In a 1911 editorial on the clothing trade, a section on "The Tyranny of Foreman" claims that:

Abusive and insulting language is frequently used by those in authority in the shops. This is especially intolerable to the girls, who should have the right to work without surrendering their self-respect. No women should be subjected by fear of loss of her job to unwarranted insults.[24]

Stories of harassed women workers were published in the magazine. While these may be composite stories, they do indicate the range of harassment, the results, and the anger of women at being sexually as well as economically exploited on the job. An example is "Rosie's story," the account of a 17-year-old worker in the needle trades.

> The boss from the shop was always fresh with the girls. He liked to see us blush, so we made a society, called "The Young Ladies Educational Society," and we was not to stand the freshness of the boss. But we was afraid of him, and so we couldn't help each other. Once he touched me, very fresh like, and I cried, and he said, "Lets be good friends, Rosie, and to show you how good I means it, you take supper mit me in a swell hotel, with music and flowers, see?" And I says, "So! Supper mit you—swell hotel! Well I ask my ma," and he said, "Don't do it. You say you going to sleep at a friend's house" and I was trembling so I couldn't nearly do my work, and when my ma sees me, she says, "What's the matter, Rosie?" and I says, "Nothing," because she's sad, my ma is, 'cause I have to work so hard and can't have no education, and she says, "Rosie, you got to tell your ma what's wrong," and we both cried together, and so the next day I went to another shop, and I told the *first lie I ever told in my life*. I told the boss I come from another city. I liked this new boss; he was not so fresh and I had a seat by a window, and my ma and me, we was so happy we laughed when I told her about the nice shop and fresh air, and then the next day the boss he come to me and he says, "I'm sorry, Rosie, we like your work, but your other boss he telephoned he no discharged you and so we can't keep you here."[25]

As did Rosie, many women reacted on an individual level. But Rosie and her friends also saw that this problem wasn't something they were asking for, and did try to meet it on a group level; they formed a "Young Ladies Educational Society" with the purpose of resisting the boss's harassment. The fact that their boss was a habitual harasser, and recognized as such by the group, was not that uncommon a situation. Dorothy Richardson in *The Long Day* (her account of how women workers were exploited at the turn of the century) wrote that after her boss approached her (". . . in a moment he had grasped my bare arm and given it a rude pinch"), ". . . the rest of my companions repeated divers terrible tales of moral ruin and betrayal, . . . wherein the boss was inevitably the villain."[26] S. R., a saleswoman, suffered repeated harassment and propositioning on a new job before she discovered that she was not the only one:

> I never heard the other girls complain, so supposed for some time that they were not bothered; but when I knew them better I found they had the same trouble. . .[27]

There were other instances of groups being formed. In some cases these were more successful than the attempt of Rosie and her friends. Alice Woodbridge, the "moving force and guiding spirit of the Working Women's Society" (the forerunner of the WTUL), was politicized as the result of such experiences,

She had held at various times positions in offices; these positions had promised to be lucrative, but because of insulting proposals from employers she had been obliged to give them up; she had been buffeted about for many a year, trying to earn an honest living and trying to live on the low wages offered her.

Protection of working women from unwanted sexual advances was a major aim of the Society.

> . . . it was her purpose to endeavor to shield other working girls from the hideous experiences which had been hers, in her efforts to lead an honest, upright, independent life.[28]

But what could be done to stop sexual harassment? The sisterly support of Rosie's group ("we was not to stand the freshness of the boss") had its obvious limits. The women were afraid of the power of the boss, and with good reason; even more than today, he had the power to fire them at will. As in Rosie's case, he could force them into a position where they felt if they didn't quit they'd be raped. Alice Woodbridge was forced to leave many jobs. When Dorothy Richardson's boss returned and "after looking me over thoughtfully, informed me that I was supposed to be promoted Monday morning to the wrappers' counter," she feared for her own safety and quit. Elizabeth Hasanovitch was so afraid of her former boss after his attempted rape that she never returned to collect her week's wages, although she was at that point almost penniless.[29] But groups to combat harassment were not common, which suggests that women had little faith in their power to change their own lives.

In the short run, less politicized women looked for ways to protect their individual personal safety. This is not to say that they denied the group aspects of the problem, for they often tried to share such knowledge. Their coping strategies included warning other women about "fresh" bosses and supervisors, quitting, finding new jobs, sharing verbal ways to reject passes, staying out of empty offices, and giving in to keep a job. In her first job in a garment shop at the age of 12, Rose Cohen often felt uncomfortable because the men told dirty jokes.

> I could never keep my face from turning red. One day when Atta (the only other woman worker) and I were alone at our table she said: "It is too bad that you have a tell-tale face. You better learn to hide your feelings. What you hear in this shop is nothing compared with what you will hear in other shops. Look at me."

Atta was an expert at dodging the boss and threatening him with her needle when he tried to grab her. The first English sentence Rosa learned from her was:

> "Keep your hands off please."[30]

A social worker posing as a cannery worker to investigate working conditions for the New York State Factory Investigating Commission (1912), was warned by sister workers to stay away from the men:

> . . . an Italian girl told me that one must be careful not to get fresh with the Italian boys, because they were dangerous.

She herself was offered an opportunity to make

> two or three dollars on the side any time, if you come up here to work at night, we can go for a stroll. That was the timekeeper and his name was Gillette.

The other workers corroborated her experiences.

> A great many girls told me he was fresh, and he was boss, and it was best to keep away from him.[31]

Occasionally women took harassers to court. In 1908, Grace Abbott and Sophonisba Breckinridge took a saloon-keeper to court in behalf of Bozena, a young Bohemian immigrant. Her employer had "abused her shamefully and then turned her out when he found that she was to become the mother of his illegitimate child." They lost the case, "because the charge was a penitentiary offense, and the judge was lenient." Not surprisingly, the judge empathized with the defendant rather than the victim.

Grace Abbott had such cases in mind when she started immigrant protection associations in Chicago. Protecting immigrant girls from lecherous bosses was, again, a major theme in organizing.[32] In this case it was because of the middle-class social workers' intervention that Bozena's case was taken to court at all; most women, feeling less able to cope with the male-dominated legal system, would hesitate to bring their case to court. And even the feminist solidarity of the Hull House activists with Bozena did not win her case.

Working women themselves wanted to resist. Elizabeth Hasanovitch's fear was replaced by anger:

> If I could only discredit that man so that he would never dare to insult a working-girl again! If only I could complain of him in court! But I had no witnesses to testify the truth; with my broken English I could give very little explanation. Besides that, if I were working in a shop and were called to court, the firm might suspect some evil in me and send me away.[33]

Her confrontation with this dilemma led her to the conclusion that working women must organize; this seems to have been one of her personal motivations for joining the Waist and Dressmakers Union. As an individual member of a union in a basically non-unionized industry, a woman might not immediately improve her own conditions. Elizabeth Hasanovitch's new foreman, who had previously treated her in a friendly if condescending manner and called her "little daughter" (though she adds he's "too young to be my father") began to criticize her work and harass her until she got terrible headaches and ultimately quit. Unions, then, did not always protect women workers. But the issue of women in unions is complex, and needs to be looked at specifically.

UNIONS AND SEXUAL HARASSMENT FROM CO-WORKERS

Looking at unions' role in combatting sexual harassment will also focus our attention on the relation of co-workers to sexual harassment. Sexual harassment was not simply a boss-employee interaction, but in many cases an interaction between co-workers. Here, of course, the dynamic was somewhat different, as co-workers do not have the power to fire a woman or offer promotions. However, sexual harassment by co-workers can make a job unbearable for a woman; if she publicly complained, she was as likely to be blamed as the harasser, for "leading him on." To the extent a woman internalized the socially conditioned guilt of being responsible for controlling sexuality (while males were allowed to initiate it), she was vulnerable to this kind of manipulation. And real consequences ensue; Brodsky's study of workers victimized at work showed that employers tended to lay them off:

> Employers are not disturbed by the fact that their female employees have been spoiled or contaminated, but they are concerned that this employee might make for further "trouble." Employers want peace. They do not want workers who disturb the tranquility of the organization in any way, not even as a result of bad luck. Employers whose workers are raped would like to have the victim disappear and not disturb the smooth functioning of their organization.[34]

Because of this tendency to "blame the victim," co-workers do have power over women's jobs and economic security. This division in the workforce, like any division, can also benefit employers.

Unions' position on women workers have been contradictory. On the one hand, unions have tried to keep women out of their occupations, or struck to avoid working with women. On the other hand, some male union organizers have been aware of the danger to workers' solidarity in ignoring women as potentially organizable workers, and have attempted to organize them. Gompers and the AFL held officially (at times) to this second position, but in practice did the opposite—ignored women workers, denied women's locals charters, or sought to exclude women from men's locals by complex rules.[35]

Union members harassed potential women members in various ways which preyed upon their anxieties and kept them home. One example was union meetings. Mary Anderson, later head of the U.S. Women's Bureau, wrote of early union meetings:

> The men met in halls that were often in back of a saloon, or in questionable
> districts, dirty and not well kept. I remember the so-called labor temples
> that were anything but temples. The girls would not go to meetings in these
> places and we could not ask them to go under the circumstances. Then,
> when it came to paying dues at the headquarters of the union, the girls
> found it very distasteful to go where there were large groups of men playing
> cards and hanging about. . . .[36]

This is a good instance of the implied threat of violence operating as a social
control mechanism. It also shows the connection of workplace-union-street
violence in women's actual experience.

Women organizers "realistically" evaluated the ways in which they
themselves were treated by their co-workers (i.e., male union officials).
After a dispute with the male leadership of the ILG in Cleveland, over the
issue of equal pay for women organizers, Pauline Newman described the
women that John Dyche (the unions' executive secretary) selected to replace her: "Well they are not too bad looking and one is rather liberal with
her body. That is more than enough for Dyche."[37]

She, like other women organizers, also tried to solve problems of sexual
harassment outside the union grievance structure. Faced with a complaint
that a factory owner's son and his superintendent had taken liberties with
female employees, she argued:

> There is not a factory today where the same immoral conditions [do] not
> exist. . . . This to my mind can be done away with by educating the girls
> instead of attacking the company.[38]

Rose Schneiderman, however, tried to use the unions to fight sexual
harassment. Having organized the Aptheker shop she received a complaint
from the chairwoman.

> She said that Mr. Aptheker had a habit of pinching the girls whenever he
> passed them and they wanted it stopped. I went to see him, and in the
> presence of the chairwoman told him that this business of pinching the girls
> in the rear was not nice, that the girls resented it, and would he please stop
> it. He was a rather earthy man and looking at me in great amazement, he
> said, "Why Miss Schneiderman, these girls are like my children." The
> chairwoman without a blink answered, "Mr. Aptheker we'd rather be
> orphans." Of course it was stopped.[39]

Mary Anderson also wrote of a strike in a broom factory in which sexual
harassment of the workers by the foreman was a major issue. Since the
foreman was one who "did not stop at anything," some of the women
carried knives to protect themselves. She went to talk with the employer:

> I told him that I had heard stories about one of his foremen, not only of his
> brutality in dealing with the women, but also that he was immoral and that

immoral conditions existed in the plant because of him. The employer said he knew this was so. . . . Finally the strike was settled, the foreman was fired, and the wages raised a little.[40]

Unions, then, have at times provided protection from sexual harassment for women. However, they have also been simply additional places where women experienced sexual harassment. This is one reason why women turned from strategies of group action to protective legislation to protect their interests at work.

CLASS DIFFERENCES AND WOMEN'S CULTURE

What type of women are harassed? The simplest answer is all types of women. No sociodemographic characteristic saved a woman in a sexist society from the possibility of sexual harassment, and the implicit threat of violence. However, there is evidence that the specific forms of sexual harassment did vary according to occupation and social class. All women were subject to at least the subtler forms of sexual harassment (verbal suggestive remarks, dress codes) but physical violence was more common and expected by women in menial jobs.

An examination of the kind of sexual harassment faced by early women doctors shows a pattern of harassment used to force women out of privileged, male-defined jobs. Women's role as professionals in the healing professions had been systematically eliminated by the mid-nineteenth century.

The first women to attempt to become licensed physicians in the United States faced much harassment—psychological, verbal and physical. Most of it came from male co-students (with the tacit approval of their supervisors?), an example of the power co-workers have over a woman's job. Alice Hamilton, an early pioneer in industrial health, suffered from similar treatment as a sex object.[41]

Emily Barringer, the first woman doctor to win an appointment to the staff of Gouvernor Hospital, the downtown branch of Bellevue (N.Y.) found her appointment was resented and opposed by the male appointees:

> But it came to me as a sickening realization that the real opposition I was to meet was to come from my own peers, educated brothers with medical degrees.

An intense campaign of psychological and verbal harassment ensued. For example, other male co-workers discussed graphic details of rape cases at the dinner table, with obvious enjoyment at her discomfort. What she wrote of this experience is revealing of the differences between the experiences of a middle-class professional and an immigrant worker in withstanding sexual harassment. She didn't expect physical violence, a reality to immigrant workers; yet her life was constrained and controlled by this harassment:

> Yes, I could and would endure any taunts or gibes or outrageous insults that these ingenious young men could think of. No matter how degrading their onslaught was, I would stand for it. But if ever in their machinations they should as much as lay a finger on me physically, there would be an immediate reckoning. They knew this perfectly well and always kept completely within bounds. I was as safe in their midst as if I had been surrounded by the strongest iron cage.

Despite this "confidence," she kept her door locked nights, and wouldn't open it to any "fellow" male students.[42]

The weight of the evidence indicates that women in working-class jobs, on the bottom of the workplace hierarchy, and also on the bottom of the social hierarchy, were the most likely victims of harassment. While this is plausible, the way the evidence is recorded also biases the sample. Much of the recorded instances of harassment are reported by middle-class observers, who would, because of the consequences and implications, be less likely to report their own similar experiences. During this period, middle-class women were ladies who were considered "above" sexuality, and thus would be "tainted" by being involved in incidents of sexual harassment. To the extent that they accepted the idea that women were responsible for controlling sexuality, they would have trouble recognizing and dealing with such incidents in their own lives.

The language used by many women in reporting such incidents in the late nineteenth century and early twentieth century indicates the inability of Victorian society to deal directly with sexuality. Women reported their boss' and co-workers' conduct as "vulgar remarks," "shameful behavior," "unspeakable suggestions," "things no lady should bear." When Grace Abbott and Sophonisba Breckinridge accompanied Bozena to court, they transgressed these bounds of ladylike behavior:

> . . . a young lawyer on the State's Attorney's staff who had known Miss Breckinridge at the University rushed over to her and said, "Oh, Miss Breckinridge, you and Miss Abbott must not stay here. This just isn't a fit place for women like you. It's a terrible case for you to hear."[43]

This inability of women to speak directly of their experiences had several implications. It led to sexual harassment being greatly underreported along with other instances of sexual violence, as rape. Women felt guilt rather than anger after such incidents; and fear, not without reason, that the stigma resulting from public association with sexual issues would outweigh any "justice" they might get by reporting the incident. If they had been friendly to the male involved, they would be accused of complicity; when a more likely explanation of what was going on was that the women were looking for husbands, and were responded to as prostitutes. This leaves us with the problem of interpreting vague accounts of behavior, and occasionally makes it hard to determine whether a specific incident really is "unspeakable behavior" or an off-hand vulgar remark.

The other issue this raises is whether women were overreacting to typical male language. If women and men in the nineteenth century were raised in separate spheres—in homosocial networks—with different customs, ways of interaction, speech patterns, and expectations, then such a response on the part of women to men's "normal" behavior seems plausible. For immigrant women to respond to the more open social mores of the United States in the same horrified manner is also plausible. This explanation implies that much of what is considered "harassment" behavior by women is simply "teasing" or "humor" or "informality" on the part of men.[44] While this may occasionally be true, this explanation fails to account for the majority of cases; doesn't account for the overtones of terror, force, domination, and violence felt by the women in such situations; and doesn't account for the many cases in which severe reprisals (firing, blacklisting, refused promotions, attempted rape, rape) were perpetrated on women who refused to accept such "teasing" as part of the job. It is also clear that sexual harassment is basically a man-against-woman interaction; there are few reported cases of either men-against-men or women-against-men harassment. Although men "tease" other men in the workplace, and use non-sexual types of harassment against each other, neither historically nor currently is there evidence that sex is a common component of this harassment.[45]

The major function of sexual harassment is to preserve the dominance of patriarchy. The use of sexual harassment to push women out of specific jobs may well be a new version of an old phenomenon. Even for older societies which accepted a "men's sphere" and a "women's sphere" as both equally necessary to the survival of the community, there is evidence that women were sexually harassed to keep them from stepping out of line in other ways.

Sexual harassment is a phenomenon that crosses class lines, though it does have a class dimension. It cannot be reduced to bosses exploiting workers, because the problem of harassment by co-workers is so extensive. In addition, harassment by supervisors and co-workers does not necessarily support the needs of a rationalized, profit-oriented production system, and may even work at cross-purposes to it. Furthermore, for many men, sexuality and domination were not entirely separate; thus social control and sexuality are not totally distinct phenomena. And for many women, being defined as sexual beings meant that sexual harassment posed both a "compliment" and a threat to their autonomy and safety.

This suggests that to understand the problems of sexual harassment we must analyze both the organization of capitalism and the organization of male dominance.

NOTES

I would like to thank Roslyn Feldberg, Susan Forbes, Alexander Keyssar and the members of the Alliance Against Sexual Coercion for their helpful criticism and discussion of the ideas presented in this paper; and Elizabeth Pleck and Judith Smith for supplying references and supporting my interest in this topic.

1. "The Girl Who Comes to the City: A Symposium," *Harper's Bazaar*, March 1908, p. 277.

2. Sources for this topic are scattered yet cumulatively persuasive. They include autobiographies, letters, social worker's reports, state investigating commissions, labor newspapers, women's magazines, oral histories, surveys of women's work, studies of women in history, studies of women in ethnic communities. Other sources include union records, personnel records, workmen's compensation claims, and legal records.

I also looked at works on protective legislation and prostitution to make connections between sexual morality, economics, and violence in society. I investigated incidents as case studies in the dynamic of sexual harassment, in order to develop a theory of sexual harassment as a mechanism of social control, which theory can be tested by further historical research.

3. Phillip Foner, *History of the Labor Movement in The United States* (New York, 1975), vol. 1, p. 26.

4. Frank Carlton, "Crusade to Improve Working Conditions," *Life and Labor* 4, no. 4 (1914): 108–109.

5. Leonora O'Reilly resigned from the WTUL in 1905–1907 over such a dispute.

6. Wanda F. Neff, *Victorian Working Women* (New York, 1929), pp. 54–55.

7. Boston *Daily Times*, Jan. 16, 1839. There were other articles in the *Times*, the Boston *Quarterly Review*, and the Lowell *Courier* similar to this. Norman Ware, *The Industrial Worker* (Chicago, 1964), p. 81.

8. "Vox Populi," *Voice of Industry*, Sept. 11, 1845.

9. Theresa Wolfson, *The Women Worker and the Trade Unions* (New York, 1926), p. 103.

10. For discussion of the "Nice Girl" construct and social control, see Greer Litton Fox, "Nice Girl: Social Control of Women Through a Value Construct," *Signs* 2, no. 4 (1976): 805–817, especially pp. 805 and 809.

11. See, for example, Rose Cohen, *Out of the Shadow* (New York, 1918); Elizabeth Hasanovitch, *One of Them* (Boston, 1918); Helen Campbell, *Prisoners of Poverty* (Boston, 1900); Mrs. John and Marie Von Vorst, *The Woman Who Toils* (New York, 1904).

12. Jeanne Westin, *Making Do* (Chicago, 1976), p. 96.

13. Robert Smuts, *Women and Work in America* (New York, 1971), p. 88.

14. Virginia Yans-McLaughlin, *Family and Community* (Ithaca, 1977), p. 199, and Alice Kessler-Harris, "Organizing the Unorganizable," *Labor History* 17, no. 1 (1976): 5–23.

15. Maud Nathan, *The Story of an Epoch-Making Movement* (New York, 1926), p. 7.

16. *Harper's Bazaar*, July 1908, p. 693. Also see *One of Them*, pp. 108–110, and *Out of the Shadow*, pp. 127–129.

17. *Harper's Bazaar*, Nov. 1908, p. 1141.

18. *One of Them*, pp. 108–111.

19. *Out of the Shadow*, pp. 127–129.

20. Isaac Metzger, ed., *A Bintel Brief: Sixty Years of Letters from the Lower East Side to the Jewish Daily Forward* (New York, 1971), p. 72.

21. *One of Them*, p. 110.

22. Andria Hourwich, ed., *I Am a Woman Worker* (New York, n.d.), p. 86.

23. Ibid., Dec. 1908, p. 123.

24. *Life and Labor* 1, no. 1 (Jan. 1911): 14.

25. Ibid., 4, no. 8 (Aug. 1914): 242.

26. Dorothy Richardson, *The Long Day*, in William L. O'Neill, ed., *Women at Work* (Chicago, 1972), p. 260.

27. *Harper's Bazaar*, July 1908, p. 693.

28. Nathan, *Epoch-Making Movement*, pp. 15–16.

29. Richardson, *The Long Day*, p. 263; Hasanovitch, *One of Them*, p. 110.

30. Rose Cohen, *Out of the Shadow*, p. 851.

31. *New York State Factory Investigating Committee*, 2nd Report, vol. 3, 1913, Testimony of Mary Chamberlain, pp. 1016, 1004.

32. Edith Abbott, *Unpublished Biography of Grace Abbott*, chap. 2, "Lost Immigrant Girls," The Abbott Papers, University of Chicago, Box 1, Folder 16, Addenda 2.

33. Hasanovitch, *One of Them*, p. 110.

34. Carroll Brodsky, "Rape at Work," in Marsha J. Walker and Stanley L. Brodsky, *Sexual Assault* (Lexington, Ky., 1976), p. 48.

35. See S. Gompers, "Don't Sacrifice Womanhood," *American Federationist* 4 (Oct. 1897): 186–187, and "Female Labor Arouses Hostility and Apprehension in Union Ranks," *Current Opinion* 64 (April 1910): 292–294.

36. Mary Anderson, *Woman at Work* (Minneapolis, 1951), p. 66. Also see *Life and Labor* 3, no. 4 (1913): p. 103, and Wolfson, *Woman Worker and Trade Unions*, p. 55.

37. Quoted in Harris, "Organizing the Unorganizable," p. 20.

38. Quoted in ibid.

39. Rose Schneiderman, *All for One* (New York, 1967), p. 86.

40. Anderson, *Woman at Work*, p. 56, incident about 1915.

41. Alice Hamilton, *Exploring the Dangerous Trades* (Boston, 1943).

42. Emily Dunning Barringer, M.D., *Bowery to Bellevue* (New York, 1950), p. 184.

43. "Lost Immigrant Girls," Abbott Papers, pp. 2–3.

44. On homosocial networks and sisterhood, see Carroll Smith-Rosenberg, "The Female World of Love and Ritual," *Signs* 1 (1975): 1–29, and Nancy Cott, *The Bonds of Womanhood* (New Haven, 1977). For differing perceptions of harasser and victim, see Carroll Brodsky, *The Harassed Worker* (Lexington, Ky., 1976).

45. On current conditions, Brodsky, *The Harassed Worker*, and interview with members of the Alliance Against Sexual Coercion, a Boston group working on this issue. Prison may be a significant exception to this as a situation in which men are frequently subjected to sexual harassment. See, for example, the interviews with prisoners in the film *Rape Culture* (Cambridge Documentary Films).

PART TWO

Organizing
the Unorganized

The articles in this section consider why labor unions have never been able to organize more than about one-fourth of the wage-earning population. Some of the answers of course lie in the capitalists' power to control the labor market, pay differentials, and job structures; not to mention their influence over the government, the courts, the police, the media, and so forth. But as the previous group of articles suggests, even unorganized workers have engaged in militant acts of resistance. If that is so, does organized labor bear some responsibility for failing or refusing to organize the unorganized?

In his influential essay "Working-Class Self-Activity," George Rawick argues that important organizational and social gains are generated by workers themselves, not by the institutions that claim to represent them. Workers' own activity created the modern labor movement through factory sit-downs, and mass strikes in the 1930s, but labor union leaders, preoccupied with their own organizational concerns, failed to follow the workers' lead. Indeed, they imposed their own agenda on the labor movement and tried to channel rank-and-file militancy into established bureaucratic channels less threatening to capital and the state.

As a case in point, Roslyn Feldberg examines the problem of organizing clerical workers. Male trade unionists argued that women office workers were "unorganizable," but clericals' own activity indicated significant discontent and readiness to take collective action. Feldberg describes the real

137

obstacles that existed to organizing the offices, but she refuses to blame the workers themselves for remaining unorganized when unions failed to offer support.

Traditionally socialist historians saw radical movements as providing an alternative to the "misleadership" of conventional trade unionists. *Radical America* historians also appreciated the historic role of the Left, but still found the radical movement wanting. Indeed, the journal was formed to explore the history of American radicalism and to learn from past mistakes. In this tradition, Roy Rosenzweig studies the radical unemployed organizations launched by Communists and Socialists in the early years of the Great Depression. The unemployed councils and leagues were most effective when they built upon the spontaneous, self-help activity of jobless workers. Indeed, militant, locally rooted struggles could even overcome racial differences. However, when the Communist Party burdened its organizing efforts with a heavy dose of sectarian rhetoric, it alienated many potential recruits. Rosenzweig is more optimistic about the potential for leftist leadership of workers' struggles than George Rawick. But both historians take a similar view of effective organizing: it has to flow from the spontaneous local activity generated by workers themselves. If outside organizers impose their strategy and political views, rank-and-file workers become alienated.

Staughton Lynd adopts a similar position in explaining how a rank-and-file movement of steelworkers rose up against the company unions and the do-nothing AFL craft unions during the early 1930s. But just as the movement broke with the AFL and looked for support from the organized Left, the Communist Party abandoned its efforts to build independent unions and began to work within the old unions. Lynd faults the Left for not taking its cue from the workers themselves. By following an international party line, the Communists cut themselves off from a real rank-and-file movement and played into the hands of established union leaders. Thus, the Left itself limited "The Possibility of Radicalism in the Early 1930's," at least in the case of the steel industry. At the time he wrote this article Staughton Lynd worked as a labor lawyer active in the effort to democratize the Steel Workers' Union. As a radical historian he showed that the Union's conservatism resulted from conscious decisions by the leadership and not from the docility or passivity of the membership. In general, rank-and-file workers acted more militantly than top union leaders or the officials of the Communist Party. Lynd's efforts to blend political activity and radical history offered an inspiring example of activist intellectual work.

Manning Marable, another activist intellectual, also considers the problem of organizing the unorganized in his essay on A. Philip Randolph, the most important black trade union leader in U.S. history. Like Baron, Marable sees the oppression of black workers as a national question as well as a matter of race and class. By ignoring the driving force of nationalism among black workers Randolph missed important opportunities to actually mobilize the black masses. Instead, the head of the Pullman Porters Union relied upon the old socialist idea that race problems could be solved through unified class struggle. He also held to the view that minority workers could not advance unless their organizations affiliated directly with the American Federation of Labor.

Finally, the Alliance Against Sexual Coercion argues that violence against women workers requires an affirmative approach based on the experience of the women's movement. The situation described by Mary Bularzik in Section I has changed little. Women workers, who remain largely unorganized, cannot count on unions to fight for equal, non-sexist treatment. The Alliance strategy draws on the model of rape crisis centers and battered women's shelters to make direct contact with workers suffering from sexual harassment. This approach is not anti-union. Indeed, it is based on collective organization rather than individual action through courts or agencies. The Alliance's study of sexual harassment indicates that women workers, organized or not, are still unrepresented and unprotected by the labor movement. Therefore, feminists with a workplace orientation have taken to other strategies just like the civil rights movement and the occupational health and safety movement. These movements show that workers are concerned about more than wages and benefits.

If the AFL-CIO is to organize the unorganized it should look to the history of workers' struggles. It shows that unorganized workers have been mobilized by the struggle for dignity and equality on the job. Indeed, if the unions are to represent more than a quarter of the wage-earning population, they must address the social issues raised in these articles as well as the traditional economic issues. They must also recognize that autonomous workers' movements, whether they attempt to organize the unemployed, demand racial equality, or fight against sexism, can contribute enormous energy and purpose to organized labor.

CHAPTER SIX

Working-Class Self-Activity

by George Rawick

The history of the American working class is a subject obscure to the Old and New Left alike. For the most part, academic labor scholarship has been institutional history focusing on the trade union, and like all institutional orientations has been quite conservative. "Radical" labor history has similarly been little concerned with the working class because of its concentration on another institution, the radical political party. Marxists have occasionally talked about working-class self-activity, as well they might, given that it was Marx's main political focus; but as E. P. Thompson points out in the preface to his monumental *Making of the English Working Class*, they have almost always engaged in substituting the party, the sect, and the radical intellectual for class self-activity in their studies.[1] As a result of this institutional focus, labor history from whatever source generally ignores also social structure, technological innovation, and the relation between the structure and innovation. In the present article I shall attempt some notes toward a study of the American working class since 1919 which strives to avoid the main errors of the old historiography. It must be clear from the outset that this article can be no more than suggestive, that it will be sparse and at times abstract. Hopefully, however, it will engender serious consideration and further probing into its basic themes.

The great steel strike of 1919 marks one beginning of the struggle for industrial unionism. Building on the tradition of the IWW, a gigantic strike

Reprinted from Vol. 3, No. 2 (March-April 1969).

of almost all American steel workers broke out that year; the workers divided into dozens of small craft unions, but under the leadership of two former IWW leaders, William Z. Foster and Elizabeth Gurley Flynn (both soon to become leaders of the Communist Party), attempted to overcome the organizational limits of the craft structure. During World War I the introduction in the steel industry of significant technological rationalization was followed by the appearance of the entire apparatus of Taylorism, which included a whole range of procedures including time-and-motion studies and the development of new equipment to significantly increase the rate of exploitation. Despite the militancy of the workers, the craft-union form of organization was not powerful enough to withstand the implications of highly rationalized industry, and the strike was broken. Taylorism had meant that workers could not gain anything significant by organization on a shop-by-shop basis. Monopoly capitalism, then at its most sophisticated in U.S. Steel, demanded industry-wide organization if the workers' struggles were to succeed.

Before World War I, many skilled workers had significant control over their own time. They had the right to fairly long breaks from work at their own discretion; they organized their work to suit their own needs and whims. Workers could regularly take off an extra day or two each month to handle personal affairs, which often included a small garden farm or other additional sources of income. Workers controlled much of the hiring process, directly handled the relationship with their workmates in such matters as sickness and death benefits, and successfully bargained informally with plant managers and foremen.

Taylorism and its greatest innovation, the assembly line, was introduced to try to expropriate from workers their previous freedoms. Factory life of the 1920s was characterized by significant rationalization in steel, automobiles, electrical equipment, and petroleum and chemical products. Although wages increased to $5 per day in the automobile industry, the amount of surplus value extracted from workers increased at a more rapid rate. Thus, while American workers received a wage level certainly higher than that known by workers in other industrially advanced countries, they also worked harder and faster than any similar group of workers in other countries. Detroit and the assembly line became synonymous on a worldwide basis in the 1920s with high wages—and a degree of alienation hitherto even unanticipated. It would take a full-length study to substantiate this; here it must be simply asserted with the hope of encouraging documentation.

The relative increase in the standard of living in the 1920s was most significant for American workers, most of whom were foreign-born or in contact with relatives in Europe, or were from poor American rural backgrounds. Under such conditions most workers who experienced an increase in the standard of living were unwilling, under conditions in which they could not see their way clear to the creation of new forms of organization, to engage in militant action. Thus in heavily capitalized and rationalized industry, the decade was one of relative peace. There should be nothing surprising about this calm, however. The problems posed by mass production and the assembly line required some time and pressure before workers could fight back again.

The changes in American capitalism during the 1920s did not alter the low-capitalized industries, most of which were in the South. There were serious workers' struggles in sectors such as textiles, clothing, and low-priced consumer goods, where only limited technological rationalizations were economically feasible, and the labor of low-paid male and female workers was substituted for new technology. Under such conditions, the margin of profit came from attempting to make workers labor harder and accept wage cuts and deteriorating conditions. Most unions ignored these industries and made the workers look to their own resources and to whatever aid they could receive from radical organizations. In strike areas like Loray, Tennessee, Danville and Gastonia, North Carolina, and Passaic, New Jersey, the Communist Party was able to play an important role precisely because the American Federation of Labor was unwilling to attempt to organize the unskilled workers. Historians often present these strikes in such a way as to suggest their impossibility without Communist Party leadership; in my opinion this is a false impression. Indeed, long conversations I had many years ago with Fred Beal, a leading organizer of strike activity in Gastonia, suggest to me that these strikes might have been more successful if the Communist Party had been willing to follow the lead of workers.

In the soft-coal mines of southern Illinois and in the bituminous coal mines of Kentucky and West Virginia in the late 1920s and early 1930s, there were constant struggles of a similar nature. Preliminary investigations of these suggest that the self-activity of the workers was often sabotaged by the conflict among radical organizations over the mythic question: "Who should lead the workers?" This kind of strike activity continued into the early 1930s in bloody pitched battle in the bituminous coal mines of Kentucky and West Virginia. Here too we have a decaying industry unable to modernize; here too the official Left was able to play a meaningful role; and here too it subordinated the struggles of the workers to its own needs. In any case, the importance of strikes in low-capitalized industries during this period should not be exaggerated.

In 1958 an article in *The New International* (an American Marxist periodical, now defunct) on the New Deal had the following conclusion about why workers supported Roosevelt:

The problem is really simple if one is willing to lay aside romantic notions based upon the experience of other countries and their working-class movements. The American working class had not yet reached a level of consciousness that enabled it to do anything but accept the concessions it was able to force out of the pro-capitalist parties. The task in the New Deal period for the labor movement was the mass organization of the industrial workers. . . . One could not reasonably expect the American working class to leap so far ahead as to reject a New Deal, with its undeniable benefits, in the interests of a more class-conscious and politically-mature radical objective.

I was the author of this article. In writing it I demonstrated the backwardness, not of the working class, but of the intellectuals who fail to understand the working class. Nor was I the only one convinced of the backwardness of the American workers. Some ten years ago I spent some time with Francis Perkins, then a professor of labor economics at Cornell, but previously secretary of labor under FDR and the person most responsible for the New Deal labor policy. Madame Perkins spoke to me along the following lines: Why didn't the working class in America ever attempt to change American society? We all expected that it would in 1933. At the first meeting of the Cabinet after the president took office in 1933, the financier and adviser to Roosevelt, Bernard Baruch, and Baruch's friend General Hugh Johnson, who was to become the head of the National Recovery Administration, came in with a copy of a book by Gentile, the Italian Fascist theoretician, for each member of the Cabinet, and we all read it with great care.

Madame Perkins was quite wrong. The American working class did change American society, despite the fact that American capitalism was very powerful and had often indicated clearly in the 1930s that it would resort to any means, if allowed to do so, to prevent a radical transformation of society.

We can estimate most sharply the power of the American working class if we look at its accomplishments comparatively. In Italy the crisis of capitalism of the decade of the Bolshevik Revolution and the World War produced Fascism as an answer to the bid of the Italian working class for power. In Germany, the crisis of capitalism produced first the Weimar Republic, which did nothing to alter the situation, and then Nazism; the consequence was the worst defeat any working class has ever known. The German working class was pulverized—unlike the Italian working class, which was never smashed to bits under Fascism and in fact survived to destroy Fascism itself. In France essentially the same pattern as in Italy was repeated, with the difference that full-fledged Fascism came only as a result of the German military advance, since the French working class had managed to defend democracy throughout the 1930s, often over the heads of the radical parties.

In the United States the situation was different. Throughout the 1920s the working class found its organizations weakened; but in the 1930s the working class struggled and created powerful mass industrial unions of a kind never known anywhere in the world, unions that organized all the workers in most major industries throughout the nation. The working class of America won victories of a scale and quality monumental in the history of the international working class. Only the capture of state power by a relatively small working class of Russia—a state power it did not retain—has surpassed the magnitude of its victory in the thirties.

The full organization of the major American industries, however, was a mark of the victories, not the cause of the victories, of the American working class. The unions did not organize the strikes; the working class in the strikes and through the strikes organized the unions. The growth of successful organizations always followed strike activity when some workers engaged in militant activities and others joined them. The formal organization—how many workers organized into unions and parties, how many subscriptions to the newspapers, how many political candidates nominated and elected, how much money collected for dues and so forth—is not the heart of the question of the organization of the working class. The statistics we need to understand the labor history of the time are not these. Rather, we need the figures on how many man-hours were lost to production because of strikes, the amount of equipment and material destroyed by industrial sabotage and deliberate negligence, the amount of time lost by absenteeism, the hours gained by workers through the slowdown, the limiting of the speed-up of the productive apparatus through the working class's own initiative.

In virtually every year since 1919, American workers have either led, or were second or third, in both the absolute and relative numbers of hours lost through strikes. In 1932 there were only 840 strikes; in 1933 there were 1,700; by 1936, 2,200; by 1937, 4,740; in 1938, only 2,500; in 1941, 4,000; in both 1944 and 1945, 5,000. In 1946, the year of the greatest militancy up to that point, there were just under 5,000 strikes involving nearly five million workers, 14½ percent of the workforce. And as the strike wave developed the unions grew. All of this occurred in the midst of a great depression and after more than a decade of inactivity in the area of industrial union organization. But most important, it all occurred not because the older unions attempted to organize industrial workers, but in spite of these unions and even against their opposition. When the crisis came, the response of the AFL unions was to protect their own members' jobs and wages from the onslaught of millions of unorganized workers placed in the pool of the proletarians.

Only John L. Lewis and the oldest industrial union, the United Mine Workers, along with a few other older semi-industrial unions such as those in clothing and printing, responded at all. For the most part, what occurred was simple and direct. The workers in a given plant organized themselves into a strike committee, went out on strike, won some limited demands or lost, but maintained their organization. Eventually they joined with workers in other parts of the industry to form a national union.

There were three obstacles to the efforts of workers to organize unions. First there was the resistance from the employers who hired spies, black-listed workers, fired activists, and finally created company unions. Second was the set of obstacles created by the top-ranking union leaders. Fearing that a strong industrial union would threaten the entrenched interests of craft-union leaders, the American Federation of Labor decreed that auto workers were to be organized in local federal unions, and that later these federal unions were to be broken up and their members divided among the craft unions. In the early years of the 1930s these tactics of the unions confused, demoralized, and slowed down the organization of workers. Only after a few years did the workers gain renewed confidence to organize, if need be against the unions. Third was the set of obstacles created by the Government under the National Recovery Administration. With the co-operation of the established unions, the NRA saw to it that demands for more money or a check on the growth of speed-up were ignored.

One recent case study of the organization of a particular union is illustrative of this process of the self-activity of the working class and the obstacles it encountered.[2]

When workers in the Briggs Manufacturing Company, in September 1933, voted to apply for an AFL federal charter, Briggs management hastily installed a company union. When a committee of the new federal union asked management for recognition, they were flatly told that the company had already recognized an association for bargaining purposes. Hearing this, the membership voted to strike the plant. The company responded by hiring strikebreakers and continuing to operate the plant, although produc-tion was crippled. The Regional Labor Board stepped in and ordered the strike ended and an election conducted to determine whether the workers wanted the federal union or the company union to represent them.

But the company had other ideas: It had no intention of laying off non-strikers. The National Labor Board answered this by referring the case to the National Compliance Board of the NRA; the Board handed down recommendations calling for an election under rules favorable to the com-pany union, and discriminating against the strikers. Finally, in March 1934, the Briggs case was included in the general settlement forced through by the Government to head off widespread strikes in the auto industry scheduled for March. The company agreed to reemploy one striker for every two men hired.

The role of the AFL was characteristic. A full month elapsed after the strike began before AFL president William Green gave it official recogni-tion (but no financial help). By the time the strike had ended, the union affiliated with the AFL in the plant was dead. The workers at Briggs turned to new organization and were among the first to create the United Automobile Workers.

Such were the experiences of auto workers throughout the industry. And after two and a half years of such defeats, inflicted by a combination of employers and government and union officials, a new movement began which would wage the sit-down strikes and from which would grow the UAW. A look at the history of the sit-downs will indicate that in this most advanced example of working-class struggle, the genuine advances of the working class were made by the struggle from below, by the natural organization of the working class, rather than by the bureaucratic elaboration of the administration of the working class from above. Symbolically, the first sit-downs came spontaneously in Atlanta, Georgia, not in Detroit under the direction of the Left.

During the early years of the Depression (before 1937), the struggles remained fairly small while workers sought a new form. In 1934 the organization of industrial unions began in earnest. With the further downswing of wages and employment in 1937, the workers in autos, then in rubber, and then in other industries occupied the plants, slept there, ate there, refused to leave or produce, protected themselves inside the plants, and organized massive demonstrations outside. Thousands of troops surrounded the factories with tanks and artillery, not firing because of the certainty that it would further radicalize the situation. Out of the strikes came the right of workers to join unions, with virtual closed-shop conditions won in many industries.

Throughout the war, workers were faced with a general wage freeze and a commodity-scarce economy. Workers made good money by working overtime and continually demonstrating that they would never accept lower wages again. However, the most basic struggles the workers engaged in were attempts to improve working conditions, slow down the speed of work, and resist the attempts of management to turn the factories into smaller military camps by disciplining the workers. Workers in coal production engaged in very militant strikes to increase wages directly, because during the 1930s coal miners had not even been able to raise their pay.

At the end of the war, there was an attempt to roll back wage increases made during the war, to force the working class to accept a smaller share of the product. Only after the greatest outpouring of strikes and militancy since 1919 did American capitalism agree to a new wage policy.

The price of the new wage policy was the further linking of the union leadership with government and management decision-making processes. Since the end of World War II the unions have been able to gain monetary wage increases, generally speaking, to keep up with increases of productivity: Unions can guarantee that the size of the unionized worker's slice of the national product does not diminish, although inflation continues to wipe out many gains. In return unions have had to insure industrial peace by disciplining the workers and curtailing their demands on all issues save money and fringe benefits. In particular unions resist demands of workers for greater shares of production and lessened exploitation.

Unions have generally given up the demand for a shorter work week. Indeed, in many industries the de facto situation now is that workers work 50 hours or more per week. Workers' pay does keep up with productivity, but only if overtime pay is included. The grievance procedure which has been the main protection of the worker in the past has all but totally broken down. With thousands of unresolved grievances common in every major plant, the speed-up has increased very rapidly without much union opposition, automation proceeds without limitation by the union, and attempts of workers to gain control over working conditions and procedures are systematically fought by the unions.

All of this must be understood as part of the necessary device whereby the State has directly transformed capitalism since the 1930s. The State regulates the flow of capital, owns outright or indirectly large bodies of capital (for example, the aerospace program in both its public and private sectors), and through the contract—enforced by the shop committeemen and union stewards, who in effect become agents of the State—disciplines the workers. On the one hand, the New Deal acts—from the NRA (declared unconstitutional) to the Federal Reserve Act, Securities and Exchange Act, Agricultural Adjustment Act, et cetera—provided the legal context in which workers raised their wages through massive strikes at the end of World War II. On the other hand, the CIO unions became through the process the political weapons of the State against the working class. Carefully legalized mass industrial unions were a necessary part of this development; industry-wide bargaining agents able to impose wage rates high enough to drive out all marginal producers who cut prices by superexploitation of workers were in effect incorporated into the State apparatus.

The full incorporation of the unions within the structure of American state capitalism has led to very widespread disaffection of the workers from the unions. Workers are faced squarely with the problem of how to find means of struggle autonomous of the unions; this problem, while always present, is more prevalent under capitalism than anywhere else. As a consequence workers struggle in the factories through wildcat strikes and sporadic independent organizations. Outside the factory only young workers and black workers find any consistent radical socialpolitical expression, and even the struggles of blacks and youths are at best weakly linked to the struggles in the factory.

There is often a very sectarian and remarkably undialectical reaction to these developments. Some historians and New Leftists argue that it demonstrates that the CIO was a failure which resulted only in the workers' disciplining. This argument ignores the gains of the CIO in terms of higher living standards, more security for workers, and increased education and enlightenment. Clearly, the victories are embedded in capitalism and the agency of victory, the union, has become an agency of capitalism as well. This is a concrete example of what contradiction means in a dialectical sense; and it is part of a process which leads to the next stage of the workers' struggle, the wildcat strike.

There are two characteristics of the wildcat strike which represent a new stage of development: first, through this device workers struggle simultaneously against the bosses, the State, and the union; second, they achieve a much more direct form of class activity, by refusing to delegate aspects of their activity to an agency external to themselves.[3]

When the wave of wildcat strikes first began to appear as the new form of working-class self-activity and organization, it was hard to see (except very abstractly) where they would lead. But after glimpses of the future afforded by the workers' councils during the Hungarian Revolution in 1956 and the French uprising of May and June 1968, the new society which can only be fully realized and protected by revolutionary struggle is clearly revealed: workers' councils in every department of national activity, and a government of workers' councils.

NOTES

1. The last work approaching a full-scale Marxist history of the U.S. working class was in the early additions to Anthony Bimba's *History of the American Working Class*, which while theoretically above average was factually far below. A mark of the backwardness of American Marxism, its failure to concern itself with its own working class, is the fact that *History of the American Working Class* by Frederich Sorge, who lived in the U.S. in the latter nineteenth century while remaining one of Marx's closest co-workers, has never been translated into English from its initial publication in Neue Zeit.

2. See Frank Marquart's study of the creation of a union at the Briggs Manufacturing Company in Detroit which appeared in *Speak Out*, no. 9. Unquestionably, hundreds of similar stories can be collected; doubters should listen to the sit-down stories of auto workers from Flint, Michigan, and compare them to the official UAW history which emphasized the strikes' leadership (none other than the present national officers and executive board of the UAW). Radical scholars should begin to collect materials while there is still time. Editor's note: See Frank Marquart, *An Autoworker's Journal* (University Park: Pennsylvania State University Press, 1975).

3. Marxists who are familiar with the basis of the Hegelian dialect, in the master-slave discussion in which Hegel indicates that the slaves must struggle against elements of their own class as well as against the masters, will not be surprised by this historical analysis. In *Facing Reality* (Detroit: Facing Reality Publishing Committee, 1956), C. L. R. James offers the following useful summary of dialectics:

a. All development takes place as a result of self-movement, not organization or direction by external forces.

b. Self-movement springs from and is the overcoming of antagonisms within an organism, not the struggle against external foes.

c. It is not the world of nature that confronts man as an alien power to be overcome. It is the alien power that he has himself created.

d. The end toward which mankind is inexorably developing by the constant overcoming of internal antagonisms is not the enjoyment, ownership, or use of goods, but self-realization, creativity based upon the incorporation into the individual personality of the whole previous development of humanity. Freedom is creative universality, not utility.

Editor's note: Also see C. L. R. James, *Notes on Dialectics* (2nd ed.; Westport, Conn.: Lawrence Hill, 1980).

CHAPTER SEVEN

"Union Fever": Organizing Among Clerical Workers, 1900–1930

by Roslyn L. Feldberg

And now the typewriter girls of Montreal, Canada have the fever and are talking about forming a union. Say, girls, *don't*; take my advice and each of you find some nice young man and form a union of two, for life; that's the best form of union.[1]

We do not know whether or not the "typewriter girls" of Montreal took the editor's advice, but we do know that by the end of the 1920s, the "fever" was spent, leaving few traces of labor unions among clerical workers. Despite numerous struggles and personal sacrifices in the previous three decades, only one union, the Bookkeeper's, Stenographer's and Accountant's Local No. 12646 of New York, continued into the 1930s as an active, vital union. Even as of 1977, only 8.2 percent of all clerical workers were unionized, and the proportion among women was certainly lower still.[2] Although this article deals only with the period 1900–1930, many of the conditions which hindered unionization then continue to exist today.

INTRODUCTION

How can we analyze this low level of unionization? It can be understood largely as a consequence of the response to women clerical workers by their male "comrades" in the labor movement. Men believed that this group of workers was "unorganizable," and therefore not worth a great deal of effort to organize. This view not only prevented labor from wholeheartedly sup-

Reprinted from Vol. 15, No. 3 (May-June 1981).

porting the organizing efforts which were made during this period, but it also formed the basis of most subsequent relationships between labor unions and women clerical workers.

Why were women clerical workers then seen as unorganizable? The answer is that women clerical workers were different from other workers. They were white-collar, mostly white, mostly native born, mostly young and single and, most important, women; whereas other workers were blue collar, often immigrant, mostly married, and most important, male. Union men saw these differences as a barrier to organizing. First, they assumed that women were less organizable because they were women: Their 'traditional' place in family life and their expectations of wifehood and motherhood were thought to reduce their long-term interest in employment and, therefore, to reduce their interest in organizing. Second, at that time clerical work was seen as relatively good work for women, and it was assumed that people (and especially women) with good jobs would not organize, especially when they could be easily replaced.[3] Third, clerical work, because it was white-collar and done in offices, was not seen as "real work," and clerical workers were not seen as "real workers." Only blue-collar or manual workers were expected to organize, while clerical workers were expected to dissociate themselves from "real" workers and from unions.

There was some truth to these assumptions. The characteristics of women clerical workers were as described. Clerical work was relatively good work for women at that time, and it did represent a degree of upward mobility for women who otherwise would have worked in factories or in domestic service.[4] Some clerical workers probably did see themselves as separate from and better than "workers." However, if we accept this line of reasoning, we would not expect to find any organizing among clerical workers—and we do find some, even in the face of an indifferent and often hostile labor movement. That finding suggests that the usual explanations of the low level of unionization among clerical workers do not tell the whole story. This paper adds new information and new analysis to that story.

The situation of women clerical workers in the early 1900s has a new importance today. Once again there are attempts to organize clerical workers—again, often initiated and supported by women outside the major labor unions—and again we hear prophesies that clerical workers will not organize. These prophesies reflect the same stereotypical notions about women clerical workers prevalent at the turn of the century. Understanding early organizing efforts, their strengths and their defeats, may help us to avoid recreating the conditions that contributed to their failure.

EARLY ATTEMPTS TO ORGANIZE CLERICAL WORKERS
Organization Before 1900

Interestingly, the first attempts to organize clerical workers came at the time when women were entering clerical occupations. The most active organizing appears to have been among stenographers—the group which, combined with "typewriters," was over 60 percent female before the turn of the century.

By 1890, stenographers in many states and cities had joined together to form "associations." At least 34 associations made public reports of their meetings, and their statements of purpose were similar. The Reading, Pennsylvania Stenographers' Association announced as its object: "to bind together all the stenographers and typewriters for mutual improvement, sociability, unity and harmony of feeling with a view to combine their efforts for the maintenance of practical efficiency in the stenographic professions." Its membership was 75, and of its 14 officers, 5 were women. An association in Chicago certified its members and assisted them in obtaining positions. Several of the associations commented on the need to *maintain wage levels*.

Formed in response to business conditions that expanded opportunities in clerical work and, at the same time, led to a mushrooming of commercial colleges whose graduates threatened to cheapen the field of stenography, these early associations were essentially craft unions. Individual (male) stenographers argued against "public school masters 'boosting' hundreds of other fellows [sic] up the same stump . . ." by teaching shorthand in the schools;[5] and the associations grew increasingly militant about the need to control entry into their craft. In 1890, the Grand Chief Stenographer of the Order of Railway and Transportation Stenographers wrote to the editor of the clerical trade magazine informing him that the requirement of 'teaching shorthand to others' had been eliminated from the constitution of the Order. "Any person with any sense at all would not be guilty of injuring his interests by increasing the supply."[6]

In the 1890s, unlike the previous decade, there were no statements blaming women for the difficulties facing stenographers, nor were there calls for their exclusion from the field or from the associations. Instead, an 1891 call for a national association explicitly included phonographers, type-writers and "all worthy members of the professions." The problem of low wages was blamed on "incompetents who will work for correspondingly low wages." The source of these "incompetents" was alleged to be the "three month schools." The failure to blame women specifically suggests that by now the job market was sexually segregated: that women were *entering new positions, not competing with men*.

Sex Segregation in Clerical Occupations, 1900–1910

As more women entered the clerical occupations, more explicit patterns of sex segregation were established. Most women entered the newer occupations of stenography and typewriting, while the traditional jobs of general clerk and bookkeeper remained male strongholds.[7] However, even within stenography, sex-based mechanisms of exclusion barred women from the best-paying jobs, reserving these for men. Overall, this pattern of sex segregation kept women in the lower levels of the occupation, making them more vulnerable to employers, more dependent on marriage, and less likely to establish ties with those male clerical workers who had had organizing experience.

The justifications for barring women varied from their competence to their moral purity. Managers for the railroads argued that women did not understand the business as well as men did. In 1902, the president of the Baltimore and Ohio Railroad announced that no more women would be hired as stenographers in the operating departments because he wanted "all clerks to fit themselves for higher places . . ." and believed that women cannot "grasp the railroad business in the way the men do."[8] A year later, the Chicago and Northwestern Railroad announced that it had "nothing against women, but that they stand in the way of regular promotion among the rank and file."[9] Other railroads were expected to adopt the same policy.

Saying that women "stand in the way of regular promotions" indicates that women were not promoted. They were hired as stenographers at a particular level and were expected to remain there until they left the organization. Restricting the levels for which they were hired guaranteed that there would be no opportunities for promotion for women stenographers on the railroads. Although the brotherhoods of male railroad clerks had been organized for at least a decade, they did not protest these limitations.

Women stenographers were also being excluded from jobs in the courts. Here the rationale was based on women's moral purity and propensity to marry. One writer argued that women stenographers were "innocent" and should not be exposed to the harsh realities of the courtroom, "an atmosphere of such distressing controversies," while the Nassau County Clerk (New York) announced an end to the hiring of "girl typewriters" because they marry and leave their positions.[10]

The more women entered the occupation, the more rigid distinctions between men's and women's positions became. Separate, non-competing labor markets were institutionalized. In the federal Civil Service, men's stenographic positions typically paid higher wages ($900 vs. $600 per year) and offered more opportunities for advancement than women's positions. In industry, too, men got preference. The Remington Typewriter Company employment bureaus announced that over 2,000 requests for male stenographers were refused in 1901 alone due to insufficient supply.[11] Women could not apply for those jobs.

Everywhere the rationale was the same: the "girl" would marry, or at least expect to marry, and leave the job; therefore, there was no point in permitting her to occupy a position that could be held by a man, who would see it as the basis of his future career. This logic served to rationalize both paying women less and reserving the best positions for men, a combination of actions which, in turn, increased the economic pressure on young women to marry. In a crowded labor market, this combination insured a changing but ample supply of low-paid women clerical workers and of young women eager to become wives. In addition, it separated women into a distinct group within the occupation. This very separateness served to keep women in their place. It cut them off from craft traditions, as well as from the organizational experience of the previously organized male clerical workers, and thus made it more difficult for women to organize or to gain control of entry into women's jobs in the occupation.

Women Begin to Organize, 1900–1930

In this context, women clerical workers began to organize. They formed their own associations of stenographers, typewriters, bookkeepers, and other clerical occupations. Interestingly, their first organizations were *not* labor unions, but mutual benefit societies. In 1902, 600 girl stenographers from Toledo, Ohio, were "seriously considering starting and maintaining a restaurant in that city for their own use."[12] Pittsburgh stenographers "subscribed to the stock of a cooperative lunchroom for female stenographers and typewriters only," no dish to cost more than five cents. The common problems female stenographers and typewriters faced were beginning to evoke a collective response.

Soon women clerical workers turned their attention to labor unions. In 1903, "stenographers and typewriters of a feminine persuasion" formed a labor union in Worcester, Massachusetts. In 1904, delegates from office locals in Washington, D.C., and Indianapolis were seated at the AFL national convention.[13] In that same year, typewriters in New York held a "secret meeting" to discuss unionization. Fifty men and women attended and agreed that typewriters and stenographers of both sexes should be admitted as members.[14]

That 1904 attempt did not succeed. In 1908, however, a new organization was formed which included "the women stenographers, typewriters and bookkeepers in Greater New York."[15] This union, open only to women, (under a local charter from the AFL) was called the Bookkeepers and Accountants Union No. 1 of New York. The organizing campaign was headed by Helen Marot, executive secretary of the Women's Trade Union League, and three assistants—all members of the League. Principal purposes of the union were regulating the hours of employment and improving the conditions of women workers in offices. They chose as their slogan "equal pay for equal work," comparing themselves to hod carriers, whose work required less skill but received more pay, and indicating that they would struggle to defend this slogan. Miss Marot explained: "We have incorporated the equal pay for equal work plan in the constitution of the union and we shall have no controversy with the men on that account."[16]

It is not surprising that the first major campaign to organize clerical workers took place under the auspices of the Women's Trade Union League (WTUL), rather than an established union. The unions were simply not organizing women clerical workers. Male industrial workers were their priority. If any organization were to support organizing among clerical workers, it would be the WTUL, which held a unique place in the labor movement. It was an organization of women, feminists and unionists, which "attempted to serve as a link between women workers and the labor movement and as a focal point for unorganized women interested in unionism."[17] Its members, drawn from both upper-class and working-class women, sought to create an egalitarian organization. They aimed to introduce unionism to unskilled and semiskilled women workers, and to help these women build unions—while at the same time maintaining connections to the male-dominated labor movement which so often ignored these women. With these aims, it is not surprising that the WTUL supplied the first known organizers to work with women clerical workers.

Soon after, women in other cities joined the organizing effort. A Chicago local of the Stenographers Union began in 1911 with 300 "girls." They aimed to have 10,000 members within a year, to enforce a minimum wage of $12/week with one year's experience, and to offer their members a free employment agency, night school in "subjects bearing on their work," physical culture classes, free medical service by women physicians, and an "out-of-work" (unemployment) fund.[18] The emphasis on *girls* in the announcement, and on medical care by women physicians, suggests a "women only" organization. The list of demands hints at their working conditions: an overcrowded labor market, low wages, and problems with unemployment. Inclusion of physical culture classes may reflect an association with the settlement house movement, as well as the Chicago chapter of the WTUL.

By 1912, "union fever" among clerical workers had run up against some obstacles to organizing. The founding of a new union for stenographers and typists in Kansas City gave organizer Helen Marot an opportunity to argue that this latest example was evidence that clerical workers can and should organize.[19] Marot described the union's founder, and its members, as "exceptional women. . . . They are, in fact, so superior, that they can afford to belong to a labor union, or anything else for that matter which seems good in itself. . . . And that is the lesson that our pretentious office workers have to learn. We are just people, but people with common interests so vital they will, if we let them, break through all the petty social distinctions and place us alongside of real men and women in touch with life." Marot saw in women clerical workers a sense of social distinction that separated them from "real" working-class men and women and prevented them from recognizing their interests in unionization. To her, this was a blindness clerical workers could ill afford.

Despite the problems Marot saw, the "fever" was not spent. Another new Stenographers and Typists Union formed in St. Louis in 1912, and the Chicago union, now working closely with the WTUL, began a campaign to encourage men as well as women to join. Even during World War I, union activity continued. A new Boston local, Accountants and Office Employees No. 14965, formed in 1916 with the assistance of the WTUL, announced a program of "street meetings" for the spring. Meanwhile, the Chicago, Washington, D.C., and New York unions remained active. The New York union, known as the Bookkeepers, Stenographers and Accountants Union, was said to be "one of the most flourishing unions" that met at WTUL headquarters.[20]

The 1920s saw a decline in organizing activities among clerical workers.[21] No new unions were formed and only a few major campaigns are reported. The Bookkeepers, Stenographers and Accountants Union of New York continued to be the most active union, but its biggest and most successful campaign, the 1923 organization of bank clerks employed in the "labor banks," concentrated on male clerical workers. In contrast, the unsuccessful 1927 drive to organize Metropolitan Life Insurance Company resulted in the firing of at least one woman organizer, who was later pictured with three other organizers holding placards in a demonstration which urged office workers to join the union.[22] The only other city in which union activity definitely continued was Boston. Here, the Stenographers Union was said to be conducting "an aggressive campaign" and to have hired a special organizer for the work, following up on earlier success in the nearby town of Quincy.

Despite these drives, the vast majority of clerical workers remained unorganized. This failure caused Rose Schneiderman, in her presidential address to the 1929 WTUL National Convention, to single out clerical work as one of three special fields requiring "intensive cultivation."[23]

ORGANIZING: CONTEXTS AND PROBLEMS, 1900–1930

It is clear from the number of organizations that were formed and re-formed during the teens and twenties, and from the current organizing drives among clerical workers, that the early efforts did not succeed in establishing lasting unions.

If current efforts are to be more successful, the problems of the earlier attempts must be understood. On the one hand, it is always difficult to organize previously unorganized workers. The possibility of success is never clear, while the possibilities of failure or loss of a job are very evident. In the period prior to the National Labor Relations Act, these latter possibilities seemed all the more likely, whatever the group of workers being organized.

On the other hand, organizing clerical workers also seemed to present particular problems. The most obvious of these problems—the attitude among clerical workers that unions were for factory workers—was recognized by the clerical organizers and outsiders alike. As Alice Bean, a clerical organizer affiliated with the WTUL said, ". . . average American office workers . . . do not feel that they are 'wage earners' but have a notion that they are professionals and, therefore, it would be degrading to join a union. They leave unions to the factory workers."[24] Unfortunately, the distance between clerical workers and the unions was assumed to be the product solely of the ideas and life situations of the clerical workers.

But attitudes are not born in isolation. They develop in particular social and historical circumstances. In this case, those circumstances included the structure of offices and the economics of clerical work, the attitudes of "the public" toward employed women, and the response of male trade unionists to women clerical workers.

The Immediate Context

The set-up of offices in this period created some special problems for clerical organizing. A small number of workers were scattered among a great many offices. In the small offices, the clerical workers were likely to have closer personal ties to their bosses than to clerical workers from other offices. Even in large offices, the clerical workers were often separated into different areas which afforded little opportunity to get to know each other, while in the early clerical pools, favoritism and competition for the best jobs undermined solidarity. It is true that many industrial workers were also located in small shops, but the situation for clerical workers was extreme. Industrial workers, even in small shops, were likely to have at least one or two workmates with whom they could freely associate, while a typist in a small office could easily be the only woman, cut off from the company of a male bookkeeper or general clerk.

If the structure of office work separated office workers from each other, it insulated them almost completely from factory workers. They worked in a different setting (usually cleaner), had different hours, did different tasks (although the degree of division of labor and the productivity measures might be similar), and had closer contact with management. Furthermore, they rarely spoke with factory workers in the course of their work, even when they worked in the offices of the factory. Thus, the presence of unions among the factory workers did not necessarily bring the unions closer to the office workers, and may have added to the view of unions as alien.

The economics of clerical work in this period also created barriers to unionization. Clerical work was expanding rapidly, but so was the clerical labor force. Wages were low and declining and fears of unemployment were very great.[25] The pattern was an extension of that noted by male stenographers in the 1890s. As one office worker wrote to the editor of *Life and Labor* in 1912:

> . . . a younger element is more and more crowding in, who because of inexperience and inefficiency, and mostly because of financial pressure, accept the most paltry wages. What follows—is that really experienced and qualified stenographers and clerks have a hard fight, getting even twelve dollars.[26]

The workers had no control over entry to the occupation. Certification was by high school diploma, a credential widely available to native-born young women, or by the diploma of a "business college" run by private entrepreneurs. There were no formal apprenticeships in clerical work in general, and few informal ones in the jobs open to women. The supply of young women prepared for office jobs was more likely to reflect the effectiveness of the schools' (public and private) publicity than the availability of jobs.

Finally, the life situations of clerical workers probably did dampen their enthusiasm for organizing. While they have been accused of viewing their work as "professional," it is more likely that many saw it more as an interval between childhood and marriage.[27] While this attitude did not make organizing easy, it did not necessarily prevent it. The same absence of "responsibilities" (especially financial ones) and of expectations for long-term employment that may lead young, single workers to accept poor working conditions may also leave them freer to be militant.

The Social Context

One factor that affects workers' responses is their perception of how appropriate and effective unions are for workers in their position. On this point, clerical workers received little encouragement. Unions were viewed as organizations for factory workers and as organizations for men. Joining a union meant proclaiming one's status as a worker. Women were not "supposed" to be "real workers." They were supposed to be working at a job only until they got married and had children. If their family circumstances were such that they "had to work" beyond that time, that was judged an unfortunate situation, but it still did not make them "real workers." Thus there were no grounds for the women to be militant, fighting for rights as workers. Nor did they have access to an alternative view. Everywhere they looked—the church, the newspapers, the social reformers, other women, even the male unionists in their own families—the message was the same: organizing unions was not appropriate for respectable women.

Journalists, reformers, and other voices of popular culture sympathized with the plight of employed women and argued for improvements. Special investigations documented both the terrible working conditions women faced and the low wages, primarily in factories, but in shops and offices as well. Appropriate methods of redress, however, were considered important. Improvements were to be won in ladylike fashion, through the exercise of quiet influence and moral suasion among men who would champion their cause. Women were not to act militantly or to wield power directly. They were to be protected, not to become their own guardians.

The paradox was clear. Lillian Wald wrote in 1906: "Protective legislation is evidence of a public sentiment as to the necessity of guarding the interests of women . . . yet, [there is] a seemingly deep-rooted prejudice

159

against regulation by [women] themselves when expressed in trade unionism, a curious confusion of democratic principles." Such a prejudice seriously restricted organizing among "respectable" single women, especially
when so many of them lived at home under the authority of parents or
relatives.[28]

Labor Movement Context

If the prevailing social opinion of the day was that women were not "real
workers" and "shouldn't" organize, the view of organized labor seemed to
add the element that women, and women clerical workers in particular,
"wouldn't" organize, and that whether or not they tried made little difference to the labor movement.

As early as 1904, the clerical organizer Elsie Diehl had invited a representative from the AFL and several other labor men to address the first
public meeting of clerical workers organizing for a labor union. Two other
office workers' unions sent delegates to the 1904 AFL convention. The AFL
did not reciprocate this interest. When the Chicago office workers local
formally requested the AFL to send a woman organizer to assist them, the
AFL executive council let the matter die.[29]

It was rare for women from clerical backgrounds to be trained as
organizers within the labor movement. In two instances women had to fight
to prove themselves real workers in order to receive training. The stories of
these women illustrate how completely the male leadership of the labor
movement continued to reject the idea of supporting organizing drives
among women clerical workers as late as 1925.

Two women interested in clerical organizing were admitted to the
Brookwood Labor College in Katonah, New York, one of several schools
run by the labor movement to train organizers. The first was Rose Goldberg
(pseudonym), a 21-year-old Jewish woman from New York who applied as a
member of the Bookkeepers, Stenographers and Accountants Union. She
had to lobby hard for admission because her two years of evening classes at
Hunter College, which she attended while working full-time since the age of
13, made her a "college girl" for some members of the admissions board.
They were also troubled by her lack of "industrial experience," the hallmark
of the real worker. At graduation from the program she faced similar
problems. She proposed employment in a large insurance office so she could
begin organizing clerical workers, but her teachers directed her to work as a
secretary or journalist in the office of a union. There was no sense of hostility
in their response—rather a sense that the organization of office workers was
not a priority issue, and that she could better contribute to the labor
movement in another capacity.

Sophie Caldron, a 19-year-old woman from a similar background, who
had been very active politically, had even greater difficulty securing admit-
tance to Brookwood. Her first application was rejected on the grounds that

she did not have "sufficiently thorough experience in the trade union movement to benefit fully from the course—and you are still young. . . ." A year later she was admitted. However, after her first year, the faculty recommended that she withdraw from the school and "go into industry" before completing her course. The basics of their decision can be inferred from the statement of the Student Body in answer to Sophie's appeal. "While the students do not consider the clerical forces of being equally important with workers in basic industries, yet they maintain that it is of sufficient important character to demand immediate consideration by the trade union movement and that people should be trained to cope with the white collar workers' problems." It is not certain whether she was allowed to complete the second year.

Even when women clerical workers were organized, they were not treated as equals by "fellow" trade unionists. During World War I, women and men were organized together in the railroad offices, but the supervisors were still able to treat the women "as jokes or pets"[30] and male co-workers were friendly only as long as rigid differentiation of jobs by sex was carefully maintained. In part, this behavior may have reflected the unionists' inability to view the women as real workers, but it may also have been an attempt to reserve preferred jobs within the occupation for the men. The distance between office workers and the industrial unions insured that neither the leaders nor members of these other unions would see unionization of women clerical workers as a goal vital to their own political strength.

Alice Henry wrote in 1914 that none of the established labor unions or associations (such as the National Union Label League or women's auxiliaries) had taken the organization of women wage-earners as their task.[31] Reviewing employed women's relation to the labor movement a decade later, she found few changes, and offered further evidence of the unwillingness of union men to organize women into their occupations.[32] The behavior of organized male clerical workers was part of the pattern. Until employed women generally were supported in their organizing efforts, there was little hope of union support for organizing women clerical workers.

CLERICAL ORGANIZING AND
THE WOMEN'S TRADE UNION LEAGUE

If the major themes in previous discussions of the failure of clerical organizing are "unorganizability" and life situations of clerical workers, then the minor theme is the influence of "middle-class" women or groups outside the labor movement. Once again, the accepted story seems incomplete.

From what we know of the various union locals, the women who organized them came from two groups. One group was clerical workers who were employed in the offices of trade unions, had long-standing commitments to unionism, and wanted to apply its principles to their situation.[33]

These women initiated unions out of the belief that all workers should be organized, including those who work for labor organizers. The second group was women from middle-class backgrounds, or women from working-class backgrounds who had been upwardly mobile. These women, many of whom were associated with the WTUL, wanted both to alleviate the common problems of working women and to help women escape from the lowest-level jobs into better ones. They were oriented to legislation as well as to organizing. Their legislative efforts aimed at extending labor laws to cover office workers in the areas of unhealthful, unsafe or inhuman working conditions and regular hours of work,[34] while their attempts to boost women clerical workers into better jobs emphasized upgrading individual qualifications.

Despite direct and indirect labor affiliations, the methods these two groups of women used did not closely parallel traditional union practices. Organized labor was male labor, and attempts to use its tactics ran into problems that reflected the social prescriptions for women's "respectability"—the prejudice against women's forming *any* trade unions, for example, the structure of clerical work, and the special problems of employed women. If women could overcome these problems, they faced further difficulties making sufficient contacts with workers who were distributed among many offices, and of finding suitable meeting rooms, since women without male escorts had little access to "public" gathering places.

In addition, the set of issues developed for male workers did not encompass the special problems relevant to women employees. While women workers were subject to the economic power of their employers in the same ways that men were, they faced the added problems of patriarchal power: the power of men to command (and judge) the behavior of women.[35] In clerical work, this meant that employers had the power to reward or punish women economically according to whether the women met the men's standards of feminine attractiveness in appearance and demeanor. Elsie Diehl called one version of the problem "companionship," explaining that companionship was the employing of typewriter girls by men who did not need them. They sought companionship instead of workers.

> We want to remedy this through a big organization like the American Federation of Labor. Now when good salaries are paid to typewriter girls it is because they have winning faces and charming manners. We want quiet girls who are not charmers to get as good pay for the same work. There are many other things that we could remedy by concerted action.[36]

Female office workers also faced employers' demands for personal services (sewing "buttons on vest, coat and trousers, and selecting Christmas presents for the employer's family"[37]) or even sexual advances—problems which were also outside the experience of union leaders.

Trade union strategy relied primarily on paid organizers employed for that purpose by the American Federation of Labor or one of the established unions, to conduct organizing campaigns. Since the AFL had never worked in clerical organizing, such resources were not available for these campaigns. Thus, clerical organizers were "on their own"—without the guiding experience, the interest, or the resources of organized labor.

That clerical organizing was carried out instead in close alliance to the WTUL, is not surprising. This was the one organization which readily accepted organizing women clerical workers as possible and worthwhile. Here workers were not suspect as workers because they were women or because they were white-collar. Furthermore, the main purpose of the WTUL was to organize unorganized women workers. While the distance between clerical workers and trade unions was troublesome to WTUL organizers, they were nonetheless accustomed to the difficulty unorganized workers often had in seeing the value of unionizing. Finally, the intertwined problems of clerical workers as workers and as women made sense in an organization whose members were unionists and feminists. The problem of absolutely low and relatively declining wages in clerical work was well known. Less fully articulated, but also familiar, was the relationship between low wages and patriarchal power. These problems did not place clerical workers beyond the scope of unions. Within the WTUL, they were evidence that clerical workers needed to organize.

The WTUL's acceptance of organizing women clerical workers was concretely expressed. From its early days (1904) the League provided organizers to assist in arranging campaigns and space for organizing meetings. Meeting space was a particular problem for women. While men could congregate in barber shops, saloons, bowling alleys, or even on street corners, there were few public places available to women. The League offered the kind of space that women could enter without fear of damage to their reputations. In addition, the WTUL developed experience in organizing employed women. In a short time, its collective experience far surpassed any that the male-dominated labor movement could offer—even if it were willing, which it was not. Finally, the organization itself, as a combination of upper-class and working-class women, lent an aura of respectability to organizing that may have made it more possible for women to join its efforts.

In relying on the WTUL, clerical organizers were not so different from organizers working with other groups of employed women. As one observer reported in 1911, "Women's unions, more than men's, have been developed and influenced by leadership from outside the ranks of wage-earners." This pattern was seen as having particular consequences: the "greatest result of the trade union movement among women has been in the direction of a united stand for protective legislation," a strategy that has been compatible with the "willingness of women to make the greatest sacrifices in conjunction with others for a common cause. . . ."[38] This implies that the association with "outside" groups has been a major factor directing women toward a legislative rather than an organizational strategy, and thus would account in part for the low level of organization among clerical workers. At first hearing, this is a convincing interpretation. Circumstantially, the backgrounds, skills, and orientations of the upper-class members of the WTUL would contribute to a shift from organizing to more inclusive legislation and worker education. I now question that interpretation. It is not "wrong," but its emphasis is misleading.

In the period 1900 to 1930, women clerical workers were employed in a sex-segregated, never-before-organized occupation. Isolated from the mainstream of labor, they were of little threat and little interest to male unionists. Organized labor wrote them off as "unorganizable," reflecting the popular view that because women, especially women clerical workers, were not "real workers" it was neither possible nor important to organize them. The women themselves learned that organizing was not appropriate for "ladies," and that unions were for male factory workers. This combination of circumstances encouraged clerical workers to see themselves as separate from organized labor, a view which was continually reinforced by organized labor's lack of support for their organizing efforts. In this context, clerical organizers came to rely on sources sympathetic to, but outside of, organized labor—primarily the WTUL. While the resources of the WTUL and backgrounds of its members *made possible* a transition from an organizing to a legislative emphasis, they cannot be assumed to have *caused* the transition. On the contrary, I would argue that the WTUL made it possible for women clerical workers interested in organizing to receive much-needed support.

The limited successes in organizing union locals from 1900 to 1920 and the decline in attempts during the 1920s reflect the possibilities for effective action. Neither the attitudes of the clerical workers, their personal characteristics, nor the backgrounds of the organizers and their supporters can adequately account for the difficulties in clerical organizing during that particular period. These "facts" are indicative of the position of women clerical workers, but they still do not preclude organization. Other "facts," such as the limited resources available to the organizers, economic and employer pressures (especially after 1920) against unionization, and the denigrating response of the labor movement contributed significantly to the failure of the early attempts to organize clerical workers. Indeed, as one reads of the persistent efforts made with so little encouragement or recognition, one wonders how those involved maintained their determination.

To me, this analysis suggests that the issue of "organizability" cannot be prejudged. It is not only a product of circumstances, but also of our responses to them. Rather than attempting such judgments, our analysis should aim at discovering the actions we can take to help create conditions which foster organization.

NOTES

Acknowledgments: I would like to thank Mary Bularzik, JoAnne Preston and Ross Feldberg for reading early drafts of this paper, and the editors of *Radical America* for suggesting revisions. Janice Weiss first introduced me to the *Journal of Commercial Education*.

Data for this paper have been gathered primarily from journals and newspapers of the period. The most important sources have been *Life and Labor*, the magazine of the Women's Trade Union League (WTUL), the bulletins of that organization, and *The Typewriter and Phonographic World* (*TPW*), a monthly magazine devoted to the interests of the stenographic professions and their practitioners, later called *The Journal of Commercial Education*. Occasional reports in newspapers and other journals supplement these materials, as do primary documents from the Brookwood Labor School Collection of the Archives of Labor and Urban Affairs, Walter P. Reuther Library, Wayne State University, and secondary sources.

1. Editorial comment, *The Typewriter and Phonographic World* 24 (1904): 90. This journal is referred to in subsequent footnotes as *TPW*.

2. U.S. Department of Labor, *Directory of National Unions and Employee Associations* (Washington, D.C., 1977).

3. "Replaceability" rested on the need for little prior training. In the case of clerical workers, the high school supplied that training. Therefore, even when the clerical function was recognized as strategic, the people who did it could be easily replaced. JoAnne Preston first suggested this point to me.

4. Elyce Rotella, "Occupational Segregation and the Supply of Women to the American Clerical Work Force, 1870–1930," paper presented at the Berkshire Conference on the History of Women, Radcliffe College, Cambridge, Mass. Clerical work continues to be relatively good work for women. In 1976, the median weekly earnings of full-time women clerical workers were \$147, compared to \$111 for women in sales, \$149 for women in crafts, \$121 for women operatives except transport, and \$218 for women in the professions. As usual, these earnings were considerably less than those for men in the same occupation. Women clerical workers earn on average 64 percent of the earnings of men clerical workers (U.S. Department of Labor, *U.S. Working Women: A Databook*, Bureau of Labor Statistics, Bulletin 1977).

5. *TPW* 1 (1885): 218.

6. *TPW* 6 (1890–1891): 101.

7. In the period 1870–1900, women stenographers and typewriters increased dramatically. From less than 1 percent of the small female clerical work force in 1870, stenographers and typists came to account for 46.5 percent of all women clerical workers by 1900. In the following decades, their rate of expansion slowed so that by 1930 they were down to 40 percent of all female clericals (calculated from Alba Edwards, *Comparative Occupation Statistics for the United States, 1870 to 1940* (Washington, D.C., 1943).

8. *TPW* 20 (1902): 242.

9. *TPW* 22 (1904): 201.

10. *TPW* 24 (1904): 113; *TPW* 26 (1905): 342.

11. *TPW* 20 (1902): 260.

12. *TPW* 20 (1902): 367.

13. Benjamin Solomon, "Project on White Collar Unionization," unpublished, held in the University of Chicago Library. This is a useful source on many areas of white-collar unionization.

14. *New York Tribune*, April 22, 1904.

15. *New York Evening Journal*, June 26, 1908.

16. Ibid.

17. Nancy Schrom Dye, "Creating a Feminist Alliance," *Feminist Studies* 3 (1975): 24.

18. *Survey* 27 (1911): 1380.

19. *Life and Labor* 2 (1912): 292–294.

20. *Life and Labor* 6 (1916): 28.

21. The period in which clerical organizing was most widespread was 1904–1916. This was a period of growing feminist activity, with renewed efforts to accomplish labor organizing and with the organizing emphasis in the WTUL. It is also a period in which college-educated women were being encouraged to take up "secretarial" work.

22. *New York Daily News*, Oct. 22, 1927.

23. Gladys Boone, *The Women's Trade Union Leagues in Great Britain and the United States of America* (New York, 1942), p. 187.

24. *Life and Labor* 5 (Jan. 1915): 6.

25. The entanglements of the wage issue are considerable. Average wages of all clerical workers did decline relative to those of all workers in manufacturing and railroads between 1900 and 1971. See Grace Coyle, *Present Trends in the Clerical Occupations* (New York, 1928), pp. 31–32; and Harry Braverman, *Labor and Monopoly Capital* (New York, 1974), pp. 286–287. But it is not clear whether the average wage of women clerical workers declined relative to the average wages of women in factory work. See Evelyn Nakano Glenn and Roslyn L. Feldberg, "Clerical Work: The Female Occupation," in Jo Freeman, ed., *Women: A Feminist Perspective* (2nd ed.; Palo Alto, 1979).

26. Coyle, *Present Trends*, pp. 31–32.

27. This was certainly the message implicit in the type of positions they could secure and explicit in the discussions of "girl stenographers and typewriters" appearing in the *TPW*. Articles on the marriageability of women stenographers and typewriters were standard fare in the first decade of the century, along with "amusing" newspaper stories of employers' problems in retaining their female employees. See Margery Davies, "Woman's Place Is at the Typewriter: The Feminization of the Clerical Labor Force," *Radical America* 8 (July–Aug. 1974): 1–28, for the images of women as office workers. Almost all clerical workers were single prior to 1920. See Roslyn L. Feldberg and Evelyn Nakano Glenn, "Who Sits Behind the Desk: An Exploration of Class Origins of Women Clerical Workers," paper presented at American Studies Association, Boston, 1978. Almost 60 percent of them were under 25 compared to 40 percent for employed women as a whole. See Coyle, *Present Trends*, p. 15.

28. Lillian Wald, "Organization Amongst Working Women," *Annals of the American Academy of Political and Social Science* 27 (1906): 640–641; Feldberg and Glenn, "Who Sits Behind the Desk."

29. Barbara M. Wertheimer, *We Were There: The Story of Working Women in America* (New York, 1977), p. 235.

30. Maurine Weiner Greenwald, "Women Workers and World War I: The American Railroad Industry, a Case Study," *Journal of Social History* 9 (Winter 1975): 154–177, 162.

31. Alice Henry, *Trade Union Woman* (New York and London, 1915), p. 60.

32. Her assessment is consistent with contemporary analyses offered by other women in the labor movement. See, e.g., Helen Marot, *American Labor Unions* (New York, 1914), and Theresa Wolfson, *The Woman Worker and the Trade Unions* (New York, 1926).

33. *Life and Labor* 5 (1915): 348.

34. Ibid., p. 7, and 6 (1916): 106.

35. For extended discussions of patriarchy as a structure of men's power over women, particularly in relation to capitalism, see Heidi Hartmann, "Capitalism, Patriarchy and Job Segregation by Sex," in Martha Blaxall and Barbara Reagan, eds., *Women and the Workplace* (Chicago, 1976), pp. 137–169; and Zillah Eisenstein, ed., *Capitalist Patriarchy and the Case for Socialist Feminism* (New York, 1979). For a more focused analysis of patriarchal power in relation to employed women, see Mary Bularzik, "Sexual Harassment at the Workplace," *Radical America* 12 (July-Aug. 1978): 25–43 (see Chapter 5 of this volume).

36. *New York Tribune*, April 22, 1904.

37. *TPW* 30 (1907): 345.

38. John B. Andrews and W. D. P. Bliss, *The History of Women in Trade Unions* (1911; rpt., New York, 1974), pp. 17, 18, 223.

CHAPTER EIGHT

Organizing the Unemployed: The Early Years of the Great Depression, 1929–1933

by Roy Rosenzweig

The reemergence of economic hard times in the 1970s raises forcefully the issue of how the left can best respond to attacks on working-class living standards. The best historical model we have for such a response is the organizing that radicals did among the unemployed in the early years of the Great Depression. Although the two historical situations are obviously not exactly the same, there is a great deal that we can learn from the experience of the activists of the early thirties. The fact that almost nothing has been written about the unemployed groups of that period makes it worthwhile to piece together the general sketch of their activity and how it evolved.

On March 7, 1930, President Herbert Hoover made his most detailed economic statement of the four months following the Wall Street Crash. "All the evidences," Hoover declared, "indicate that the worst effects of the crash upon unemployment will have passed during the next sixty days."[1] Although Hoover's veneer of optimism remained untarnished during his next three years in office, unemployment mounted steadily. At the time of this very speech, even according to moderately conservative government estimates, joblessness had already increased almost ten-fold from 492,000 to 4,644,000. By the following March it had almost doubled again, and before peaking in March 1933 it had practically doubled once more to 15,071,000.[2]

Reprinted from Vol. 10, No. 4 (July-August 1976).

Although virtually no industry or community escaped the scourge of unemployment, the impact was not uniform. Autos, textiles, and other durable-goods industries were particularly hard hit in the early years of the Depression. Between March 1929 and August 1931 the payroll of the Ford Motor Company dropped from 128,142 to 37,000 persons. Even within industries and communities, unemployment was selective. The poor, the unskilled, the young, and the foreign-born suffered disproportionately. Managerial employees suffered least, and whites did much better than blacks. The unemployment rate for Harlem blacks, for example, was between one and a half and three times that of the whites in New York City. Yet, for all these variations, what was truly remarkable about thirties joblessness was its pervasiveness—one third of a nation was out of work.[3]

How did these unprecedented millions of unemployed respond to their plight in the early years of the Great Depression? Although many observers on both the right and the left expected them to turn to radicalism, the jobless, of course, never composed the shock troops of revolution. Still, it is a serious mistake to conclude on this basis, as did one historian, that "most of the unemployed meekly accepted their lot."[4] The jobless employed a number of spontaneous survival strategies such as informal and formal cooperative movements, family and neighborhood networks of assistance, individual and group looting of supermarkets, coal bootlegging, determined searches for work, and innovative stretching of income.[5] At the same time, radical organizers helped stimulate more formal and political jobless actions such as sit-ins at relief stations, national and state hunger marches, demonstrations at City Halls, and direct resistance to evictions. Organized into a variety of groups under the leadership of several left-wing organizations, the unemployed compiled an impressive record in the early thirties. Not only did these radical organizations of the unemployed stop evictions and raise relief payments, they also helped to intensify the class consciousness of many of their members.

But we must be wary of exaggerating or romanticizing the past. While no one would deny the heroism, energy, and imagination of the radical leaders and rank-and-file militants active in the unemployed movement, we must realize that their organizations constituted neither a revolutionary force nor even a truly mass movement. The core active membership of the unemployed movement—perhaps 100,000 in 1933—never included even 1 percent of that third of a nation that was out of work at the height of the Depression. While the radical unemployed movement often succeeded in winning immediate concrete gains for the jobless on the local level, it was much less successful in its efforts to create a revolutionary movement based on the unemployed.

What were the barriers to the development of such a mass-based, revolutionary unemployed movement? Were the radicals themselves responsible, as many commentators of both the right and the left have argued?

Or was the problem in external social, economic, and political conditions that made a jobless-based revolutionary movement an impossibility in the early thirties?

Passing judgment on the record of 1930s radicals is a difficult and painful process for the present-day Left.[6] The dismal record of the American Left in the last few years should make us distressingly aware of our own failures and limitations as radical organizers and strategists. Consequently, while judgments are inevitable, they must be made with a consciousness of both the difficult conditions faced by thirties organizers and the limited range of options open to them. This article, then, explores the experience of Communists, Socialists, and Musteites in organizing the unemployed within the context of the external barriers that limited their successes. It focuses primarily, however, on the Communist Party's efforts, since in the Hoover years of the Depression it was both the first to act and the strongest radical group. Moreover, the problems faced by the Communists were typical of those faced by other groups trying to do the same kind of organizing.

COMMUNISTS AND THE UNEMPLOYED:
THE UNEMPLOYED COUNCILS

Organizationally, the Communist Party (CP) faced the Depression in a weakened state. The post-World War I Red Scare, the political lethargy of the twenties, and the expulsions of the Cannon and Lovestone factions had reduced the Party to a mere 7,500 members at the start of the thirties. Moreover, the CP of 1930 did not represent a cross-section of the American working class; rather, it was dominated by foreign-born and urban workers.[7] Ideologically and strategically, on the other hand, the Communists were uniquely well prepared for the Depression. The Tenth Plenum of the Comintern Executive Committee, meeting in Moscow in the summer of 1929, had proclaimed the "Third Period" of capitalist crisis and revolutionary offensive.[8] In August 1929, while most Americans were still celebrating Republican prosperity, the Communists were in Cleveland organizing a new labor federation, the Trade Union Unity League (TUUL), which included as one of its objectives, "to set up Councils of Unemployed Workers."[9]

The Communists' new Third Period line directed them to take an aggressive approach to decaying American capitalism. As a result, even before the Wall Street Crash, energetic young Communist activists sought out the jobless on breadlines, at flop houses, outside factory gates, in relief offices, and, most often, in their neighborhoods. With the coming of mass unemployment in 1930, organizational activity accelerated and organization of the unemployed became a top priority for Communist activists. In March 1930 the Party's theoretical journal declared that "the tactical key to the present state of class struggle is the fight against unemployment."[10] Organizational activities took very concrete and visible forms. In Chicago, for example, Communists led, organized, or participated in 2,088 mass demonstrations in the first five years of the Depression.[11] Not just mass demonstrations, but also leafleting, personal contacts, and eviction protests were used to build a core of local activists around whom to organize a local unemployed council. Any issue of immediate concern to the jobless was seen as a potential organizing tool. "The Councils," writes one historian, "did not consider any issue too small or unimportant to fight for: brooms for housewives in Seattle, milk for a baby in Detroit, breaking down barriers against Negro relief in St. Louis, coffee instead of cocoa for welfare recipients in New York, . . . an anti-spaghetti crusade at a Minneapolis relief commissary."[12]

The early successes of the Communist unemployed movement grew directly out of the spontaneous discontent that was sweeping through the urban unemployed. "So desperate were the unemployed," wrote two Chicago observers, "that protest was seething through the disadvantaged neighborhoods of the city." The Chicago CP was unable to fulfill all the requests for organizational assistance from protesting groups.[13] The Communist unemployed associations, usually known as Unemployed Councils, built on a cooperative neighborhood solidarity that emerged in response to the disorganization and inadequacy of local relief. Consequently, the Communist Unemployed Councils were most effective when they seized upon potent neighborhood issues.[14] Because of the unemployed movement's initial connection to the Trade Union Unity League, Communist organizers were told to form unemployed groups on a shop or factory basis. But, as unemployed leader Herbert Benjamin has recalled, "down below people weren't concerned with" these directives. They were "just concerned with finding any means they could of acting."[15] Most often this meant local, ad hoc neighborhood councils mobilized around specific grievances.

Out of this combination of aggressive organizing and spontaneous discontent emerged a vital Communist-led unemployed movement beginning in January and February 1930. These months saw demonstrations of the unemployed in such places as New Britain, Connecticut; Passaic, New Jersey; Buffalo, New York; Pontiac, Michigan; Detroit; Boston; Philadelphia; and New York City.[16] These early stirrings climaxed dramatically on March 6, 1930. The Party mobilized all its resources behind nationally coordinated demonstrations on March 6, which it called International Unemployment Day. Within the first month of the campaign the Party distributed over one million leaflets. Chicago Communists distributed 200,000 leaflets, 50,000 stickers, and 50,000 shop papers in the last few days before the demonstration.[17] These energetic efforts paid off. Throughout the United States huge numbers of unemployed workers, many of whom had never before taken part in radical demonstrations, took to the streets. Although precise figures are impossible to arrive at now, the Communist Party at the time claimed a nationwide mobilization of one and one-quarter million people.[18]

The March 6 demonstrations awakened many to the existence of mass unemployment and large-scale unrest in America. In Detroit, where over 35,000 jobless workers had been mobilized by the Unemployed Council, business leaders "were shocked by the emergence of truly radical agitation, and by the support it received." Even local Communists were surprised by the size of the crowd.[19] In many cases, government repression—a problem that was to bedevil the unemployed movement throughout its history— came immediately. The scene of carnage at the bloody Union Square Demonstration in New York prompted even the *New York Times* to strong description:

> Hundreds of policemen and detectives, swinging nightsticks, blackjacks and bare fists, rushed into the crowd, hitting . . . all with whom they came in contact, chasing many across the street and adjacent thoroughfares. . . . A score of men with bloody heads and faces sprawled over the square with policemen pummeling them.

The blood spilled on March 6 was only the beginning. In the next five months over 4,000 people were arrested at radical demonstrations. The battle lines were drawn.[20]

Despite these repressive measures, the Unemployed Councils blossomed in the period immediately following the March 6 demonstrations. Unemployed workers around the country began constituting themselves as loosely organized, neighborhood-oriented councils of the unemployed. By mid-summer Chicago had twelve locals and Philadelphia seven. Minneapolis, Milwaukee, and Indianapolis also had strong groups.[21]

Of particular significance was the emergence at this time of interracial unemployed councils. As early as December 1929 Party leader Earl Browder had stressed that the organization of black workers had to be a top priority of the unemployed councils. The March 6 demonstrations provided an opportunity to implement this call, and throughout the country they attracted large numbers of black participants. Black Communist leader Cyril Briggs felt that March 6 revealed "the successful breaking down of the wall of prejudice between white and Negro workers fostered by the employers and the substitution of working-class solidarity and fraternization." Not all unemployed groups cut across racial lines, but many, especially those in Southern cities like Chattanooga and Atlanta, were the first interracial organizations in their areas. Even in the North black and white solidarity threatened public officials. "Here was something new," black sociologists St. Clair Drake and Horace Cayton have commented about the frightened reaction in Chicago: "Negroes and whites *together* rioting against the forces of law and order." "The beginnings of a breaking down of barriers between whites and Negroes," unemployed leader Aurelia Johnson has recalled, were among the central achievements of the unemployed movement.[22]

In the spring of 1930 the CP made its first efforts at national coordina-

172

tion of the unemployed movement. Out of a Preliminary National Conference on Unemployment in New York at the end of March and a Chicago Convention in early July emerged a new national organization—The Unemployed Councils of the U.S.A. Although officially under Trade Union Unity League control, the Unemployed Councils, in practice, remained a largely autonomous neighborhood movement based on the anger and confusion of the jobless.[23]

This local, ad hoc quality was a strength, but also an important weakness of the unemployed movement. Particularly in the early years of the movement, large numbers of unemployed mobilized around specific grievances or demonstrations, but rarely maintained a regular organizational connection. One Party official complained in the fall of 1930 that "despite millions of leaflets and hundreds of meetings, not to speak of the half-dozen demonstrations in every city, organized unemployed councils are almost nonexistent." Where there was a regular membership it was usually dominated by CP members.[24] The problem of impermanence plagued the unemployed movement throughout its history. Many people drifted in and out of jobs in the thirties; they were not continuously available for membership in an unemployed group, and this led to a continual churning of membership. This churning had a particularly severe effect on rank-and-file leadership, since it was often the most talented and aggressive among the unemployed who first secured reemployment.[25] (The Party itself also suffered from this problem of membership instability. In 1930, 6,000 new members joined the CP, but actual membership rose only about one thousand.)[26]

The Communist Party's Third Period line, although it had helped the Party anticipate the economic crisis, created additional problems for the unemployed movement. Its revolutionary anticipations were too sanguine for the period, and thus inspired slogans and demonstrations which either frightened or confused the rank-and-file unemployed worker. Few unemployed saw the connection between their immediate need for relief and demonstrations against the "Imperialist war danger," slogans about Defense of the Chinese Soviets, or even electoral campaigns for CP candidates. Nor was it clear why Norman Thomas was being denounced as an "undercover" agent at the same time that he was speaking out against repression of the unemployed movement, or why Socialists and Musteites were regularly labeled "social fascists" and "tools of the bosses."[27] Such revolutionary posturing inevitably alienated unemployed workers, especially outside of the big cities. Moreover, it seriously handicapped efforts to recruit the jobless into the radical movement. The use of terms like "rightist deviation," "agitprop," and "theoretical levels" "invariably frightened . . . off" the average worker, observed Mauritz Hallgren, a *Nation* editor sympathetic to the Left. "These Communists," a worker complained to Louis Adamic, "thought Shamokin, Mount Carmel, and Shenandoah were just like Union Square."[28]

The Communist Party itself soon reached a similar conclusion. In September 1930, CP leader Clarence Hathaway complained of the Party's tendency to raise issues of no immediate concern to the jobless: "Crises, war, contradictions, colonial revolts, defense of the Soviet Union, etc. too often become merely a string of phrases having no connection with the class struggle in a given locality." And two months later the Party's Central Committee called for a reorientation of the Unemployed Councils toward more direct work among the unemployed and away from revolutionary sloganeering. It also directed that the Councils should operate on two levels: nationally, they would work for direct federal aid for relief and unemployment insurance; locally, they would represent the unemployed in their relations with relief authorities.[29]

This new "bread and butter" focus dominated the Councils on the local level through 1933, and with some modifications for the rest of the thirties. Although they never again reached the level of nationwide visibility achieved on March 6, 1930, the Councils successfully won limited concrete gains for the local unemployed. Particularly in the period 1931–1933, when local relief efforts were disorganized and woefully inadequate, the Councils were able to force important concessions from the relief authorities through demonstrations at relief offices, city halls, and state capitals. In Chicago, for example, the Unemployed Councils on several occasions blocked citywide relief cuts.[30]

Yet the real effectiveness of the Councils rested not on their ability to occasionally force increased relief appropriations, but on their capacity to resolve *individual* relief grievances. By 1932 the Chicago Unemployed Councils had already handled several thousand individual cases, and in the process had helped establish important precedents on adequacy and quality of relief. Moreover, in many localities the Unemployed Councils successfully fought relief discrimination and liberalized administrative thinking regarding the right of clients to complain. It was this function of the Unemployed Councils as grievance representatives for the jobless that constituted their greatest attraction to the rank-and-file unemployed worker. A study of Cleveland Unemployed Council members confirmed that individual relief grievances were most often the "precipitating factor" in creating Unemployed Council members.[31]

The prevention of evictions was another concrete service that the Unemployed Councils performed for the jobless in the early thirties. A variety of techniques came into play: blocking the sheriff's entrance; returning the furniture; packing the courts to pressure judges to stop evictions. As the Depression deepened in 1931 and 1932, eviction struggles occurred with increasing frequency. In March 1931 Edmund Wilson reported that the Unemployed Councils had "practically stopped evictions" in Detroit, and that one landlady had actually called the Unemployed Council to ask whether she could evict her tenant yet.[32]

This new "bread and butter" focus implemented in the fall of 1930 proved particularly effective in black communities. Mark Naison, in his recent study of Communists in Harlem, notes a shift at that time from agitational work into practical organizational activity. According to Naison, this policy, combined with the aggressive leadership of a committed, interracial group of organizers, helped the Harlem Unemployed Council "develop into a mass movement with solid roots in the community, one of the major sources of Communist influence among the least privileged sectors of Harlem's population." The two major tactics employed by the Harlem Council were the relief-bureau sit-in and eviction resistance. Unemployed Council sit-ins, demonstrations, and disruptions at the home-relief bureaus sought— and sometimes won—immediate relief for hard-hit Harlem residents. The eviction struggles brought concrete results, not only in Harlem, but in other urban black communities as well. When Chicago blacks received eviction notices, "it was not unusual," according to Cayton and Drake, "for a mother to shout to the children, 'Run quick and find the Reds!'" These struggles persisted despite vicious police attacks which led, for example, to the killing of three black eviction protesters in August 1931.[33]

The Unemployed Councils aimed for direct approaches to the immediate needs of the jobless. But how direct? Soliciting food donations for the hungry or, alternatively, seizing food from the grocery store? The Councils briefly flirted with both of these tactics, but ultimately rejected them. In early 1931 directives from both the Comintern and the Trade Union Unity League urged that the Councils set up relief kitchens and undertake direct food collections. By July, however, the Party had reconsidered, and Browder had denounced communal charity schemes as an "open right-wing opportunist deviation." But this new policy sometimes caused problems on the local level. In Harlem, according to Naison's study, Council leaders concluded that the rejection of "spontaneous efforts of rank-and-file Council members to collect food, money, and clothing for starving neighbors, or to cook communal meals for the unemployed . . . had isolated the Harlem Council from many sincere workers who saw no contradiction between taking a collection for their neighbors and resisting an eviction or marching on City Hall." Consequently, by the fall of 1931 the Harlem Council began to take up food collections, although such collections never became a central focus of the Council's work.[34]

Unemployed Council participation in food seizures similarly reflected both an ambivalence at the top and a tendency of some local unemployed groups to set their own course in accordance with local conditions. In the early thirties individual and group looting of supermarkets was not an isolated phenomenon. "Grown men, usually in two's and three's, enter chain stores, order all the food they can possibly carry, and then walk out without paying," the *Nation* reported from Detroit in the summer of 1932. Although most such incidents took place outside of the organized unemployed movement, Unemployed Councils in Toledo and Oklahoma City joined in the food looting in early 1931. Such actions, however, frightened not only authorities, but also some top Communist leaders. In the summer of 1931 Browder condemned food seizures as "an effort to substitute an idealistic, 'heroic' action to 'inspire' the masses, in the place of the necessary Bolshevist organization and leadership." Unemployed Council leader Herbert Benjamin recalls that "those of us who were politically more responsible" continually advised against food riots, and he believes that more such rioting would have occurred without the Unemployed Councils. "It seems probable," conclude two academic writers unsympathetic to the Left, "that the Communist Party exercised an important influence in restricting the amount of violence against persons and property during the depression."[35]

While the CP helped to restrain the violence of the out-of-work, it could do little to restrain police violence directed against the jobless. As an examination of the dispatches of the *Federated Press* or even the *New York Times* shows, police violence against unemployed demonstrators was almost a daily occurrence. One of the most dramatic incidents came on March 7, 1932, when the Detroit Unemployed Councils led 3,000 in a march on Henry Ford's River Rouge Plant in Dearborn to demand jobs, fuel, and food. The Dearborn police responded with bullets. By the end of the day four marchers lay dead and over fifty had been seriously wounded.[36] Such incidents were all too common in the thirties.

The successes of the Unemployed Councils as a local pressure organization between 1930 and 1933 were not equaled on the national level. The Unemployed Councils did not receive effective national leadership until the fall of 1931, when Herbert Benjamin was assigned by the CP to direct this work. Even then the national office remained a "nominal sort of thing," as Benjamin has recalled. In fact Benjamin himself *was* the national organization—he initially had no supporting staff.[37]

In the early thirties national Unemployed Council activity revolved around petition drives for the CP's unemployment-insurance bill and two national hunger marches in December 1931 and December 1932. The marches did much to publicize the unemployed cause, although neither was a dramatic success. The Communists limited participation in the marches to elected representatives of local Unemployed Councils, and as a result only 1,600 marched in the first and 3,200 in the second. More importantly, the marches failed to mobilize many jobless outside of those already in the Communist Party; over 70 percent of the 1932 hunger marchers, for example, belonged to the Communist Party or the Young Communist League.[38]

The national organization of the Unemployed Councils strengthened and solidified in the years after 1933. Yet these same years saw the loss of much of the vitality and spontaneity of the unemployed movement, particularly on the local level. The local Councils settled down as a more orderly movement that sought to represent the unemployed in their dealings with relief authorities; they became in many areas the bargaining agent for both relief recipients and WPA workers. Large demonstrations or eviction resistance occasionally flared up, but more often the unemployed organizations quietly carried out their trade-union functions. In 1940 Irene Oppenheimer, a sociologist, noted that each year the unemployed organizations tended to have fewer sit-ins, strikes, and picket lines; she concluded that unemployed activity "has been characterized by a gradual evolution from the position of a purely conflict group to an organized and responsible relationship with the authorities."[39]

Along with this decreasing activism on the local level came the nationalization and unification of the unemployed movement. By 1936 the Workers' Alliance of America, originally a federation of Socialist unemployed groups, encompassed most of the Communist, Musteite, and independent jobless leagues as well. Increasingly, the Workers' Alliance focused its attention on Washington (where it had its headquarters), and it developed into a relatively effective lobbying organization for national-relief and unemployment-insurance measures. Basically, the Workers' Alliance accepted the terms of the New Deal; it adopted the politics of the popular front—a left-wing New Deal liberalism—and developed a close symbiotic relationship with New Deal relief officials. In 1938, for example, Workers' Alliance locals campaigned actively for New Deal candidates. Both nationally and locally the unemployed movement after 1933 moved from insurgency to respectability. "The organized unemployed," wrote a *Saturday Evening Post* reporter in 1938, "are no longer merely an undecorative and troublesome fringe on the body politic."[40]

It was not just the Communists with their popular-front politics who shifted their unemployed organizing into more "respectable" channels in the late thirties. Other unemployed groups led by Socialists and Musteites also made that transition. An examination of the organizing efforts of these groups before the New Deal shows how their tactics evolved in a way similar to those of the CP.

SOCIALISTS AND THE UNEMPLOYED

That the Socialists formulated their basic approach to the problem of unemployment six months before the Wall Street Crash, and retained that approach unaltered for three more years, testifies to the unimaginative way many Socialists initially confronted the gravest crisis of twentieth-century capitalism. In May 1929 the National Executive Committee of the Socialist Party (SP) urged local Party branches to form "Emergency Conferences on Unemployment," not as mass pressure organizations of the unemployed, but rather as lobbying agencies for three traditional Socialist demands: unemployment insurance, old-age pensions, and abolition of child labor.

Throughout the early thirties most Socialist activity on behalf of the jobless continued to emphasize traditional Socialist propagandizing and disdained direct organization of the unemployed.[41]

Why this inertia on the part of the party of Debs? Whereas the Third Period line of the CP predisposed it to respond aggressively to the Great Depression, the political conditions within the SP led it initially to offer traditional Socialist panaceas rather than aggressive organizing. The American Socialist Party had declined precipitously in the 1920s, with membership plummeting from 105,000 in 1919 to less than 8,000 in 1928. Those who had stuck it out during the lean years of the twenties no longer had any immediate expectations of a Socialist victory. These so-called Old Guard Socialists—often over 60, foreign-born, and closely tied to the trade unions—believed that Socialist propaganda and educational activities would lead inevitably and gradually to Socialism—but only in the long run.[42] In the meantime, campaigns to organize the unemployed were perceived as unnecessary diversions which would "take time away from Socialist propaganda." Anyway, the Old Guard felt that the unemployed were too unstable and heterogeneous to make good Party members. They condemned, as one critic observed, "any 'backdoor' entrance into Party membership by way of 'mass struggle' rather than rigorous intellectual education."[43]

Only with the entrance into the Socialist Party of a newer generation of young, college-educated, and native-born members did the SP begin to abandon its passive approach to the unemployed question. Starting with the 1928 Norman Thomas presidential campaign, and accelerating after the onset of the Depression, the SP benefited from a rapid influx of young, activist Socialists, who clamored impatiently for "Socialism in Our Time." Many also belonged to the League for Industrial Democracy (LID), a Socialist Party offshoot which appealed largely to college students, professionals, and white-collar workers. Prior to the Depression the LID had devoted most of its energies to educational activities, but from 1931 on its members often took a leading role in helping to organize the jobless.[44] By far the LID's most impressive achievement was the Chicago Workers' Committee on Unemployment, which by mid-1932 had organized 25,000 jobless into over 60 locals.[45] Inspired by the Chicago success, LID members in Baltimore initiated the People's Unemployment League, which had about 20 locals and 7,000 to 12,000 members.[46]

While many LID members were out aggressively organizing the unemployed, the Socialist Party was just beginning to stir out of the bog of lethargy. A combination of factors—the growing power of the younger activists with the Party, the fear of Communist domination of the unemployed, and the increasingly grave economic situation—pushed the SP's National Executive Committee, in February 1932, to finally endorse the idea of direct organization of the jobless.[47] Yet, while the National Office of the SP provided some programmatic and organizational guidance to local

Party branches interested in organizing the jobless, the success or failure of most efforts rested largely on the local initiative of both Socialists and the unemployed. The real growth of Socialist influence among the unemployed did not come until the beginning of the New Deal, and in some ways was tied to that development. In the mid-1930s the Socialist unemployed groups provided the impetus for the nationalization and centralization of the unemployed movement under the Workers' Alliance.[48]

Both the LID and Socialist unemployed groups tended to employ the same techniques as the Communist Unemployed Councils—acting as grievance representatives at relief stations, fighting evictions, and holding demonstrations and parades to urge higher relief appropriations. On the whole, however, Socialists tended to use confrontations and disruptions less than the Communists. They often tried to intercede with relief authorities to get money for a family threatened with eviction rather than trying to block it bodily. This moderation often gave the Socialist organizations a certain respectability the Communists lacked. "We were not a pariah organization," one leader of the Baltimore People's Unemployment League (PUL) recently recalled. To a much greater degree than the Communists, the Socialist unemployed groups subordinated Socialist ideology to the quest for fulfillment of the immediate economic needs of the jobless. "We were so busy with local problems," remembers another organizer of the PUL, that "indoctrination" of members in "Socialist principles" was often neglected.[49]

MUSTEITES AND THE UNEMPLOYED:
THE UNEMPLOYED LEAGUES

When Socialist organizing of the unemployed finally got underway in the early years of the New Deal, it tended to mirror both the organizing approach and constituency of the Communist Unemployed Councils. But the third major radical movement of unemployed workers, that led by the followers of A. J. Muste, the Dutch Reformed Minister turned labor educator and organizer, differed in organizing methods and support.[50]

Beginning around 1932, the Musteites sought to transform their propaganda and educational organization—the Conference on Progressive Labor Action—into an independent working-class center competitive with the AFL, CP, and SP. The unemployed offered a possible power base for this transformation, and in 1932 the Musteites began organizing Unemployed Leagues. The Musteites, like the Communists and Socialists, met with their greatest success when they pitched their efforts toward the bread-and-butter needs of the unemployed. But to this immediate-needs focus they added their own unique "American Approach"—an effort to identify their Unemployed Leagues with popular patriotic symbols such as the Rattlesnake Flag and the slogan "Don't Tread on Me." This approach made the Musteites somewhat more tolerant and flexible in dealing with existing non-political unemployed groups than the Communists or Socialists. They

179

worked closely and successfully with jobless self-help groups—organizations devised by the unemployed to meet their needs through barter and exchange of labor for produce and fuel. While other unemployed groups stigmatized self help as "collective picking in garbage cans," the Musteites initially condoned this approach, calling it "a cement . . . to keep the organization together . . . that would push the members into further action."[51]

This flexibility and Americanism paid off: The Musteites were able to attract more native-born and less politicized members, and to build a following in areas that the Communists and Socialists were unable to penetrate. From the small industrial and mining towns of Ohio, the steel mills of Pittsburgh, the coal fields of eastern Pennsylvania and West Virginia, and the textile mills of North Carolina, thousands of unemployed enlisted under their banners. While the CP Unemployed Councils in Ohio were confined to the cities and towns with large immigrant populations, like Youngstown, the Musteite Leagues found support in much smaller and more rural towns.[52]

The attractiveness of patriotic rhetoric for many Depression unemployed is further evidenced by the success of the Washington marches of Father James Cox and the Bonus Expeditionary Force. In January 1932 Father Cox, a round-faced, spectacled Pittsburgh radio priest active in the labor movement, led 15,000 unemployed from the Pittsburgh area to Washington to present their demands for immediate relief.[53] The following summer the famous Bonus March gathered over 20,000 jobless World War I veterans in the capital.[54]

Why were these marches able to attract many who were immune to the appeals of radical unemployed groups? One important reason was that the radicals had to recruit the jobless in the face of well-ingrained cultural assumptions that identified radical activity with anti-Americanism, alienism, and deviance. E. Wight Bakke, a Yale economist who made an extremely careful and sensitive study of the New Haven unemployed, found that "the identification of all radical ideas with Russia is all but universal." In New Haven, at least, these patriotic and anti-Communist cultural assumptions militated against the success of radical groups.[55] Father Cox and the Bonus Marchers, like the Musteites to a lesser degree, played effectively on this patriotism and anti-Communism. Cox's March was, in part, a reaction against the Communist Hunger March of 1931. In explaining his march, Cox said:

> Some weeks ago I read of the invasion of Washington by a Communistic group of marchers waving the red flag, singing the Internationale and demanding all sorts of fantastic things. This is repugnant to me, and I so stated casually over the radio. I remarked that, while I condemned these demonstrations, I believed a body of real American citizens should go to Washington and protest against unemployment conditions which exist in the United States today.

This Americanist rhetoric carried through Cox's entire march. His followers arrived in Washington singing the Star Spangled Banner and waving American flags; they concluded their visit at the Tomb of the Unknown Soldier.[56] The Bonus Marchers also manipulated patriotic symbols to cultivate an image of respectability.[57]

This patriotic posturing apparently enabled Cox and the Bonus Army to attract followers who disdained the radical unemployed movements. Most workers were used to frequent periods of joblessness, but small entrepreneurs and white-collar workers were not. In the thirties, for the first time, unemployment was an experience shared by both the middle and working classes; but, it was the middle-class unemployed who experienced the greatest shock and attitude changes as a result of the Depression.[58] Hence, although these middle-class jobless were important potential supporters for thirties protests, they were unlikely to join avowedly radical groups like the Unemployed Councils. The Bonus Army and Father Cox, with their patriotic rhetoric, could and did mobilize the middle-class unemployed. According to one recent historian, the "vast majority" of the Bonus Marchers were "middle-aged and middle-class—small businessmen, skilled tradesmen, white-collar workers, with a sprinkling of professionals, such as teachers, lawyers, and dentists."[59] Although little is known about Father Cox's marchers, his financial backing came from the small store owners of the Allegheny County Retail Merchants Association.[60]

Although to a lesser degree, the Musteites shared with Cox and the Bonus Army the ability to attract more middle-class, native-born, and "Middle American" unemployed. Yet, the Musteites' Americanist rhetoric also brought its problems. At the Unemployed League's first national convention, held in Columbus, Ohio, on July 4, 1933, the Musteites had to quell a revolt led by a "Stars and Stripes" faction over the Musteites' failure to open the Convention with a prayer and the National Anthem. In the long run, much of this native-American and small-town support evaporated as the Musteites became more and more revolutionary in their gradual movement toward Trotskyism, and as the New Deal liberalism of Franklin Roosevelt competed for the allegiance of the out-of-work.[61]

CONCLUSIONS

We see, then, that between 1929 and 1933 the three main radical unemployed movements varied in ideological assumptions, organizing personnel, geographic bases, and organizing strategies. Yet they shared some common achievements. First, they resolved the immediate individual grievances of their members with particular success: They won relief adjustments, blocked evictions, and reconnected the gas and electric for thousands of unemployed. Second, on a collective level, the unemployed organizations helped create pressure not only for higher levels of relief and larger relief appropriations, but also for more equitable and less degrading administrative procedures at relief stations. And, third, they were the first groups in the thirties to propagandize and agitate openly and actively for unemployment insurance. Although there were a number of elements involved, such as the pressure on FDR from Huey Long, their agitation did help to pave the way for the Social Security Act of 1935, which included provisions for unemployment insurance. The battle for unemployment insurance had a long history going back to the early twentieth century, but the radical unemployed movement can be credited with helping to revive it as a serious issue in the Great Depression.[62] The psychological impact of the unemployed movement should, similarly, not be minimized. Jobless workers became convinced that their condition was not their own fault, that larger economic forces had thrown them out of work.

Perhaps most importantly, the unemployed movement helped raise the political and social consciousness of the thousands of workers who passed through its ranks. For many the unemployed movement was their first experience in any sort of mass pressure organization, and through this affiliation many learned the power of organization as a weapon. Sam Brugos, a leader of a Cleveland Unemployed Council, had no contact with radicalism or trade unionism prior to the Depression. Yet, he told an interviewer of his determination to "join a union and organize a strike" as soon as he found a job.[63] Obviously many jobless workers did just that in the late thirties. Many leaders of the CIO came directly out of the unemployed movement, and it appears that many in the rank and file had similar training. "It was a period of great schooling," black Communist leader William Patterson recalled.[64] Schooling was available in organizational techniques as well as in interracial cooperation. The greatest educational achievement of the Baltimore People's Unemployment League, according to one of its founders, was "getting white men and women to work with and under Negro men and women."[65]

These were substantial and significant achievements, particularly from the perspective of the rank-and-file jobless worker. To the extent that the unemployed movement fostered trade-union consciousness and helped break down barriers between black and white workers, it contributed importantly to the strength of the American working class. Yet, to state the obvious, neither this gain nor the more tangible improvements in living conditions won by the unemployed movement were accompanied by the creation of a mass revolutionary movement of the unemployed. To return, then, to the question raised at the outset: Was this limitation the product of mistakes internal to the radical movement, or was it determined by broader external forces?

The comparative experience of Communists, Socialists, and Musteites in organizing the unemployed suggests that the basic limitations on the thirties unemployed movement lay outside the Left. The Socialists and Musteites, in their efforts among the jobless, offered variations on the basic

Communist theme, but neither achieved markedly better results. Being less prone to the use of confrontation politics, the Socialists could sometimes attract less politicized workers or win a more respectful hearing from authorities. But there was a political price to this approach. As one top leader of the People's Unemployment League wrote to Norman Thomas: the "loyalty of the members . . . is to the league and its leaders and not in any sense to the SP."[66] The aggressive grassroots organizing and the "American Approach" of the Musteites offers a contrasting strategy to that of both Communists and Socialists. Yet there were problems here as well. The Musteites' Americanist rhetoric attracted many workers who were indifferent to the Communists and Socialists, but some of these workers soon lost interest in the Musteites when they realized that the radicals' patriotism did not run very deep. Moreover, as a relatively small left-wing sect built around one man, the Musteites were never able to expand their movement beyond Ohio and Pennsylvania.

All of the radical unemployed groups suffered at one time or another from opportunism, sectarianism, factionalism, dogmatism, and mechanical party control of a mass movement. In particular, one could easily criticize some of the programs and practices of the Stalinized Communist Party of the thirties. Yet Stalinism did not permeate the unemployed movement. And, rank-and-file organizers often ignored Party directives that were irrelevant to their concrete and practical organizing efforts. Indeed, in general, the organizers of the radical unemployed movement evidenced creative and aggressive leadership on both the local and national levels. While others merely talked about the "forgotten man," these organizers actually did something.

In the end, the similar levels of success achieved by the varying organizing approaches of the Communists, Socialists, and Musteites suggest that no slight shift in the party line would have made any fundamental difference. Hence, although an awareness of the errors of the Left organizers in the thirties may help to prevent their repetition, to understand fully the limitations of the unemployed movement it is necessary to examine the basic external factors that shaped its history: the repressive response of the government and the upper classes; the dominant ideological and cultural currents in 1930s America; and the composition and condition of the jobless themselves.

The American upper classes were not about to passively accept a jobless-led revolution. Virtually any signs of incipient rebellion were met by swift and often violent repression. An American Civil Liberties Union pamphlet, "What Rights for the Unemployed?," summarized the grim situation: "Bans against assembly, refusal of permits to speak, the stationing of squads of police at relief stations, attacks by the police on peaceful meetings, clubbings, arrests, abuse of prisoners, infliction of maximum sentences, prosecution for criminal syndicalism or conspiracy—these have become in relation to the activities of the unemployed monotonously familiar." Yet it was fear of repression, not repression itself, that deterred many jobless from supporting the radical unemployed groups in the first place. Yale economist E. Wight Bakke learned in talking to New Haven jobless that they had discovered in their working days that radicalism was a "surefire demoter," and they "cannot forget it now."[67]

But the organizers of the radical unemployed movement confronted more than just police batons and tear gas. They sought to win the allegiance of the unemployed in the face of powerful ideological and cultural assumptions that militated against their success. Although the Depression did much to erode working-class faith in American capitalism, this breakdown had not led to a new consciousness, at least by the early thirties. As the Lynds found in Muncie, Indiana, during the Depression, "fear, resentment, insecurity, and disillusionment were largely an *individual* experience for each worker, and not a thing generalized by him into a *'class'* experience."[68] Workers had a culture of their own, of course, which rejected many of the values of middle-class American society. But many of the values of that very working-class culture—patriotism, distrust of politics, and a frequent anti-radicalism—also discouraged membership in radical unemployed groups. "In the face of Communism," Bakke found in talking to the New Haven jobless, "the most insecure American workman becomes a hero by defending American conditions."[69]

Moreover, unemployed organizers had to try to mobilize an American working class that was divided within itself along ethnic, racial, religious, and geographic lines. Although occasionally the shock of unemployment did break down racial and ethnic barriers, the basic divisions remained. Homer Morris, an American Friends Service Committee worker, described the persistence of racial, national, religious, and family feuds in the impoverished coal-mining camps of West Virginia and Kentucky. Similarly, one New Haven worker blamed his unemployment on the "Jews in control who had no use for Italians."[70] Among the Depression unemployed the problems in developing class consciousness were exacerbated by the presence of large numbers of jobless men and women from middle-class backgrounds. Given this context, most unemployed people in the early thirties did not come to see themselves as part of a common group united by their lack of work.

Finally, the jobless, as a group, were particularly difficult to organize for a number of reasons. As one thirties radical leader has commented: "I don't know of any task in the revolutionary movement more discouraging and disheartening than the task of trying to keep an unemployed organization . . . together."[71] One problem was the continual churning of leadership and membership caused by the impermanence of unemployment. Another was the debilitating effects of unemployment: Joblessness, for some, often led to despair, apathy, and listlessness, rather than rebellion.[72] Because of the persistence of the work ethic throughout the Depression,[73] many of those without work began to see themselves as worthless. Such men and women were more likely to withdraw from society than to actively protest against it; the last thing they wanted was to publicly identify themselves as "reliefers" by participating in jobless associations. Finally, there was the battle for survival itself: Unemployed workers often were too absorbed in their own personal struggles for food and housing to concern themselves with political action. Not only individualist efforts, but also collective sharing and cooperation among kinship networks, neighbors, and ethnic groups absorbed the full energies of many unemployed workers.

Given these formidable barriers—persistent and often violent repression by government and business, the strength of cultural values which inhibited jobless political activity especially of the radical variety, and the inherent problems involved in basing a revolutionary movement on the unemployed—it becomes clear that the accomplishments of the thirties unemployed movement are more notable than its failures. It remains a significant example of a locally based, grassroots organization under radical leadership that worked creatively and militantly to meet the concrete, immediate needs of the unemployed.

NOTES

I would like to sincerely thank the following people for their helpful comments and suggestions on this article: Herbert Benjamin, Elizabeth Blackmar, Ellen Malino James, Jim O'Brien, Frances Fox Piven, Marion Shapiro, and Ann Withorn. None of these people is responsible for my interpretations, and Mr. Benjamin, in particular, is critical of some of my formulations.

1. *The New York Times*, March 8, 1930.

2. Robert R. Nathan, "Estimates of Unemployment in the United States, 1929–1935," *International Labour Review* 33 (Jan. 1936): 49–73.

3. Irving Bernstein, *The Lean Years* (Baltimore, Md., 1966), pp. 255–257; John A. Garraty, "Unemployment During the Great Depression," *Labor History* 17 (Spring 1976): 134; Mark Naison, "The Communist Party in Harlem: 1928–1936," unpublished Ph.D. dissertation, Columbia University, 1975, p. 49.

4. William Leuchtenberg, *FDR and the New Deal* (New York, 1963), p. 26.

5. The definitive work on cooperative self-help is Clark Kerr, "Productive Self-Help Enterprises of the Unemployed," unpublished Ph.D. dissertation, University of California, 1939. See also "Cooperative Self-Help Activities Among the Unemployed," *Monthly Labor Review* 36 (March, April, May, and June 1933); Daniel J. Leab, "Barter and Self-Help Groups, 1932–33," *Midcontinent American Studies Journal* 3 (Spring 1966): 15–24. On stealing and coal bootlegging see *Federated Press*, Dec. 10, 1933, and Oct. 4, 1932; Louis Adamic, *My America* (New York, 1938), pp. 316–324; Bernstein, *Lean Years*, pp. 422–425. E. Wight Bakke discusses the unemployed worker's struggle to maintain his self-reliance in *The Unemployed Worker* (New Haven, 1940), pp. 363–385.

6. For a discussion of some of the issues involved in radical historiography of radicalism see Aileen Kraditor, "American Radical Historians on Their Heritage,"

Past and Present, No. 56 (Aug. 1972), pp. 136–153, and James R. Green, "American Radical Historians on Their Heritage," *Past and Present*, no. 69 (Nov. 1975), pp. 123–130.

7. Irving Howe and Lewis Coser, *The American Communist Party* (Boston, 1957), p. 225; Nathan Glazer, *The Social Basis of American Communism* (New York, 1961), pp. 38–89.

8. Howe, *Communist Party*, p. 178.

9. *Labor Unity*, Sept. 14, 1929.

10. "Notes of the Month," *The Communist* 9 (March 1930): 198.

11. Harold D. Lasswell and Dorothy Blumenstock, *World Revolutionary Propaganda—A Chicago Study* (New York, 1939), p. 44.

12. Daniel J. Leab, "United We Eat: The Out-of-Work, the Unemployed Councils, and the Communists, 1930–1933," unpublished M.A. thesis, Columbia University, 1961, p. 72.

13. Lasswell, *Propaganda*, pp. 43–44.

14. *Labor Unity*, July 16, 1930.

15. Interview with Herbert Benjamin, Washington, D.C., Feb. 7, 1973.

16. *The Daily Worker*, Jan. 16, 21, 22, 27, 31, and Feb. 4, 5, 6, 1930; *The New York Times*, Feb. 12, 15, 22, 28, 1930.

17. "Notes of the Month," *The Communist* 9 (March 1930): 198; Lasswell, *Propaganda*, pp. 191–193. See also *Labor Unity*, Feb. 1, 22, 1930.

18. While *The Daily Worker* claimed that 110,000 gathered in New York's Union Square, *The New York Times* reported that only 35,000 demonstrated. *The Daily Worker*, March 7, 1930; *The New York Times*, March 7, 1930. See also *Labor Unity*, March 15, 1930; M. J. Olgin, "From March Sixth to May First," *The Communist* 9 (May 1930): 417–422; S. Mingulin, "The Crisis in the U.S. and the Problems of the CP," *The Communist* 9 (June 1930): 500–518.

19. Martin E. Sullivan, "On the Dole: The Relief Issue in Detroit, 1929–1939," unpublished Ph.D. dissertation, Notre Dame University, 1974, p. 45.

20. *The New York Times*, March 7, 1930; John Dos Passos, "Back to Red Hysteria!," *The New Republic* 63 (July 2, 1930): 168.

21. Daniel J. Leab, "'United We Eat': The Creation and Organization of the Unemployed Councils in 1930," *Labor History* 8 (Fall 1967): 313. See also for example *Labor Unity*, March 29, May 10, June 18, and Sept. 10, 1930.

22. Naison, "Harlem," pp. 54, 57; *The Daily Worker*, Jan. 31, 1930; St. Clair Drake and Horace Cayton, *Black Metropolis* (New York, 1945), p. 87; Johnson quoted in Leab, "United," M.A. thesis, p. 71.

23. *Labor Unity*, April 5 and July 16, 1930. The Program of Action adopted at the July Convention declared: "The local TUUL Council shall lead and direct the activity of the unemployed movement."

24. Clarence A. Hathaway, "An Examination of Our Failure to Organize the Unemployed," *The Communist* 9 (Sept. 1930): 789; A. Allen, "Unemployed Work—Our Weak Point," *The Communist* 11 (Aug. 1932): 684. Both *The Party Organizer* and *The Communist* are filled with complaints about the "organizational weakness" of the Unemployed Councils. See for example Earl Browder, "Report of the Political Committee to the 12th Central Committee," *The Communist* 10 (Jan. 1931): 7–31; Jack Johnstone, "Overcome Looseness in Our Mass Work," *The Communist* 10 (March 1931): 324–329; Clarence A. Hathaway, "On the Use of

'Transmission Belts' in Our Struggle for the Masses," *The Communist* 10 (May 1931): 409–423.

25. Robert E. Asher, "The Influence of the Chicago Workers' Committee on Unemployment Upon the Administration of Relief, 1931–1934," unpublished M.A. thesis, University of Chicago, 1934, p. 72.

26. Glazer, *Social Basis*, p. 101.

27. *Labor Unity*, Aug. 1, 1930; Leab, "United," *Labor History*, p. 310; *The New York Times*, March 15, 17, 1930; "Notes of the Month," *The Communist* 9 (April 1930): 294; Israel Amter, "The Revolutionary Upsurge and the Struggles of the Unemployed," *The Communist* 12 (Feb. 1933): 115.

28. Mauritz Hallgren, *Seeds of Revolt* (New York, 1933), p. 336; Adamic quoted in Leab, "United," M.A. thesis, p. 75. For a similar assessment see Edmund Wilson, *The American Jitters* (New York, 1932), p. 12.

29. Hathaway, "Failure to Organize," p. 791; *The Daily Worker*, Nov. 8, 1930; Leab, "United," *Labor History*, pp. 314–315.

30. Lasswell, *Propaganda*, p. 343. Probably the most dramatic and effective of the Chicago demonstrations was that of October 31, 1932, which mobilized 25,000 jobless. Asher, "Chicago," pp. 21–22; *Chicago Tribune*, Nov. 1, 1932; *Chicago Defender*, Nov. 15, 1932.

31. Charles R. Walker, "Relief and Revolution," *The Forum* 88 (Sept. 1932): 115; Helen Seymour, "The Organized Unemployed," unpublished M.A. thesis, University of Chicago, 1937, p. 108; Virginia C. Searls, "Cuyahoga County Relief Administration Clients as Members of the Unemployment Council," unpublished M.S. thesis, Western Reserve University, 1935, pp. 34–35.

32. Edmund Wilson, "Detroit Motors," *The New Republic* 66 (March 25, 1931): 145. Ellen James, who is studying relief in New York City in the Depression, aruges that pressure from City Hall was the major force in stopping evictions in New York, at least. Ellen Malino James, "Reform in NYC Welfare Before the New Deal," paper read at American Historical Association Convention, Atlanta, 1975.

33. Naison, "Harlem," pp. 71, 122, 138, 140; Drake and Cayton, *Black Metropolis*, p. 87; *The New York Times*, Aug. 4, 5, 1931; Lasswell, *Propaganda*, pp. 196–201. See also Horace R. Cayton, "The Black Bugs," *Nation* 133 (Sept. 9, 1931): 225–256.

34. "Directives of the Political Secretariat of the ECCI to the CP of the U.S.A. Relative to the Decisions of the 12th Plenum of the C.P.U.S.A.," *The Communist* 10 (May 1931): 403; *Labor Unity*, March 28, 1931; Earl Browder, "Faith in the Masses—Organization of the Masses," *The Communist* 10 (July 1931): 609; Naison, "Harlem," pp. 120–121.

35. Bernstein, *Lean Years*, p. 422; Mauritz Hallgren, "Grave Danger in Detroit," *Nation* 135 (Aug. 3, 1932): 99; Leab, "United," M.A. thesis, p. 68; *The New York Times*, Jan. 21, 1931; Browder, "Faith," p. 609; interview with Benjamin; Lasswell, *Propaganda*, p. 346.

36. Alex Baskin, "The Ford Hunger March," *Labor History* 13 (Summer 1972): 331–360.

37. Interview with Benjamin.

38. *Labor Unity*, Sept. 5, Oct. 17, and Dec. 5, 1931, and Jan. 1932; *New York Times*, Dec. 7–9, 1931, and Dec. 3–7, 1932; John Dos Passos, "Red Day on Capitol Hill," *New Republic* 69 (Dec. 23, 1931): 153–155; Edward Dahlberg, "Hunger on the

March," *Nation* 135 (Dec. 28, 1932): 642–644; Edward L. Israel, "Hunger and Clubs," *The World Tomorrow*, Dec. 21, 1932, pp. 587–589; Labor Research Associates, "Analysis of the Questionnaires Filled Out by Certain Hunger Marchers Who Participated in the National Hunger March to Washington, December 6, 1932," in Unemployed Council Folder in University of Michigan Library, Ann Arbor. The hunger marches deserve a fuller treatment than space permits here, or than they have received from most historians.

39. Irene Oppenheimer, "The Organizations of the Unemployed, 1930–1940," unpublished M.A. thesis, Columbia University, 1940, p. 36. Frances Fox Piven, "The Depression Movement of the Unemployed," unpublished paper, discusses the post-1933 history of the unemployed movement.

40. Stanley High, "Who Organized the Unemployed?," *Saturday Evening Post*, Dec. 16, 1938, p. 35.

41. Minutes of the National Executive Committee (NEC), Feb. 28–March 1, 1931, Socialist Party mss., Duke University; Labor and Socialist Press Service (hereafter cited as LSPS), March 15, Nov. 22, and Dec. 13, 1930, and Jan. 3, March 7, and March 14, 1931; "Suggested Program for Unemployment Councils, July 1, 1931," SP mss.

42. Membership Report, 1935, Thomas mss., New York Public Library. On the SP in the twenties and thirties, see Daniel Bell, *Marxian Socialism in the United States* (Princeton, N.J., 1967); Harry Fleischman, *Norman Thomas* (New York, 1964); Bernard Johnpoll, *Pacifist's Progress* (Chicago, 1970); David Shannon, *The Socialist Party of America* (New York, 1955).

43. Clarence Senior to members of the NEC, July 13, 1935, Thomas mss.; Seymour, "Organized Unemployed," p. 23. See also *New Leader*, Dec. 12, 1931.

44. The LID was formed out of the old Intercollegiate Socialist Society in 1921. LID, *Thirtieth Anniversary Report* (New York, 1935).

45. Asher, "Chicago," passim.

46. "People's Unemployment League of Baltimore," *Monthly Labor Review* (May 1933); Roy Rosenzweig, "Radicals in the Great Depression: Socialists and the Unemployed, 1929–1936," unpublished paper, Jan. 1974.

47. *New Leader*, Feb. 6, 13, and March 12, 1932.

48. Rosenzweig, "Socialists."

49. Asher, "Chicago," p. 23; interview with Frank Trager, New York, May 17, 1973; Naomi Ritches to author, May 3, 1973.

50. Roy Rosenzweig, "Radicals and the Jobless: The Musteites and the Unemployed Leagues, 1932–1936," *Labor History* 16 (Winter 1975): 52–77.

51. Ibid.; Louis Budenz, "Jobless—A Longtime Job," *Labor Action*, Jan. 21, 1933.

52. Rosenzweig, "Musteites," passim.

53. Fred Donaldson, "Father Cox's Hunger Marchers," *Labor Age* 20 (Feb. 1932): 11–13; *The New York Times*, Jan. 3, 6, 7, 8, 9, 17, 24, 1932; *Federated Press*, Jan. 4, 1932.

54. Donald J. Lisio, *The President and Protest: Hoover, Conspiracy, and the Bonus Riot* (Columbia, Mo., 1974); Roger Daniels, *The Bonus March: An Episode of the Great Depression* (Westport, Conn., 1971).

55. E. Wight Bakke, *Citizens Without Work* (New Haven, 1940), pp. 59–64.

56. Donaldson, "Cox," p. 12.

57. Lisio, *Protest*, pp. 317–318.

58. On middle-class unemployed see Alfred Winslow Jones, *Life, Liberty, and Property* (Philadelphia, 1941); O. Milton Hall, "Attitudes and Unemployment: A Comparison of the Opinions and Attitudes of Employed and Unemployed Men," *Archives of Psychology*, no. 165 (March 1934), pp. 5–65; Bernard Sternsher, "The Other America in the Twenties and Thirties," paper read at American Historical Association Convention, Atlanta, 1975.

59. Lisio, *Protest*, p. 82.

60. *The New Leader*, Jan. 23, 1932.

61. Rosenzweig, "Musteites," passim.

62. On unemployment insurance see Daniel Nelson, *Unemployment Insurance: The American Experience, 1915–1935* (Madison, Wis., 1969).

63. Searls, "Cuyahoga County," pp. 74–75.

64. Studs Terkel, *Hard Times* (New York, 1970), p. 339.

65. Frank Trager to Norman Thomas, March 7, 1934, Thomas mss.

66. Ibid.

67. American Civil Liberties Union, "What Rights for the Unemployed?" (New York, 1935), p. 4; Bakke, *Citizens*, p. 65.

68. Robert S. and Helen M. Lynd, *Middletown in Transition* (New York, 1937), p. 41. See also Robert S. McElvaine, "Thunder Without Lightning: Working-Class Discontent in the United States, 1929–1937," unpublished Ph.D. dissertation, SUNY at Binghamton, 1974; Jones, *Life, Liberty*; Sternsher, "The Other America."

69. Bakke, *Citizens*, p. 61.

70. Homer L. Morris, *The Plight of the Bituminous Coal Miner* (Philadelphia, 1934), p. 111; Bakke, *Unemployed Worker*, p. 189.

71. James Cannon quoted in Leab, "United," M.A. thesis, p. iv.

72. Philip Eisenberg and Paul Lazarsfeld, "The Psychological Effects of Unemployment," *Psychological Bulletin* 35 (1938): 358–390; Sternsher, "The Other America."

73. See for example Warren Susman, ed., *Culture and Commitment, 1929–1945* (New York, 1973), p. 68.

CHAPTER NINE

The Possibility
of Radicalism in the
Early 1930s:
The Case of Steel

by Staughton Lynd

Recent historians associated with the Left have found industrial union organizing in the 1930s puzzling. We have declined to join in the liberal celebration of its results, pointing to "the partial integration of company and union bureaucracies" in administering CIO contracts (C. Wright Mills)[1] and the CIO's "definition of union organizing that made it impossible . . . to concentrate on political organization that challenged capitalist institutions" (Mark Naison).[2] We have dwelt on happenings which for liberal historians are merely preliminary or transitory, such as the mass strikes in Toledo, Minneapolis, and San Francisco in 1934,[3] the improvisation from below of local industrial unions and rank-and-file action committees,[4] or the many indications of interest in a Labor Party or Farmer-Labor Party.[5]

But this is not enough. In the 1890s, the drive for industrial unionism under Eugene Debs led to a confrontation with a Democratic president, recognition of the need for independent labor politics, and the formation of the Socialist Party. There was a step-by-step transition, first to economic organization on a broader scale, then to political organization, very much in the manner outlined in *The Communist Manifesto*. This did not happen in the 1930s (or at first glance *appears* not to have happened), and we must ask why. I believe that there is a connection between the difficulty experienced

Reprinted from Vol. 6, No. 6 (November-December 1972).

by New Left historians in answering this question, and the difficulty experienced by New Left working-class organizers. If we had a better idea how radicals should have acted while unions were being organized, we might better understand how they should act today. This essay considers the case of steel.

When the National Recovery Administration came into existence in June 1933, the feeble AFL union in the steel industry—the Amalgamated Association of Iron, Steel, and Tin Workers—reported less than 5,000 members. By the time of the Amalgamated's annual convention in April 1934 its membership had increased to a number variously estimated at 50,000 to 200,000.[6] Harvey O'Connor, then a labor reporter living in Pittsburgh, remembers it this way:

> Along came the New Deal, and then came the NRA, and the effect was electric all up and down those valleys. The mills began reopening somewhat, and the steelworkers read in the newspapers about this NRA Section 7A that guaranteed you the right to organize. All over the steel country union locals sprang up spontaneously. Not by virtue of the Amalgamated Association; they couldn't have cared less. But these locals sprang up at Duquesne, Homestead, and Braddock. You name the mill town and there was a local there, carrying a name like the "Blue Eagle" or the "New Deal" local. These people had never had any experience in unionism. All they knew was that, by golly, the time had come when they could organize and the Government guaranteed them the right to organize![7]

This remarkable organizing drive was carried out by rank-and-file steelworkers with little help from full-time organizers of the Amalgamated. At the U.S. Steel Edgar Thomson Works in Braddock, for example, an Amalgamated organizer provided membership cards and volunteer organizers from the mill returned in a week with 500 of them signed.[8] Walter Galenson wrongly terms the Amalgamated organizing campaign of 1933 "unsuccessful."[9] As a matter of fact, the Amalgamated drive between June 1933 and April 1934 signed up about the same number of steelworkers that the Steel Workers Organizing Committee, using 200 full-time organizers, signed up in a comparable period of time, from June 1936 to March 1937.

The self-organization of the rank and file was at least as effective as the top-down professionalism of the CIO, which had far greater resources at its disposal. Galenson himself quotes Lee Pressman as saying that as of the spring of 1937 SWOC could not have won an NLRB election "on the basis of our own membership or the results of the organizing campaign to date" in either Big or Little Steel.[10] The best testimony to this effect comes from the man who collected SWOC dues, David J. McDonald, later president of the United Steelworkers of America. "Contrary to union propaganda—some of which I helped to write—the steelworkers did not fall all over themselves to sign a pledge card with the SWOC," McDonald states in his autobiography.

What we hoped would be a torrent turned out, instead, to be a trickle. Under our arrangement with the Amalgamated, it would charter a local union as soon as we had enough men signed up in a plant to form the nucleus of an effective organization. Oftentimes the locals consisted of the half-dozen men daring enough to sign the charter application. When these skeleton requests straggled in, we assigned impressively high lodge numbers in the hope that outsiders would think we had that many locals. Only Murray and I knew how thin the tally was, although Lewis would insist on the truth whenever I visited Washington, then would shake his head in wonderment at the lack of progress.[11]

According to McDonald, SWOC membership was a "shaky 82,000" at the end of 1936, and when U.S. Steel signed a contract in March 1937, SWOC had signed up only 7 percent of its employees.

McDonald offers a hatful of explanations for steelworkers' absence of response to SWOC: a 50-year tradition of non-unionism, the fear of losing jobs, and the fact that some workers "were as apprehensive about dictatorship from an international union as they were of arm-twisting from their employer." Only the last of these makes any sense when one recalls that just three years before the same steelworkers had enthusiastically organized local unions. The question presents itself: Why did the organizing drive of 1933–1934, strongly supported by the rank and file, fail to achieve the union recognition accomplished by the SWOC drive of 1936–1937 with weaker rank-and-file backing?

The rank and file sought to achieve union recognition through the Amalgamated in 1933, 1934, and 1935. The 1933 effort was the by-product of a spontaneous strike by coal miners in the "captive mines" of western Pennsylvania owned by the steel companies.[12] These miners joined the United Mine Workers after the passage of the NIRA just as steelworkers were joining the Amalgamated. Late in July, miners at the H. C. Frick mines owned by U.S. Steel struck for recognition of their new UMW locals and the right to elect checkweighmen. UMW president John L. Lewis agreed with President Roosevelt that the men would go back to work and that their grievances would be referred to a special government board. The men refused, their representatives voting 123 to 4 against returning to work for the present. A 44-year-old Irish immigrant named Martin Ryan emerged as their spokesman. By the end of September 1933, 70,000 miners were on strike.

Then the strike spread to steelworkers. On September 26 miners marched into Clairton, Pennsylvania, where the largest coke plant in the United States made fuel for U.S. Steel mills throughout the Monongahela Valley. Hundreds of coal miners and an estimated half of the workforce at Clairton "circled the gates of the Clairton steel and by-products works in an endless march, day and night." Meanwhile at Weirton, West Virginia, 50 miles away, 12,000 more steelworkers went out demanding recognition of their new lodges of the Amalgamated. The national president of the Amalgamated, Michael Tighe, declared both the Clairton and the Weirton strike "outlaw."

John L. Lewis and Philip Murray, leaders of the UMW and future leaders of the SWOC and CIO, persisted in attempting to get the miners back to work. O'Connor describes the part played by Murray:

> Vice President Murray of the United Mine Workers summoned the rank-and-file leaders to Pittsburgh. "Today," he warned them, "you are fighting the coal companies; but tonight, if you remain on strike, you will be fighting the Government of the United States. Today you are conducting a strike; tonight you will be conducting a rebellion. Today we may say we are going to defy the greatest friend we've ever had in the history of this nation (President Roosevelt). But I tell you, friends, he can turn against you as strong as he's been for you. He can call out the Army and Navy."

Martin Ryan, leader of the striking miners, answered Murray: "Why do you ask 75,000 men to go back to work instead of telling one man [President Moses of the Frick Company] to sign the contract?" The rank-and-file delegates returned to Fayette County and called 20,000 miners together to consider Murray's back-to-work order. The miners voted to continue their strike until the Frick Company signed a contract.

Finally, on October 30, 1933, Lewis and Murray signed a contract on behalf of Frick's miners with none other than Myron Taylor, the same man who would sign a contract with them in March 1937 concerning steelworkers employed by U.S. Steel. Historians differ as to how much this contract achieved for the miners, but whatever it achieved was thanks to the pressure from below of men who struck without authorization and who refused Lewis's and Murray's orders to go back to work. The striking steelworkers achieved nothing. At Weirton, the strikers returned to work with a promise that an election for union representation would be held on December 15. The election turned out to be an election for company-union representatives. In the words of O'Connor: "The grand tactical plan for the united front of steel's mine and mill workers, conceived on the spur of the moment by local rank-and-file leaders in both industries, had been scuttled by a stronger united front, that of Washington, the union leaders, and the steel companies."

The leaders of the Weirton strike, Billy Long and Mel Moore, now joined with other presidents of new Amalgamated lodges to launch a second effort to unionize steel. On March 25, 1934, 257 delegates from 50 of the newly formed lodges met in Pittsburgh to plan strategy for the Amalgamated convention the following month.[13] First among equals was Clarence Irwin, president of the Amalgamated lodge at the Brier Hill works of

Youngstown Sheet and Tube, Youngstown, Ohio, and of the Sixth District of the Amalgamated, which included Youngstown, Canton-Masillon-Mansfield, and Cleveland.

Irwin is dead now, but Robert R. R. Brooks of Yale University interviewed him in the late 1930s, and further information can be gleaned from a scrapbook in the possession of his wife. Irwin was the antithesis of the demagogue usually placed at the head of crowds by historians. In 1934, at the age of 42, he had worked at steel mills in the Mahoning Valley since 1906, and had belonged to the Amalgamated since 1910. He was chairman of the strike committee in his mill during the 1919 steel strike. He was married and had three children. He was a skilled roller and had voted Democratic all his life, except in 1932, when he voted for Norman Thomas.

Irwin describes the other rank-and-file leaders as very much like himself:

> Almost all of us were middle-aged family men, well paid, and of Anglo-Saxon origin. Most of us were far better off than the average steelworker and didn't have much to gain from taking part in the movement except a certain amount of personal prestige. Almost all of us could have done better for ourselves if we had stuck with the companies and not bothered about the rest of the men. But for various reasons we didn't.

We were sure, he goes on,

> that the mass of steelworkers wanted industrial unionism, and so did we. But it wasn't clear to us until we set out to get it that we would have to fight not only the companies but our own international officers and even the Government. The process of learning was slow and painful, and a lot of us dropped by the way.[14]

Contrary to John L. Lewis's subsequent allegations, "All these fellows had a union inheritance of one kind or another." Long's father had been a militant in the Amalgamated Association of Iron, Steel, and Tin Workers, and Earl Forbeck's father had been a Knight of Labor.[15] Moreover, the rank-and-file presidents of the new lodges developed the practice of calling together lodge representatives in district conferences. These district meetings had no constitutional standing. They had been used years before for the purpose of informal discussion of common organizational problems, and in the course of time had died out. Now they were revived, at first with the sanction of the national officers, who attended and spoke at many of the conferences. In time more or less permanent officers were chosen for each district.[16]

The March 25 gathering brought together delegates from lodges all over the country. A general strike was in progress in Toledo; the very day the steelworkers met a national strike in auto had been averted; general strikes in Minneapolis and San Francisco were little more than a month in the future. Steelworkers, too, turned to the strike weapon. Delegates decided to take back to their lodges, for proposed presentation to the Amalgamated

194

convention on April 17, the following strategy: All lodges should request recognition from management at the same time; if recognition is denied, a strike date should be set; the Auto Workers, the Mine Workers, and the Railroad Workers should be approached with the idea that these three groups, together with steelworkers, should act together if necessary to gain collective bargaining for any one group. What was envisioned was a national strike, and if need be a national general strike, for union recognition.

The Amalgamated convention adopted this strategy. The convention also adopted resolutions to the effect that the Committee of Ten rank-and-file leaders which had drawn up the strike program should be included in all negotiations arising from it, that no lodge should sign an agreement until all could sign at once, that full-time Amalgamated organizers should be elected rather than appointed, and that the national union should no longer have the power to declare locally initiated strikes unauthorized.[17] The new members of the union appeared to have taken it over from the incumbent leadership.

The rank-and-file leaders understandably found this historic opportunity frightening. "Most of us were capable local or district leaders," Irwin recalls, "but we had very little idea what the national picture was like. . . . We were completely unprepared for a strike. We had no funds, no central leadership, no national organization except the Amalgamated's officers, and they were opposed to strike action." Irwin and his co-workers began to look for help.

They turned first to a group of four intellectuals: Heber Blankenhorn, Harold Ruttenberg, Harvey O'Connor, and Stephen Raushenbush. Blankenhorn had edited the Interchurch World Commission report on the 1919 steel strike. He was close to John L. Lewis and Senator Wagner, and later helped to create the LaFollette Civil Liberties Committee. Ruttenberg was a student at the University of Pittsburgh doing research on the steel industry, O'Connor a labor journalist who during this period published *Mellon's Millions*, and Raushenbush an investigator for the Nye Committee.

Appearing at the 1934 Amalgamated convention with a typewriter, Ruttenberg (and O'Connor) assisted the rank-and-file delegates in "putting together the resolutions they wanted the way they wanted them and getting things going."[18] Thereafter they functioned as a behind-the-scenes leadership group cryptically known (because Blankenhorn in particular was concerned lest his association with the rank and file become public) as "The Big Four." "Although they had no money and had to work on the q.t.," remembers Irwin, "[they] gave us something like national leadership. In a way, they were a forerunner of the Steel Workers Organizing Committee."

I believe it is fair to characterize the Big Four (with the partial exception of O'Connor) as Social Democratic intellectuals, in the sense that they had a tendency to rely on publicity and government intervention rather than on the collective power of the workers, and to avoid co-operation with the Communist Party.

But four men with typewriters and connections could not really be the functional equivalent of a SWOC. According to the decisions of the Amalgamated convention, all lodges were to ask for recognition on May 21, and if recognition was refused a strike date was to be set for the middle of June. On May 7 Irwin wrote to Ruttenberg asking if Ruttenberg could get him the addresses of the men who had led the 1933 strike in the captive mines, and of the leaders of the Steel and Metal Workers Industrial Union (SMWIU).

The SMWIU was one of the dual unions sponsored by the Communist Party during the so-called Third Period of international Communist strategy.[19] It was founded in August 1932 and claimed a membership of 10,000 to 15,000. The SMWIU justly denounced the NRA. It called on working people to rely on their own power rather than on presidential promises, government boards, and so-called labor leaders. By May 1934 it had led local strikes, for instance in Warren, Ohio; East Chicago, Indiana; and Ambridge, Pennsylvania. These had often ended in violent defeat.

After the Warren strike, which resulted in the discharge of many strikers and the departure from the city of an entire community of Finnish steelworkers, the local Communist Party "was convinced of the impossibility to organize independent labor unions in opposition to the old AFL"[20] and sought to persuade William Z. Foster and other national Party leaders to abandon dual unionism in steel. The rank-and-file movement in the Amalgamated offered the SMWIU an opportunity to overcome its isolation from the mass of steelworkers. And the SMWIU offered the rank-and-file movement, which had lost its own local strikes at Clairton and Weirton, the national structure and resources so badly needed if a national steel strike were to become a reality.

The difficulty was that in May 1934 the SMWIU had not abandoned the dual unionist line. SMWIU literature urged its members and sympathizers simultaneously to "take the lead in the organization of united committees" to implement the decisions of the convention and to prepare for a strike— and "to build the SMWIU into a powerful organization in their mill."[21] This was a tactic which looked two ways at once. It never has worked, it never will work, and it did not work in the spring of 1934.

Irwin and Ruttenberg arranged a meeting with the SMWIU leadership for May 20. They urged all members of the Committee of Ten and of the Big Four to be there so as "to determine [in Irwin's words] a central plan of attack, set up a central office with a secretary, determine a uniform method of demanding recognition, find out what help the SMWIU could give us, and discover what the national officers were going to do to bust up our plans." Three days before the meeting, Irwin wrote to Ruttenberg that the only alliance which should be sought with the SMWIU was cooperation on the conduct of the strike. That cooperation should be basically through local joint committees which would work in unison even against the orders of the Amalgamated national office, Irwin believed.[22]

Tragically, Irwin was unable to attend the meeting because his wife was seriously ill. He was represented by Ruttenberg, subsequently research director for SWOC, co-author with Clinton Golden of *The Dynamics of Industrial Democracy*, and steel company executive. Blankenhorn was apparently not at the meeting, but his taped reminiscences make it clear that he was part of the discussion.

> There were telegrams to me, and as a matter of fact I was in Pittsburgh when that meeting was held, and talked with Pat Cush [one of the SMWIU leaders] and the SMWIU boys, and tried to get the brass tacks on it, and in front of them I advised the rank-and-filers: "If these boys won't walk out of here and keep their mouths shut instead of making public pronouncements, you have no choice but simply to say that they came and saw you but you had nothing to do with them. If they have any paid members to deliver, let them deliver them quietly."

Blankenhorn and Ruttenberg persuaded the rank-and-file leaders not to work with the SMWIU.[23]

Yet responsibility for the failure of the May 20 meeting falls equally on the SMWIU. In contrast to Irwin's proposals for cooperation visible at a local level but behind the scenes nationally, "They [the SMWIU] wanted the rank-and-file group and the SMWIU to issue a joint statement from this meeting, a joint call for a joint convention to focus public attention on the issues, and local organizations to issue joint statements and call joint mass meetings. It was perfectly clear that they wanted to formalize the whole affair, and to be sure that the SMWIU was in the limelight as an organization. As soon as they had withdrawn [from the meeting], the rank-and-file group voted thumbs down on the whole proposition. We'd have been smeared immediately as Communists if we had accepted."

These words from Irwin's interview with Brooks are perhaps more those of Ruttenberg than those of Irwin, who was not at the meeting.[24] But the fact remains that the SMWIU approach counterposed a Left dual union not only to the national structure of the Amalgamated, but also to the independent local lodges that the steelworkers had built for themselves. Then and later the rank-and-filers showed themselves quite able to stand up to Red-baiting, and had the SMWIU not placed so much emphasis on its own organization, I believe united action might have been possible. The fact that (to look ahead) the rank-and-file leaders and the former SMWIU leaders easily established a working relationship the next November, after the SMWIU finally abandoned dual unionism, is strong evidence to this effect.

In May and June, after the failure of the May 20 meeting, things went from bad to worse. On May 22 five of the rank-and-file leaders went to the national office of the Amalgamated and demanded $100,000 from the union to help run the strike, the use of the union's printing press, and rooms in the union's building for strike headquarters. They were contemptuously refused. Irwin then proposed to the rest of the Committee of Ten "that we would take over the running of the strike altogether, call upon the lodges for money (my lodge had already put up a hundred dollars), and select a secretary from our own group." Only two other members of the Committee supported this leap into the unknown. "I was never so disgusted in my life," Irwin remembers.

At this point the four intellectuals stepped back onto center stage, urging the rank-and-filers to take their campaign to Washington, where they could attract national press attention and hopefully embarrass the president into intervening on their behalf. Desperate, the rank-and-file leaders agreed. They got the publicity, but killed the possibility of a successful strike. As one of them commented after it was all over, "They spent most of their time in Washington in a futile attempt to 'see Roosevelt.' This running around after Roosevelt created the impression among the steelworkers that a strike was unnecessary, that Roosevelt would step in at the last minute and help them. . . ."[25] The precious weeks which might have been used for local strike preparation were squandered, as the national secretary of the SMWIU rightly observed.[26] In the First District of the Amalgamated near Pittsburgh, where more than a thousand steelworkers gathered to support the strike movement on May 27, a meeting a month later, after the strike had collapsed, attracted only 53.[27]

It now appears that in directing the rank-and-file leaders to Washington, Ruttenberg, Blankenhorn, and Raushenbush acted as agents for John L. Lewis. In interviews conducted by the Pennsylvania State Oral History Project in 1968 and 1969, Ruttenberg stated that a steel strike "did not come off because of the intervention of John Lewis and Philip Murray, who counseled against it for fear that an abortive strike would thwart their contemplated plans to move in and really organize the steel industry." The UMW had no contact with rank-and-file steelworkers until spring of 1934, Ruttenberg went on. "At that point they began to exercise influence through myself, and they assigned John Brophy from the UMW to be the liaison man." "Blankenhorn was the one who kept telling John Lewis and Philip Murray that they should get control of the rank-and-file committee and use them as a basis for their unionizing work." "And so the counsel that I got from Blankenhorn, which I in turn passed on to the steelworkers, was not to strike now because John Lewis was going to come here and have a big organizing campaign that would stand a chance of being successful." Raushenbush, for his part, "said that we have to show strength among the rank-and-file steelworkers in order to encourage John Lewis to take the risk. . . . And so you had the whole threatened strike and activity to influence John Lewis to come in as well as to influence Congress to pass a National Labor Relations Act."

Through Ruttenberg, Blankenhorn, and Raushenbush the rank-and-file leaders were brought before Senator Wagner, the sponsor of that act, who "gave them a lecture about not engaging in a premature strike and gave them a lecture that John Lewis was 'going to come in here and do this job right and don't you fellows mess it up'."[28] Putting this evidence together with Lewis's role during the coal and steel strikes of 1933, the hypothesis suggests itself that if Lewis succeeded in 1937 where the rank and file failed in 1934, it was partly because Lewis did his best to make sure that industrial unionism would come to steel only if he controlled it.

Meantime the steel companies had disdainfully refused to recognize the Amalgamated lodges, and the strike date approached. The companies placed large orders for the purchase of arms and, at least in Gary, arranged to house strike breakers in the mills should a strike occur.[29] As tension mounted the Amalgamated leadership called a special convention in Pittsburgh for mid-June, the time at which, according to the mandate of the convention, a strike date was to be set if recognition had been refused. Reporters, government mediators, delegates, and a confused group of rank-and-file leaders assembled for the convention.

The strategy of President Roosevelt, of the Amalgamated leadership, and apparently of Ruttenberg and associates and of John L. Lewis, was to have William Green, AFL president, come to the convention and propose yet another government labor board as an alternative to a walkout. Ruttenberg reports on the mood of labor officials and government representatives at the convention: "Social revolution was on hand. Bill Green was their only hope." Clinton Golden was one of three people who met Green at the train and "coached him as to what to say. He said it."[30] The strike was called off. As the news came over the radio in the bars in Braddock, steelworkers tore up their union cards.[31] Ruttenberg also tells us that Irwin got dead drunk and lost the confidence of many delegates, a situation for which Ruttenberg appears to feel he had no responsibility.

There was to be one more effort at unionization by the rank and file, in 1935. During the summer of 1934, Irwin "tried to keep the rank-and-file movement together by supporting the rank-and-file slate of officers that was running in the Amalgamated's fall referendum." In the October 1934 convention of the AFL a resolution was passed urging the AFL executive council to take action in organizing steel. Meanwhile the government board created in June to head off the threatened walkout had done nothing. "Production was picking up," Irwin remembers, "and the steelworkers were stirring again."

More important than any of these events was the fact that—six months too late—the Communist Party abandoned dual unionism. SMWIU chapters dissolved so that their members could join the Amalgamated. According to Irwin, in November 1934 rank-and-filers and SMWIU finally got together. Money became available for steelworkers to travel to conferences,[32] and a series of meetings began to heat up the idea of a national strike again. But whereas in the spring of 1934 the Communist Party wanted a steel strike only if the SMWIU could publicly help to lead it, in the spring of 1935 the Communist Party wanted a strike only if expulsion from the Amalgamated could be avoided. Remaining part of the organization they had previously scorned became the primary goal of Party members in steel.

These forces came to a head at a meeting of 400 rank-and-file steelworkers and 100 rank-and-file miners in Pittsburgh February 3, 1935. Our four intellectual friends played their by now familiar role. Ruttenberg wrote to Irwin before the conference warning him of Communist influence, and O'Connor wrote to Irwin after the conference, acting as an intermediary for an unnamed third party in Washington, to urge the rank and file not to act by itself but to consider cooperation with a committee on the AFL executive council to organize steel.[33]

Lewis, too, played a predictable part. Just as Michael Tighe, president of the Amalgamated, threatened to expel from the Amalgamated any steelworkers who attended the February 3 meeting, so Pat Fagan, district director of the UMW, issued similar warnings to dissident miners. After the meeting both men carried out their threats, Fagan stating: "You can't be a member of the UMW and be affiliated with a Red group. That meeting was absolutely Red. Those fellows don't believe in authority or law and order or anything else. They're an asinine crowd of parlor bolshevists!"[34] This is the same Pat Fagan who in April 1936 led a delegation of the Pennsylvania AFL state convention to the national Amalgamated convention nearby, and proposed that the Amalgamated accept $500,000 from John L. Lewis and work with him to organize steel.

Ruttenberg, Tighe, and Fagan notwithstanding, the gathering of rank-and-file steelworkers and miners took place as scheduled. It was an extraordinary occasion. Mr. and Mrs. Irwin, Bill Spang, Mel Moore, Roy Hallas, Cecil Allen, and Lew Morris represented the rank-and-file leadership in the Amalgamated. Present on behalf of the rank-and-file miners was Martin Ryan, leader of the 1933 strike in the captive mines. The lesson of 1933–1934 had been learned. A resolution was adopted that "the steelworkers know from their own experience that they can secure no help in their struggles from the labor boards or other Federal agencies, but that their only defense . . . is the power of their own organization, exercised by the calling of strikes if and when necessary."

This time, organization was not left to afterthought. A committee was named to open headquarters in Pittsburgh. Local finance committees were to be pressed into service at once. Most remarkable, in view of subsequent history, were speeches by Martin Ryan and (according to the press) numerous other speakers equally denouncing Michael Tighe and John L. Lewis. The one had betrayed the steelworkers and the other had betrayed the miners, according to the prevailing sentiment at this meeting. "Lewis and

Tighe have crucified you for years," declared Ryan, "and will continue to do so until you demand and get their resignation and removal."[35]

Why did these rank-and-file steelworkers and miners fail to press on toward a national organizing campaign? This time around, the Amalgamated leadership were not going to permit their national convention to be captured and used to legitimize a rebel movement. Within days of the February 3 meeting Tighe expelled the lodges represented there. What was critical was the rank and file's response to the expulsions. Here the Communist Party, with its newfound concern for labor unity, and John L. Lewis, jockeying in Washington for passage of the Wagner Act and Guffey Act, again had determining influence.

The expelled lodges represented the overwhelming majority of the Amalgamated membership.[36] They might simply have declared that they were the Amalgamated, or reorganized as federal unions directly affiliated with the AFL, and in either case proceeded to organize steel. It appears that many members of the rank-and-file movement—the rank and file of the rank and file, so to speak—wanted to do this. O'Connor reports that at the February 3 meeting "some difficulty was experienced in stemming the apparently powerful sentiment of many delegates . . . that an independent union should be started now."[37]

An independent union was exactly what the Communist Party had been trying to build the year before, but now no longer desired. The resources which might have financed an organizing drive were used instead to campaign for reinstatement in the Amalgamated. The National Organizing Committee set up by the February 3 meeting distributed 50,000 leaflets in April calling for "Unity For All Steel Workers." "Our program," the leaflet stated, "is the restoration of unity in the union and the organization of the unorganized steel workers."[38] Lawsuits followed to compel Tighe to reinstate the expelled lodges. These were successful, and on August 1, 1935 it was announced that unity had been restored. In the meantime, however, another strike threat had swelled up and been dissipated, with the result that the Amalgamated, to which the expellees won reinstatement in midsummer 1935, had by then been reduced to the empty shell it was two years before.

In dissipating the strike threat of 1935, Lewis's misleadership augmented the misleadership of the Communist Party. Early in March a meeting to implement the February 3 decisions was held in Weirton, attended by steelworkers from Illinois, Indiana, Ohio, Pennsylvania, and West Virginia. Conference speeches, the Federated Press reported, showed great sentiment for a strike in steel. Clarence Irwin declared that "The kind of union we are going to have will not depend on courts, but on organization and the picket line."

Later that month William Spang, president of District 1 of the Amalgamated, tied a steel strike to a strike of 400,000 soft-coal miners threatened for April 1. "Rank-and-file committees of steel workers and coal miners have been meeting to set up plans to strike April 1. If the United Mine Workers of America does not get a new contract, both unions will join in united strike action," Spang said. He added: "We have decided to disregard all arbitration boards. . . . There is only one way we can win our demands—by an industry-wide strike. That's just what we're building up for now."[39]

But there was no coal strike April 1. On the eve of the miners' walkout, John L. Lewis postponed action till June 16 "out of consideration of the President of the United States and the National Industrial Recovery Board."[40] On Memorial Day 1935, just two years before the Memorial Day strike sacred in CIO annals, the steel strike almost happened from below.

What at first seemed to the Federated Press "the long-expected clash in the steel industry" began in Canton, Ohio. "Rank-and-file leaders led it; not one union-paid official had a directing hand in it," Ruttenberg wrote. The strike began at the Berger Manufacturing Company, a wholly owned subsidiary of Republic Steel employing 450 persons. An AFL federal union at the plant struck to enforce a government finding that the company was refusing to bargain collectively. Two-hundred-fifty thugs attacked the strikers with tear gas and lead pipes. One striker, Charles Minor, had the side of his face torn off, and in all 14 persons were hospitalized. As so often in those years, this picket-line brutality triggered a general strike. Within 24 hours 4,000 Republic Steel employees in the Canton area had walked out in protest, led by Lewis Morris, one of the Committee of Ten of 1934.

Two other members of the Committee from nearby communities, Mel Moore from Weirton and Clarence Irwin from Youngstown, apparently tried to call a national strike. On May 29 they asked "all Republic mills to send delegates to Canton to formulate plans for spreading the strike nationally." On May 31 "The Central Strike Committee (in Canton) issued a call for support from all lodges of the Amalgamated." The only response, or parallel action, which has come to light was by Bill Spang's Fort Dukane Lodge in Duquesne, Pennsylvania. There a strike at the U.S. Steel mill was called for 3 P.M. May 31, but short-circuited when Spang and other officers of the lodge were arrested for parading without a permit. Meanwhile in Canton an attempt to spread the strike to neighboring Masillon collapsed when non-union employees flooded the Amalgamated lodge meeting and voted not to go out. County and city police broke up the Canton picket lines, and the men started back to the mills.[41]

Once more the rank and file looked to the UMW. "Following Spang's release, the Fort Dukane Lodge decided at a mass meeting to issue a call to other lodges to 'strike all Carnegie Steel Company [U.S. Steel] mills June 16,' the date set by the United Mine Workers of America for its strike in the bituminous fields." But Lewis postponed this strike too. On June 14 he promised President Roosevelt not to strike till June 30 so that Congress could act on the Guffey bill. On July 1 the coal strike was postponed for a third time, and on July 29 for a fourth. Meanwhile on July 5 the Wagner Act became law, and late in August the Guffey Act, setting up NRA-like machinery for the coal industry, finally made it through both houses of Congress.[42]

Two philosophies of industrial union organization expressed themselves in these events. Lewis's approach stressed governmental intervention so as to make possible a "responsible" unionism which would avoid strikes. As Len DeCaux summarized it at the time, Lewis and a number of other union officials told the Senate Education and Labor Committee considering the Wagner Act: "Allow the workers to organize, establish strong governmental machinery for dealing with labor questions, and industrial peace will result." DeCaux noted that some employers favored this approach, and that the expectation in Washington of international war made its adoption more likely.[43]

The second approach relied on strike action, and insisted on writing the right to strike into any labor-management contract which resulted. No one can prove that a national steel strike in 1934 or 1935 would have been any more successful than the defeated national steel strike of 1919. Yet it was Blankenhorn's retrospective judgment that "without even the pretense of Amalgamated leadership" the rank-and-file movement would have involved 75,000 to 150,000 steelworkers in a national strike; and O'Connor argued at the time that any strike in steel was likely to reach a climax within a few weeks, because the Government could not allow it to continue "in view of the restiveness of workers in the auto industry and other industries."[44]

Seeking proof in the experience of SWOC, one can argue that the Little Steel strike of 1937 shows what would have happened had steelworkers struck in 1934 or 1935. One can also argue that SWOC would never have gotten its contract with U.S. Steel in March 1937 had auto workers for General Motors not been willing to strike and occupy their plants just previously.

The trade-union line of the Communist Party after mid-1934 dovetailed neatly with the approach of John L. Lewis. The Party maneuvered brilliantly within the skeleton Amalgamated to have Lewis offer $500,000 to the Amalgamated for a steel drive, with the understanding that the money would be administered by Lewis, and to have the Amalgamated accept that offer.[45] When SWOC was formed, the Party made available 60 organizers.[46] The rank-and-file dream passed into the hands of Lewis in the bastardized form of an organizing committee none of whose national or regional officers were steelworkers, an organizing committee so centralized that it paid even local phone bills from a national office, an organizing committee, in De-Caux's words, "as totalitarian as any big business."[47]

It could have been otherwise. The critical weakness of the rank and file was its inability to organize on a national scale. Had the Communist Party thrown its organizers, its connections, and its access to media, lawyers, and money in a different direction, there might have come about an industrial unionism not only more militant and more internally democratic, but also more independent politically.

Coming about as it did, industrial unionism in steel lacked any thrust toward independent political action. By 1935 the rank-and-file leaders had lost confidence in the "National Run Around" and, to a considerable degree, in President Roosevelt. Experience daily brought more and more workers to the position that "we are through forever with Washington" (Mel Moore), "we're through with weak-kneed appeals to government boards" (Clarence Irwin).[48] They were prepared to defy the national government through strike action and to seek parallel strike action from workers in other industries. In effect they wanted to duplicate Toledo, Minneapolis, and San Francisco on a national scale. And despite Roosevelt's genius in letting local Democrats take the onus of state action against striking workers, a national steel strike might have brought steelworkers into collision with Roosevelt just as a national rail strike had brought Debs into collision with Cleveland in 1894.

Even as it was, there were indications of support among steelworkers for independent political action. In 1935, along with many other unions in that extraordinary year, the Fort Dukane and South Chicago lodges of the Amalgamated passed resolutions for (in the South Chicago wording) an "anti-capitalist Labor Party."[49] In 1936, Clarence Irwin stated that "I am in favor of a real Labor Party with no connection with any of the existing parties." The last clipping in his scrapbook describes a 1939 regional SWOC meeting which passed a motion stating: "Whereas labor's experience in the political field has been anything but satisfactory, therefore be it resolved that our ultimate goal be the fostering of a third party called the Labor Party."[50] Given the existence of this sentiment, at the very least it should have been possible to organize local labor parties which, after the death of Roosevelt in 1945, could have joined to form a deeply rooted national third party.

But industrial unionism came to steel and to the CIO generally under the auspices of a longtime Republican who at no point favored a third party, and of a national radical party which, by mid-1936, was uncritically supporting the incumbent Democratic President. The new industrial unions lost little time espousing the political company unionism of the two-party system.

NOTES

This essay brings together material some of which was initially presented in "Guerrilla History in Gary," *Liberation*, Oct. 1969; "What Happened to the Militancy of the CIO? Some Rank-and-File Views," a paper read at the American Historical Association meeting, Dec. 1970; and "Personal Histories of the Early CIO," *Radical America* 5, no. 3 (May-June 1971), reprinted as a pamphlet by the

New England Free Press. A collection of the interviews which are the basis of this work will be published by Beacon Press in 1973 under the title *Rank and File: Personal Accounts of Working-Class Organizing*, edited by Alice and Staughton Lynd. I should like to thank Professor Carroll Moody of Northern Illinois University for his remarkable scholarly generosity during my work on rank-and-file movements in steel. He permitted me to examine not only a first draft of a study on the rank-and-file movement in the Amalgamated Association of Iron, Steel, and Tin Workers, but the notes on which that study is based. I have made clear in the notes those few cases in which a statement in the present essay is made on the authority of Professor Moody's research. In general, however, this research makes it possible for me to advance more confidently conclusions which I had reached independently on the basis of personal recollections of steelworkers and of documents they had saved.

1. C. Wright Mills, *The New Men of Power: America's Labor Leaders* (New York, 1948), p. 224.

2. Mark Naison, "The Southern Tenant Farmers' Union and the CIO," *Radical America* 2, no. 5 (Sept.-Oct. 1968): 53. The present essay attempts to carry a step further the argument of Naison's splendid article.

3. Art Preis, *Labor's Giant Step: Twenty Years of the CIO* (New York, 1972), chap. 4.

4. Jeremy Brecher, *Strike!* (San Francisco, 1972), chap. 5 et passim.

5. Staughton Lynd, "Prospects for the New Left," *Liberation*, Winter 1971, p. 20.

6. Carroll Daugherty, Melvin de Chazeau, and Samuel Stratton, after stating, "What the actual membership strength of the Association was at different times under the Steel Code—how much the total number of fully paid-up and partially paid-up members came to—apparently no one knows," estimate the total membership in February 1934 at 50,000. *The Economics of the Iron and Steel Industry* (New York and London, 1937), vol. 2, p. 947 n. Vincent D. Sweeney, a Pittsburgh reporter in the early thirties and later public-relations director for SWOC (which would have had no reason to exaggerate the achievements of the Amalgamated), states: "No official figure of the growth of the union in that campaign has ever been made public. The peak was probably around 200,000." *The United Steelworkers of America Twenty Years Later, 1936–1956* (n.p., n.d.), p. 7. The rank-and-file leaders claimed 150,000 signed up as of April 1934. Harvey O'Connor, Federated Press dispatch April 30, 1934, Columbia University.

7. Harvey O'Connor, quoted in Staughton Lynd, "Personal Histories of the Early CIO," *Radical America* 5 (May-June 1971): 52–55.

8. My authority for this statement is a novel written by a steelworker which very closely follows the events of the 1930s and includes extracts from the minutes of the company union at the Edgar Thompson Works. Thomas Bell, *Out of This Furnace* (New York, 1950), p. 290.

9. Walter Galenson, *The CIO Challenge to the AFL: A History of the American Labor Movement, 1935–1941* (Cambridge, 1960), p. 75.

10. Ibid., p. 94.

11. David J. McDonald, *Union Man* (New York, 1969), p. 93ff.

12. This account of the captive mine strike of 1933 is based on: almost-daily dispatches of reporters for the Federated Press, July-Dec. 1933; Harvey O'Connor, *Steel—Dictator* (New York, 1935), chap. 14; Irving Bernstein, *Turbulent Years: A*

History of the American Worker, 1933–1941 (Boston, 1971), pp. 49–61; and Muriel Sheppard, *Cloud by Day: The Story of Coal and Coke and People* (Chapel Hill, 1947), chap. 10.

13. Harold Ruttenberg, "Steel Labor, the NIRA, and the Amalgamated Association," a detailed narrative of the rank-and-file movement of 1934 (Ruttenberg Papers, Pennsylvania State University). Unless otherwise indicated, statements about the 1934 movement are based on this source.

14. Robert R. R. Brooks, *As Steel Goes . . . : Unionism in a Basic Industry* (New Haven, 1940), chap. 3. This is an extraordinary interview, but must be used with care. Brooks interviewed Clarence Irwin, for Mrs. Irwin remembers the occasion. But the text of the so-called interview as published in *As Steel Goes . . .* draws on several sources, including Ruttenberg's narrative, as Brooks explicitly acknowledges. (See his footnote on p. 262.)

15. Interview with Heber Blankenhorn, Columbia University Oral History Project, pp. 437a and 438a. According to the minutes of the AFL executive council meeting of February 12, 1935, Lewis told this body: "You have to utilize the services of these young men in the steel industry. They have no training, no background in trade unionism, no experience in the labor movement." Professor Carroll Moody kindly called this statement to my attention.

16. Daugherty and associates, *Economics of the Iron and Steel Industry*, vol. 2, p. 959n.

17. The rank and file in the United Steelworkers of America, AFL-CIO, have repeatedly attempted to modify the USWA constitution in these same three ways—referendum vote on new contracts, election of staff men, local right to strike—and repeatedly failed.

18. O'Connor, "Personal Histories of the Early CIO."

19. This account of the SMWIU is based on Horace B. Davis, *Labor and Steel* (New York, 1933), especially pp. 257–258 and 264, and on interviews with three SMWIU organizers.

20. Address by Leon Callow, former SMWIU organizer in Youngstown, at Youngstwn State University, April 14, 1972.

21. SMWIU "Steel Workers! Organize and Prepare to Strike!" leaflet, O'Connor Papers, Wayne State University, n.d. (May or early June 1934). Professor Carroll Moody kindly made this document available to me.

22. Clarence Irwin to Harold Ruttenberg, May 17, 1934, Exhibit 10 attached to Ruttenberg's narrative.

23. Interview with Heber Blankenhorn, Columbia University Oral History Project, p. 444a. In Daugherty and associates, *Economics of the Iron and Steel Industry*, vol. 2, p. 1059, the statement is made that one or more of the Big Four persuaded the rank-and-file leaders to "turn down united-front offer from Leftwing Steel and Metal Workers" on May 20. Since Ruttenberg was a student of Daugherty's and did research for this study, we can be sure that this statement reflects Ruttenberg's views.

24. The quoted words are identical to words which Ruttenberg, in his narrative, has himself saying to Forbeck: "Number 3 (Ruttenberg) told Forbeck that they wanted to institutionalize the whole affair," and so forth.

25. Cecil Allen, open letter to "Fellow Steel Workers" (undated, but around July 1, 1934), Exhibit 34 attached to Ruttenberg's narrative. The Weirton leaders

had been to Washington prior to May 1934 to testify in their own behalf before the National Labor Board. As early as April, Bill Spang stated: "We're tired of sending delegations to Washington and of the endless run-around we get there." Federated Press dispatch, April 18, 1934.

26. Statement by James Egan to Harold Ruttenberg on June 5, 1934, Ruttenberg narrative, p. 23. On the same day an SMWIU delegation in Washington stated this criticism to the press. Federated Press dispatch, June 5, 1934.

27. Harold Ruttenberg to George Soule, July 6, 1934, Ruttenberg Papers.

28. Arthur S. Weinberg interview with Ruttenberg, May 12, 1968, and Don Kennedy interview with Ruttenberg, April 24, 1969, Pennsylvania State Oral History Project.

29. The statement about strike breakers is made on the basis of an interview with John Morris, March 30, 1972. He was hired by the Calumet Protective Association at its office on the fifth floor of the Hotel Gary, issued a uniform and a gun, and housed in the Youngstown Sheet and Tube Mill in East Chicago, Indiana, for three days before the Amalgamated special convention in mid-June 1934.

30. Harold Ruttenberg: "The Special Convention . . . ." Professor Carroll Moody kindly made this document available to me.

31. Bell, *Out of This Furnace*, pp. 323–324.

32. Clarence Irwin to "Dear Brother," Nov. 19, 1934, NSLRB files. This was an invitation to the secret meeting of representatives from several districts of the Amalgamated with SMWIU representatives in Cleveland on November 25. Professor Carroll Moody kindly made this document available to me.

33. Clarence Irwin to Harold Ruttenberg, Jan. 23, 1935, Ruttenberg Papers, and Harvey O'Connor to Clarence Irwin, Feb. 12, 1935, O'Connor Papers. Professor Carroll Moody kindly made the latter document available to me.

34. *Youngstown Vindicator*, Feb. 8, 1935, Irwin scrapbook.

35. *Pittsburgh Post Gazette*, Feb. 4, 1935, Ruttenberg Papers.

36. Prior to the Amalgamated convention of 1935, the rank and file asserted that they represented between 75,000 and 90,000 expelled members. At the convention a careful check was made and the figure scaled down to 50,000. Federated Press dispatches, March 28 and April 2, 29, and 30, 1935.

37. Federated Press dispatch, Feb. 5, 1935.

38. *Daily Worker*, April 15, 1935. Professor Carroll Moody kindly made this document available to me.

39. Federated Press dispatch, March 28, 1935.

40. Federated Press dispatches, April 1 and 2, 1935.

41. Harold Ruttenberg, "A Rank-and-File Strike," Ruttenberg Papers; Federated Press dispatches, May 29 and 31 and June 3, 4, and 5, 1935. Clarence Irwin was fired as a result of this strike and thenceforth worked full time, first for the rank-and-file movement and then for SWOC. Brooks, *As Steel Goes . . .* , p. 70.

42. Federated Press dispatches, June 3 and 14; July 1, 5, and 29; and August 22, 1935.

43. Federated Press dispatch, April 2, 1935.

44. Interview with Heber Blankenhorn, Columbia University Oral History Project, p. 475a; Federated Press dispatches, April 19 and May 4, 1934.

45. A group of rank-and-file steelworkers confronted Lewis when he spoke at Greensburg, Pennsylvania, April 1, 1936 and demanded that he make good on his

rhetoric about organizing steel. Lewis invited a committee of three to meet with himself and the CIO executive committee in Washington the next week. The result was the decision to offer $500,000 to the Amalgamated convention meeting in Canonsburg, Pennsylvania, on April 28. There are three accounts of the April 1 encounter: by Irwin, in Brooks, *As Steel Goes . . .* , pp. 71–72; by Albert Atallah, in an interview with Alice Hoffman, Sept. 20, 1967, Pennsylvania State Oral History Project; and by George Powers, in *Monongahela Valley: Cradle of Steel Unionism* (East Chicago, Ind., 1972). My statement about the connection of the Communist Party with this event is based on an interview with a participant.

46. "Foster, who should know, wrote later that 60 of the first organizers hired by SWOC were members of the Communist Party." Len DeCaux, *Labor Radical: From the Wobblies to CIO* (Boston, 1971), p. 279.

47. Brooks, *As Steel Goes . . .* , pp. 157 and 177, and DeCaux, *Labor Radical*, p. 280.

48. Statements made to Harvey O'Connor at the February 3, 1935, meeting. Federated Press dispatch, Feb. 5, 1935.

49. *Daily Worker*, March 2 and July 24, 1935. Professor Carroll Moody kindly made these documents available to me.

50. Press clippings, March 31, 1936 and May 21, 1939, Irwin scrapbook.

CHAPTER TEN

A. Philip Randolph and the Foundations of Black American Socialism

by Manning Marable

Asa Philip Randolph was the most influential black trade unionist in American history. He may also have been, next to W. E. B. Du Bois, the most important Afro-American socialist of the twentieth century. His accomplishments in black union organizing, militant journalism, and political protest were unequaled for decades. His controversial newspaper, *The Messenger*, published from 1917 to 1928, was the first Socialist journal to attract a widespread audience among black working- and middle-class people. In 1941 he led the Negro March on Washington Movement to protest racial discrimination in federal hiring policies, establishing a precedent which was to be revived over two decades later at the high point of the civil-rights movement. Early in his career, Randolph earned the hatred and fear of the capitalist elite and federal government officials. President Woodrow Wilson referred to the black socialist leader as "the most dangerous Negro in America."

Later in his life, Randolph's contributions to the Afro-American freedom struggle were severely criticized. In the late 1960s, young black industrial workers condemned Randolph and other black trade union leaders for not representing their problems and vital interests. To the black activists in the League of Revolutionary Black Workers he came to represent a modern Booker T. Washington, without the Tuskegee educator's skill at political

Reprinted from Vol. 14, No. 3 (May-June 1980).

compromise and power. In 1968 when blacks demanded greater decision-making authority in New York's public school system and charged the United Federation of Teachers with racism, Randolph heartily defended the UFT and its leader, Albert Shanker. In 1976 he lent his support to Daniel Patrick Moynihan, a conservative, racist Democrat, when Moynihan was running for the U.S. Senate from New York. By then, Randolph's image as a radical Socialist and militant trade unionist had been utterly erased. Upon his death in May 1979, Vice President Walter Mondale glorified the black leader, declaring that "America can speak out for human rights around the world, without hypocrisy, because of the faith A. Philip Randolph . . . showed in our country."

Thus we approach the great legacy of Randolph with some sadness and uncertainty. So many questions are left unanswered by the path of his brilliant and yet contradictory career. Some Marxists suggest that the "decisive break" in Randolph's career occurred in 1919, when he parted company with other black Socialists like Grace Campbell, Cyril V. Briggs, and Frank Crosswaith, who joined the fledgling Communist Party. "The issue was clear cut," argued Irwin Silber of the *Guardian*, "not support for socialism in general or in the abstract, but support for and defense of the Bolshevik revolution." Randolph's decision to choose "the path of social democracy" was "the decisive turning point in a political life devoted to preventing revolutionary forces from winning leadership of the Black liberation struggle."[1] As we shall observe, this split was not as decisive as Silber or others suggest. Randoph admired and supported the Russian Revolution for many years. Throughout his early career, especially in the periods 1919–1922 and 1935–1940, he welcomed the support of Marxist-Leninists, although differing with them politically. In general, there is much greater continuity of political ideology and practice from the younger to the older Randolph than is usually thought.

This essay does not attempt to present a comprehensive view of Randolph's political life. (Numerous books and articles document his long and productive career, usually in a very positive light.[2]) Instead, this essay will examine Randolph's early career as a militant journalist, Socialist Party candidate, and trade unionist, from his arrival in New York in 1911 until the late 1920s. Many of Randolph's major accomplishments, such as founding the National Negro Congress during the Great Depression, the March on Washington Movement of 1941, and the civil-disobedience campaign against military conscription in 1948, are discussed here only briefly, if at all. This is because, first, the fundamental outlines of Randolph's Socialism and political activism were firmly established during an earlier period. The roots of his thought were in the chaotic experiences of World War I and its aftermath. Second, the foundations for subsequent black working-class activism and modern black nationalism were established in the twenties. The competing political forces in Harlem of that period—Garveyism, left

210

black nationalism, militant integrationism, Marxism-Leninism—are themes which recur within the black movement today. The political decisions Randolph made during the 1920s, for better or worse, set much of the pattern for Socialism and trade-union work within the black community. The attempt here is to criticize Randolph's emergent theory of social transformation during his formative decade of political activism and to develop an understanding of the consequences of his sometimes eclectic political practice. The legacy of Randolph's politics and trade unionism which is carried on by his protegé Bayard Rustin will also be considered in this light.

A BLACK PROLETARIAT

The historical period of World World I and the immediate postwar years brought substantial changes to black Americans in general and to blacks in industrial labor in particular. For the first time in history, a substantial number of Southern, rural blacks were moving to the industrial urban North. Against the paternalistic advice of Booker T. Washington, almost half a million black men, women and children left the South before and during World War I. Simultaneously, writes Philip Foner, "the first black industrial working class in the United States came into existence." The number of blacks employed in industry between 1910 to 1920 rose from 551,825 to 901,131. By 1920 about one third of all Afro-American workers were employed in industry. However, only about 15 percent of those workers held skilled or semiskilled jobs. The great majority of black workers earned a living in the very lowest paying and most physically difficult jobs.[3]

As the political economy of black America took a decisive shift toward the industrial North, competing political interests began organizing, leading, and interacting with the new black labor force. Broadly conceived, four potential political forces presented alternative agendas to black industrial workers during this period. They were: (1) the old Booker T. Washington–capitalist alliance, which included conservative black ministers, businessmen, and journalists who preached cooperation with the capitalist class; (2) the American Federation of Labor, which in theory called for organizing black workers, but in practice upheld a strict Jim Crow bar; (3) the Marxist trade unionist in the Workers party, later the Communist Party and many members of the Socialist Party, which advocated black-white labor unity; (4) independent all-black labor organizations, including black nationalist groups influenced by Marcus Garvey, which operated on the outside of the "House of Labor."

The success of Booker T. Washington in attracting white captial to his many enterprises, from the National Negro Business League to Tuskegee Institute, was dangerous for the new black working class in the North. Washington's Northern constituency, the aggressive but fragile black entrepreneurial elite, firmly supported a capitalist-Negro alliance against white labor. Washington had argued that blacks should appeal to white

211

employers to hire black workers, since they were "not inclined to trade unionism" and not in favor of strikes. (Tuskegee scientist and inventor George Washington Carver was a friend of auto industrialist Henry Ford.) Thus, a major black newspaper such as the Chicago *Defender* supported Washington's strategy of alliance with the capitalist class. Many prominent black ministers, Republican politicians, and businessmen counseled black workers to reject unionism. Despite this influence, the overwhelming majority of new immigrants from the rural South saw this strategy for what it was, a "dead end" Jim Crow policy which only perpetuated low economic status for the black working class.

On paper, the American Federation of Labor sought to recruit the budding black proletariat to its cause; in actual practice it was scarcely less reactionary than the Ku Klux Klan. Between 1919 to 1927 the number of black locals in the AFL dropped from 161 to 21. Many unions had a long established Jim Crow policy. Sometimes blacks were admitted to separate lodges, and then forced under the authority of a white local. The new president of the AFL, the United Mine Workers' former secretary-treasurer William Green, was not a friend of black workers. Green had tolerated Ku Klux Klan influence within the UMW, and had never taken a strong stand against racial segregation. Green's concern for black labor was only stimulated in the 1920s when it appeared that many Afro-American workers were moving toward Marxism and/or independent trade union activism.[4]

The only white groups which defended black workers' rights during this period were on the Left. Growing out of the militant tradition of the Industrial Workers of the World (IWW), thousands of socialist organizers of both races campaigned for worker unity against the issue of white racism. When the "Wobblies" split over the question of the Soviet revolution, many, such as William Z. Foster, joined the Communist Party. In 1920 Foster brought together a biracial coalition of Marxists and reformist trade union activists to create the Trade Union Educational League. The TUEL advocated the building of a workers' and farmers' political party, greater racial egalitarianism inside the AFL, and the creation of militant unions for non-craft workers. In 1925 the CP was also active in the formation of the American Negro Labor Congress, an all-black labor group which advocated the building of "interracial labor committees" to promote the introduction of black workers into previously segregated crafts. As the Communists grew more influential in organizing black workers, the fears of AFL leaders mounted.[5]

Related to these developments in the labor Left was the rapid growth of independent black workers' organizations. As thousands of black laborers came to the North, the base for all-black, militant activism in labor increased dramatically. In 1915 a national organization of black railroad workers was created, the Railway Men's Benevolent Association. Within five years it had 15,000 members. In 1917 the Colored Employees of America was founded, one of the first of many groups which attempted to organize all black laborers. Two years later the National Brotherhood Workers of America was established, a coalition of black workers from almost every occupation, including blacksmiths, electricians, dock workers, porters, riveters, and waiters. Until its demise in 1921, it represented a potential alternative to the racist policies of the AFL. To the left of these organizations, black radicals and Marxists urged the development of independent socialists strategies for black labor.[6] Randolph's entire life must be viewed against this initial period of his activism, a time of tremendous growth and opportunities for black labor in the industrial North.

RANDOLPH'S SOCIALISM

Randolph's personal background conformed in most respects to that of other first-generation black immigrants from the South. Born in Crescent City, Florida, in 1889, he grew up in Jacksonville during the nadir of black-white relations. Inspired as a teenager by Du Bois's *Souls of Black Folk*, young Asa decided to leave the South and settle in New York City. Arriving in Harlem in the spring of 1911, Randolph first tried to become an actor. Failing at this, he drifted from one job to another. From 1912 to 1917 he attended courses at the City College of New York. A leftist philosophy professor, J. Salwyn Shapiro, acquainted Randolph with Marx's writings and other Socialist literature. His discovery of Socialism was so "exciting," he later reflected, that he studied "Marx as children read *Alice in Wonderland*."[7] He formed a group of radical "free thinkers" called the Independent Political Council, and began to follow the IWW closely. He began to identify himself with Harlem's premier black Socialist and "leading street-corner orator," Hubert Harrison. He joined the Socialist Party in the end of 1916, and began to lecture on black history and political economy at the Socialist Party's Rand School. By the beginning of World War I, Randolph and his new black friend, Chandler Owen, a fellow Socialist, had become "the most notorious street-corner radicals in Harlem, exceeding even Harrison in the boldness of their assault upon political and racial conditions in the country."[8]

Randolph and Owen became involved in a series of efforts to organize black workers in their community. After several weeks' work they won the support of 600 black elevator operators for starting the United Brotherhood of Elevator and Switchboard Operators. The new union's demands included a minimum wage of $13 a week, and an eight-hour day. Receiving a federal charter from the AFL, the short-lived organization tried, and failed, to organize a strike to force recognition. Randolph and Owen were also active in the Headwaiters and Sidewaiters Society as editors of the union's journal, the *Hotel Messenger*. After a dispute with the Society's president, William White, the young Socialists were fired. Within two months, they organized their own monthly magazine, the *Messenger*, with the critical financial support provided by Randolph's wife, Lucille, who earned a living as a popular and successful Harlem hairdresser. Over the next months, the new publication acquired the enthusiastic support of older radicals like Harrison and younger militants like Jamaican Socialist W. A. Domingo.[9] Between 1917 and 1918 the journal received the support of a wide variety of Harlem radicals and liberal black intellectuals of various shades: William Pickens, a field secretary of the NAACP; Robert W. Bagnall, NAACP director of branches; Wallace Thurman, Harlem Renaissance author; essayist George S. Schuyler, a Socialist who evolved into a right-wing, Goldwater Republican.

The theoretical basis for Randolph's Socialism in his early years, between 1914 to 1920, was an uneven combination of traditional religious reformism, economic determinism, fervent internationalism, and Karl Marx. His father, the Reverend James Randolph, was a pastor in the African Methodist Episcopal Church. Upon his move to Harlem, the first organization he joined was the Epworth League, a social club whose principle activity was Bible study and prayer. Later friends recalled that Randolph was the outstanding participant in all Epworth forums. Throughout Randolph's youth his father regarded him "as a fine prospect for the AME ministry."[10] Randolph rejected the orthodoxy of the cloth, but not the meaning of black spirituality in his politics. The language of the Old Testament would inform many of his speeches, as he deliberately used religious principles of brotherhood and humanism in organizing black workers. Even at the high point of their radicalism, Randolph and Owen spoke at black churches and worked closely with progressive clergy. "There are some Negro ministers," the *Messenger* declared in March 1920, "who have vision, intelligence and courage. There [are] some upon whose souls the Republican Party has no mortgage."[11] Randolph continued to believe that the black church was "the most powerful and cohesive institution in Negro life." Like his friend Norman Thomas, Randolph's Socialism was never rooted in an atheistic outlook.[12]

Like many other Socialists of the day, especially those influenced by the intellectual debates between Eduard Bernstein and Karl Kautsky of German Social Democracy, Randolph believed that Socialism was a series of economic reforms taking place between management and labor. Through the vehicle of the trade union, the working class seized an increasingly greater share of the decision-making power within the means of production. The expression of working-class politics was, of course, the Socialist Party. The revolution against capital would be a revolt of the majority against the selfish interests of a tiny, isolated elite. Randolph's definition of Socialism limited all of his subsequent work. If the Socialist Party was, as Randolph believed, the highest expression of working-class consciousness, and if blacks were profoundly working class, then no other political formation could address blacks' interests as well as the party. Race and ethnicity played no role in the "scientific evolution" of class contradictions; class was an economic category without cultural or social forms. Randolph increasingly viewed any form of black nationalism as a major obstacle between white and black workers in the struggle toward socialist democracy.

The outbreak of World War I deepened Randolph's commitment to militant pacifism and "revolutionary socialism." Like Debs, Randolph and Owen opposed World War I on the principle that "wars of contending national groups of capitalists are not the concern of the workers." The *Messenger*'s first issue denounced the "capitalist origins" of the conflict in a fiery essay, "Who Shall Pay for the War?" The editors told black men that they should not serve when drafted, and charged that the Wilson administration's claim that it was "making the world safe for democracy [was] a sham, a mockery, a rape on decency and a travesty on common justice."[13] In 1918 Randolph and Owen participated in a Socialist Party anti-war speaking tour. On August 4, 1918, the two were arrested by federal agents after a mass rally in Cleveland and charged with violating the Espionage Act. Freed with a warning, the young men continued their lecture tour, visiting Chicago, Milwaukee, Washington, D.C., and Boston, where black radical Monroe Trotter joined their mass anti-war rally. In mid-August, Postmaster General Albert Burleson denied second-class mailing privileges to the *Messenger*. Owen was drafted and sent to a Jim Crow army base in the South. Only the armistice kept Randolph out of the draft.[14]

The Bolshevik Revolution inspired Harlem's radicals, seeming to vindicate their faith in revolutionary socialism. "Lenin and Trotsky . . . are sagacious, statesmanlike and courageous leaders," the *Messenger* proclaimed in January 1918. "They are calling upon the people of every country to follow the lead of Russia; to throw off their exploiting rulers, to administer public utilities for the public welfare, to disgorge the exploiters and the profiteers."[15] For several years, Randolph argued that the Communist revolution meant the "triumph of democracy in Russia." He praised the Soviet Army's defeat of the White Russians in 1920, stating that the capitalist opponents of Socialism "had not reckoned with the indomitable courage and the cold resolution born of the unconquerable love for liberty."[16] Randolph boldly predicted that Bela Kun's Hungarian Communists would eventually defeat the Social Democrats and send the aristocracy "to that oblivion and obscurity from which they ought never to emerge";[17] he also believed that British capitalism was on the brink of "an impending financial revolution."[18] Domestically, Randolph participated eagerly in the Socialist Party's activities. In 1917, the *Messenger* campaigned for Morris Hillquit, Socialist Party candidate for mayor. In 1920 Randolph ran as the party's candidate for state comptroller and polled 202,361 votes, only 1,000 less than Socialist presidential candidate Eugene V. Debs in the state! In 1921 he ran another unsuccessful campaign for secretary of state. Despite these failures, Randolph's belief in a democratic socialist revolution remained uncompromised.[19]

CONFLICT WITH DU BOIS

Randolph's strong anti-war position led to a decisive break with Du Bois—the major black leader of the NAACP and Randolph's intellectual mentor—in 1918, when the editor of the *Crisis* urged black Americans to support the war effort.[20] Up to this point, the *Messenger* had praised Du Bois as a race leader and opponent of "disfranchisement," condemning only his attitude on labor. "One has not seen where the doctor ever recognized the necessity of the Negro as a scab," Owen wrote, "allaying thereby the ill feeling against him by working white man."[21] Now Du Bois's advocacy of the war crystallized Randolph's and Owen's opposition to his entire political line—from the "Talented Tenth" theory—the idea, used in *The Souls of Black Folk*, of a black intellectual leadership which would act as a vanguard for the black masses—to his views on segregation. By July 1918, Randolph condemned almost every major essay or book that Du Bois had ever written. Du Bois was a "political opportunist," simply representing "a good transition from Booker Washington's compromise methods to the era of the new Negro."[22]

Never one to avoid a fight, Du Bois defended his anti-Socialist Party, anti-trade unionist, anti-Bolshevik, and prowar positions head on. As early as January 1912, when he was a member of the Socialist Party, Du Bois complained about racism within the organization. He left the party to endorse the election of Woodrow Wilson later that year.[23] His opposition to trade unionism was well established.[24] Du Bois's position on the war evolved from examination of the colonial and racist origins of the conflict. The destruction of the German empire, Du Bois reasoned, might have resulted in the possibility of greater African self-determination.[25] Meanwhile, black Americans would be rewarded for their loyalty to America's war effort against Germany.[26]

About Russian Socialism Du Bois was profoundly skeptical. After the "February Revolution" in early 1917, Du Bois suggested to his *Crisis* readers that the event "makes us wonder whether the German menace is to be followed by a Russian menace or not."[27] Although he criticized Alexander Kerensky's "blood and iron methods" in governing Russia, he said nothing about the Bolsheviks' rise to power.[28] When radical Harlem Renaissance writer Claude McKay questioned why Du Bois "seemed to neglect or sneer at the Russian Revolution," he replied curtly that he had "heard things which [were] frighten[ing]" about the upheaval. I am "not prepared to dogmatize with Marx or Lenin."[29]

For the new Negro generation, these opinions relegated "the Doctor" to the status of "the old, me-too-Boss, hat-in-hand Negro generally represented by Robert Russa Moton of Tuskegee."[30] Randolph declared that Du Bois was "comparatively ignorant of the world problems of sociological and economic significance."[31] In 1920, the *Messenger* charged that the *Crisis* had an editorial policy of "viciousness, petty meanness" and "suppression [of] facts pertaining to the NAACP." It attacked Du Bois's associates, especially field secretary William Pickens, as advocates of "sheer 'claptrap.'"[32] It laughed at Du Bois's provincial liberalism and staid social conformity. By the end of Wilson's administration, the Justice Department reported that the *Messenger* was "by long odds the most dangerous of all the Negro publications." Throughout Harlem, Randolph and Owen became known as "Lenin and Trotsky," the most revolutionary black Bolsheviks on the scene. Their political break from Du Bois seemed complete.[33]

RANDOLPH AND GARVEY

Having declared war against Du Bois and the NAACP leadership, Randolph and Owen sought the support of other black activists in Harlem. They needed support because, by their own admission, Du Bois remained "the most distinguished Negro in the United States today."[34] Marcus Garvey seemed a likely addition to their struggle against the *Crisis's* editor. Born in Jamaica, Garvey had established his Universal Negro Improvement Association (UNIA) in 1914. Inspired by the racial "self-help" slogans of Booker T. Washington, the young black nationalist eventually settled in New York City in 1916. Randolph claimed the distinction of having been the first prominent black radical to invite Garvey to Harlem. He recalled years later that "when he finished speaking . . . I could tell from watching him then that he was one of the greatest propagandists of his time."[35] Garvey was attracted to Harrison, who by 1917 had left the Socialist Party to form his own Left black nationalist movement, the Afro-American Liberty League. Although Garvey was one of the main speakers at the League's first rally on June 12, 1917, he quickly established separate UNIA offices near the *Messenger* on 135th Street. Randolph and Garvey worked together in the International League of Darker Peoples, an organization which demanded that the African territories and colonized nations be represented at the Versailles peace conference. Some Garveyites began to assist Randolph's efforts. Domingo, who was editor of Garvey's *Negro World*, worked as a contributing editor on the *Messenger*.[36] Randolph certainly welcomed Garvey's public attacks on Du Bois as an "antebellum Negro."[37]

The first major disagreement between the black nationalists and Randolph probably occurred over the creation of the Liberty Party, an all-black political coalition of former Socialists, Republicans, and Democrats, in late 1920. The stated slogan of the party was "Race First"; it advocated running a black presidential candidate and independent candidates at local levels. Randolph condemned the notion on all conceivable grounds. First, the Negro party was criticized because it had no prospects for support from white workers. "A party that has no hope of becoming a majority has no justification for independent action; for it can never hope to be of positive benefit to its supporters." Second, the party had no economic platform. Third, the proposition of a Negro president was "tragically inane, senseless, foolish, absurd and preposterous. It is inconceivable that alleged intelligent, young colored men could take such obvious, stupendous political folly seriously." Last, the Liberty Party consisted of "opportunists, discredited political failures who are now trying to capitalize race prejudice of the Negro." The basis for this vituperative attack was Randolph's view that it was in the interests of "Negro workers to join and vote for the Socialist Party."[38]

It is probable that Harrison's Liberty League supported the new party. Another more menacing factor, of course, was Garvey, who had long been a proponent of an all-black political party.[39] J. W. H. Easton, the UNIA leader for U.S. blacks, was the party's nominee for president. [40] The idea of a separate, race-conscious, political organization, rather than the Liberty Party per se, was the real issue. Randolph and Owen had begun to view black nationalism as being even more dangerous than the threat presented by Du Bois and his *Crisis*.

The *Messenger* began to challenge the Garvey movement for hegemony within Harlem's black working-class population. In December 1920, Randolph issued an editorial, "The Garvey Movement: A Promise or a Menace," which argued that "the class-struggle nature of the Negro problem" was missing from the UNIA's work. Revolutionary black nationalism "invites an unspeakably violent revulsion of hostile opposition from whites against blacks." In Randolph's view, any all-black organization could "only misdirect the political power of the Negro. All party platforms are chiefly concerned with economic questions" and not with race. Therefore, the *Messenger* concluded, Garvey's entire program "deserves the condemnation and repudiation of all Negroes."[41] Relations with Garveyites swiftly worsened. Randolph insisted that Garvey's advocacy of an independent Africa for the Africans was unrealistic, because the Africans do not possess "the ability . . . to assume the responsibilities and duties of a sovereign nation."[42] By mid-1922 the *Messenger* concentrated on opposition to Garvey. "Here's notice that the *Messenger* is firing the opening gun in a campaign to drive Garvey and Garveyism in all its sinister viciousness from the American soil."[43]

Nowhere in the black press of the time was the anti-Garvey campaign expressed so bluntly, and with such anti-West Indian sentiments, as in the *Messenger*. Every significant aspect of Garvey's program was denounced as "foolish," "vicious," "without brains," or "sheer folly." The UNIA's proposal for a Booker T. Washington University will have "neither students nor teachers" since the former "will not trust it to give out knowledge" and the latter "will not trust it to give out pay." Garvey's wildest claim, that the

UNIA had 4.5 million dues-paying members, proved that he was "a consummate liar or a notorious crook." But Randolph failed to explain the reasons for Garvey's massive popularity among black workers in Harlem, and ignored the hard evidence of the UNIA's progressive positions on African and international affairs.[44]

RANDOLPH BREAKS WITH BOLSHEVISM

As the Bolshevik Revolution forced the creation of a Third International, Randolph felt himself pulled gradually toward the Right. For the first time in several years he was no longer "the first voice of radical, revolutionary, economic and political action among Negroes in America."[45] Revolutionary black activists outside both UNIA and *Messenger* factions were making political waves across Harlem. In the fall of 1917 Cyril V. Briggs founded the African Blood Brotherhood (ABB), a leftist and black nationalist group. A native of the Dutch West Indies and a former editorial writer for the New York *Amsterdam News*, Briggs began to edit his own nationalist journal, the *Crusader*. Many members of the ABB, which included Lovett Fort-Whiteman, Richard B. Moore, and Otto Huiswood, were quickly recruited into the newly formed Workers, or Communist, Party. (Harrison did not go over to the Communists, according to Harold Cruse, but he did "assist" them in certain situations.)[46] By 1922, the Communists had begun "to assail Garvey's program as reactionary, escapist and utopian" while simultaneously trying "to influence, collaborate with, or undermine his movement."[47] As Marxist-Leninists, the ABB also attacked Randolph's firm ties with the Socialist Party, his reformist and quasi-religious theories for social transformation, his bitter hostility toward black nationalism, and growing tendency toward political and economic conservatism.[48]

The *Messenger* turned on its former Left friends almost as viciously as it had turned against Garvey. Declaring all black Communists "a menace to the workers, themselves and the race," Randolph judged their policies "utterly senseless, unsound, unscientific, dangerous and ridiculous." Black Marxist "extremists" were hopelessly out of touch with the mentality of Negro laborers, since the latter had not "even grasped the fundamentals and necessity of simple trade and industrial unionism!" As further proof that "Communism can be of no earthly benefit to either white or Negro workers," Randolph pointed out that the Soviet Union's new economic policy of "State Capitalism" had replaced the radical socialist economics of the war communist years.[49]

Opposition to "Communists boring into Negro labor" united Randolph and Du Bois.[50] Their joint opposition to Garvey's success was even stronger, and drove them back into some collaboration. There was no indication that Du Bois had changed his views on any of the major points that had separated him from Randolph during the war. If anything, Du Bois's opposition to

"State Socialism" and the "class struggle," and his advocacy of black "capital accumulation to effectively fight racism," placed him to the economic right of many Garveyites, and perhaps even Garvey himself at this time.[51] But the distance that had separated Randolph and Du Bois had now narrowed due to Garvey's gospel of black nationalism. The *Crisis* and the *Messenger* concurred in opposition to all forms of racial separatism and distrust of Garvey's business methods and honesty.

Working closely with the NAACP's assistant secretary, Walter White, Randolph coordinated an elaborate campaign against Garvey, which included the distribution of anti-Garvey handbills throughout Harlem. In January 1923, Randolph, Owen, Pickens, and several other black leaders drafted a memorandum to Attorney General Harry M. Daugherty asking for the conviction of Marcus Garvey on charges of mail fraud, various criminal activities, and "racial bigotry." Garvey was eventually convicted of mail fraud, and imprisoned in February 1925. By the late 1920s the UNIA had virtually collapsed, partially due to Randolph's anti-Garvey activities. The irony of this entire episode was that Randolph, a would-be leader of the black working class, had participated in the destruction of the largest black workers' and peasants' organization in American history.

THE BROTHERHOOD OF SLEEPING CAR PORTERS

Unlike Garvey, Randolph at first met with little success in his efforts to organize black workers. Randolph and Owen created the Friends of Negro Freedom in 1920, a biracial group which promoted black entrance into trade unions and held lectures on economic and political issues. Friends of Negro Freedom included Domingo, Baltimore *Afro-American* newspaper editor Carl Murphy, and black intellectual Archibald Grimke. In 1923 Randolph attempted unsuccessfully to establish a United Negro Trades organization to bring black workers into independent trade unions. Finally, in August, 1925, a few Pullman porters asked Randolph to help them establish the Brotherhood of Sleeping Car Porters. Despite the fact that several black Pullman employees such as W. H. Des Verney and Ashley Totten had been more instrumental in organizing rank-and-file support for the Brotherhood, Randolph was named president. The initial prospects for this union's success looked just as dim as all the other groups that Randolph had led, however. The eleven thousand black porters working on Pullman cars faced the united opposition of the federal government, the Pullman Company, and its black conservative allies.

Given Randolph's early inability to build a successful and popular mass organization of black workers, it is not surprising that he began to reassess his overall theoretical outlook and political practice. Gradually, Socialism was given less emphasis in his writings; by 1923 the *Messenger* had succeeded in attracting several black businessmen and merchants to advertise in its pages. Articles by Emmett J. Scott, the former secretary of Booker T.

Washington, and even Robert Russa Moton, of Tuskegee, began appearing in the journal.[52] Quietly, editorial policies began to change. In January 1925, Randolph declared that "Negro businessmen are rapidly rising to the high mark of responsibility." Many black entrepreneurs were "splendid, courteous," and a "*delight* to deal with."[53] Randolph's blanket condemnation of the AFL and his earlier critical descriptions of Gompers—a "conservative, reactionary and chief strikebreaker"—mellowed into fawning praise. The AFL was no longer "a machine for the propagation of race prejudice," but a progressive and democratic force. Randolph banned articles critical of William Green, newly elected AFL leader.[54]

The editors endorsed Hampton and Tuskegee Institutes' five-million-dollar fund drive by defending Washington's position on industrial education against Du Bois's Talented Tenth ideal. "Dr. Du Bois has probably been responsible for a great deal of misunderstanding about industrial education in America," they argued. "We need more brick masons, carpenters, plasterers, plumbers, than we do physicians; more cooks than lawyers; more tailors and dressmakers than pupils."[55] Yet there were only 40,000 black secondary and elementary teachers, 3,200 black physicians and 900 black lawyers in the United States at this time. Only 50 percent of black children between the ages of five and twenty were enrolled in school: 25 percent of all adult blacks in the South were illiterate.[56] Randolph had moved toward a defense of private property and capitalism—a posture which he would never relinquish.

Thus Randolph persuaded the Brotherhood to apply for an international charter from the AFL in 1928, after it had spent several years as an independent, all-black union. The AFL rejected the application for equal membership, and instead proposed a "compromise" of "federal union" status inside the organization. Despite criticism from leftists, black workers, and some journalists, Randolph agreed to these terms. Both parties got something in the deal: Green and the AFL acquired a major black union, silencing their Marxist and black critics like Du Bois; Randolph received the promise of assistance from organized white labor in his growing struggle with the Pullman Company.

Randolph built the Brotherhood with characteristic enthusiasm. Appeals to porters to join were made in racial and religious terms. "Ye shall know the truth, and the truth shall set you free," was the slogan on Brotherhood stationery. In language reminiscent of some Garveyites, the Brotherhood's literature declared its faith in God and the Negro race: "Fight on brave souls! Long live the Brotherhood! Stand upon thy feet and the God of Truth and Justice and Victory will speak unto thee!"[57] Randolph's efforts to organize the porters received a boost in 1926, when the Garland Fund, administered by the American Civil Liberties Union, donated $10,000 to the Brotherhood. The money allowed Randolph to hire Frank W. Crosswaith, a West Indian Socialist and graduate of the Party's Rand School in New

York City, as a professional organizer and executive secretary of the Brotherhood.[58] Randolph also benefited from many intelligent and creative leaders among the porters: Morris "Dad" Moore and C. L. Dellums of Oakland; T. T. Patterson of New York City; Des Verney, and Totten. Chief among them was Milton Webster. Two years Randolph's senior, he had been fired by Pullman because of his militancy. In the twenties he became a bailiff and was one of Chicago's influential black Republican leaders. As assistant general organizer of the Brotherhood and chief organizer for the Chicago area, next only to Randolph, the aggressive yet politically conservative Webster became the major spokesperson for the porters.[59]

Randolph's leadership was soon tested against the Pullman Company.[60] After the Board of Mediation, established by the Railway Labor Act of 1926, ruled the following year that the parties could not reach an agreement and recommended voluntary arbitration, Randolph's only alternative was to call a strike to force Pullman Company into collective bargaining. The strike was set for June 8, 1928.[61]

Across the country, porters were excited at the prospect of a confrontation between themselves and the Pullman Company. Despite red-baiting against Randolph, random firings, and veiled threats, the porters backed the Brotherhood leadership almost unanimously. The strike vote, 6,053 to 17, astonished even Randolph. Some porters made plans for a long siege, even blocking the use of strikebreakers. Ashley Totten and his associates in Kansas City began collecting "sawed-off shotguns, railroad iron taps, boxes of matches, knives and billy clubs" and storing them in a local black-owned building. Facing the prospect of an extensive and probably violent strike which would disrupt Pullman railroad service nationwide, Randolph began to have doubts. Could an all-black workers' strike succeed without some measure of white trade-union and working-class support? Three hours before the scheduled strike, Green sent Randolph a telegram stating that "conditions were not favorable" for a strike. He suggested that the Brotherhood engage in "a campaign of education and public enlightenment regarding the justice of your cause." Randolph called the strike off.[62]

It is difficult to know whether the strike would have been successful. Throughout the remainder of his life, Randolph insisted that the possibilities were nil. The historical evidence points in the opposite direction, however. William H. Harris's research on Brotherhood correspondence suggests that Webster had a great deal of difficulty in convincing his local members not to strike by themselves. "Aside from disruption of peak travel, what could be more damaging to interstate commerce than to tie up the rails during the time when both national political parties were holding conventions in such remote cities as Houston and Kansas City?" Harris asked. "Even the Pullman Company recognized this as a potential danger."[63] The union was "in shambles after the abortive strike." The *Messenger* was forced to halt publication; porters lost confidence in the Brotherhood and stopped paying their regular dues. Black newspapers like the New York *Argus* attacked the leadership of "A. Piffle Randolph."[64] The Communists accused him of "betraying Negro workers in the interest of the labor fakers."[65] The American Negro Labor Congress charged that Randolph had "forsaken the policy of militant struggle in the interest of the workers for the policy of class collaboration with the bosses and bluffing with the strike." Within four years, the Brotherhood's membership declined from almost 7,000 to only 771 in 1932.[66]

It was only in April 1937 that the Pullman Company agreed to bargain seriously with the Brotherhood. On August 25 of that same year Pullman agreed to reduce the porters' monthly work load from 400 to 240 hours, and provide a substantial pay increase. But many of his critics, black and white, suggested that these and other accomplishments would have been achieved much sooner if A. Philip Randolph had had a little less faith in the system and a little more confidence in the militancy of the black working class.

NATIONAL CIVIL RIGHTS STRUGGLES

In the Depression, Randolph again exhibited courage and some of his former political independence. Contrary to Du Bois, Randolph charged that "the New Deal is no remedy" to black people's problems. It did not "change the profit system," nor "place human rights above property rights." Assisted by Alain Locke, Ralph Bunche, and other Left-oriented black intellectuals, Randolph initiated the National Negro Congress in February, 1936. Hundreds of black trade unionists, radical civic reformers, and communists participated in a black united front in blunt opposition both to Roosevelt's "welfare capitalism" and to the do-nothing acquiescence of the NAACP. Despite the breakup of the Congress in the early 1940s over the issue of "Communist control," the organization represented one of the most advanced coalitions of black activists ever assembled.[67]

With the onset of World War II in Europe, the Roosevelt administration began expanding production in defense industries. Prior to America's direct involvement in the war, thousands of new jobs were created in industrial, clerical, and technical fields related to wartime production. Black workers were largely kept out of these positions because of a tacit policy of Jim Crow followed by white labor, big business, and the federal government. Although Congress had forbidden racial discrimination in the appropriation of funds for defense training, the law was essentially a dead letter. With Randolph's resignation from the National Negro Congress in 1940, he turned his energies toward the issue of black employment in defense industries with federal contracts. Working again with Walter White, who by this time was secretary and dictatorial leader of the NAACP, Randolph sought to influence Roosevelt to initiate action against white racism.

By January 1941, Randolph was prepared to take what was, for that time, radical action. Randolph urged blacks to organize a militant march in Washington, D.C., on July 1 to protest the discrimination against black workers. The idea of a "March on Washington Movement" seized the imagination of the black working class, the unemployed, and even the petty bourgeoisie. The Brotherhood of Sleeping Car Porters was the central force behind the campaign. Hundreds of March-on-Washington Movement meetings were held in black churches, union halls, and community centers. With able support, Randolph succeeded in committing over 100,000 black people to the march. Foner observes that the "March on Washington Movement represented the first occasion in American history when a black labor organization assumed leadership of the struggle of the Negro masses on a national scale and became the spokesman for all black Americans, conservative and radical alike." Neither Garvey, Washington, nor Du Bois had ever succeeded in forging a popular coalition of the black business and professional elites, the working class, and rural blacks toward a single, progressive cause.

The driving force behind the 1941 March on Washington was black nationalism. Taking another page from Garvey's book, Randolph insisted that only blacks participate in the march. It was important for blacks to show white America that they were able to build an effective, militant, national organization without white assistance. C. L. Dellums explained that the Brotherhood informed its "white friends over the country why this had to be a Negro march. It had to be for the inspiration of Negroes yet unborn." White progressives and trade unionists were asked to offer "moral support, to stand on the sidelines and cheer us on."[68]

The demand for an end to discrimination in defense plants appealed to the typical black industrial worker who, like porters in the 1920s, was on the verge of class consciousness. But its expression among blacks was nationalism, a force involving religious, cultural, and ethnic qualities which Randolph was forced to deal with in a concrete manner. Randolph's biographer emphasizes that "a certain strain of black nationalism . . . ran through his social and religious heritage." Not surprisingly, "when the chips were down," Randolph had to return to his own origins to find the means to understand his own constituency and to articulate their aspirations. His biographer writes, "It is a wonder that black nationalism did not become the central activating force and principle of Randolph's political life."[69]

Roosevelt used his considerable power to force the organizers to stop the march. As black workers in Harlem, Washington, D.C., Chicago, and every major city prepared for the confrontation, Roosevelt finally agreed to sign an executive order prohibiting the "discrimination in the employment of workers in defense industries because of race, creed, color or national origin." The Democratic administration promised to create the Fair Employment Practices Committee, a commission which would supervise the compliance of federal contractors with the executive order. Although this was not everything that the March on Washington Movement had asked for, Randolph and other leaders agreed to call off the demonstration on June 24.[70]

Historians August Meier and Elliott Rudwick point to the March on Washington Movement as the real foundation for the Civil Rights Movement of the 1950s and 1960s. "Though its career was brief, the former organization prefigured things to come in three ways," they note. It was, first, "an avowedly all-Negro movement"; second, it involved the direct "action of the black masses"; third, "it concerned itself with the economic problems of the urban slum-dwellers."[71] Two additional points can be made. The FEPC was the beginning of today's Federal Office of Contracts Compliance Programs, the Department of Labor's affirmative-action watchdog. The principle of equal opportunity for black people in employment was, for the first time, considered a civil right. Randolph's ideology behind the march also "prefigures" the 1950–1960s because of the impact of Gandhi's approach to social change. In an address before March-on-Washington associates given in Detroit in September 1942, Randolph called attention to "the strategy and maneuver of the people of India with mass civil disobedience and non-cooperation." Huge, nonviolent demonstrations "in theaters, hotels, restaurants, and amusement places" could be a potential means to gain full equality. Years before Martin Luther King, Jr., Randolph envisioned the basic principles of *satyagraha* applied to the fight against Jim Crow.

Yet for all his foresight and commitment to the ideals of black struggle, Randolph's subsequent political behavior did little to promote the creation of a permanent organization. The March-on-Washington Movement's last major conference was in October 1946, and it lapsed completely the next year. Randolph's ongoing fights with AFL officials still produced meager results. As in the past, Randolph's failure to carry out the threat of militant action compromised the pursuit of his long-range goals. Even at the peak of his influence throughout black America, during the March-on-Washington Movement of 1940–1941, Randolph failed to establish a mass-based, permanent force which promoted his rhetorical commitment to democratic socialism and black economic equality. Again and again, especially later in his career, he failed to trust the deep militancy of the black working-class masses, relying instead upon tactical agreements with white presidents, corporate executives, and labor bureaucrats. Curiously, like Booker T. Washington, Randolph always preferred class compromise to class struggle.

With the end of World War II and the beginning of the Cold War, Randolph's creative contributions to the struggle for black freedom had largely ended. Like other labor leaders and Socialists such as Norman Thomas, Randolph capitulated to the posture of extreme anti-Communism. Randolph and Thomas traveled to the Far East lecturing against the evils of radical trade unionism, for instance, under what later was revealed to be the auspices of the CIA. Randolph became an acknowledged "elder statesman" during the Civil Rights Movement of the 1950s. Making his peace with those black leaders he had formerly opposed in the NAACP and Urban League, he had little to offer in the way of guidance or political theory to a new generation of black radicals, the rebels of SNCC, CORE, and SCLC. Ironically, it was during this period that Du Bois, now in his eighties, moved toward a thoroughly radical condemnation of America's political economy. The old so-called "political opportunist" had become the active proponent of world peace and international liberation, while his "Young Turk" critic had become a defender of the conservative status quo.

Since the 1960s, Randolph's role in the AFL-CIO hierarchy has been filled by his trusted assistant, Bayard Rustin. Like his mentor, Rustin is a Socialist and pacifist with a long history of principled and at times even courageous struggle. As a participant in CORE's "Journey of Reconciliation" campaign of 1946, he tested local Jim Crow laws by sitting in white sections on interstate buses in the South. With other early "freedom riders" he received a 30-day jail term on a North Carolina chain gang. Rustin was one of the major organizers of the 1963 March on Washington, and inspired a generation of younger black activists like SNCC's Stokeley Carmichael and Phil Hutchings. But when he became head of the A. Philip Randolph Institute, founded by George Meany and the AFL-CIO in 1965, he acquired the language and outlook of white labor's elites. Rustin bitterly denounced Malcolm X as a "racist,"[72] and condemned the Black Power movement as "anti-white" and "inconsistent." Rustin and Randolph defended the Vietnam War and criticized King for linking domestic civil rights with America's involvement in Southeast Asia.

In the 1970s Rustin's position within the black movement drifted increasingly toward the Right. At the September 1972 convention of the International Association of Machinists, he attacked black rank-and-file activists and defended the AFL-CIO's shabby record on integration. The next year he was critical of the creation of the Coalition of Black Trade Unionists, arguing that the Randolph Institute should be viewed as the "catalyst" for black advancement in union leadership positions. On the international front, at the time of Randolph's death in 1979, Rustin participated in a "Freedom House" delegation to Zimbabwe which declared that the white minority regime's fraudulent elections were democratic. Cruse analyzed him best in 1968, observing that "Rustin's problem is that in thirty years he has learned nothing new. He has done nothing creative in radical theory in American terms. . . ."[73] Put another way, Rustin is a victim of what Marx postulated in "The Eighteenth Brumaire of Louis Bonaparte"; that "all great personages occur, as it were, twice—the first time as tragedy, the second as farce." Randolph's life is tragic, because of his greatness and yet untapped potential. Rustin's is a caricature, in another historical period, of that lost greatness.

Despite Randolph's changes and shifting images certain consistencies remain. Throughout his career, Randolph perceived union organizing as a "top-down" rather than a mass-based strategy. Although he was not a porter, he asked for, and received, the presidency of the Brotherhood in 1925; he left the presidency of the National Negro Congress after realizing that he could no longer control the leftists in it. He consistently preferred compromise and gradual reform to confrontation and class/race struggle. The capitulation of the Brotherhood's 1928 strike and the 1941 March on Washington were the most outstanding instances, but not the only ones. He made a similar compromise in December 1965, after the establishment of the Randolph Institute. After years of criticizing the racial policies of the AFL-CIO. Randolph reversed himself at the San Francisco national convention by announcing that racism had virtually disappeared from organized labor.

Another of Randolph's central characteristics was his inability to appreciate the relationship between black nationalism, black culture, and the struggle for Socialism. Randolph's and Owen's editorials in the *Messenger* declared that "unions are not based upon race lines, but upon class lines," and that "the history of the labor movement in America proves that the employing class recognize no race lines." This crude and historically false oversimplification led Randolph into pragmatic alliances not only with the white Marxists, but also with the AFL after 1923, and later the Kennedy and Johnson administrations. His successes in winning higher wages and shorter working hours for the Brotherhood were achieved at the expense of building an autonomous, all-black protest movement which was critical of both racism and capitalism. The *Messenger*'s vicious attacks against Garvey did not stop hundreds of thousands of rural and urban black workers from defending black nationalism. Randolph was ill equipped to understand the rank-and-file revolt of black industrial workers in the past two decades who were influenced by Malcolm X, Franz Fanon, and their Black Power disciples.

Cruse's comments on the entire generation of Harlem radicals, both in politics and the arts, are an appropriate critique of Randolph as well. Because "the Negro intellectuals of the Harlem Renaissance could not see the implications of cultural revolution as a political demand," Cruse notes, "they failed to grasp the radical potential of their own movement." Like the Renaissance poets and novelists, Randolph was hesitant to place black culture, ethnicity, and nationalism on the same agenda with other social and political concerns. "Having no cultural philosophy of their own, they remained under the tutelage of irrelevant white radical ideas."[74]

This same assessment was also made by Du Bois in 1933. He criticized the literary Renaissance as "literature written for the benefit of white readers, and starting primarily from the white point of view. It never had a real Negro constituency and it did not grow out of the inmost heart and frank experience of Negroes. . . ."[75] Similarly, Randolph's economic determinism, his political pattern of compromise and reconciliation, his narrow definitions of class and culture, proved harmful throughout his entire career. In the first Negro March on Washington when he did turn to the black workers with an avowedly nationalistic style and a program for political confrontation of the segregationist status quo, he was dramatically successful. When he overcame his Socialist Party training and used the language of the black church and Southern black political protest traditions to appeal to his Brotherhood's rank and file, he reached a potentially revolutionary force. But his ambiguous hostility toward the Negro's nationalism negated the full potential of his efforts.

Randolph's contribution to the ongoing struggle for black self-determination was unique and important. His activities in creating the Brotherhood of Sleeping Car Porters, the National Negro Congress, and the March on Washington Movement of 1940–1941 were necessary preconditions for the black activism of the 1950s and 1960s. Harold Cruse is correct that "not a single Negro publication in existence today matches the depth of the old *Messenger*." Randolph was the first great leader of the black urban working class. But unlike Du Bois, he was unable to reevaluate himself and his movement dialectically; ultimately he became a prisoner of his own limited vision for black America.

In the next stage of history, black working people and activists must transcend Randolph's contradictions. If they succeed, as they must, they will begin to realize the possibilities of socialism within the means and relations of production. In doing so, they will carry out the legacy of Randolph that he was unable to achieve for himself and his own generation.

NOTES

1. Irwin Silber, "Randolph: What Was His Role?," *Guardian*, May 1979.

2. Jervis Anderson's biography, *A. Philip Randolph: A Biographical Portrait* (New York, 1972), examines the black Socialist's personal and political life. There are two excellent sources on the Brotherhood of Sleeping Car Porters: William H. Harris's recent study, *Keeping the Faith: A. Philip Randolph, Milton P. Webster, and the Brotherhood of Sleeping Car Porters* (Urbana, Chicago, and London, 1977), and Brailsford R. Brazael, *The Brotherhood of Sleeping Car Porters: Its Origin and Development* (New York, 1946). Theodore Kornweibel's Ph.D. dissertation, "The *Messenger* Magazine, 1917-1928" (Ph.D. dissertation, Yale University, 1971), examines Randolph's early years as a political activist.

The list of popular and scholarly articles published about Randolph or his role in the black movement are almost endless. See, for example, L. W. Thomas, "Three Negroes Receive 1964 Presidential Freedom Medal," *Negro History Bulletin*, Dec. 1964, pp. 58–59; M. Kempton, "A. Philip Randolph," *New Republic*, July 6, 1963, pp. 15–17; Arna Bontemps, "Most Dangerous Negro in America," *Negro Digest*, Sept. 1961, pp. 3–8; John Henrik Clarke, "Portrait of an AfroAmerican Radical,"

A. Philip Randolph and Black American Socialism

Negro Digest, March 1967, pp. 16–23; A. Morrison, "A. Philip Randolph: Dean of Negro Leaders," *Ebony*, Nov. 1958, pp. 103–104.

3. Philip S. Foner, *Organized Labor and the Black Worker, 1619–1973* (New York, 1974), pp. 129–135.

4. Ibid., pp. 169–172.

5. Ibid., pp. 164–166, 171–172.

6. Ibid., pp. 147–160.

7. Anderson, *A. Philip Randolph*, pp. 32, 50, 51, 52.

8. Ibid., pp. 76–77; Harris, *Keeping the Faith*, pp. 28–29. In 1944 Randolph commented that his "extensive reading of Socialist literature" was one of the "fundamental forces that had shaped his life." The Socialist Party theorists and authors he named included Morris Hillquit, Algernon Lee, Norman Thomas, Frank Crosswaith, and Eugene V. Debs. Until 1964, when he voted for Lyndon Johnson, he had consistently endorsed the Socialist Party ticket. Anderson, *A. Philip Randolph*, p. 343.

9. Anderson, *A. Philip Randolph*, pp. 79–82.

10. Ibid., pp. 48, 59.

11. Editorial, "Some Negro Ministers," *Messenger*, March 1920, p. 3.

12. Anderson, *A. Philip Randolph*, p. 25. Randolph stopped attending church within a year after his arrival in Harlem in 1911. But in December 1957, the Reverend Richard Allen Hildebrand, an AME minister in Harlem received a request from Randolph to become a member of his church. Randolph seldom attended, if ever; nevertheless, he probably rested somewhat easier with the spiritual knowledge that he was a member.

13. Anderson, *A. Philip Randolph*, pp. 97–98.

14. Ibid., pp. 107–109.

15. "The Bolsheviki," *Messenger*, Jan. 1918, p. 7.

16. "The Russian Triumph," *Messenger*, March 1920, pp. 3–4. Randolph's mechanistic, economic determinism is evident in his faulty commentary on the Bolsheviks and the coming American revolution. "The Government of the United States . . . is located in Wall Street. When the large combinations of wealth—the trusts, monopolies and cartels are broken up . . . a new government will then spring forth just as the Soviet Government was an inevitable consequence of the breaking up of the great estates of Russia and assigning the land to the peasants, and the factories to the workers. It is as impossible to have a political machine which does not reflect the economic organization of a country, as it is to make a sewing machine grind flour." "The Negro Radicals," *Messenger*, Oct. 1919, p. 17.

17. Editorial, *Messenger*, Sept. 1919, pp. 9–10.

18. Anderson, *A. Philip Randolph*, pp. 92–96.

19. "When British Capitalism Falls," *Messenger*, March 1920, p. 3.

20. One of Du Bois's most controversial prowar editorials was "Close Ranks," published in the July 1918 issue of the *Crisis*. He argued, "Let us, while this war lasts, forget our social grievances and close our ranks shoulder to shoulder with our white fellow citizens and the allied nations that are fighting for democracy."

21. Chandler Owen, "The Failure of the Negro Leaders," *Messenger*, Jan. 1918, p. 23.

22. Randolph, "W. E. B. Du Bois," *Messenger*, July 1918, pp. 27–28; editorial, *Messenger*, March 1919, pp. 21–22.

23. W. E. B. Du Bois, "Socialism Is Too Narrow for Negroes," *Socialist Call*, Jan. 21, 1912; Du Bois, "A Field for Socialists," *New Review*, Jan. 11, 1913, pp. 54–57; Du Bois, "Socialism and the Negro Problem," *New Review*, Feb. 1, 1913, pp. 138–141. This does not mean that Du Bois disavowed Socialism. In May 1914, Du Bois joined the editorial board of the Socialist Party's journal, *New Review*. His criticisms of some Socialists' explicitly racist platforms in the South did not lessen his intellectual commitment to Socialist economic goals.

24. W. E. B. Du Bois, "The Black Man and the Unions," *Crisis*, March 1918.

25. W. E. B. Du Bois, "The African Roots of the War," *Atlantic Monthly*, May 1915, pp. 707–714.

26. W. E. B. Du Bois, "The Reward," *Crisis*, Sept. 1918.

27. W. E. B. Du Bois, "The World Last Month," *Crisis*, March 1917.

28. W. E. B. Du Bois, *Crisis*, Sept. 1917, p. 215.

29. W. E. B. Du Bois, "The Negro and Radical Thought," *Crisis*, July 1921. Du Bois's attitude toward the Bolshevik Revolution warms as Randolph's attitude wanes. See Du Bois's "Opinion" on Russia. *Crisis*, April 1922, pp. 247–252, and his essay, "The Black Man and Labor," *Crisis*, Dec. 1925, where he states, "We should stand before the astounding effort of Soviet Russia to reorganize the industrial world with an open mind and listening ears."

30. "The Crisis of the *Crisis*," *Messenger*, July 1919, p. 10.

31. Anderson, *A. Philip Randolph*, pp. 100–101, 10.

32. "A Record of the Darker Races," *Messenger*, Sept. 1920, pp. 84–85; Owen, "The Failure of the Negro Leaders," p. 23.

33. Anderson, *A. Philip Randolph*, pp. 115–119.

34. "W. E. B. Du Bois," *Messenger*, July 1918, p. 27.

35. Anderson, *A. Philip Randolph*, p. 122.

36. Ibid., pp. 122–123; Tony Martin, *Race First: The Ideological and Organizational Struggles of Marcus Garvey and the Universal Negro Improvement Association* (Westport, Conn., 1976), pp. 9–10. On the Garvey Movement, also see Amy Jacques-Garvey, ed., *The Philosophy and Opinions of Marcus Garvey*, vols. 1 and 2 (rpt., New York, 1977).

37. Martin, *Race First*, p. 182. After Harrison's newspaper, *The Voice*, closed in 1919, Garvey offered him a position on the *Negro World*. During 1920–1921 Harrison was "joint editor" of the paper. Martin, *Race First*, p. 92.

38. "A Negro Party," *Messenger*, Nov. 1920, pp. 130–131.

39. Martin, *Race First*, p. 320.

40. "The Garvey Movement: A Promise or a Menace," *Messenger*, Dec. 1920, p. 171. Throughout the entire history of the *Messenger* one finds an anti-nationalistic bias. Randolph and Owen even took the extreme position that the greatest danger to American Socialism and the trade union movement was not the racist, conservative white worker, but the Negro! "Negroes must learn to differentiate between white capitalists and white workers," the editors declared. Since they do not, "this makes the Negro both a menace to the radicals and the capitalists. For inasmuch as he thinks that all white men are his enemies, he is as inclined to direct his hate at white employers as he is to direct it at white workers." In the *Messenger*'s opinion, the only hope was for organized labor to "harness the discontent of Negroes and direct it into the working-class channels for working-class emancipation." "The Negro—A Menace to Radicalism," *Messenger*, May-June 1919, p. 20.

41. Ibid., pp. 170–172.

42. Editorial, *Messenger*, Nov. 1922, p. 523.

43. Editorial, *Messenger*, July 1922, p. 437.

44. A. Philip Randolph, "The Only Way to Redeem Africa," *Messenger*, Jan. 1923, pp. 568–570, and Feb. 1923, pp. 612–614. Du Bois's comments against the Garvey organization were provocative. He defended the *Negro World* against Attorney General Palmer's attacks during the Red Summer of 1919, and in late 1920 described Garvey as "an honest and sincere man with a tremendous vision, great dynamic force, stubborn determination and unselfish desire to serve." In 1921, he admitted that the "main lines" of the UNIA's activities "are perfectly feasible." It was only in 1922 and 1923, when Garvey began to consider the Ku Klux Klan as a potential ally to the black liberation movement, that Du Bois registered his strongest denunciations. See "Radicals," *Crisis*, Dec. 1919; "Marcus Garvey," a two-part essay in *Crisis*, Dec. 1920 and Jan. 1921; "Back to Africa," *Century Magazine*, Feb. 1923, pp. 539–548.

45. Anderson, *A. Philip Randolph*, p. 82.

46. Harold Cruse, *The Crisis of the Negro Intellectual* (New York, 1967), pp. 45, 75. At its peak in 1921, the ABB had 2,500 members in 56 chapters throughout the country. It demanded the right for black self-defense, "absolute race equality," a "free Africa," and political suffrage. In many respects, its platform was strikingly similar to the agendas of Malcolm X's Organization of Afro-American Unity, over 40 years later. See "Cyril Briggs and the African Blood Brotherhood," WPA Writers' Project No. 1, Schomberg Collection, New York Public Library.

47. Ibid., p. 46.

48. The final break between the black Marxist-Leninists and Social Democrats does not come in early 1919, as many have suggested, but much later. As late as mid-1920 Briggs was a participant in Randolph's Friends of Negro Freedom. Martin, *Race First*, p. 320.

49. "The Menace of Negro Communists," *Messenger*, Aug. 1923, p. 784. The division between black Socialists and Communists tended to be along ethnic as well as political lines. Cruse observes that "after 1919, the split among Negro Socialists tended to take a more or less American Negro vs. West Indian Negro character. The Americans, led by Randolph, refused to join the Communists, while the West Indians—Moore, Briggs and Huiswoud—did." There were several exceptions; Fort-Whiteman, an American, joined the Communists. It is interesting to note that Cruse does not fully discuss the fate of Harrison, a revolutionary Socialist who abandoned the Socialist Party because of its racism and never joined the Marxist-Leninists; a black nationalist who nevertheless did not wholeheartedly embrace the Garvey phenomenon. His primary concerns were generating independent black political activity and developing a greater race-consciousness among all Socialists. See H. Cruse, *The Crisis of the Negro Intellectual*, p. 118.

50. Du Bois, "Communists Boring into Negro Labor," *New York Times*, Jan. 17, 1926, pp. 1–2.

51. Du Bois, "Socialism and the Negro," *Crisis*, Oct. 1921, p. 245; Du Bois, "The Class Struggle," *Crisis*, Aug. 1921, p. 151.

52. Emmett J. Scott, "The Business Side of a University," *Messenger*, Nov. 1923, p. 864. Early in its career, the *Messenger* was not reticent in its denunciations of Moton. "Moton has neither the courage, education or the opportunity to do any-

thing fundamental in the interest of the Negro," Randolph declared in 1919. "He counsels satisfaction, not intelligent discontent: he is ignorant of the fact that progress has taken place among any people in proportion as they have become discontented with their position. . . ." "Robert Russa Moton," *Messenger*, July 1919, p. 31.

53. "High Types of Negro Business Men," *Messenger*, Jan. 1925, p. 21.

54. "Samuel Gompers," *Messenger*, March 1919, p. 22; "Why Negroes Should Join the I.W.W.," *Messenger*, July 1919, p. 8; and "Unionizing of Negro Workers," *Messenger*, Oct. 1919, pp. 8–10.

55. "The Knowledge Trust," *Messenger*, May 1925, pp. 197, 209.

56. "Black Persons in Selected Professional Occupations, 1890–1970," "Percent of Persons 5 to 20 Years Old Enrolled in School," and "Illiteracy in the Population 14 Years Old and Over for Selected Years," in U.S. Department of Commerce, Bureau of the Census, *The Social and Economic Status of the Black Population in the United States: An Historical View, 1790–1978* (Washington, D.C., 1979), pp. 76, 89, 91.

57. Brazeal, *The Brotherhood of Sleeping Car Porters*, p. 40. At this time Randolph also began a modest effort within the AFL to drum up support for the Brotherhood's position against Pullman. See Randolph, "Case of the Pullman Porter," *American Federationist*, Nov. 1926, pp. 1334–1339.

58. Ibid., p. 18; Anderson, *A. Philip Randolph*, p. 140. Crosswaith eventually became a member of New York City's Housing Authority, appointed by Mayor Fiorello LaGuardia in the early forties. Earlier, he had been a leading political opponent of Marcus Garvey, and revolutionary Socialist Party theorist.

59. Anderson, *A. Philip Randolph*, pp. 171–174; Harris, *Keeping the Faith*, pp. 76, 78–79, 91. It is significant to note that Du Bois had anticipated Randolph's interest in the porters by at least a decade. In a brief essay for the *New York Times*, Du Bois suggested that the porters should organize as a union and strike for higher wages and better working conditions. See Du Bois, "The Pullman Porter," *New York Times*, March 16, 1914, p. 5.

60. Robert L. Vann, conservative black editor of the Pittsburgh *Courier*, argued that "the company will not deal with [Randolph] because of his history as a socialist. It is known that American capital will not negotiate with socialists." *Courier*, April 14, 1927. A more fundamental reason was provided by one lower-level Pullman boss to his black employees: "Remember, this is a white man's country, white people run it, will keep on running it, and this company will never sit down around the same table with Randolph as long as he's black." Anderson, *A. Philip Randolph,* p. 181.

61. Harris, *Keeping the Faith*, p. 110; Foner, *Organized Labor and the Black Worker*, pp. 183–184.

62. Harris, *Keeping the Faith*, p. 111; Foner, *Organized Labor and the Black Worker*, p. 185.

63. Harris, *Keeping the Faith*, p. 112.

64. Ibid., pp. 113, 114.

65. Foner, *Organized Labor and the Black Worker*, p. 184.

66. Anderson, *A. Philip Randolph*, pp. 204–205. It should be noted as well that after 1928 Randolph remained "the dominant figure" in the Brotherhood, but no longer wielded "absolute power." Webster demanded and won the right to have all

major union decisions made within the Brotherhood's Policy Committee, which he chaired. Historian William H. Harris describes Randolph as the union's "national black leader," whereas Webster was "a union organizer. Randolph thought in wider terms; he saw the problem of black sin the totality of American society, whereas Webster thought mainly of the porters and of finding ways to improve their conditions at Pullman."

67. Ralph J. Bunche, "A Critical Analysis of the Tactics and Programs of Minority Groups," *Journal of Negro Education*, 1935, pp. 308–320; Ralph J. Bunche, "The Programs of Organizations Devoted to the Improvement of the Status of the American Negro," *Journal of Negro Education*, 1939, pp. 539–550; A. Philip Randolph, "The Trade Union Movement and the Negro," *Journal of Negro Education*, 1936, pp. 54–58; Walter Green Daniel, "A National Negro Congress," *Journal of Negro Education*, 1936, A. Philip Randolph, "Why I Would Not Stand for Re-Election as President of the National Negro Congress," *American Federationist*, July 1940, pp. 24–25.

68. Anderson, *A. Philip Randolph*, p. 254.

69. Ibid., pp. 254–255.

70. Ibid., pp. 241–261.

71. August Meier and Elliot Rudwick, *From Plantation to Ghetto* (rev. ed.; New York, 1970).

72. On the question of Malcolm, we confront again the inconsistencies of Randolph's views on black nationalism. According to one source, Randolph was "a friend and admirer of Malcolm" even during his years as minister of Harlem's Temple Number Seven of the Nation of Islam. In 1962, Randolph invited him to serve on the Committee on Social and Economic Unity, a multiethnic coalition in Harlem. Several conservative black ministers threatened to leave when Malcolm arrived. Randolph replied that he would leave immediately if Malcolm was denied a voice on the committee. See Anderson, *A. Philip Randolph*, pp. 13–14.

73. Harold Cruse, *Rebellion or Revolution* (New York, 1968).

74. Harold Cruse, *The Crisis of the Negro Intellectual*, p. 65.

75. W. E. B. Du Bois, "The Field and Function of the Negro College," in Herbert Aptheker, ed., *The Education of Black People, Ten Critiques, 1906–1960* (New York, 1973), pp. 95–96.

CHAPTER ELEVEN

Organizing Against Sexual Harassment

by the Alliance Against Sexual Coercion

In 1976, when the Alliance Against Sexual Coercion was founded, sexual harassment was not a topic of public concern. That same year, *Redbook* magazine included a questionnaire asking women if they received unwanted sexual attention on the job. Of the 9,000 women who responded, a startling 88 percent reported harassment. The response was a complete surprise to almost everyone at that time.

Today, sexual harassment stories are featured in newspapers and magazines; TV specials and movies address the issue explicitly. Sexual harassment has been made illegal under the Title VII sex discrimination law, as well as other statutes. Women who are harassed can (sometimes) collect unemployment if they quit their jobs. Feminists have won some victories.

In the process feminists and leftists have come to understand more of the subtle dynamics of power and sex in workplaces (and in universities, where many cases have been documented). Some of us have come to recognize as harassment, dynamics which formerly we accepted as inevitable aspects of male-female interaction in the workplace. Our definitions of what we will accept as "normal" have changed. Along with these changes, our confidence in ourselves as women and as workers defining what we want and need in our lives has grown.

But work on the issue of sexual harassment is not simple. Legal solutions do not encourage the kind of workplace organizing which would

Reprinted from Vol. 15, No. 4 (July-August 1981).

ultimately give women greater power vis-a-vis management. Historically in the U.S. the women's liberation movement, particularly the violence-against-women movement from which AASC evolved, has been separated from the labor movement. Both labor leaders and leftists have been indifferent, suspicious, or even hostile toward organizing around "women's issues." Yet sexual harassment is an issue which combines insights from both the labor and women's movements.

In the Alliance Against Sexual Coercion, we see sexual harassment as the intersection of two perspectives: first, as a working women's issue, since the harassment is affected by the unequal power relationships of the workplace; and second, as an issue of violence against women. We feel that these aspects of sexual harassment are interrelated and interdependent. The economic insecurity of working women is intensified by the threat that sexual harassment might escalate from subtle to much more serious and blatant actions involving physical and sexual assault. The threat of such violence has always kept women "in their place" as defined by men, and in the workplace it serves to keep women isolated and powerless.

AASC was founded by three women who had worked in the movement against rape. The violence-against-women movement identified the inequality of men and women and showed how our society was structured around male power and sexism. But because sexual harassment occurs at work and is only one issue among the many problems women workers face, AASC found that it was necessary not only to create separate services for sexually harassed women but also to expand our analysis and explore strategies for dealing with sexual harassment and sexism on the job. The violence-against-women movement had initiated certain strategies and institutions such as rape crisis centers for women to deal with emotional aspects of rape, and shelters for battered women. On a small scale, self-defense skills were shared and women became much more aware of their own relationship to the social system. But these strategies were not viable within a job context. These women had to go to work every day and deal with the harassment each day. Dealing with the emotional aspects of violence against women, or being more self-aware or knowing self-defense, helps to give a woman more control, but it does not confront the issue of economic dependence and survival.

Violence is an underpinning to social control in this society, and the use of it to control women is readily accepted. A woman will not complain to another woman or to a man about sexual harassment if she feels that they condone the behavior. But this is not the only reason why a woman might not complain: the strict hierarchies and regimentation of the workplace discourage any complaint from men *or* women. People are tracked and expected to stay tracked; it is much easier to fire those who balk than to change the hierarchy of the institution. There is no assumed level of worker support, particularly in cases involving sexual harassment. All of these factors are part of our analysis of sexual harassment in the workplace, as both issues of violence against women and as an economic issue facing women workers.

Any woman who strives to be economically independent knows consciously or unconsciously, that she is stepping out of place. The threat of violence is a means of pushing her back to validate herself according to a male definition—to "go back to the home" psychologically or actually. Whether women work out of necessity (as most do) or out of choice, the threat of violence tells them they should understand themselves as marginal to the world of paid work. In 75 percent of our cases, subtle harassment does escalate to a more blatant form. Whether women are conscious of it or not, this is part of the reason that women remain powerless and fear to do anything. Women are conditioned to feel that if they confront the issue directly, it will most likely escalate, for sexual harassment at the workplace is an issue of power, and experience shows that pressing the issue will bring on an intensified response. It seems easier to do nothing than to complain, because complaining is stepping out of line, and stepping out of line brings on a display of power and control in our society.

These are some of the reasons why creating strategies to deal with sexual harassment in the workplace is a difficult task. The first step is to challenge women's socialization, to reveal how it disempowers them, and to show how society is structured around their lack of control. The next step is to challenge the workplace structure and to show how women and Third World people are oppressed as workers in a capitalist society. There is no single course of action which will bring about these changes.

THE DEFINITION

In some early articulations, violence against women was more or less synonymous with the existence of a sexist, racist, and capitalist system in which women were, as members of our sex, race, and/or class, violated by individuals (men) and institutions. Now violence against women is more often narrowed to acts of physical harm caused by individual men, like rape or battering and violence in the media.

In the remainder of this article, we use the narrow definition. Work on sexual harassment has gained some focus by narrowing the definition but has lost some insight which came from the broader definition. We have gained a focus on the importance of the ever-present threat of physical violence as a means of maintaining sexism and preventing women from speaking out against more subtle harassment. Sexual harassment threatens not only a woman's job, but also her safety. Narrowing the definition, however, tends to obscure the way subtle acts which degrade a woman or treat her solely as a sex object are violations of her person; violations have strong emotional impact and generate a sense of powerlessness, regardless of whether the woman feels a greater threat to her safety or her job.

The ultimate message of the violence that is present in all aspects of our lives is that there is no escape from male power. That message remains in the linking of rape, battering, and sexual harassment, along with media violence as the core of violence-against-women organizing. The street, the home, the workplace, and even the world of fantasy and escape are dominated by male power, backed up by the threat of physical harm.

There are difficulties here. Power is also the basis of masculinity in our culture. Many women are attracted to men because they are, or at least appear to be, powerful. This attraction, however, is not to men who appear likely to be violent or cause harm. Rather, power seems to offer protection from violence or actual harm. Passive submissiveness, or at least its pretense, is a part of the definition of femininity. It is likely that powerful men will be attracted to women who play out this definition of femininity. Mutual attraction in the workplace can be the beginning of a fulfilling relationship for both people. It can also be a setup for a woman for the abuse of power the man has due to his position in the workplace—one quite likely to be over hers in the hierarchy. It can also be a setup for her due to his ability to wield male social power, regardless of his position in a workplace hierarchy.

Sexual harassment may often stem from a confusion of issues of sexual attractiveness, power, and violence against women on the part of the harasser. The harasser may fail to recognize the power he does have, denying the importance of the fact that he is above the woman in the workplace hierarchy, claiming that he is just approaching her "as a man" and that she is attracted to him because of who he is, not what he does. A woman may find it hard to sort out confusion as well. We suspect that such a confusion would be particularly difficult for a young woman (e.g., student) to sort out in relation to an older man (e.g., her professor) where other issues such as mentoring may come into play. One test of such a relationship is what happens when one person decides to end it. Can they come to a mutual decision about how to handle the resulting tensions? Or is the decision made by the more powerful person, resulting in negative effects on the woman's school or work life?

It is clear that what counts as a violation to one woman will not necessarily violate another. And it is important that women begin to define their own needs, to regain a sense of their own power. It is also important that men begin to see *real* women, to see women as individuals. Together, these three points are the basis for the Alliance's insistence that only a subjective definition of sexual harassment, one which incorporates the point of view of the person harassed, is adequate politically.

AASC defines sexual harassment as follows:

> Any unwanted sexual attention a woman experiences on the job, ranging from leering, pinching, patting, verbal comments, and subtle pressure for sexual activity, to attempted rape and rape. The sexual harasser may be the woman's employer, supervisor, co-worker, client, or customer. In addition

237

to the anxiety caused by sexual demands, there is the implicit message from the harasser that non-compliance will lead to reprisals. These reprisals can include escalating the harassment, poor work assignments, sabotaging a woman's work, sarcasm, unsatisfactory job evaluations, threatened demotions, transfers, denial of raises, promotions and benefits, and in the final analysis dismissal and poor job references.

CAPITALISM AND SEXUAL HARASSMENT

Sexual harassment is possible because sexism is an integral part of capitalism. Male dominance in the family or at home also means male dominance in the workplace (and vice versa). Sexual harassment expresses and reinforces this power relationship at work. Bosses, supervisors, managers, and owners are almost always men, and such occupational segregation not only perpetuates a close link between sex roles and job functions but also props up the system of depressed wages for women workers.

Recognizing male dominance under capitalism helps us to understand sexual harassment at the workplace because men have not only social control over women, but economic control also. This places women in a situation of double jeopardy. The two spheres of male power mutually reinforce each other, creating a situation in which men are socially and psychologically dominant—sometimes even when women are more highly placed in the workplace hierarchy. In other words, men can and do exert power over women even when they are lower in a job hierarchy or are not "economically fit" in providing for their families.

The leering boss chasing his secretary around the desk is a universal image of sexual harassment. Implicit here is the threat of job-related reprisals for not complying with his demand, a threat which results from the "office-wife" mentality. This view represents the secretary as the girl in the office who takes care of the boss at work while he's away from his wife at home. The "office-wife" mentality or the creation of the home in the workplace sets up a situation in which a woman is there to meet the needs of her boss. The boundaries concerning what a secretary actually has to do to fulfill her job responsibilities can and often do get fuzzy. The experience of women in these traditional jobs illustrates the fact that male power and dominance forms the basis for male-female relationships in the workforce.

The following are all ways in which capitalism has incorporated sexism, reinforcing male power and reaping increased benefits by the "superexploitation" of women:

1. The ideology that views women as a reserve labor force that works only when men are preoccupied with other activities, such as war.
2. The ideology that women belong at home, when in fact women must work to support themselves and/or their families.

3. The reserving of high-paying jobs for men by tradition and by current practice. This is justified by the myth of men's natural superiority as well as the definition of women as wife and mother, not worker.
4. The idea that women workers are only part-time or transitory help, rather than full-time steady help.

The function of these myths and ideologies is to increase the vulnerability of women workers and to justify the discrimination women face at work. Sexual harassment is only possible because of these myths and it, in turn, makes the position of women workers even more vulnerable.

Sexual harassment is a complex phenomenon. The two sources of power we are dealing with—male power and class power—overlap and support each other in a variety of ways.

Sexual harassment plays an important function in maintaining sexism and the exploitation of women at work. The effects of sexual harassment on women lead to low productivity, low morale, and high turnover among women workers. This simply reinforces sexist beliefs that women are not good workers, that they should only work certain jobs, and that men should have more power, higher wages, and higher status.

It is clear that sexual harassment is a function of sexism in society and of the sexist organization of work. Sexual harassment, as one expression of male power and sexuality, is a tool to maintain the system of male domination. Our understanding of this problem and of the possible strategies to challenge it must include an analysis of both male power and the structure of the capitalist workplace.

FIGHTING SEXUAL HARASSMENT

AASC's work around sexual harassment reflects two goals: (1) assisting women who have been sexually harassed in their workplace or school, and (2) challenging sexual harassment as a built-in condition of work and education for most American women. Challenging the institution of sexual harassment requires a confrontation with the structures of power that perpetuate it: capitalism, sexism, racism, heterosexism, and ageism.

AASC has assisted individual women from unorganized and unionized workplaces. We have worked with women who organized themselves to work as a group against particular harassers or for workplace and school grievance procedures. We have worked with women in workplace-based women's groups, both union and non-union.

Sexual harassment, like all other occupational hazards, is more difficult for unorganized workers to confront than for those in unions. Too often, workplace advocacy groups have failed to seriously address the situation of unorganized workers because the unions have traditionally acted as the primary avenue for providing information and resources about occupational hazards to workers. This has been particularly true in the occupational safety and health movement as most advocacy groups work closely with regional labor councils and do very little outreach to unorganized workers.

Only 11 percent of women workers are unionized. And until recently most unions have not been interested in "women's issues," meaning that it has taken some struggle to place sexual harassment on the union agenda. For both of these reasons, AASC has chosen to make contact with women workers independently through a telephone hotline rather than by working through unions or other workplace organizations.

We have found in our work, whether with unionized or with unorganized workers, that at times our goals conflict. A strategy that most expediently stops the harassment of an individual woman is not necessarily the same tactic that challenges the power structures and ideologies that allow and create harassment. Many women find that the best way to deal with particular situations of harassment is to leave them. This reaction might be the best "solution" for the individual woman, but it leaves the woman who takes her place vulnerable to the harasser. Many women are fearful, often with good reason, of the risks involved in pursuing strategies which might have a more lasting effect on the workplace.

Although we recognize the conflicts between these goals and try to raise consciousness about the importance of challenging the institution of sexual harassment while fighting a specific harasser, we also remain committed to a woman's right to decide what action she wants to take in a given situation. As an advocacy group, we offer support and information about possible risks and benefits, but women who are harassed must make their own decisions if they are to regain a sense of their own power, a sense which is generally undermined by harassment. Furthermore, they are in the best position to assess the possibilities and risks of various actions. And they must live wih the results. This means that we are limited in our ability to challenge an individual's decision, even if we disagree.

There are times, for example, when an individual woman may get more immediate results in her efforts to stop sexual harassment by complaining to a sympathetic person in the hierarchy than by organizing with other women. We've seen a concrete instance in a local hospital. A high-ranking hospital official was dismissed for sexual harassment after a secretary complained to a powerful doctor in the hospital. The doctor was a woman and understood her complaint; the doctor's father had also been a prominent figure in the history of the hospital. Even so, nothing was done by Personnel until the doctor put her complaint on behalf of the secretary in writing and threatened further action if the secretary was not protected. Although the harassment stopped, the secretary felt no greater sense of power in the workplace. Personnel went on to suggest that she should be transferred, and she had to continue to rely on the good will and understanding of the doctor.

Several other secretaries had been harassed by this hospital official.

Their organizing against him might have been less effective in stopping the harassment than the doctor's intervention was, given the harasser's power in the hospital and the expendability of the secretaries. On the other hand, they might have formed the core of a secretaries' organizing group that could eventually force changes with more long-term and truly empowering effects. Taking up sexual harassment as an organizing issue would have been more progressive over the long term. In the meantime, though, a number of secretaries might have lost their jobs or undergone intensified harassment.

Even if the secretaries had filed a joint complaint with the Equal Employment Opportunity Commission, a sex discrimination complaint leading to suit against the hospital, they would have faced a trade-off in their lives. They *might* have forced the hospital to pay for damages and forced it to institute grievance procedures. Thus they might have gained some power vis-a-vis the hospital. But they would have given several years of their lives over to a stressful court battle for whatever they gained in money or in precedents. A lawsuit becomes an act of self-sacrifice to try to establish even a meager legal precedent for other women. And these legal protections may be revoked (as we now see Reagan attempting to do with current guidelines against sexual harassment) by hostile presidential directives or legislation. In the end, the secretaries might wish they had simply found other jobs. Thus the goals of assisting individual women may conflict with the goal of challenging sexual harassment as an institution, along with the power structures which perpetuate it.

This conflict exists both in unorganized and unionized workplaces, but it is more prominent in the unorganized workplace where detailed channels for grieving do not exist. We have also seen cases of union women who face these same dilemmas because they have no real representation of their interests as women by the union. This backdrop is an important one to keep in mind as we look at potential strategies for fighting sexual harassment. We will first look briefly at sexual harassment and unions and then move on to look more closely at the situation of unorganized workers.

SEXUAL HARASSMENT AND UNIONS

AASC has provided information and programs for various union locals about sexual harassment and has helped women who approached us to raise the issue in their unions. Over the years, we have seen an improvement in the response of unions to this problem, but the basic framework from which unions approach workplace issues—as a simple conflict between management and workers—tends to obscure conflicts based on gender or race. Current controversies over affirmative action and the threat to traditional seniority rights illustrate the bind many unions are in—Which workers' rights are to be protected and which are to be sacrificed? The rights of women workers are not generally seen as a priority.

In fact, sexual harassment and affirmative action often go hand in hand.

Complying with affirmative-action guidelines is often a condition of receiving public money. Many companies initially hire women, then systematically subject them to sexual harassment; the women either quit or are fired during their probation period. In many contracts, management is not required to justify the firing, and employees on probation are not entitled to union representation. Either way—quitting or being fired—the company can claim it met its responsibility in good faith.

Evidence of sexual harassment being used as a union-busting technique also exists. When the Steelworkers were attempting to organize Canadian bank workers several years ago, members of management began harassing those tellers who were most prounion. Again, some women chose to quit, while others agreed to stop their union organizing efforts if the harassment would stop.

Given the widespread attention to sexual harassment as a serious problem, most unions would probably support a union member who was harassed by a member of management. Happily, the cases that have come to AASC's attention in which union officials chose to ignore such complaints are greatly outnumbered by the success stories. The most dramatic of these occurred in October 1979, when 1,400 workers walked out at Simpson Plywood in Washington state to protest several instances of women in the International Woodworkers of America being sexually harassed during job interviews. Women were asked to take off their blouses, asked if they wore a bra, and asked if they were willing to have sex with the supervisor. One woman filed sex discrimination charges with the Washington Human Rights Commission and the EEOC. She was fired after filing. The firing triggered the strike, which spread to Simpson plants in California and eventually involved over 3,000 workers.

We acknowledge the conflicts for unions in handling sexual harassment between co-workers. As mentioned earlier, most unions are not prepared to step in to resolve sex- or race-based complaints and need to develop methods of intervening in such conflicts between union members. The results of this neglect are seen in increasing friction between female and Third World workers and the white men who control the unions.

Examples of unions creatively handling cases of coworker harassment are quite rare. Union women around the country report being discouraged from filing a grievance against a union brother. Grieving is often viewed as a divisive act, one that allows management to discipline union members. In contrast, the harassment itself is not often seen as divisive, nor as violating a union's "brotherhood" codes. In cases where grievances are filed, the union is placed in a difficult position; they are obligated both to support the woman's grievance (by EEOC guidelines) and to represent the harasser if he is disciplined by management.

Of course there are strong positive reasons for unions to take sexual harassment seriously, and to deal with it before it takes place. In times where unions need to increase membership and organize workers in new fields, a firm stand against sexual harassment can make a difference. This proved to be a pivotal issue in a recent strike at Boston University by clerical and library workers. District 65 of the UAW won a specific clause in its contract which prohibits harassment, provides a definition, and indicates that grievances will be handled quickly. Fearing similar success during an organizing drive at hospitals in the Harvard Medical Complex, administrators launched a series of training sessions on sexual harassment for all women employees.

Sexual harassment also forms an important bridge between traditional health and safety issues (e.g., noise levels in factories, presence of toxic substances) and other issues relating to the quality of the working environment. After a black woman was raped by a white man in a bathroom at a General Electric plant in Massachusetts last year, the Women's Committee of Local 201 of the International Union of Electrical Workers took action. In addition to responding to the specific event, they distributed a survey to women on all shifts of all of GE's plants. The survey sought to determine the extent of sexual harassment and sexual assault experienced by women, and how safety concerns affected their choice of shifts with pay differentials. By linking sexual harassment and sexual assault with other workplace safety issues, they increased the awareness of all union members. Women from the United Mine Workers and United Steel Workers of America have also included sexual harassment and sexual discrimination with traditional health and safety issues when picketing or taking other job actions.

The legal (EEOC) requirement for workplace training on sexual harassment can be useful for initiating educational programs in locals where they don't already exist. Following the incident at GE described above, the union incorporated workshops into its regularly scheduled business meetings. Films and speakers from community women's organizations were used to encourage internal discussion between men and women on societal images of women, the effects of these images on men and women who work side by side, and sexual harassment. Co-workers can learn to respect each other's definitions of appropriate workplace behavior as they become conscious of sexism and its effects. Unions can distribute literature from sexual-harassment groups, sample contract clauses, and case histories from other locals or unions. Stewards can be trained to assist women and to mediate between co-workers. Women's committees, health and safety committees, or union officials can use general membership meetings to inform members about how to report sexual harassment (a specific person, preferably a woman, should be designated as the recipient of such complaints) and how to meet the required standards of proof.

SEXUAL HARASSMENT AND UNORGANIZED WORKERS

As mentioned earlier, AASC's work is largely conducted via a telephone hotline. This approach has both positive and negative consequences. We do reach the unorganized woman worker who often has no other resources to help challenge the workplace problems. From the vantage point of offering emotional support and basic information about potential strategies and options, our work is both valuable and successful; however, from an organizing perspective, there are many limitations. Our contact is almost always with an individual woman in a workplace who is experiencing sexual harassment in isolation. The one-to-one nature of this contact places us in the service-provider role rather than in a position to catalyze organized action. We can (and do) make suggestions that involve soliciting co-worker support and taking action in conjunction with other workers, but collective action in an unorganized workplace is so difficult (and often even harder when sexual harassment is the issue) that many women choose to pursue a strategy that does not involve a lot of publicity and reliance on co-workers.

Whatever theories we hold, it is crucial to understand the ways in which sexual harassment and complaints resulting from it are experienced in the unorganized workplace.

Being sexually harassed often means losing your job no matter what you do. A woman's job is on the line whether she rebuffs the harasser but doesn't tell anyone, acts to stop the harassment, decides under pressure to comply with the demands, or ignores the harassment and hopes it will go away. In each of these cases, we have seen women who were eventually fired on the pretense of poor work performance or insubordination, or who were forced to leave an intolerable situation of constant harassment. We are not saying that it is useless to fight sexual harassment in the workplace or that a woman should leave as soon as the harassment begins. Rather, we are saying that there is no safety in staying quiet and trying to keep the problem between herself and the harasser. In fact, we have found that a woman's greatest protection in keeping her job is to speak out and let everyone know exactly what is happening and how she feels about it.

We cannot emphasize strongly enough how important it is to overcome the many myths and fears that cause women to remain silent. Many people still believe that sexual harassment doesn't really occur unless the victim provokes it or tries to "sleep her way to the top." Thus, a woman who complains of sexual harassment is often confronted with a barrage of questions that implicate her and play on any feelings of self-blame she may already be experiencing. Women who complain of sexual harassment are often seen as troublemakers and humorless prudes who "just can't take a joke." The chances of retaliatory action, ranging from increased harassment and work sabotage to firing, are high. Some co-workers will be afraid to associate with the "troublemaker" in the workplace. Harassers are often in a position to fire employees who step out of line, so taking any action at all entails great risks. And finally, for many people sexual harassment is difficult to talk about because it means talking about sex and sexual violations—taboo topics in our culture.

These factors forcefully keep women isolated and silent about their experiences with sexual harassment. Many women feel too embarrassed or afraid to speak out about the harassment and also believe that it is safer to remain silent. Remaining silent ensures that a woman will remain isolated and unprotected from any action the harasser chooses to take. If the harassment continues and a woman decides to try to grieve at a later point, she will have no witnesses or support, or if it gets to a point that she can no longer tolerate, she has no verification that she has been *forced* out of her job.

These real experiences are a starting point for evaluating the options for confronting sexual harassment. On the one hand, our understanding of the many dangers and complex power struggles does not allow us to paint a hopeful picture for sexual harassment victims, but on the other hand, our experience does suggest that taking collective action in an unorganized workplace may well be worth the risk.

With this in mind, we would like to suggest some specific tactics that can be used to fight sexual harassment. The first option we will discuss involves varying levels of co-worker support and does not rely on utilizing formal grievance procedures within the workplace. The first step in pursuing any course of action is to break the isolation of sexual harassment. This can be done in a number of ways. Placing leaflets about sexual harassment in bathrooms or publicizing the name of the harasser can be an effective means of communication. Another option might be to survey your workplace to determine what the incidence of sexual harassment actually is. This information is particularly helpful in validating individuals' experience and in convincing those who might be skeptical that sexual harassment is a "real" workplace problem. This can be done discretely and safely. There is also the option of discussing your situation with as many co-workers as possible, and then perhaps forming a workplace safety committee that would meet regularly to discuss the situation and to decide on group action.

The following is an example from our caseload of a successful strategy that resulted from the women in a workplace talking and acting together. A new man/boss was hired, and he soon began harassing many of the 14 secretaries in the typing pool on the sly. Their tentative efforts to talk to each other about it made them aware of the problem and revealed that each of them felt threatened and isolated as well as very angry. Together the women decided that each time he called one of them into his office, a co-worker would accompany her so no one would ever be alone with him. If he insisted on speaking with only one woman, then the other would leave the door to his office open as she went out. The situation placed the man in an extremely awkward position and made it very difficult for him to continue his harassment. He quit within a month. This story exemplifies one of the wide range of options available to women who truly have the support of their co-workers.

Each of the tactics offers a chance to fight sexual harassment but they all require a willingness to raise the subject within the workplace and then to take responsibility for educating those who don't take it seriously. These strategies certainly help a woman who is actually being harassed by creating a network that can help develop a plan of action as well as offer support. It is also very helpful to pursue one or all of these tactics *before* a situation of harassment actually occurs. If sexual harassment has already been discussed in a workplace, the climate is better for responding to a specific instance of harassment.

We have successfully used two other options for fighting sexual harassment outside of traditional workplace solutions to problems. The first is an educational picket in front of the worksite. For obvious reasons, this strategy is not realistic unless a woman has quit her job or knows that she will inevitably have to leave anyway. Pickets certainly have the advantage of drawing public attention to the problem of sexual harassment and embarrassing the employer by pointing a finger at a specific workplace.

The second tactic is to send a warning letter to the harasser. At the request of a worker, AASC sends warning letters that let the harasser know that his behavior is illegal, and perhaps more importantly, that someone else knows what he is doing. We have found, however, that warning letters sometimes have the effect of escalating rather than stopping the harassment. This option should be chosen only if a woman is prepared to deal with more blatant and direct forms of harassment. Another type of warning letter is one that is sent to the employer rather than the harasser. The employer is legally liable for providing a harassment-free environment, and this type of warning has been helpful in forcing companies to adopt policy statements and grievance procedures concerning sexual harassment.

Another option is to file a grievance through company policy if such a grievance policy exists. Most women will utilize this type of strategy more readily than they will pursue one of the other options outlined here. Filing a grievance is an individual action that does not involve public outcry such as telling the story of being harassed to other co-workers. It is a legitimate channel for grieving (from the employer's perspective) so that it is *seemingly* safer in terms of keeping your job. The reality is that many women who file grievances for sexual harassment are subjected to harsh recriminations on the part of the employer, the harasser, and even some co-workers. These women are often without support or protection of any kind because they have filed as an individual without soliciting support and aid within the workplace. Even so, the myth tells us that we should be "good" workers and follow company policy. If a woman chooses to pursue a legal strategy ranging from filing for unemployment to lodging a complaint with the EEOC, she must first use the employer's existing channels for complaints and give him or her an opportunity to rectify the situation.

We recognize that a workplace policy on sexual harassment is something to get excited about only if workers maintain some awareness about its potential misuse. It doesn't necessarily offer much protection for a sexual harassment victim; it implies that individual solutions to the problems of sexual harassment are possible, and that women workers can rely on management to take care of their problems. In many cases, the harasser and the person administering the policy are so close that a woman might not even be able to file a complaint.

The issue of using company policy only becomes more complicated when the harasser is a co-worker rather than a supervisor or part of management. We have seen instances in which a worker files a complaint against a male co-worker out of desperation and lack of options and then is appalled to find out that she looses complete control over the process and over what might happen to resolve the situation.

In other words, when the harasser is disciplined or fired, it may be for reasons other than the harassment: perhaps he is personally disliked; maybe he is not wanted in the workplace because of union work, his color, or his national background; possibly the management is religiously or moralistically opposed to sex, or the owners fear negative publicity or legal action. Issues of worker harassment, union harassment, and racism then come into play. Any individual "victory" in getting a harasser fired can also be a defeat for those of us who see sexual harassment as being rooted in broader power relationships. When anti-sex attitudes prevail then the liberation we seek is undermined by a limited vision of who we are as people and a view of sexuality which is ultimately anti-woman. If only women who can afford a lawyer and are not intimidated by the legal system (or by publicity about the actions taken against them) can be effective in stopping harassment, men will simply choose easier victims. Here the conflict between helping a woman and confronting power structures is deepest.

It is still worthwhile to have a policy against sexual harassment on the books. There are those occasions in which the policy provides just enough legitimacy and safety for a woman to pursue some form of direct or collective action with a minimal amount of protection. A stated policy and grievance procedure also helps clarify before the fact how the employer might respond to sexual harassment and helps to make that response consistent. With no clear policy outlined before, the employer can justify any action he or she chooses to take and simply use sexual harassment as a tool for selective punishment of certain employees. Given that women who are being sexually harassed often feel forced to go to Personnel at some point during the experience, it is better to have a policy than not to have one. The key is to be very clear about the limits and potential abuses of such a policy.

Sexual harassment is a complicated issue. Fighting it requires an understanding of how sexism, racism, and class privilege operate in our society and in the workplace. Sexual harassment occurs within the work setting because of strict hierarchies which result from and reinforce capitalist economic organization. These class hierarchies are not always structured along race and gender lines, although we have found that race, class, and gender often coincide. When trying to decide what to do about sexual harassment, we have to take all of these exploitative systems into account.

As leftists and feminists, we can understand why sexual harassment occurs and in many ways it comes as no surprise that it does. What has not been acknowledged to date is the very real bind a woman experiencing harassment is in. We constantly hear about all the problems with the legal system and with using formal or institutional channels to grieve. But along with these very necessary critiques must be a serious understanding of the limited options that do exist. We must be *as concerned* with protecting the woman being harassed and her right to take action as we are with the potential (and probable) misuse of formal complaint channels. This requires not only extensive education about sexual harassment and ways to fight it, but also concerted action by both female and male workers within a workplace before harassment ever occurs.

PART THREE

Militancy,
Union Politics,
and Workers' Control

The articles in this section focus on the relationship between organized workers and union leaders, and specifically on the tension between rank-and-file concerns on the one hand and the demands of large labor organizations with national contracts on the other hand. The authors explore various kinds of militant activity ranging from wildcat strikes during World War II to recent demands for black power and health and safety in the workplace. In general more radical demands seem to be brought to the surface by rank-and-file workers, as the Black Lung Association and the Miners for Democracy did for the United Mine Workers union. Then rank-and-file insurgency becomes part of union politics. Union officials can see militancy from below as a threat or they can respond by introducing reforms and incorporating rank-and-file leaders into the organization.

In most of the cases described here union politics have been unresponsive to rank-and-file demands. On the other hand, as Stan Weir says in his discussion of worker movements in the early seventies, militants found it difficult to break out of their isolation and create alternative forms of organization. As the economic crisis worsened in the late seventies, labor union leaders, mainly at a local level, began to react more creatively to rank-and-file discontent. Dave Wagner and Paul Buhle explain, for example, how fairly traditional craft unions joined with other workers to collectively run a worker-owned strike newspaper in Madison, Wisconsin. And in his concluding article David Montgomery describes how some local unions have sought to take over plants abandoned by their owners. He suggests that the struggle for control, identified in Section I, has taken on a new dimension as a result of plant closings. In addition to demanding collective bargaining rights and asserting the need for greater democracy and dignity on the job, workers now have to exert some control over investment decisions. If they do not, and their plants are moved to low-wage areas, all of their other struggles will have been fought in vain.

Clearly, the international unions and the labor movement generally have to be more responsive to the kind of struggles described in this section. At a time when experts are seriously discussing the "fall of the house of labor" and the eclipse of organized labor in the industrial states, it is time for radical departures from the conservative past. Instead of experimenting with new policies conceived and executed by top labor leaders, the union officialdom might do well to encourage the creative militancy erupting at the local union level. The AFL-CIO might also begin to see that workers' struggles initiated outside the ranks of organized labor have the energy, solidarity, and sense of purpose the official movement lacks.

CHAPTER TWELVE

The Conflict in American Unions and the Resistance to Alternative Ideas from the Rank and File

by Stan Weir

Socialists have remained for over 20 years trapped within objective conditions, unable to perform their necessary roles and often indifferent to the very necessity of social theory. As a consequence, there is not one revolutionary Socialist organization, in the full meaning of the term. "Socialist" and "revolutionary" are often used, but rarely have more than rhetorical, anti-capitalist content. As individuals most Socialists have developed their own vision of a better society, and have often shared their vision unsystematically with those closest to them, but can find no organization devoting itself (that is, its collective membership) to the job of concretizing and giving life to that vision. For all the admirable expenditure of energy and self-sacrifice, individuals and groups work with limited tools that stunt growth. Therein lies much of the unhappy and even surly atmosphere that surrounds and infuses existing organizations. Slogans are offered, for instance, which may be good, but have little to support them. Those in the general working public reached by the slogans have little opportunity to distinguish between transitional and reformist efforts: Without some supportive efforts, the former can be as unappealing, dry, and husklike as the latter. What ideas Socialists do obtain are for the most part gained empirically, with little if any mediation between practical activity and theory. Within the Socialist groups, education is generally seen as a process of

Extensively abridged from Vol. 6, No. 3 (May-June 1972).

exposure to the writings of the Marxist greats, histories of the class struggle, critiques of specific areas of bourgeois society (generally related to factional self-justification), and little more. The full-time theoretical pursuits that can merge the intellectual life of an organization with its day-to-day functions in the outside world generally do not exist, or do so parasitically as the perpetual self-replication of the organization as is. . . .

YESTERDAY'S THEORY, TODAY'S REALITY

The industrial-union revolution of 1932 to 1941, out of which the CIO was born, allowed American radicals a very high degree of identification with the official organizations and leadership of the labor unions. Communist, Socialist, Trotskyist, and anarcho-syndicalist parties and groups, each in almost exact ratio to their size, had members who became official labor leaders or who became influential advisors to new official leaders. Particularly from the time of the outbreak of general strikes in San Francisco and Minneapolis, through the inception of the CIO (first as a committee within the AFL and then as an independent federation), to the time of the outbreak of World War II, alliances between radical intellectuals, rank-and-file workers, and a new generation of labor officials came easily. Most often with different goals, though there were many illusions to the contrary, they agreed on one major issue: Industrial unionism as an institution was a progressive development. The alliances were unique and short-lived, but it was under the influence of this period that the American radical movement last developed a full set of attitudes and theories on the labor movement.

Now, thirty years almost to the day after the close of that period, there is no ideological basis for a healthy or ongoing relationship between the ranks and the officialdom of labor. And, it has been so many years since radicals have been a presence within the unions that it is difficult for them to learn and articulate clearly the ideological basis for the historically demanded realliance between themselves and the ranks. The once fresh and progressive young workers who rose from the ranks to the top positions of leadership in many of the unions have long since succumbed to bureaucratic conservatism.

The depth of the bureaucratic degeneration of the labor leadership and the speed with which the bureaucratization process occurred is a principal, and in some cases the principal, cause of demoralization, skepticism, and cynicism among labor militants and socialists—former, present, and potential. Without a full theoretical analysis of the causes of past examples of bureaucratic degeneration and a positive prognosis for the future that is scientifically based, Socialists appear to operate on no more than impressionistic assertions of faith in the working class. The volume of cynical academic literature on the question of bureaucracy grows, undealt with by Socialists. Socialists seem unaware that works like Robert Michels's *Political Parties*, given ever new life by the work of Seymour Martin Lipset, provide a formidable challenge to the very theoretical foundations of working-class socialism as long as they remain unanswered. In fact, the tenets—both implied and explicit—on which the writings of Lipset and Michels are based have almost biblical importance for those who live in the ignorance that bureaucratism is an eternal inevitability. This crisis alone provides a major task for socialists and their theoretical publications. Failure to attack it means failure to win respect and support in the intellectual community.

From the outset of the industrial-union revolution, the followers of the Communist Party in the labor unions set the tone for radicals. Their primary focus was on obtaining official power in the unions. Those with Marxist and other radical tendencies separated themselves from the Communists mainly by their adherence to the democratic principles of internal union government and their lack of opportunism, but their focus was still on obtaining official power for themselves or independent militants. The entire process was aided by the fact that rank-and-file militants were themselves focused primarily on the problem of who would obtain power over formal and official union bodies. It was natural that this should be their concentration because (a) official union machinery was needed just to make the new unions operative, (b) the unions were new in many industries and there were widespread and panacean illusions about what they could accomplish, and (c) the power of the informal work-group organizations in the workplace was at a peak and they were able to exercise a great deal of control over the formal local union structures.

But the industrial-union revolution did not institutionalize around the goals and aspirations that were foremost in the minds of the workers who made it. The primary motivation for industrial unions in labor's ranks came out of the alienation and indignities that workers experienced on the job. Almost spontaneously, it seemed, they formed unions in the workplace; but they were dealing for the most part with nationwide corporations. The power of local unions in each workplace had to be centralized in order to keep the employers from playing off the workers in one workplace against the workers making the same product in another. The major fight to humanize working conditions had to be postponed until nationwide contracts were obtained. This facilitated the transfer of local autonomy to the top union leaders in the international headquarters. The postponement, with the aid of World War II, has lasted for more than a generation. The outbreak of rank-and-file revolts in the early 1960s served notice on a now case-hardened bureaucracy that the ranks intended to resume the fight to win dignity at work.

Disillusioned with their unions, though not about to reject them, rank-and-file militants today do not focus primarily on obtaining power per se within the formal union governmental structure. They have learned that that is not the means to the end they seek. Instead they often bypass that power fight and seek a direct and radical expansion of their powers or their democratic rights in the total collective-bargaining process. They want autonomy over the grievance procedure, the choice of bargaining goals, and contract administration.

Thus far the main tactics they have employed to pressure for these goals have been voting against the acceptance of contracts negotiated by their leaders, and wildcat strikes. At times these have assumed mass character, particularly the former tactic. Neither of the tactics has been coordinated on a regional or national level in more than a handful of instances, and even then the coordination has not come out of strong centralized organization. No large-scale progress toward the goals has been made. Dozens and dozens of local unions within an international have elected rebel delegates to conventions, and again because of the lack of regional or national coordination little advance has been made.

Does progress await the formation of stronger local rank-and-file caucuses whose power is then centralized nationally? Hundreds of locals have elected new and more militant leaders from the ranks. This has helped, but it has been insufficient to achieve the needed degree of change. Is the problem again the lack of coordination of revolt on a national basis? If so, the task of militants is somewhat simplified and is one of building and waiting, seeking to win power locally and parlay that power by trying to unite rebel locals on a regional and then a national basis. The task would then be to use that power to put collective bargaining to work improving working conditions and real wages rather than for the distorted purposes the leadership used it for after winning multiplant or multiemployer contracts. This view can only lead militants to resume the power struggles of the thirties, albeit for different ends. It includes and speaks to only a small part of the change that has taken place in three decades.

INSTITUTIONALIZATION OF UNIONS

When collective bargaining institutionalizes, unions undergo qualitative changes ideologically, administratively, and even structurally. Bargaining did not institutionalize for the new unions of the 1930s with the signing of their first contracts. The process of bargaining could not routinize and solidify for any one of the new mass unions as long as any one of the major corporations in the industry they were organizing held out and sustained a threat to the rest of their contracts.

Also, the first of the major contracts obtained in steel, auto, rubber, or electric, for example, were most often documents guaranteeing little more than union recognition. Signatures were applied, but the corporations in most cases continued to resist the process, and open conflict continued. In the steel industry the first real breakdown of resistance became noticeable after Germany's invasion of Poland in 1939. That tragic act caused a flood of orders for American steel from as-yet-uninvaded European countries. The crisis that the steel employers had experienced in 1938 was ended. The first real breakthrough and establishment of a contract more nearly resembling the detailed contracts of today was not accomplished until the signing of the Carnegie-Illinois contract in late 1941. And the rest of the steel corporations did not follow suit until the early years after formal American entry into the war.

The story was generally the same in auto, rubber, and electrical appliances. The differences can be measured by matters of months. The sit-down period in rubber did not end until 1938. Slim contracts were won at Sieberling (U.S. Royal in Detroit), Goodrich, and General. Firestone continued resistance. Goodyear held out altogether, and not until it was put under contract in 1941 could the top leaders of the Rubber Workers begin to achieve stability in their lives. Collective-bargaining rights were won at General Motors as a result of the 1937 Flint sit-downs. Ford held out until 1940, and it is likely that Henry Ford and Harry Bennett would have resisted even longer were it not for the fact that NLRB investigators, most of them former members of the LaFollette Senate Investigating Committee staff, had uncovered evidence indicating Ford's use of Detroit's organized gangsters to fight union organization. In electric a contract was won with General Electric as early as 1938, but it was not until the early years of the war that the industry became organized in a substantial way.

At the start of World War II, the majority of America's top labor officials gathered before Franklin Roosevelt like "feudal princes offering their services to a king," and most of the leaders of the new unions were among them. The wartime restrictions that were imposed upon the ranks of labor freed the leadership to complete the organization process begun by the ranks, but on a bureaucratic basis. Institutionalization of collective bargaining thus occurred on the worst terms. Compulsory arbitration of grievances became a general pattern through the initiatives of the War Labor Board that labor accepted seats on. The degenerative socialization process labor officials undergo was cemented through a tripartite arrangement between official labor, employers, and government bureaucrats. However, it is incorrect to view the war by itself as the major culprit. Its function was to accelerate the negative process that goes into high gear with institutionalization of bargaining.

The atmosphere in and character of the local unions in particular during the initial organizing period was one of conflict. The new self-organized federal locals of the early 1930s and the new and often self-organized locals of the CIO a few years later had a character that, for the U.S. and Canada of that time, could almost be described as revolutionary. Open battle and constant confrontation were the methods of the employers and in turn of the workers. The sitdown strikes and the mass slowdowns were the more dramatic of the tactics used by the members and leaders of the new locals. Equally if not more important were the mass meetings held on company property—in parking lots, in company cafeterias, and even on the workplace floor. The confidence and sense of security made possible by the very physical nature of these meetings freed the participants to release the depth of their feelings about their work and their employers and to put forth and consider the most radical and sophisticated ideas.

The early memoranda of union recognition and minimal wage and seniority awards could not immediately cause great change in the attitudes of the ranks or change the character of their locals. The formal contractual victories only whetted appetites for even greater ones. The momentum of "just yesterday" could not easily be stopped. A new consciousness was growing. Moreover, the employers regularly reneged on conditions to which they had agreed, or began new campaigns to quash the drive of the workers, necessitating immediate returns to direct action.

Only when the employers recognized that they no longer had the needed legitimacy to act as the full disciplinarians of the people in their employ, and that the union leadership could be used as a substitute disciplinary force, were they willing to join in building the institution of collective bargaining. The beginnings of qualitative change in the character of the unions from the international to the regional and finally to the local level followed upon this fact.

The process by which union leaders become disciplinarians of the rank and file need not and seldom does involve conscious and overt dishonest conduct at the start. The process becomes a natural one once the employers decide that it is possible for them to live with the unions. The establishment of systematized collective bargaining and of "full range" contracts is usually viewed as the cure for most if not all current problems by both ranks and leaders of labor. Unavoidably the hope grows that the contract will allow the making of gains against the employers without the constant conflict, insecurity, and disruption of personal and family lives that characterize the organizing period for new unions.

For the ranks, this is an illusion that must soon vanish. Routine, home life, and income may become more stable after bargaining is institutionalized, but the conflict at work goes on. Grievance bargaining that denies the right to strike at the local level mutes it and makes it less explosive. There is no record or official admission of its existence unless the production process is stopped. There is even the pretense that some major slowdowns or brief wildcats did not occur, after they have been ended, and in the new world of make-believe that is created, bargaining occurs under unconditional no-strike pledges and compulsory grievance arbitration. It takes some time, however, to intimidate the ranks into an acceptance of that make-believe world.

As soon as the employers accept collective bargaining as a fact of life and their signatures are put on contracts that they do not intend to break in other than a piecemeal way, the top labor leadership particularly must undergo a full change in attitude. For a time they may remain bitterly angry at some or all of the employers or their representatives, *but they must now show concern about the employers' competitive position.* The successful delivery of all of the things in the contract that have for so long been striven for cannot be made unless the firms under contract prosper and grow. The open and total conflict relationship of the precontract days has to go. Now, a care has to be shown for how hard an employer is to be hit. The new situation demands "flexibility" and attentiveness to what the limits are or "you might kill the goose that lays the golden eggs." The rank and file by its very size and the nature of the condition in the workplace cannot, of course, be expected to show the needed care. Decision-making powers in the grievance procedure must therefore be placed outside the reach of the ranks and in the hands of the union officials who are responsible for the administration of the contract so that those grievances, which if won would set precedents to undermine the competitive position, can be watered down or discarded.

The ranks, however, do not share the change in attitude of their leaders. They too want to retain and maintain the contracts, but they see no reason for pulling back from a struggle to win a grievance that is legitimate. Their method for fighting a grievance is one of continued battle until won or lost. For moments at a time in the meetings down at the union hall it is possible for them to see the logic of their leaders on the necessity to keep the company in business. That reason is destroyed the moment they physically or mentally return to work. The attitude of the company toward them is one of total antagonism and disrespect whenever the production process is in motion. Schizophrenia cannot live in a reality where there is so much immediate pain and unhappiness. For each one of them and their immediate associates the task becomes how to cheat the employer out of what is expected. If the company survives it will have to come from the labor of the others in the workplace besides themselves. The local-level leaders developed during the organizing period find it difficult to act any longer as a link to the top leaders. If they continue to work daily in the production process, they share the attitudes of the people who elected them. Even if they are freed from work, it is they, the local leaders, whom the ranks will move against first in a showdown, and not the leaders at the regional or international level. They must stay with the ranks in order to survive.

The union administrators of the contract at the top cannot tolerate this situation. "Yes, the work is hard and the damned foremen and supervisors of the companies are so stupid that they continue to cause our people to be boiled up; but can't they see that if they continue in bull-headed battle, the contract and all they fought for will be lost?" The ranks will have to be disciplined. The hottest heads among the leaders will have to come around to a reasonable attitude or be eliminated. "It's a hell of a thing to have to do, particularly after all the hard work those guys did; in fact, without some of them we never could have done the job in the first place . . . but a few cannot be allowed to stand in the way of the welfare of the many. . . . This after all is the real world." And for the leadership it is, if the contract is to survive under existing relationships. It is true that when workers in a workplace begin to make justifiable inroads on the ability of their employer to exploit them, they can put that employer in an uncompetitive position, or make it difficult or impossible for that employer to become competitive.

So unassailable was the new logic of the new bureaucrats' new world during the transition period that was the early 1940s, that they spoke openly about their new role due to the existence of contracts. So without alternatives were they that it did not occur to them to show shame. In 1942 Clinton Golden and Harold Ruttenberg wrote a book entitled *The Dynamics of Industrial Democracy*. In it they describe in detail how the leadership of the Steel Workers Union dealt with militant leaders who resisted compromise. The book is a unique document not only because of its contents, but also because Golden was at that time the veteran director of the Eastern Region of the Steel Workers Organizing Committee and Ruttenberg was the educational director of the entire union.

The title they chose to give their book provides some indication of their ignorant innocence. Their self-image was a good one. They were key figures in the building of a giant union that was going to benefit and had already benefited hundreds of thousands. Their ends, both present and potential, justified any means. The social-political value of their long-out-of-print document has increased with time, yet it has been forgotten except by students of management. In the wisdom of our retrospection it seems incredible that not one organization on the left has ever grasped it for the tremendous educational tool that it is. It is probable that the book was passed over because even the most top-flight of revolutionaries are prone to resist recognition that a period of intense radical activity is past and a transition period of Thermidorian reaction has begun.

The outward pacification of the rank and file requires that the official power center of the union have control over all staff jobs. There is no easier way to remove a dangerously "hot-headed" militant from a sensitive area than to appeal to his or her sense of responsibility to the larger struggle. And so rank-and-file militants with roots deep in their native workplaces accepted organizing jobs that took them considerable geographic and psychological distances from their home bases.

But though the number of staff jobs is relatively large, it is never large enough to allow the officials to divert the militancy of more than several score at a time. The staffs of the Auto Workers and Steel Workers are each just under one thousand, and the workhorses on those staffs can carry only a limited number of newcomers at one time. Thus, other avenues have to be found for handling militants who resist making the transition to the Thermidor and beyond. It is at this point that sections of the union leadership enter into collusive relationships with the employers. Employers are always in need of talent to fill management vacancies. The recruitment of a rank-and-file leader not only removes a thorn, but usually provides management with someone of top capabilities and energy. No one on the union side need ask them to conduct these raids. The corruption of the union results when by its silence it gives tacit approval to them.

Nor is it necessary for union officials to make formal arrangements with management in order to designate a rank-and-file leader whom they would like to see removed from the job. A staffer comes into the local and baits a particular militant. The news leaks back to management. It is during this aspect of the reaction process that the fearful, the conservative and opportunistic rank-and-filers, receive signals and come forth as an alternative leadership to the one that organized the local.

Even the names of the bulk of the workplace heroines and heroes of the industrial-union revolution have been lost to us. The new and more conservative local leaders are the ones who survive to accept credit for the gains made by the formation of the unions. They are generally—except during periods of rank-and-file assertiveness—in debt to officials on the staff, and thus are in a weak position in relation to the employer. They owe their new office and status to their willingness to concede local autonomy in the bargaining and internal governmental apparatus to the upper echelons of the union. In short and in a sense, they are willing to abide by Bonapartist relationships, and to see whatever change and reform that occurs be initiated bureaucratically from above.

The turnabout of the labor leadership's purpose made necessary by the employers' agreement to institutionalize collective bargaining eventually instills in the leadership a contempt for the ranks. Add in the guilt that has appeared half-recognized and unadmitted, and all the ingredients for a recipe for cynicism are present. Ingestion of it for any extended period frees the leadership to exploit their new position to in turn improve their economic and social status. Externally or internally, there is no longer anything present to help ward off full infection by the virus of bureaucratic conservatism. Kafkaesque metamorphoses occur. Consciously corrupt elitism can now be pursued.

The establishment of contracts with what appear to be comprehensive grievance procedures establishes a formal dual power within an industrial-type local union. Now not only is there an entire set of officers—headed by the president, vice-president, treasurer, and recording secretary—all holding offices divorced from the workplace and process, but there must be a series of committeemen, committeewomen, and stewards inside the workplace to administer the contract and grievance procedure. They are the most accessible to the ranks and thus potentially the most dangerous to the bureaucracy. They have no responsibility for presenting the face or the official policy of the union to the public. They cannot be trusted to assume full authority in the grievance process. By contractual definition the international or staff representatives had to be given the power to determine with top local management the destiny of all grievances that departmental-level management denied.

The on-the-job officers of the union are not immune from bureaucratic conservatism. If they are freed from the oppression of the work process to spend all or part of their time at work processing grievances and handling union business, both management and the international union get in position to cheat stewards and committeemen and committeewomen of their basic militancy. As bad as the buying and selling that goes on is the change in plant union structure from that which existed during the organizing period. The early period of the union's life demands that the union have at least one key person, representative or steward, for each foreman so that a maximum number of workers in every corner of the workplace get signed up and stay organized in the union. Most of the good ratios of steward representation established in the 1930s have been eliminated. Ratios as low as one to fifteen have become as high as one to several hundred. The ranks in such cases were promised that full-time stewards with their own offices and telephones in the plant would allow better representation. But experience has shown the opposite. Their aristocratic position and the impossibly large size of the workplace territories they represent negated the advantage gained in their becoming full-time, along with the negation of the freedom gained by the checkoff dues system and union shop.

Despite the estrangement caused between ranks and union workplace officials and the increasing number of contracts which widen the ratio of steward representation, they remain the most accessible, the most often challenged and changed, and the most important stratum of official leadership to the rank and file of the unions. It is no accident that there are few unions that provide the workplace officials with any automatic standing in the local union governmental apparatus. That government is officially controlled by the officers elected to preside over the business of the union that can be conducted outside the work place. It is the president, vice-president, and so forth who are most likely to side with the international in any conflict between the local and national center, particularly if the local is large enough to afford part-time or full-time employment positions for one or more of its outside-the-workplace officers. The 1967 wildcat strike of GM workers in Mansfield, Ohio, provides the classic example. The disenfranchisement of the shop stewards in turn disenfranchises the ranks.

The reactionary changes in union structure that began apace in the early 1940s continue to this moment. The reform of the Steel Workers grievance procedure that I. W. Abel has been promising the ranks of that union since 1965 is right now being instituted. It weakens the right of the stewards to bargain with the foremen and places that right solely with the assistant grievers or grievance committeemen. This automatically changes the representation ratio from roughly 1 to 30 to 1 to 200 or more. In the face of these changes the ranks of labor are demanding a reversal. Since the early 1960s, and particularly at the Special Bargaining Convention of the Auto Workers in April 1967, the demand for a ratio more like that of management, or 1 to 15, has been in the forefront of the rank-and-file demonstrations. The right to strike at the local level has become a major issue all over the mass-production industries as a result of the upsurge in militancy. The steel workers have not yet had the opportunity to respond to Abel's latest move. By contract, union government and ideology, the relationship of the ranks of labor in the mass-production and transportation industries to their officials is today very different from that period in which most radicals last defined attitudes, long-range programs, and perspectives.

Another factor in the weakening of formal rank-and-file democracy has been a major population shift. Since the early 1940s Americans have been a population on the move. The old ethnic and cohesive working-class neighborhoods nearby the industrial workplaces have become all but extinct. Informal organization in the work process no longer has supplemental aid from informal organization in the neighborhood. Only as racial and ethnic minorities in the central city cores gain more employment in city industry does the advantage return. Thus, on two counts separated from and in addition to changes already discussed above, the institution that is the local union, using the monthly meeting to legitimize its authority, has lost much if not most of its use, value and authority within the ranks of labor.

The post-World War II automobile "explosion" and high employment levels have (a) destroyed living-area organizational formations that were used to promote attendance at union meetings, and (b) created working-class suburbs that are distant from the workplaces. Not only have they atomized former living-area concentrations, but they have made it a considerable physical and nervous strain to get to and from union meetings in city core areas. With the disappearance of the "taken liberty" to meet in mass on company property when necessary, it was the local union meeting that was supposed to provide a total forum for the ranks. No substitute has yet been conceptualized. . . .

To organize all the major workplaces owned by a corporation within the U.S. and Canada is no longer sufficient even for the needs of the labor bureaucracy. The new mobility and flexibility of the corporations threaten the ability of officialdom to produce for the ranks at the present levels of success—particularly in the areas of wages and fringe benefits. The loss of jobs to foreign countries poses still greater threat to their power base. In sum, the very basis on which they have maintained their position in the tripartite arrangement established between themselves, the employers, and government bureaucrats is being chipped away.

Due to the changes indicated above in regard to the globalization of American capitalism, for the first time in American working-class history objective conditions demand that workers develop a consciousness of their international role and lead in the establishment of international solidarity. If the present official labor leaders are to make a beginning at a solution of the crisis presented to them by the development of conglomerate and multi-national corporations, they will have to make considerable changes in the structural, governmental, and administrative forms of the unions they lead. If they do, it is highly improbable that they will make efforts on their own to increase the levels of rank-and-file participation. The real likelihood is that if left to themselves they will attempt to parallel corporate change and further centralize the decision-making processes within the total union structure. The questions are: Will rank-and-file militants simply counter-punch by only putting obstacles in the path of the changes, offering no alternatives to the present structure? Or, will they take the opportunity to fight for long-overdue changes in institutional forms from bottom to top of the unions, changes that centralize the power of the working class through stuctural forms and procedures that for their very success demand the full participation of the rank and file?

THE NEW WORK FORCE

American society has experienced only a fraction of the social change that automation must inevitably bring. We have but to look backward. The introduction of the assembly line on a mass basis began as early as World War I, but not till the mid-twenties were there enough semiskilled jobs to create the basis for large-scale industrial unionism. Regardless of all the education to the idea accomplished by socialists like Eugene Debs and the Wobblies, the workers who could benefit by industrial unionism had not until that time the power to make the vision a reality.

Three further ingredients were necessary before industrial unions could appear and stabilize their existence nationally. A societal shock was needed to jar the feelings, ideas, and consciousness to such an extent that Americans could free themselves enough to break with the routine, traditions, values, institutions, and ideas on the basis of which they had been operating. The outbreak of the Depression in 1929 provided that shock; it was a release that allowed workers to begin creative construction of new institutions. Independently organized industrial-union locals formed by rank-and-file workers, who had the day before been on the bread lines, made their appearance with the first upturns in employment in 1932. Through the twenties and earlier, they had endured the disruption, exhaustion, and anxieties that assembly-line methods brought to their lives without being able to retaliate openly or on a large scale. For this new level of struggle they not only had to establish their union securely at the workplace, but also had to reach out to obtain economic and social solidarity with those in other workplaces of the same industry. An entire communications network had to be created. To accomplish this, the workers needed to acquire very rapidly a second ingredient: a source of writing, legal, and other technical skills, which were ready and available in the radicalized sections of the middle class. Freed to leave their class mainly by the Russian revolution and the plague of unemployment that had hit the middle classes, intellectuals in hundreds of large and small industrial cities offered themselves to the industrial-union revolution. Although radical political organizations many times played a role in this development, it was not essentially accomplished on the basis of national directives from the side of either the workers or the intellectuals. Who made the first contact with whom is not important for the discussion here. What is vital is that the basis for an industrial-union network stretching over the U.S. and Canada began with independent alliances between workers and radicalized intellectuals on a city-by-city and region-by-region basis.

By 1935, the viability of the industrial unions had been proven to the point that a section of the labor bureaucracy was compelled to recognize and incorporate the movement. Rebellions and revolts in the steel plants had already forced the companies to improve conditions somewhat in the hope of keeping out unions, or co-opting the newly formed unions that had just appeared. Consequently the coal operators were often losing numbers of workers to nearby mills. John L. Lewis, leader of the United Mine Workers—the only large, fully industrial union on the continent—thus found his own position unstable and needed unions in steel particularly with which his own union could deal easily. As the independent and often federally-chartered union locals demonstrated the inevitability of unionization in mass production and transportation, Lewis—through the coal miners—provided the third ingredient. To establish industrial unionism on a North American continent officially dominated by Anglo-Saxon law, tradition, and values, the UMW provided funds and personnel for the creation of a national organizational structure in the U.S. and Canada. When Lewis and the cadre of young organizers with whom he had surrounded himself inside the AFL's Committee for Industrial Organization walked out of the old federation's convention to set up the independent CIO, they signaled the end of the automatic domination of the aristocratic building-trades unions over organized labor.

We know today that the combination of new levels of mechanization and computer science which have come to be identified as automation have caused and will cause further technological unemployment and dislocation. We know that automation deskills workers, technicians, and professionals. These realities have been argued by liberals and radicals to the point at which they bore readers of liberal and radical publications: To continue simply agitating against these negative results makes a humdrum cliche of human tragedy. But what are the feelings and attitudes of Canadians and Americans who have experienced automation, or who sense that automation could soon reach into and disrupt life in their workplaces? What shocks have occurred and what forces have been broken loose? Is it possible that the terror of automation exists without at the same time freeing the thinking of those involved to consider new ideas involving basic institutional change? What new ideas are already being "batted around" among past, present, and future victims of automation? What new ideas does the new objective and subjective condition call forth for possible testing that have not as yet been articulated or conceptualized? Does automation present the possibility for the creation of new vehicles for social change as did the introduction of assembly-line techniques?

What other possible positive conditions are created by automation? We must ask if automation has for example done anything to create the basis for a new alliance between sections of the working and middle classes. If so, why, on what magnitude and level, and what type or types of organizational vehicles are needed to make it operationally progressive and stable? Even potential answers to these questions will develop our ability to stimulate enthusiasm among our public and ourselves.

A historic parallel of considerable importance exists. Eric Hobsbawm asserts that the period of industrialization in Britain (roughly 1790 to 1840) and the present period of automation are more like each other than like any of the periods in between, from the point of view of the eruptive changes in working-class and middle-class consciousness and worklife and the consequent potential alliances between the two classes. Industrialization created violent ruptures in the nature of work and the ability of workers to make decisions about the planning of work processes, creating technological unemployment for both cottage-industry workers and middlemen. In the resulting "Luddism," middlemen joined workers in the bands that roamed in search of new machines to destroy. The destruction was not, however, wanton as many historians have reported. Rather, the bands directed their activities against the giant looms built for factory use, but not against the smaller ones in use in the cottages. Giant harvesting machines were dismantled and their full introduction delayed until the 1840s, when an expanded labor market could absorb the surpluses created by the new machines. All labor-saving machines were considered reactionary as long as their introduction hurt the human condition of the workers. The British Government put a larger army into the field against the bands than it sent against Napoleon. American Socialists have yet to appreciate the importance of this parallel, to integrate the ideas of Hobsbawm, E. P. Thompson, and George Rude on Luddism and mob action into a view of current reality.

PUBLIC SECTOR WORKERS

The unionization and radicalization of workers in the public sector, particularly at the state and city levels, is directly related to the national crisis in urban and suburban centers. In the last two decades city professionals like social workers and teachers had been forced to do the dirty work of the society in a way similar to that of police. Professionalism survives with great difficulty and sacrifice. In sections of many of our cities it is impossible for city employees to perform their jobs without fear. To solve the tax-base crisis would provide only partial solution to the problems of city, county, and state employees. For them a decent work life cannot be obtained without a democratic stabilization of city and suburban life. . . .

An understanding of the new public unionism and of the angers and enthusiasms behind it demands recognition of still another phenomenon only indirectly related to low wages. For over two decades, from the beginning of World War II until the mid-1960s, civil servants were bilked through a set of widely held myths. During the Depression and before, millions of working-class and middle-class civil service workers traded off higher hourly wages for what amounted to a guaranteed annual wage. But in the War and for 20 years afterward, near-full employment destroyed these workers' "trade-off" advantage. In private industry, workers were now employed year-round, while civil servants were stuck without the right to strike, generally without union protection, and with what appeared to be permanently depressed wages. As the myth crumbled, government workers at all levels grew impatient with life-long commitments to compromise on what were socially considered low-status, stodgy jobs.

The radicalization of the American working class in the 1930s had found little open expression from public workers. Now, with workers in the private sector, they seek new values and demand more gratification from their work. A small, tidy home with a good roof, a lawn, and a surrounding fence is no longer considered the formula for happiness. Public workers are, in fact, by their recently self-earned release from old prejudices and by their objective position in a social crisis, in a vanguard position of today's class struggle. Their ranks contain occupations ranging from professional categories to blue-collar and unskilled classifications, including Third World Americans in great numbers. The bulk of them perform their labors in the large central city cores abandoned at night by most people of middle and upper incomes. They do away with the city's refuse, run the transportation systems, and provide all the services necessary for the performance of business and industry during the day and the entertainment services of the evening. As the bedroom communities begin to fill, the cities are left to them and in a sense appear to be theirs—a quite different condition from three decades ago when the middle and upper classes maintained constant visibility in the "downtowns."

Historically, great advances have been registered in the class struggle on a national basis, within particular industries; but the most dramatic manifestations of advance have been within single metropolitan areas. The Seattle General Strike of 1919 was the highest point reached in the class struggle of that time. The San Francisco and Minneapolis General Strikes of the 1930s encouraged the growth of the CIO. The Oakland General Strike led by city transportation workers and truckers after World War II raised the level of its participants ten-fold more than those whose industry-wide strikes created the 1946 Strike Wave. Since the 1940s, no private-industry struggles have individually shaken the ruling class as much as those of public employees at the city level. In city after city, as in St. Louis in June of 1971, union officials who were not known for revolutionary conduct have entered city council chambers with council in session to observe crucial votes of city monies and, after witnessing decisions that denied their members' demands, exited to make immediate strike calls. . . .

A dramatic example of the explosiveness of "routine" unionism among public employees was provided by Manhattan workers in the late sixties and early seventies. Here as elsewhere, negotiations and strikes of teachers, sanitation workers and police, subway and food-produce workers all immediately take on a political character and challenge governmental authority—all the more so because of the breakdown of legitimacy and credibility of governmental authority at the national level. (Big-city mayors, it should be noted in passing, have become national figures of importance, and city workers are in a position to make or destroy their aspirations for national office.) In the strike of New York sewage workers, water workers, and bridge tenders, called by locals of the AFSCME and the Teamsters, the purported original strategy of the unions was to first shut off the water in Rockefeller Center and Wall Street, as a direct warning to Governor Rockefeller, who was holding up monies for already negotiated pensions. If that failed to be effective, the sewage systems were to be shut down, followed by the shut-down of many of the bridges connecting Manhattan to the mainlands. This strategy was supposed to have become fouled when the bridge workers pulled out first, thus creating an immediate near-general strike. The results were instantly felt in public worker-management relations across the nation. Plans for collective-bargaining bills pending in many state legislatures were halted in panic and indecision. Not for some time will the full effects of this new spectre on the power establishment be known.

"PROFESSIONALS" AND THE NEW UNIONS

There is now an independent base in organized labor for artists and intellectuals who have a working-class orientation and are no longer dependent on labor officialdom. Moreover, because school teachers and social workers particularly are simultaneously city workers and "professionals," these sectors provide a bridge between the unskilled and semiskilled workers and highly trained white-collar workers.

Simultaneous with the appearance of mass "professional" unions has been an increase in unionization among other white-collar employees and technical workers. During the labor struggles of the 1930s the national power establishment could count on active or passive support for its position among the counterparts of those who are now themselves forming unions and becoming involved in strikes, frequently breaking injunctions. . . .

Professionals have been organizing into unions for many of the same reasons as public and blue-collar workers. Technological advances and the long period of relative full employment have raised expectations of the rewards they expect from life and work. Many of them join unions with untarnished enthusiasm and very high hopes. They find, however, that their unions are run by men who do not share their enthusiasm, but rather run these institutions on the basis of ideas that are very nearly those of the labor officialdom in the long-established unions. More than most blue-collar workers, they expect unions to be politically involved. The salaries of many professionals are determined by legislation as in the case of teachers and social workers. Freed from the control of conservative bureaucrats, they have conducted struggles in which the best union veterans could take pride.

Contrary to the belief of some, the new radicalization in the middle class is not simply the result of the mechanization, routinization, and computerization of what formerly were relatively gratifying career positions. With the growth of the demand for workers with greater amounts of formal education and the simultaneous deteriorization of the quality of work experience has come the inevitable social response. The system as it is equips ever larger numbers of people with sophisticated skills and then places them in jobs where they are denied the dignity of making the most elementary decisions connected with their work. Consequently they develop many of the same strivings and attitudes as workers on heavy industrial assembly-line jobs. Thus, as never before there exists a basis for working-class and middle-class unity. This both supplements and complements the Hobsbawm thesis mentioned above. . . .

YOUTH AND THE WAR

Analysis of radicalization or change in attitudes among working-class youth has yet to be assembled. The best opportunity so far provided is presented by the crisis in 1972 at the General Motors plant in Lordstown, Ohio. The Lordstown workers, whose average age is 24, have supplied the first pure test of the generation of workers who entered the work force in the last decade and who experienced the accelerated motion for societal change that began in the mid-1960s. The weakness of the test lies precisely in its purity. Few workplaces have so low an average age, and no other assembly-line technology is as "advanced" as that in Lordstown. . . .

The Lordstown workers made attempts at the beginnings of working-class solidarity both on a national and on an international basis. They wanted to send a rank-and-file delegation to the ILWU to get the longshoremen to extend their strike in order to temporarily keep off the market the small Japanese cars that compete with Vega. They also wanted to send a rank-and-file delegation from their plant to Japan to talk to auto workers about the necessity of establishing humanized work standards in auto production on an international basis. Their attempts were frustrated by the leadership of the UAW, but the important aspect is the effort to break out of established, conservative, and official methods of labor struggle. . . .

Most important, the Lordstown crisis revealed a widespread basis for a

267

real consciousness of class. In their fight against "Gee-mad" (GMAD), the General Motors Assembly Division, and the computerization of work they have made clear: "We don't want to end up like our mothers and fathers who have worked for you, worn out by the time we reach middle age. We want to make this a better job and a better life." Contained in this message is the realization that they are stuck in industrial employment, not far from the further realization that the division of labor is institutionalized on the basis of class and perpetuated largely on a hereditary basis. Secondly, the Lordstown strike momentarily revealed what American mass-production workers have been attempting to accomplish since the 1930s: the escalation of the drive against the speed-up to a drive for obtaining power over the standards of production. The gigantic amount of publicity given Lordstown made it impossible to avoid this revelation or bury it (as has been done before) through institutionalized collective bargaining. Finally, the national press attention served to dramatize the countercultural lifestyles of young workers. Perhaps no other single event has done so much to increase tolerance of such styles among older generations of workers.

In many instances it is clear that the appearance of countercultural styles in the young working class is related to the War in Southeast Asia. Vietnam veterans appear at plants in increasing numbers with clothing and hair styles more similar to their middle-class peers than to their parents' styles. In general, they have become accepted and respected by older workers. Yet they have no organizations, forums in the unions, or other vehicles to talk out their experiences among themselves. Unions have done nothing to help assimilate them socially or to help them overcome the trauma of their war experience, and politicals have made no apparent effort to push the matter. Yet it is certain that these veterans, like those of previous wars, have a commonality of experience and will seek to establish some sort of common external identity.

In the struggles of the 1930s, one of the major bases for reactionary attacks on unions were the war veteran organizations. Whole posts of the American Legion commonly acted as strikebreakers, as in the infamous attack on San Francisco maritime workers in 1934. Today, on the other hand, Asian war veteran committees in local unions around the country could become the basis for a new labor-oriented veteran organization which could, among other things, reunite the working-class and middle-class youths who fought that war. Continued recession and deepening economic crisis will further unite the veterans as an autonomous force. If progressive and Socialist forces fail to gain these young workers' allegiance, reactionaries will make their own bid more successfully. An attentiveness to working-class youth as an entity in itself as well as a part of the total workforce is essential to success in this struggle. . . .

CHAPTER THIRTEEN

Defending the No-Strike Pledge: CIO Politics During World War II

by Nelson Lichtenstein

During the Second World War the new industrial unions born in the mid-thirties achieved much that would characterize them in the postwar era. National trade-union membership increased from about 9 to 15 million while the CIO just about doubled in size as mass-production war industries expanded. Anti-union holdouts like Ford, Little Steel, and some meatpackers were brought under contract and collective bargaining was "routinized" under the aegis of a powerful War Labor Board. For the first time many union-management negotiations began to take place on an industrywide basis and "fringe" issues like vacation pay, shift bonuses, and pensions were put on the bargaining table.

Of course all this growth and consolidation took place under the most extraordinary circumstances. Depression-era levels of unemployment virtually evaporated as the economy was mobilized and then regimented as never before. The nation was at war, and all institutions in American society were expected, and if necessary compelled, to conform to a patriotic consensus. As its contribution to the war effort the CIO offered the government an "unconditional no-strike pledge" for the duration of the conflict. By exploring the ideology behind this industrial "burgfrieden," this essay will try to show how the enforcement and defense of the pledge contributed to the general decline in political independence and militancy of the industrial

Reprinted from Vol. 9, Nos. 4–5 (July-October 1975).

unions and advanced a pattern of internal bureaucratization during and after the war.

An assessment of the impact of the wartime no-strike pledge can only be made in light of the CIO's prewar character and potential. Something of a debate now swirls about this issue. Before the 1960s most American historians called industrial unions of the depression era militant and radical because of their use of the sit-down tactic, their mass activity, and the influence of Communists and Socialists within their ranks.[1] In recent years, however, a number of commentators, including but not limited to the "New Left," have called attention to the conservative origins of the CIO, or at least of its early leadership. Writers as different as Ronald Radosh and David Brody have emphasized the conservative trade-union program of CIO leaders like John L. Lewis, Philip Murray, and Sidney Hillman, all of whom consciously sought to channel working-class militancy into a stable and responsible unionism rooted in the AFL tradition.[2]

Both views shed light on the early industrial-union phenomenon, because like any social movement the CIO was not merely the product of the ideology of its leadership, but contained within its bounds a whole series of divergent social elements and political tendencies, some conscious about their political and economic goals, others inchoate and tentative.

After the great advances of 1937 the CIO did not immediately consolidate its power or bargaining relationships. The depression continued for almost four more years and the new unions were turned back at Ford and Little Steel. In this context trade unionists like Philip Murray could not fit their unions into the conservative mold they might have wished. Instead, mere survival put a premium upon local union initiative and rank-and-file activity. In the UAW, for example, forceful action by Detroit- and Flint-area secondary leaders helped preserve and extend the gains the union had won in 1937.[3] And even in the tightly controlled and bureaucratically structured Steel Workers Organizing Committee, union leaders like Clinton Golden admitted that in this era a sort of guerrilla warfare was inevitable, even necessary, so long as a section of the industry resisted full recognition of the union.[4]

In the late 1930s the ultimate character of the new CIO was not foreordained. The industrial unions gave new power and clarity to working-class interests, yet at the same time the union apparatus and its bargaining relationship with individual business units served to rationalize social conflict and accommodate the government's demand for order and the corporate drive for profits and efficiency. The steady pressure of the business system reinforced a pattern of bureaucratic timidity within the unions while the lingering depression, the healthy activism of the rank and file, the momentum of 1936 and 1937 were powerful countertendencies. It was only with the coming of the war that the drive for production and social order on the home front would immensely strengthen the tendency toward hierarchical control and dependence on the government within the new industrial unions.

When the question of American intervention arose in 1940, most CIO unionists—like American liberals generally—came to the conclusion that a military defense had to be built against German fascism. Unsure of the stability of their newly formed organizations and unwilling to break their alliance with the Roosevelt administration, most in the CIO also acquiesced in the shift of government energy from a faltering New Deal to a business-dominated war-production effort.

Few unionists could see any alternative to Roosevelt's defense program. Although John L. Lewis realistically forecast the conservative economic and social consequences of total war, his attempt to project an isolationist defense against European Fascism seemed both politically naive and militarily impractical.[5] Meanwhile the Communists moved from a policy of collective security to non-interventionism after the Stalin-Hitler pact and the dismemberment of Poland, but once Germany invaded Russia in June 1941 they demanded outright American belligerency. Finally, the idea of an opposition to the war on either pacifist or revolutionary grounds seemed virtually nonexistent—a situation in sharp contrast to the First World War, during which large sections of the working class had been influenced by such views.

The political and economic symbol of union cooperation with the war effort was an unconditional no-strike pledge, formally ratified by both CIO and AFL officials in a White House conference shortly after Pearl Harbor. The decision to sheath the strike weapon was made without any reciprocal agreement by the government on wartime wage, price, or production policies. Instead the adminstration set up a tripartite War Labor Board composed of representatives of labor, management, and the public. The board was empowered to arbitrate most union-management disputes, but its policies were to be guided almost entirely by decisions made in the executive branch alone.[6]

During most of the war CIO leaders were the foremost defenders of the no-strike pledge in the labor movement. Most of the industrial-union federation's leading officers—men like Sidney Hillman, James Carey, Walter Reuther, and Philip Murray—were political liberals and close allies and supporters of President Roosevelt. Because they held military success as the first essential step in a larger program of social reconstruction at home and abroad, they thought it both politically wise and socially progressive to accept wartime sacrifices and limit normal trade-union activity in the interests of a speedy victory. Since they had faith in the progressive character of the war, they thought it could not but have progressive consequences at home, regardless of the immediate demands the government made upon the union.[7] In this light many in the CIO, including but not limited to those influenced by the Communists, proposed that the unions be transformed into agencies of production for the duration. Lee Pressman, CIO general counsel, told the War Labor Board that the steelworkers' union wished to "forget their trade unionism as usual." Instead the USW was "anxious not to continue the presentation of the same grievances that it has in the past . . . but [is] anxious to turn the entire machinery, to turn all the energy of the union and of the members toward increasing production."[8]

Government policymakers recognized that such an orientation imposed a dangerous burden on the industrial unions. The traditional web of loyalties which bound workers to their unions might unravel when labor ceased to exercise the strike weapon, grievances went unresolved, and wages were held in check by government fiat. Industrial-union leaders worried that the surge of brand-new war workers would prove extremely difficult to organize under these conditions. In the spring of 1942 a few important CIO locals had already begun to disintegrate, while serious dues-collection difficulties were encountered in steel, textiles, and aircraft.[9]

In this potential crisis the government sought to strengthen the institutional power of the CIO's politically cooperative leadership. In prewar years CIO leaders had unsuccessfully demanded union-shop contracts as a guarantee that hostile employers would not seek to weaken the new unions during periods of slack employment. Now the government's WLB gave CIO unions a modified union shop—maintenance of membership—in order to assure membership stability and a steady dues flow during the difficult war years. The WLB's policy solved the chronic financial problems of many CIO unions, assured their steady wartime growth, and made cooperative union leaders somewhat "independent" of rank-and-file pressure.[10]

The no-strike pledge also seemed a necessary prerequisite to labor's bid to shape and help administer the wartime economy and lay plans for a liberal postwar order. Like the right-wing socialists and New Republic progressives of the First World War, CIO leaders hoped that the collectivist tendencies inherent in the mobilization of the society for total war might provide the opportunity to restructure industry on a basis in which labor could have a real say. In 1941 Roosevelt appointed Sidney Hillman codirector of the Office of Production Management, and for a time it looked as if the CIO vice-president might play the same influential role in America's domestic high command that the British Labour Party's Ernest Bevin played in Churchill's War Cabinet.[11] Meanwhile the CIO advocated a thorough reorganization of the production setup through the formation of a series of industry councils in which representatives of management, labor and government would jointly participate in the administration of each war industry. Walter Reuther's famous proposal to convert Detroit automobile factories to the production of 500 planes a day would have demanded a massive rationalization of the entire industry. In the process his automobile-industry council would have ignored corporate boundaries, markets, and profits as it presided over the conscription of machine tools, working space and man-power where and when needed.[12]

Labor's hopes for a progressive administration of the war economy were soon dashed. With Republicans Henry Stimson at the head of the War Department and Frank Knox at the head of the Navy, and dollar-a-year business executives flooding the new defense agencies, Roosevelt had already committed his administration to a mobilization effort designed to conciliate the business community and eschew new social initiatives. As FDR himself later put it, Dr. New Deal had been replaced by Dr. Win-the-War. CIO plans for a reorganization of production based on the industry-council model were flatly turned down where they were not ignored. And by the spring of 1942 Sidney Hillman was eased out of a top policymaking role and most defense agencies were staffed with only token labor representatives.[13] Of course these setbacks disappointed CIO officials, but such reverses did little to shake their faith in FDR personally or in their allegiance to the war effort. Instead the CIO characteristically blamed "defeatist" and "reactionary" elements in the Congress and the war-production agencies and reaffirmed its commitment to the no-strike pledge.[14]

An alternate perspective to the ambitious if thwarted plans of the CIO can be found among those unionists who took a more parochial view of the role a labor leader should play in the wartime mobilization. These unionists generally came out of an older AFL tradition and were less politically linked to the Roosevelt administration and rather less concerned with using the wartime experience as a platform for social reform. John L. Lewis is the penultimate example of this type. He was uncommitted to Roosevelt's stewardship of the economy and unwilling to long subordinate immediate trade-union interests to the government's demand for continuous production and stable industrial relations. When in 1943 he concluded that the government had taken advantage of labor's no-strike pledge to impose a rigid wage formula on the unions, he did not hesitate to defy the WLB and lead the UMW in four nationwide strikes.[15] Ironically it was the very backward-looking and socially unimaginative business unionism of figures like Lewis which led some conservative unionists to defend bread-and-butter labor standards in a more consistent fashion than the liberal patriots of the industrial-union federation.

A 1942 contest between the UAW and the International Association of Machinists provides a graphic example of this wartime phenomenon. Under the prodding of Walter Reuther and Richard Frankensteen and at the request of the government, the UAW agreed to relinquish certain types of overtime pay in the interests of a general "Victory Through Equality of Sacrifice" program. UAW organizers thought this plan would help organize new war workers through its patriotic appeal.[16] For example, they told southern California aircraft workers: "The best way [you] can speed up war production, and contribute even more to the war effort, is to join the CIO, which has made this business of winning the war its main objective."[17]

In contrast the machinists' union emphasized wages and hours and the maintenance of overtime pay standards. The IAM attacked the UAW: "Can the CIO's masterminds tell you why they know what's good for the worker better than he knows himself? . . . The CIO sacrifices workers' pay, workers' overtime as the CIO's contribution to the war effort. Big of them, huh?"[18] In a series of 1942 NLRB elections the IAM decisively defeated the UAW on this issue. UAW and CIO leaders who had pitched their election campaigns on an exclusively patriotic level were stunned. In defeat they quickly appealed to the WLB and the Administration, not to restore overtime pay, but to force the IAM and the rest of the AFL to give it up as well. This FDR soon did by issuing a special executive order on the problem.[19]

This incident points to an important aspect of working-class consciousness during the war. Most workers were patriotic and backed the war effort, but they resisted the consequences of the wartime regimentation and mobilization, especially if it entailed the sacrifice of prewar conquests their unions had made in the late thirties. Many war workers retained an aggressive distrust of big business and their own plant management, even in the first intensely patriotic months of the war. Many thought their employers would try to use the wartime emergency as an occasion to weaken their unions and roll back labor standards.[20] In short they did not believe or, more important, act as if the war had suspended class conflict.

In any work situation conflicts inevitably arise between workers and their supervisors over working conditions, individual wage rates, promotions and transfers. In prewar years the strike weapon often backstopped local grievance procedures and provided an incentive for management to resolve grievances at the lowest possible level. But with the adoption of the no-strike pledge this incentive evaporated and grievances left unresolved were dumped into the lap of a distant and cumbersome War Labor Board. Local unions found themselves "plagued by a malady of unsettled grievances" which undermined the solidarity and effectiveness of the union.[21] The *Wage Earner*, organ of the Association of Catholic Trade Unionists, summed up the local union's dilemma:

> Workers may remain loyal to their unions even when no wage increases can be obtained. . . . But if the union loses its capacity to represent its members effectively when they get into trouble with the management, it has lost its primary reason for being.[22]

Many local leaders—the stewards, committeemen, and officers who represented the backbone of an industrial union—now faced an excruciating dilemma. They could enforce CIO national policy, defend the no-strike pledge, and watch the power of their locals disintegrate as management prerogatives grew and rank-and-file respect and loyalty for the union declined. In the process they might easily find themselves turned out of office by a sullen membership.

Or they could ignore and defy international policy and revert to what they called "prewar" methods—the slowdown, the work to rule, the wildcat strike—to resolve pressing shop-floor grievances. The tension inherent in this decision is captured in the minutes of a meeting between a UAW regional director and a Cleveland local president who had just led his union on a wildcat strike in defense of two members fired by the company.

> UAW Regional Director Paul Miley: . . . I instructed you to get the plant back in operation. . . . Do you understand that the production of some four or five hundred aircraft engines has been lost already . . . doesn't [that] affect your judgment in this case at all?
> Local 91 President Lawrence Wilkey: I wouldn't say, Paul, that it doesn't affect my judgment, but I wasn't elected by those people to win the war. I was elected to lead those people and to represent them. I have tried my best to abide by the Constitution [of the UAW] but at this time my conscience will not let me because of my duty to those people.[23]

By the middle years of the war a growing list of local union leaders began to follow Lawrence Wilkey's example. These unauthorized strikes resembled the work stoppages which flared in the auto and rubber industries before the organization of the national CIO unions: uncoordinated except on the department or plantwide level, short in duration, led by a shifting and semispontaneous leadership. The strikes bypassed and ignored the international's formal apparatus for the resolution of grievances because these procedures had proven themselves ineffective, in fact an obstacle, to the genuine defense of what many union activists considered an elementary trade-union presence in their shops and factories.[24]

Beginning in the spring of 1943, and coinciding with the nationwide coal strikes launched by John L. Lewis, a wave of wildcat strikes swept through Detroit, Akron, and the East Coast shipyards. The commissioner of labor statistics called the strike wave a "fundamental swell of industrial unrest."[25] In unionized industries like auto, steel, and rubber, the level of wildcats rose steadily until the end of the war.[26]

Faced with this challenge to industrial order and internal union discipline, top CIO officials renewed their commitment to the no-strike pledge. In this they were backed and prodded by the government, which now demanded "union responsibility." The WLB threatened to withdraw or deny maintenance of membership and the dues checkoff to any union whose leadership led or condoned wartime work stoppages. In 1943, for example, the WLB denied Chrysler locals of the UAW maintenance of membership because the board felt local leaders had been insufficiently vigorous in their opposition to recent strikes.[27] Later Richard Leonard, who headed the

UAW's Ford Department, reported to the union executive board that unless the union took a "constructive position" the labor board would deal harshly with the UAW in forthcoming Ford and Briggs decisions.[28]

Therefore, in early 1944, the UAW executive board decided to crack down hard on wildcat strikes. The union announced that henceforth wildcat strikers could no longer use local union grievance procedures to appeal company discipline. Local leaders who continued to defend these strikers would be suspended from office and their locals placed under an international administratorship.[29] "The kid-glove tactics of yesterday have been discarded" reported *Ford Facts*, organ of the UAW's giant local at the Rouge.[30] During the remaining 19 months of the war hundreds of UAW members were fired or otherwise disciplined by the auto companies while their national officers stood aside. Several locals were taken over by the international and their leaders suspended from office.[31] Much the same process was taking place in the rubber, steel, and shipbuilding internationals as well.[32] Thus the WLB's "union responsibility" doctrine encouraged union officials to discipline rank-and-file militants and reshape their unions in a more conservative pattern.

Top leaders of the CIO were not unaware of the internal problems created by the no-strike pledge, and they felt a certain anguish in their new role as government-backed disciplinarians of their rank and file. Yet they felt they had little choice: "We may have to take it on the chin here and there for a time," admitted R. J. Thomas, president of the UAW, but he thought only a policy of self-restraint could avoid a union-smashing assault from the right.[33] Since these unionists feared to mobilize the economic and social power of their own membership to stem the conservative drift in wartime domestic politics, they relied ever more heavily upon FDR and his administration as a bulwark against the right. Hence in 1943 the CIO stood as the staunchest defender of the WLB in its fight with John L. Lewis because most industrial-union officials feared, with good reason, that if Lewis won a stunning victory over the government board, then the strike weapon would become legitimate once again and rank-and-file agitation for unionwide work stoppages would increase.[34] Already in May 1943 the national mine strikes during that month had touched off massive wildcats in Detroit and Akron.

At the same time the CIO also linked itself more closely to the national Democratic Party through the formation, in July 1943, of the CIO Political Action Committee. The PAC was organized by top CIO officials to meet a dual threat. Its most publicized function was to counter the conservative drift in domestic politics symbolized by and in part culminating in the passage of the Smith-Connolly Act over FDR's veto in June 1943. But an equally important purpose of the committee was to deflect and defeat a growing internal union demand for some form of independent political action in the 1944 elections. In Michigan a number of important UAW secondary leaders, led by Emil Mazey and Paul Silver, had revived the moribund state Labor Non-Partisan League and begun a remarkably successful agitation in favor of a CIO-based labor party. During the spring of 1943 they linked their break with Roosevelt and the Democratic Party to an attack upon the no-strike pledge and strong support of the mine strikers.[35] At an important Michigan CIO convention in late June the radical Mazey forces joined with a more moderate group led by Victor Reuther and Gus Scholle to pass, over strong Communist and conservative opposition, a resolution endorsing a labor-based third party in the state.[36]

Meanwhile, on the East Coast, a section of the old social-democratic union leadership in retail trade and the garment and textile industries came to advocate more aggressive electoral tactics. As the ILGWU paper *Justice* editorialized, "The present Congress is the best argument for independent political action the country has had in years."[37] Led by David Dubinsky, these New York Social Democrats hoped to link up with the Michigan radicals and spread their American Labor Party to other industrial states. While neither Dubinsky nor the Reuther-Scholle group favored outright opposition to Roosevelt on the national level, they did support direct labor-party challenges to state and local Democratic machines, thereby undercutting FDR's conservative base and forcing him (they hoped) to the left.[38]

"When the move to create an ultraliberal political party in the name of the workingman began to gather steam," recalled then USW secretary-treasurer David J. McDonald in his autobiography, "Murray and Hillman decided that they should counter it with a specific, labor-oriented political-action organization that could function within the two-party system."[39] Under Hillman's leadership the new PAC attacked the labor-party idea on the ground that it would "divide progressive forces." Although the Political Action Committee was able to defeat some conservative Democrats in the 1944 primaries, the national PAC encouraged its state units not to challenge local Democratic parties, but to reach an accommodation with them in order to "weld the unity of all forces who support the Commander-in-Chief behind a single progressive win-the-war candidate for each office."[40]

Where labor sentiment for an independent political voice remained strong and threatened to disrupt an alliance with the Democrats, Hillman mobilized PAC forces to defeat it. In New York, Hillman linked his once anti-Communist Amalgamated Clothing Workers with the Communist unions of the city to win control of the ALP from the Dubinsky Social Democrats and make the state labor party an uncritical adjunct of the Democratic Party there.[41] In Michigan, where a viable Democratic Party hardly existed, the PAC successfully fought efforts by some UAW radicals to put the state Political Action Committee on record as supporting only those Democratic candidates pledged to a guaranteed annual income and other well-publicized CIO bargaining demands.[42]

Part of the reason for the wartime political timidity of the PAC was that in looking forward to the immediate postwar months CIO leaders like Philip Murray foresaw a 1920-style political reaction combined with a major postwar recession. In this context Murray hoped to avoid at almost any cost a potentially disastrous postwar strike wave after the fall of Japan. Murray's CIO reconversion strategy forecast a new labor board which would impose a government-backed accommodation with industry along with a somewhat more liberal wage-price formula.[43] As we shall see, the CIO's neat corporativist blueprint for the postwar future ran into major opposition from the industrial-union rank and file, whose insistent demand for a restoration of the strike weapon forced a section of the CIO leadership to break with Murray's cautious program.

Before turning to this new situation, one must take into account another ideological tendency, the Communists and their close followers, and examine their relationship to the defense of the no-strike pledge. Although their organizational influence was extensive, the main impact of the Communists stemmed less from the offices they held than from the ideology they advanced. They defended the no-strike pledge with passion and prided themselves on their support of Philip Murray and the official CIO line. Yet the Communist policy only coincidentally meshed with that of other CIO leaders. Murray and Thomas thought the best way to defend their unions was through a policy of close alliance with FDR and temporary appeasement of the resurgent right. Communist spokesmen urged the CIO to agree to all concessions demanded by the government, not so much as a tactical retreat, but as a progressive step in and of itself, one which mirrored on the home front the "Big Three Unity" forged by Churchill, Roosevelt, and Stalin at the Teheran conference.[44]

The persistent theme of the Communists during the war was the need for the unity of all "progressive win-the-war forces." Yet the success of this new popular front would be possible only on a basis agreeable to conservative elements in the government and the military.[45] Hence those in the CIO high command who were influenced by this ideology—men like Harry Bridges and Joseph Curran—initially supported the Army and Navy call for compulsory National Service Legislation even when Philip Murray opposed it as destructive of trade-union principles.[46] And the New York and Detroit CIO councils, in which Communists held important posts, refused to help the CIO-authorized strikes of Montgomery Ward's unionized employees even after Ward's chairman Sewell Avery defied a WLB directive favorable to the retail clerks' union.[47]

Ultra-conservative though it seemed to many, the appeal of this ideology during the war should not be underestimated. By giving the conflict an uncritically progressive quality, the Communists provided a rationale for those in the union movement who sought to reconcile the waning power of domestic labor-liberalism with their own radical and anti-capitalist sensibilities. Thus otherwise reactionary programs, like national service legislation, imposition of undemocratic forms of internal union discipline, or alliance with anti-labor big-city bosses, were justified as strengthening the "win-the-war" forces in the world battle against Fascism. The ultimate commitment of domestic Communist leaders, therefore, was less to the defense of the American working class in its day-to-day struggles than to the political/military success of the Russian regime and the new bureaucratic social system it represented.

Despite continued defense of the no-strike pledge by a coalition of Communist and non-Communist CIO leaders, pressure from below began to crack the strike prohibition in 1944 and 1945. In retail trade and in textiles, where the CIO had only secured a shaky foothold, low wages and employer violation of basic labor rights literally forced union leaders to authorize a series of strikes to prevent the imminent disintegration of their organizations.[48] In the United Rubber Workers the big four Akron locals virtually seceded from the international as they struck repeatedly in the last year of the war.[49] Debate on the no-strike pledge flared briefly in the Steelworkers and in the UE as well.[50]

But the movement against the pledge reached its climax in the million-and-a-quarter-strong auto union, where the growth of rank-and-file sentiment had an important influence on the postwar decision to strike GM and on Walter Reuther's rise to the UAW presidency. Wildcat strikes led by UAW members were soon echoed by outright demands for repeal of the no-strike pledge itself. At the 1943 Michigan CIO convention, a resolution easily carried which called on the national CIO to rescind the pledge unless substantial changes were soon made in WLB wage policy. As we have seen, the state CIO, the most important of its kind in the industrial-union federation, also went on record in defense of the UMW strikes and in favor of some form of independent political action by the wartime labor movement.[51] Support for these initiatives was led by a group of UAW secondary leaders who became convinced that abolition of the no-strike pledge was necessary to remobilize labor's own forces both in their factories and in the larger political arena.

Some of these individuals were Socialists, others were influenced by the Trotskyists, some were members of the Anti-Marxist Association of Catholic Trade Unionists. But most who came to oppose the pledge did not do so out of a conscious commitment to radical politics, but rather because their day-to-day experience convinced them of the destructive impact it was having on their locals and their international.[52] They were especially alarmed when the UAW officers used "strikebreaking" tactics to crack down on wildcat strikes. As Chicago's Buick Local Six put it, "The gap between the rank and file and their elected leaders will grow so wide that our whole structure will collapse. Vote against the no-strike pledge and save your union."[53]

This movement soon had an important impact on the internal politics of the auto union itself. Until 1944 all of the top leaders of the UAW were firm supporters of the pledge, but Walter Reuther favored a somewhat more vigorous opposition to other restrictions and demands the government made upon the union. Therefore Reuther opposed government-sponsored incentive-pay schemes in UAW-organized factories and sharply criticized the War Labor Board and other federal agencies.[54] Despite Reuther's growing popularity on these issues, he did not associate himself with the movement for outright repeal of the pledge, and in 1944 he backed the efforts of the UAW executive board to discipline wildcat strikers.[55]

This proved a near fatal mistake. Since most of the opposition to the pledge came from those who normally supported the UAW vice-president, Reuther began to lose his internal union strength as the movement against the pledge picked up steam. At the 1944 UAW convention Reuther tried to straddle the issue with an ungainly compromise, keeping the no-strike pledge in some factories, ending it in others. The idea pleased no one. Outright opponents of the no-strike pledge, now organized into an independent Rank and File Caucus, demanded and won a unionwide referendum on the issue and fielded candidates for union office against both Reuther and his factional rival, Richard Frankensteen. Reuther's caucus strength now began to disintegrate, and for the first time he lost a convention vote to Frankensteen. Reuther retained his union vice-presidency only by winning the second-ballot contest against another less-prominent opponent.[56]

Reuther's close call at the 1944 UAW convention proved a turning point in his wartime career. Thereafter Reuther sought an accommodation with the militant and rebellious sentiment growing in the ranks, if only to retain his own power in the UAW. In early 1945 Reuther urged that the CIO withdraw from the WLB until that government agency was reorganized and adopted a more liberal wage policy.[57] A couple of months later he reversed his position on enforcement of the pledge and insisted that the UAW executive board not impose the usual disciplinary measures against the two Detroit locals then on strike.[58] With the fall of Germany those who had long fought for an end to the pledge now insisted upon an immediate industry-wide strike vote to back CIO demands for an end to government wage ceilings. Alone among prominent members of the UAW leadership, Reuther backed this proposal.[59] By shifting to the left, Reuther was rapidly winning back the support he had lost the year before.

With the end of the war against Japan, the rash of unauthorized strikes in the UAW, which reached epidemic and uncontrollable proportions, threatened to disrupt Philip Murray's plan to forge a new postwar wage-price formula in return for a promise of renewed labor peace and cooperation. Therefore R. J. Thomas and UAW Secretary-Treasurer George Addes opposed any new initiatives on the part of the auto workers until Murray and the national CIO had had time to work out a comprehensive program at a government-sponsored labor-management conference in November 1945.[60]

Of course the problem was that in the absence of a patriotic wartime ideology order in the UAW could not be restored by appeals to follow national CIO policy. R. J. Thomas declared the situation "chaotic" as local after local struck to reassert its power in the shops.[61] In this crisis Reuther came forward with his proposal for an early company-wide strike against General Motors, a proposal which provides a classic example of the characterization C. Wright Mills once gave to the labor leader as a "manager of discontent."[62]

Reuther's GM strike plan would harness the restlessness of the auto workers, restore legitimacy to top union authority, and advance his own fortunes in the internal union scramble for office. The GM strike demand— for a 30 percent wage boost without an increase in the price of cars—was but a militant restatement of then current, but soon to be abandoned, CIO postwar wage policy. Yet the idea excited union ranks because it was demanded directly of the corporation and backed by union strike power, rather than offered up to a government agency for tripartite negotiation.[63] At the same time the strike had its conservative side as well. It offered a new rationale for ending wildcat strikes at GM competitors, which were now to be kept at full production in keeping with the "one at a time" strike strategy. In fact "company security" clauses were soon negotiated with Ford and Chrysler which gave plant management their broad powers to discipline those who pulled unauthorized strikes.[64]

Reuther's plan for and conduct of the GM strike climaxed his accommodation to the radical forces within his union which the wildcat-strike movement and campaign against the no-strike pledge had set in motion. Reuther won the UAW presidency in 1946 by winning the wartime militants back into his caucus.[65]

Ironically, Reuther's aggressive GM strike policy indirectly aided the more timid leaders of other CIO unions. Without the auto strike Philip Murray might have been able for a time to reach the bureaucratic accommodation with government and industry for which he had long planned. But the GM strike made such an immediate postwar agreement difficult and helped precipitate the general 1946 strike wave—the largest since 1919.[66] In turn this massive work stoppage restored to conservative or mainstream leaders of the CIO a good deal of the prestige and publicity which they had lost during the era of wartime cooperation with the government and enforcement of the no-strike pledge.

In conclusion, one can make three observations about the experience of workers and their unions during the war. The first is that despite the maintenance of a patriotic consensus unparalleled in American history, many war workers still felt use of the strike weapon vital to the defense of those standards by which they measured their dignity and power in the shops. The wildcat strikes themselves were not designed to slow overall war production, but they were nevertheless explosive social phenomena because they challenged the wartime industrial-relations "system" and cut across the formal ideology of labor-management cooperation and common purpose. In the act of striking, war workers put their evaluation on the conduct of the home front. They measured concrete shop-floor reality against official propaganda and found the latter inadequate. Hence the implicit threat these strikes posed and the determined opposition they evoked from the government and union leaders.

A second point follows from the first. The call for political conformity in the new industrial unions had been present from the founding of the CIO in the mid-thirties. But the campaign to really enforce internal political discipline began not with the anti-Communist purges of the early Cold War, but under the aegis of the wartime mobilization. The political and institutional requirements of the War Labor Board were no less exacting than those of the Taft-Hartley Act five years later. In this context the Cold War crackdown on Communists in the unions represented not so much a break with a wartime popular front as a continuation of an era during which the society has been organized and regimented in the interests of a military-minded foreign policy. An important domestic requirement of this war economy has been a policy of essential cooperation from the labor movement. During the war the Communists defended this drive for political conformity; in 1948 and 1949 they were its victims.

Finally, the experience of American industrial unions during World War II stands as an important stage in the transition of the new unions from the aggressive and turbulent 1930s to the relative quiescence of the postwar years. The wartime routinization and expansion of collective bargaining was in one sense a step forward for the unions, but it took place under circumstances which put a premium upon internal union discipline and a penalty upon self-activity and militancy. Authority in the large industrial unions moved continually upward under these conditions as labor officials looked to Washington to set the guidelines for war and postwar economic and political policy.

NOTES

1. James O. Morris, *Conflict Within the AFL* (Ithaca, 1958), pp. 171–290; Bernard Karsh and Philips L. Garman, "The Impact of the Political Left," in Milton Derber and Edwin Young, eds., *Labor and the New Deal* (Madison, 1957), pp. 79–119; and Thomas R. Brooks, *Toil and Trouble: A History of American Labor* (New York, 1964), pp. 172–173; Richard A. Lester, *As Unions Mature* (Princeton, 1958), pp. 21–34.

2. See for example David Brody, "The Emergence of Mass Production Unionism," in John Braeman, *Change and Continuity in Twentieth Century America* (Columbus, 1964), pp. 221–262; Ronald Radosh, "The Corporate Ideology of American Labor Leaders from Gompers to Hillman," in James Weinstein and David

Eakins, eds., *For A New America: Essays in History and Politics From "Studies on the Left*," 1959–1967 (New York, 1970), pp. 125–151; also Lorin Lee Carey, "Institutionalized Conservatism in the Early C.I.O.: Adolph Germer, a Test Case," *Labor History* 13 (Summer 1972): 475–504.

3. Irving Bernstein, *Turbulent Years* (Boston, 1969), pp. 559–563; Clayton W. Fountain, *Union Guy* (New York, 1949), pp. 101–103; Joseph Ferris Oral History, Archives of Labor History, Wayne State University, pp. 25–30.

4. Harold Ruttenberg and Clinton Golden, *Dynamics of Industrial Democracy* (New York, 1942), pp. 48–57.

5. "Report of President John L. Lewis to 1939 CIO Convention," in *Proceedings of the Second Constitutional Convention of the CIO* (San Francisco, Oct. 10–13, 1939), pp. 6, 79, 80–81, 106–107; Saul Alinsky, *John L. Lewis: An Unauthorized Biography* (New York, 1949), pp. 161–191; see also Lewis's speech endorsing Wendell Willkie in *UMW Journal*, Nov. 1, 1940.

6. Joel Seidman, *American Labor From Defense to Reconversion* (Chicago, 1952), pp. 80–81; William H. Davis and Elbert D. Thomas, "Memorandum Report of the Deliberations of the War Labor Conference Convened by the President in the City of Washington, December 17, 1941," Official File 4684, Roosevelt Papers, Hyde Park.

7. See for example Philip Murray's famous speech "Work, Work, Work, Produce, Produce, Produce" in *CIO News*, March 9, 1942; also see the CIO's justification for wartime sacrifice in *CIO News*, March 30, 1942.

8. Bethlehem Steel et al., *War Labor Reports* 1 (July 16, 1942): 397–398.

9. Philip Murray to Wayne Coy, March 6, 1942, Box 18, Coy papers, FDR Library, Hyde Park; United Steelworkers, *Proceedings of the First Constitutional Convention*, May 1942, pp. 41, 48, 81; see also Walker-Turner Company, *War Labor Reports* 1 (April 10, 1942): 108–109; Marshall Field and Co., *War Labor Reports* 1 (Feb. 25, 1942): 47–53; Transcript, National War Labor Board, March 26, 1942.

10. Federal Shipbuilding and Drydock Company, *War Labor Reports* 1 (April 25, 1942): 141–143.

11. Matthew Josephson, *Sidney Hillman, Statesman of American Labor* (Garden City, 1952), pp. 506–508, 529–534.

12. For surveys of Reuther's plan and its demise see George R. Clark, "Strange Story of the Reuther Plan," *Harpers*, May 1942, pp. 645–654; Eliot Janeway, *The Struggle for Survival* (New York, 1951), pp. 221–225; Walter P. Reuther, "500 Planes a Day—A Program for the Utilization of the Automobile Industry for Mass Production of Defense Planes," in Walter P. Reuther, *Selected Papers* (New York, 1961), pp. 1–12. For industry resistance to the introduction of the plan see Barton Bernstein, "The Automobile Industry and the Coming of the Second World War," in *Southwestern Social Science Quarterly* 47 (June 1966): 24–33; Paul A. C. Koistinen, "The Hammer and Sword, Labor and the Military During World War II," unpublished Ph.D. thesis, University of California at Berkeley, 1964, pp. 602–606.

13. For narratives of the conservative drift in the administration of the war economy see Janeway, *Struggle for Survival*, pp. 125–185; and Bruce Catton, *War Lords of Washington* (New York, 1948), passim; recent studies include Koistinen, "Mobilizing the World War II Economy: Labor and the Industrial-Military Alliance," *Pacific Historical Review* 42 (Nov. 1973): 443–478; and Richard Polenberg, *War and Society* (New York, 1972), pp. 5–36, 73–98.

14. For example see *CIO News*, July 3, 10, 1943, for reaction to the passage of the Smith-Connally Act over Roosevelt's veto.

15. Lewis justified his strikes on the ground that the government had violated its "agreement" with labor to maintain wages at a constant relationship with rising prices. He therefore considered his no-strike pledge null and void. UMW Journal, February 15, 1943. For a full account of Lewis's fight with the government see Nelson Lichtenstein, "Industrial Unionism Under the No-Strike Pledge: A Study of the CIO During the Second World War," unpublished Ph.D. thesis, University of California at Berkeley, 1974, pp. 448–521.

16. *Proceedings UAW War Emergency Conference*, April 7 and 8, 1942, Detroit, pp. 6–10, 34–37.

17. Radio script, Los Angeles CIO Council, April 7, 1942, Box A7-32, John Brophy Collection, Catholic University.

18. As quoted from *IAM Aircraftsman* in Curtiss edition, *American Aircraft Builder (UAW-CIO)*, July 24, 1942, in OF 142 Roosevelt papers.

19. *CIO News* July 27, 1942; WLB Transcript, July 24, 1942, pp. 437–440; *Proceedings UAW Convention*, Aug. 3–9, 1942, pp. 86–111, passim; George Addes circular letter to UAW locals, Sept. 11, 1942, copy of executive order attached, Box 27, Addes Papers, ALHWSU.

20. A May 1942 survey by the government found a diffuse but nevertheless real political and economic disaffection among factory workers in Detroit and Pittsburgh. According to the political criteria of the survey, less than half of the war workers in the two cities were rated as wholeheartedly behind the production effort. Office of Facts and Figures, "Labor Morale in Detroit and Pittsburgh: Survey of Intelligence Materials No. 22" (marked secret), May 6, 1942, in Entry 35, Record Group 202, National Archives. See also "What's Itching Labor?," *Fortune* 26 (Nov. 1942): 101–236.

21. *Ford Facts* (UAW Local 600), Feb. 15, 1943.

22. *Wage Earner*, May 28, 1943.

23. "Meeting of the International Executive Board, UAW-CIO, for the Purpose of Requiring Officers of Local 91 to Show Cause Why They Should Not Comply with the Provisions of Article 12 of the Constitution," Cleveland, July 17, 1944, pp. 16–18, Box 3. UAW Executive Board Collection, ALHWSU.

24. For contrasting descriptions of the wartime wildcat strike phenomenon, see Rosa Lee Swafford, *Wartime Record of Strikes and Lockouts, 1940–1945*, 79th Congress, 2nd Session, Senate Document No. 136 (Washington, D.C., 1946), pp. 1–37, passim; Jerome F. Scott and George C. Homans, "Reflections on Wildcat Strikes," *American Sociological Review* 12 (June 1947): 278–287; and Lichtenstein, "Industrial Unionism Under the No-Strike Pledge," pp. 326–367, 596–641.

25. Memorandum, Isidor Lubin to Harry Hopkins, May 27, 1943, in President's Personal File, Box 145, Roosevelt Papers.

26. Swafford, *Wartime Record*, pp. 3–4.

27. Chrysler Corporation, *War Labor Board Reports* 10 (Aug. 27, 1943), pp. 553–555; War Labor Board Hearing Transcript, July 28, 1943, pp. 25–29.

28. UAW Executive Board Minutes, Feb. 7–16, 1944, pp. 83–84, Box 3, Thomas Papers, ALHWSU.

29. *United Auto Worker*, March 1, 1944.

30. *Ford Facts*, April 1, 1944. The local's leadership made this remark after the

UAW executive board had used its new powers to allow Ford management to discipline 126 unionists who had participated in a recent wildcat strike at the Rouge.

31. *Detroit Free Press*, May 22, 25, 27, 1944; *Labor Action*, June 5, Aug. 28, 1944, UAW Executive Board Minutes, Aug. 1, 1944, Box 5, UAW Executive Board Collection, ALHWSU.

32. In the United Rubber Workers the WLB and the Army worked closely with the URW national leadership to try to break the wildcat strike tradition in the "Big Four" Akron locals. See *Proceedings, Eighth Convention, United Rubber Workers of America*, Toronto, Sept. 20–24, 1943, p. 58; Harold S. Roberts, *The Rubber Workers* (New York, 1944), pp. 362–364; Big Four Rubber Companies, *War Labor Board Reports* 8 (May 21, 1943): 594–598; U.S. Rubber Company, *War Labor Board Reports* 21 (Jan. 16, 1945): 182–183; *United Rubber Worker*, Feb., March 1944, July 1945.

In the United Steelworkers the Pittsburgh bureaucracy already held more institutional power than their counterparts in Detroit or Akron, but wildcat strikes were still a problem which required stepped-up measures of control from the national union leadership. See Memorandum, Lee Pressman to Van Bittner, January 18, 1943, Entry 406, RG 202, NA; Pressman to Murray, June 21, 1944; Murray to William H. Davis (chairman WLB), Sept. 28, 1943; Clinton Golden to Daniel P. Sheehan, Staff Representative, Oct. 18, 1944; David J. McDonald to Murray, May 28, 1943; and "Work Stoppages and Slowdowns," Report of Policy Committee Meeting, Feb. 11, 1944, all in Box A4-6, Murray Papers, Catholic University.

For brief accounts of WLB discipline in the International Union of Marine and Shipbuilding Workers of America see Victor H. Johnson, "Case History of a Shipbuilding 'Wildcat,'" *Nation*, Jan. 15, 1944; New England Shipbuilding Corporation file, Case No. 25-175-D, Entry 53, RG 202, NA.

33. *United Auto Worker*, June 1, 1944; for similar comments by Philip Murray see *Proceedings . . . USW*, May 9–13, 1944, p. 135.

34. Of course Lewis stood as an alternative leadership to the existing CIO hierarchy and posed for a time as a threat to internal CIO stability. See Malcolm Ross and Richard Deverall to Harold Ickes, "CIO-AFL-RR Strategy on Wage and Price Policy and Its Relation to the John L. Lewis Situation," May 11, 1943, vol. 2, p. 270, Deverall Notebooks, Catholic University; *CIO News*, May 24, 1943.

35. Deverall to Clarence Glick, "A Summary: The Michigan CIO Council Convention, Detroit, Michigan, 28 June to 3 July," July 7, 1943, vol. 1, p. 483, Deverall Notebooks.

36. *Proceedings 1943 Michigan CIO Convention*, pp. 169–214.

37. *Justice*, July 1, 1943.

38. Deverall to Glick, June 24, 1943, vol. 2, p. 53; *New York Times*, May 23, 24, 1943; *United Auto Worker* (Local 174 edition), July 1, 1943. Dubinsky demonstrated the ALP's newfound independence from the Democrats when in 1942 his party ran a gubernatorial candidate opposed to a Roosevelt-backed Democrat for the first time. See Robert C. Carter, "Pressure from the Left: The American Labor Party, 1936–1954," unpublished Ph.D. thesis, Syracuse University, 1965, p. 158.

39. David J. McDonald, *Union Man* (New York, 1969), p. 169. *Aero Notes*, organ of UAW Local 365 on Long Island, commented upon the formation of the PAC from the point of view of those who favored a third party: "One is startled by the CIO Executive Board attempting to knock off in its infancy a regenerative

spontaneous movement for labor action instituted by the rank and file. Murray and Hillman would rather substitute an impotent program for political action than have a genuine independent mass movement because they fear that they will be unable to control the direction of this movement." *Aero Notes*, Oct. 6, 1943.

40. Joseph Gaer, *The First Round: The Story of the CIO-PAC* (New York, 1944), p. 60. A generally sympathetic account of the PAC, which nevertheless reaches some of the same conclusions put forward here, is found in James C. Foster's new book *The Union Politic: The CIO Political Action Committee* (Columbia, Mo., 1975), pp. 3–48, passim.

41. Josephson, *Sidney Hillman*, pp. 600–602; *Labor Action*, Feb. 14, 1944. In Minnesota much the same process took place when PAC officials forced merger of the radical Farmer-Labor Party there with the Hubert Humphrey-led Democrats. Foster, *Union Politic*, pp. 34, 41.

42. *Labor Action*, May 8, 1944.

43. In March 1945 Murray signed a "Labor-Management Charter" with William Green of the AFL and Eric Johnson of the U.S. Chamber of Commerce. The charter was important not for what it said, which consisted of a list of often irreconcilable platitudes hailing the virtues of unfettered free enterprise and the rights of labor, but as an indication by union leaders that they hoped to cooperate with the liberal wing of American capitalism in stabilizing postwar labor relations roughly upon the basis established during the war. In August 1945, Green, Murray, and Johnson reached an interim agreement granting labor an immediate 10 percent wage increase in return for a continued no-strike pledge and a new government labor board. Murray hoped a more substantial wage-price formula could be worked out at the President's Labor-Management Conference in November. *Chester Wright's Labor Letter*, March 31, July 21, 1945; *PM*, March 29, 1945; see also Barton Bernstein, "The Truman Administration and Its Reconversion Wage Policy," *Labor History* 6 (Fall 1965): 214–231.

44. See for example the remarks of Nat Ganley, CP leader in the UAW, in *Proceedings of the 1943 Michigan CIO Council*, 1943, p. 68; and Irving Howe and Lewis Coser, *The American Communist Party: A Critical History* (New York, 1957), p. 427.

45. The leadership of the United Electrical, Radio and Machine Workers, strongly influenced by the Communists, advanced this point of view in their official "Officer's Report to the Convention." Admitting that Roosevelt had not done all the labor movement might have wished, the UE nevertheless declared the "more imminent the destruction of Fascism the more daring will be the moves by anti-democratic forces to create suspicion against the administration." The UE leadership called for criminal indictments against those "undermining . . . Administration win-the-war policies." These elements included not only the right-wing Republican Press, but also John L. Lewis and others who favored wartime strikes. *Proceedings 1943 UE Convention*, pp. 63–65, 81.

46. Koistinen, "Hammer and Sword," pp. 483–485.

47. *Labor Action*, Jan. 1, 8, 1945; *Wage Earner*, Feb. 2, 1945; *Daily Worker*, Dec. 24, 1944; see also Aaron Levenson, *Labor Today and Tomorrow* (New York, 1945), pp. 160–169.

48. *PM*, Feb. 16, 21, 1945; *Textile Labor*, March 1945; *Labor Action*, March 26, 1945.

49. *United Rubber Worker*, May, June, July 1945; *New York Times*, July 6, 13, 1945. *Labor Action*, July 2, 9, 16, 1945.

50. *Proceedings 1944 USW Convention*, pp. 130–137; *Proceedings 1944 UE Convention*, pp. 65–77.

51. *Proceedings 1943 Michigan CIO Council*, pp. 128–140 passim.

52. Irving Howe and B. J. Widick, *The UAW and Walter Reuther* (New York, 1949), pp. 120–125; *Proceedings 1944 UAW Convention*, pp. 147–225, 447–464.

53. *The Hi-Flyer* (UAW Local 6), Nov. 1944.

54. The incentive-pay issue illustrates the extent to which Reuther was willing to disagree with his factional rivals in the UAW, but still not go so far as his more militant supporters would have wished. For more on this issue see Lichtenstein, "Industrial Unionism Under the No-Strike Pledge," pp. 392–429.

55. UAW Executive Board Minutes, Aug. 1, 1944, Box 5, UAW Executive Board Collection, ALHWSU.

56. *Proceedings 1944 UAW Convention*, pp. 147–225, 468–469, passim. Many left-wing Reutherites supported the Rank and File Caucus program and criticized the GM director's equivocation on the no-strike pledge issue. Jack Conway Oral History, pp. 14–16, ALHWSU.

57. UAW Executive Board Minutes, Jan. 26, 1945, Box 23, Addes Papers, ALHWSU.

58. UAW Executive Board Minutes, March 5–8, 1945, Box 23, Addes Papers.

59. *Wage Earner*, June 22, 1945.

60. UAW Executive Board Minutes, Sept. 10–18, 1945, p. 46, Box 4, Thomas Papers, ALHWSU; *United Auto Worker*, Sept. 1, 1945.

61. UAW Executive Board Minutes, Sept. 10–18, 1945, p. 46.

62. *Ibid.*, pp. 47–48; the Mills quote is from his *New Men of Power* (New York, 1948), p. 9.

63. For accounts of the strike see Howe and Widick, *UAW and Walter Reuther*, pp. 126–148; Barton Bernstein, "Walter Reuther and the General Motors Strike of 1945–46," *Michigan History* 49 (Sept. 1965): 260–277; Victor Reuther's critical comments on Murray's reconversion wage strategy are found in V. Reuther, "Look Forward Labor," *Common Sense* (Dec. 1945), p. 8.

64. *Wage Earner*, Dec. 7, 1945; *New York Times*, Jan. 27, 1946; for left-wing criticism of these company security clauses see *Labor Action*, Dec. 17, 24, 1945, and *The Militant*, Jan. 12, March 23, 1946.

65. This statement is based upon an analysis and inspection of the voting lists in the 1944 and 1946 UAW conventions. Of the 70 largest locals in the union, about three-quarters of those who had voted against the no-strike pledge in 1944 cast most of their ballots in favor of Reuther's presidential bid in 1946. Conversely, about three-quarters of those locals which had backed the no-strike pledge in 1944 voted for Thomas in 1946.

66. The unorthodox character of the GM strike demands alarmed leaders of the steel industry who insisted that a wage settlement with the USW allow ample room for an increase in the price of steel. By late January 1946 they actually welcomed a steel strike as a means of putting pressure of the Office of Price Administration to raise its price ceilings. Bernstein, "The Truman Administration and the Steel Strike of 1946," *Journal of American History* 52 (March 1966): 791–803.

287

CHAPTER FOURTEEN

The League of Revolutionary Black Workers: An Assessment

by Ernest Allen, Jr.

Many an observer of the 1960s noted with surprise and approval the remarkable surfacing of the civil rights, Black Power, and New Left movements so soon after the stench of McCarthyism. Within this context, equally remarkable was the fact that an organization such as the League of Revolutionary Black Workers (LRBW), with a leadership in its twenties and thirties, could have emerged with such a relatively coherent political line and practice. The League was born from the ashes of the 1967 Detroit rebellion, and passed from the scene in late 1971. To the extent that this organization developed a coherent politics, it seems to me, credit should be given in part to the presence in Detroit of a number of older and more experienced individuals and organizations. One could mention, for example, the Socialist Workers Party and its "spinoffs": the "Facing Reality" group of C.L.R. James and Martin Glaberman; the discussion circles organized by Grace and James Boggs; as well as present and past members or fellow travelers of the Communist Party. Whether one disagrees either partially or substantially with the politics of these organizations or individuals is quite beside the point; what should not be overlooked is that collectively they functioned as ongoing radical institutions which preserved and transmitted historical information and revolutionary values to a fresh generation of Detroit activists. And this, I would affirm, is what helped to

Reprinted from Vol. 11, No. 1 (January-February 1977).

make the ideology and practical activities of the League so radically different from other black political organizations of the period—League leadership did not have to start from scratch.

Obviously all the credit should not be attributed to Detroit's relatively unique political climate. If LRBW leadership had merely replicated that climate organizationally, there would be little else to discuss here. What made the LRBW different from most other radical organizations was that it moved beyond the stage of leafleting at plant gates, and actually organized black workers to oppose exploitative conditions inside the plant. Its vision and internal structure were decidedly not those of an opposition "caucus" within existing unions, but were those of an independent organization dedicated to the fundamental transformation of social relations in the United States.

At their height in the 1968–1969 period, the LRBW's in-plant organizations were able to organize hundreds of black workers and command the respect of thousands more. The League's political influence spread far beyond the geographical confines of metropolitan Detroit. The LRBW itself became involved in a number of community-organizing projects, owned and operated a modest printing plant, set up an independent legal-defense operation, and was in the process of developing a revolutionary alternative to the United Fund—the International Black Appeal—on the eve of its demise in the early 1970s. Ultimately, it is true, the LRBW succumbed to the same critical deficiencies characteristic of other political organizations of the period.

Detroit: I Do Mind Dying is a highly readable and accessible book, available in both hardcover and paperback editions. It should be considered imperative reading for anyone wishing to acquire an understanding of the radicalization of Detroit's black production workers in the late 1960s and early 1970s. A little more than half the book is devoted to the organizing efforts of the League of Revolutionary Black Workers. The details of that story, unfortunately, are not revealed in the Surkin/Georgakas book, and will have to await another format.

In the introduction to the book, the authors' purpose is stated succinctly:

> At various moments in this effort by working people to gain control of their own lives, different individuals and organizations became more important than others. Our purpose has been to follow the motion of the class which supported them rather than to trace particular destinies or to speculate on the possible future importance of specific individuals, ideologies, or organizations (p. 5).

Detroit: I Do Mind Dying is more an account of the actions and ideas of leading individuals within a specific organization—the LRBW—than one of "the motion of the class which supported them. . . ." Moreover, though speculation with regard to the future of individuals is wisely avoided by Georgakas and Surkin, by means of a process of omission, surface description, and relativism, greater weight is subtly lent to the actions and ideas of specific individuals within the League as it then existed. That the viewpoints of the book in many instances one-sidedly reflect the outlooks of Executive Board members John Watson, Ken Cockrel, and Mike Hamlin will not be immediately apparent to those readers who had no first-hand experience with the organization. We shall return to that point shortly.

The authors are essentially correct when they characterize the primary concern of General Baker and Chuck Wooten as that of plant organizing; that of Watson/Cockrel/Hamlin as more visionary, in the sense of advocating a greater political involvement of the LRBW in the larger Detroit community as well as beyond; and that of Luke Tripp and John Williams as steering a cautious middle course between these two positions (pp. 85–94). Surkin and Georgakas fail to take into account two critical points, however. Although aside from one or two exceptions one can present solid political justification for supportive and other organizational activities carried on outside the plants, the truth is that the League's Executive Board failed to integrate such activities into any comprehensive and centralized developmental plan. In other words, the proliferation of offices and activities of the LRBW throughout the Detroit metropolitan area, while no doubt illustrating "the depth and vision of the League's approach," (p. 93) as Surkin and Georgakas would have it, was, at the same time, a series of helterskelter operations which often drained the organization of precious human and financial resources. In the worst of cases, such activities assumed the form of purely personal projects, where individual Executive Board members appeared to be carving out semi-independent organizational fiefdoms. For example, there was the "Cortland office," main center for worker organizing; the "Linwood office," where Parents and Students for Community Control as well as the International Black Appeal were housed; the "Dequindre office," where the Black Star Bookstore and an abortive community-organizing project were launched; the "Fenkell office," headquarters for the Black Star Printing operation. There were also geographically separate offices for Black Star Film Productions, the Labor Defense Coalition, and UNICOM, a community-organizing center. To outsiders the operation appeared quite impressive; rank-and-file insiders often saw it as an organizational and bureaucratic nightmare.

Second point: by the time of the first general meeting of the LRBW in July, 1970, the workers' components (DRUM, ELRUM, etc.) had literally ceased to exist; at the very most only a handful of members remained in each. This latter revelation, especially, places in appropriate perspective the essential character of a key division within the League's Executive Board— that between plant organizers and those who pushed for wider community and national involvement. In reading Georgakas and Surkin, one is left with the impression that Baker and Wooten were hopeless provincials incapable of extending their vision beyond the big gates of Chrysler's Hamtramck plantation. The point, however, is that they were attempting to regain lost terrain. By mid-1970, when the LRBW was becoming increasingly well known among radical black workers throughout the United States, as well as in domestic and international Left circles, it had also lost its working-class base at home. Hence by glossing over the substantive underlying realities confronting the LRBW, Surkin and Georgakas lend greater credence to the Hamlin/Watson/Cockrel position that the principal task of the League in the 1970–1971 period was that of expansion rather than consolidation. Quite obviously I take the directly opposite view.

Let us now concentrate on what I consider to be another of the book's major shortcomings: its generally negative treatment of Afro-American nationalism. The League itself (more precisely, its predecessor, the Revolutionary Union movement) was launched on the crest of a mass nationalism unleashed during the July 1967 Detroit Rebellion. It should not be too surprising to learn, then, that nationalist sentiment in one form or another thoroughly pervaded the organization from bottom to top. Ironically, though the LRBW (through its top leadership) widely projected itself as a Marxist organization, such categorizing had little to do with the concrete political sentiments of its rank and file. Aside from its leading body, the Executive Board, all sorts of ideological eclecticism prevailed within the League, from nationalist distrust of all whites, to Christianity, astrology, pro-Socialist sentiment, and even anti-Marxist sentiment. Here is reason enough why the LRBW as a whole could not be justifiably characterized as a Marxist-Leninist organization at any single stage of its development. On the other hand, an apparent majority of the membership at least nominally accepted the proposition that Marxist theory and practice were vital to the liberation of Afro-American workers, but most seem to have done so more out of faith in the political correctness of the Executive Board than out of any deep ideological conviction rooted in study. (The political gulf between the top leadership and the membership is manifestly evident in the League film "Finally Got the News." On one hand there is John Watson lecturing on the question of surplus value and of the need for socialist revolution; on the other there is Ron March, one of the many dedicated inplant leaders of DRUM, who states, "We of the League organized to show management and the union that the workers will not tolerate these type of conditions.")

Surkin and Georgakas completely underplay the positive role of nationalism in the formation of the LRBW, mention only its negative aspects, and correspondingly overstress its Marxist-Leninist side—which, as we signaled above, remained mostly the "property" of its leading body. In this way the authors' analysis lacks comprehension of one of the principal "fueling sources" of Afro-American political movements of the past decade—and that of the League in particular.

The League of Revolutionary Black Workers was undoubtedly the most coherent and capable black political organization of the late 1960's, this in spite of its tremendous internal problems and leadership deficiencies. Shortcomings aside, *Detroit: I Do Mind Dying* is the most comprehensive attempt thus far to place the activities of the League in perspective.

CHAPTER FIFTEEN

Beneath the Surface: The Life of a Factory

by Dorothy Fennell

INTRODUCTION

The focus of the following essay is a small factory which makes electrical connectors. Situated in a rural community in the Great Lakes industrial belt, Electric Inc. employs some 400 industrial and 100 white-collar workers. The study is taken from interviews and discussions with men and women who worked or are working in this factory. While some of the history and many of the operational details of Electric Inc. could be learned without talking to the people who actually worked there, much of the history and all of the factory experience had to be collected from the men and women who shaped them.

Beginning in November 1972, I worked in this shop intermittently for 14 months until July 1974, when I was fired for "absenteeism." I and many of my co-workers suspect that the real reason for my dismissal was my union and extraunion activity. During the latter two of my stints in the factory, I acted as shop steward for the women on second shift in the aluminum-assembly department. As a steward I began to see and study the connection between the patterns of social interaction in the shop and the informal resistance to management that I saw around me. After my dismissal, I continued my research, interviewing dozens of workers and studying seniority lists, union contracts and files, strike papers, shop memos, newspaper

Revised version of an article that appeared in Vol. 10, No. 5 (September-October 1976).

articles, tax and property records, and numerous other items that workers either saved and shared with me or pilfered for me. This article, with the names altered, is a condensed version of their story.

CLARENCE LONG'S SHOP

Electric Inc. was founded in 1927 when George and Leo Heilemann began to manufacture electrical connectors in an old garage behind their house. Within a decade they had moved their business to an abandoned machine shop in the nearby industrial city of Lakeside, where they employed some 50 workers. (The experiences of these workers, which include trade-union activity with all three of the major electrical workers' unions between 1936 and 1964, have been deleted to save space.) In 1942, the Heilemanns began an experiment to cut production costs. They arranged for one of their foremen, Clarence Long, to distribute the shop's assembly work among his friends and relatives living in a rural area some 20 miles south of Lakeside. Most of those home-industry workers were either handicapped persons, senior citizens, or young mothers whose husbands had been drafted.

This putting-out system continued until 1945, when Federal inspectors investigated the operation. Long's business violated the Fair Labor Standards Act of 1938 which prescribed a minimum wage, regulated hours, required an operator's license, and outlined special provisions for the employment of handicapped persons. Rather than meet the standards, Long and the Heilemanns centralized the work of the home industry in an old garage located in Town, a rural community some 20 miles from Lakeside. Former employees who were physically able came to work in the Town shop. According to Clarence Long, "even some of the children who had helped their mothers with the assembling and packing work at home" became employees, "when they were old enough to work in a shop." The original workforce was composed chiefly of older women and men, who Long said were "people too old to get work elsewhere."

In 1946 the Heilemanns leased their entire assembly department to Long, and he installed a few more machines and hired more workers. Production continued at the old garage until the floors began to sag under the weight of the machinery. Sometime around 1950 Long moved from this building to a renovated horse stable located just a mile from Town. Thomas Kyper, a handicapped worker, recalled that there were about 50 workers in the new shop, and "90 percent of them were local women." In most cases they were supplementing marginal farm incomes with factory wages.

Of the many hats Long wore, owner, president, chief mechanic, janitor, he excelled at being the social director. Over the years he developed what one worker described as "a very special relationship with his workers." Workers recalled that he was fair about giving time off to farmers in the workforce when agricultural chores were especially pressing. Harriet Johnston remembered that:

> Farmers were given time off to do haying, planting, harvesting. Women with children in school could come in late after they had gotten the kids off to school. It was one big happy family. Long worked right alongside of the workers.

According to Thomas Kyper:

> Some of the workers borrowed money from Long. Often times he advanced pay checks. All holidays, birthdays, and departures were celebrated with parties held during shop time and gifts from Long. Mr. Long had an ideal relationship with his workers. He made coffee for the people in the morning.

Doris Blake expressed the recurring theme of discussions about the early period of the shop's history when she described Long's shop as

> one big happy family. We were the happiest bunch anyone had known. Every holiday was celebrated. . . . Ham and turkeys for Easter, Thanksgiving and Christmas.

Jason Sheldon recalled that:

> Clarence was more on the ball than any other subsequent management. Long was a lenient employer, although his motives were not always pure. It was one big happy family under Long. [He] socialized with the people in the plant—went hunting and fishing with them. They were all friends [who] knew each other's personal problems. Long was friendly with all his help. He visited the workers at their homes. If he arrived at suppertime, he would have dinner with them.

Relationships between Clarence Long and the workers may have been ideal, but working conditions were not. By 1950, production included assembly work, machine tooling, packing, shipping, and chemical processing, work identical to that being done in Lakeside. But wages were 30 to 50 percent lower. At least one worker in Long's shop of the early fifties protested against unhealthy working conditions.

Helen Fields had gone to work because she had to support her family while her husband was bedridden with a serious illness. Her brother, sister-in-law, aunt and niece, many friends and neighbors already worked for Long. When Fields complained that the ventilation system in the degreaser room was inadequate and that the fumes were making her sick, Long showed her a recent state inspector's report which certified the system. Unsatisfied with this response, Fields quit her job and took Long to court, not for compensation, but to force him to install the proper ventilation system and to warn other workers of the potential health hazard. Although the court took no action, pressure from Long's insurance company achieved the same end.

Helen Fields explained her suit against Long by saying that she was "for the working people." She claimed to have no grudge against Long. Rather she held the state inspectors and insurance agents responsible for the bad working conditions. As evidence of her admiration for Long, she recalled an incident when she had defended him against some women who were complaining about Long and his work practices. In response to their complaints, she told them to go and take "a look in that piece of glass over there. See those gray hairs. Now be thankful that there is a Clarence Long who would hire old women like us and give us an opportunity to earn a living."

To compensate for the low wages, which in 1952 averaged 50 cents per hour, there were "good" health-insurance benefits, steady work, and "plenty of overtime." Throughout the shop's history, workers could recall only one slowdown, sometime in the fifties, presumably during the recession which followed the Korean War. But even this slowdown was not taken too seriously. Doris Blake recalled that during this time:

> Mr. Long went around to the women and asked them if any of them wanted some time off to clean their homes or to get caught up on their sewing, or what have you . . . , or if there was something they cared to do that they were behind in. . . .

Doris Blake also recalled that many farmer husbands of the women workers took advantage of the insurance benefits to have operations for hernias, "which they had been carrying around for years." Other fringe benefits included the "good deals" on hunting and fishing gear Long could get through his connections with local merchants. Equally important to the farmers and housewives was the flexible work schedule, which could be adjusted to meet specific needs. Given these conditions it is not surprising that just about all the workers felt that they could best represent their interests as individuals.

Thus when organizers from the United Electrical Workers came "to talk" to Long's employees, they did not receive an enthusiastic response. At least four other factors contributed to the workers' lack of interest in the union. First, there is evidence that the UE international representative may have been an FBI agent paid to sabotage the union's efforts here and elsewhere. Second, the late forties were hard times, leaving Long's workers in no position to risk their jobs. Third, Long did not want a union in his shop, and he talked against it. According to Long, "a union is hard on a small shop." Harriet Johnston, who never saw the need for a union throughout her 30 years of working experience, remembered that:

> Clarence used to say [to his workers] "now I don't want a union in here. . . .
> You get a union and I'll close the doors." Or [he would say] "If you get a union in here, I'm leaving, I'm not sticking around."

At the one informal "free election" the UE organizers held, Long watched while the workers raised their hands to defeat the union.

Fourth, the workers already had something of an informal shop decision-making procedure. Harriet Johnston recalled the "big meetings" held during company time when Long would ask for people's opinions and advice "on things." Mary Ellen Paulson remembered that the workers and Long "communicated" at the shop meetings he organized.

> He'd tell the workers that he had so much money to spend on wages and would ask how they thought it should be divided. One decision we made was whether to have longer breaks or extra paid holidays.

These informal arrangements began to deteriorate in 1955 when Lawrence Dunlitz bought the Lakeside factory and its Town branch. He "retired" the Heilemann brothers, retained Long as president of Electric Inc., and moved the company from the remodeled horse stable to a recently constructed machine shop located on the east side of Town, just two miles from the old shop. Too old to get work elsewhere most of the workers "stuck with Long," though Harriet Johnston remembered that "some of the younger ones went to Westinghouse in Lakeside, to get higher wages." Those who stayed behind had reached, according to Harriet, that "certain age" when employers "just don't hire you anymore."

Shortly after this move, Dunlitz had a foundry built behind the new machine shop. According to Matt Conda, one of the first men to work in the foundry, his co-workers "were older men who came to work at Long's foundry through friendships," even though wages were low and the foundry was not close to their homes. Conda recalled that these men left other jobs to work for Long, and he suspected that they hoped to find more relaxed working conditions than existed in other foundries in the vicinity. Electric Inc. had acquired a reputation for having lax work rules, and stories are still told about Conda's frequent trips to local bars after lunch breaks to round up his crew for the second half of the shift. It is also rumored that beer was a popular summer beverage in the foundry.

Drunk or otherwise, the foundry workers were responsible for bringing the first union to Town. Unlike their counterparts in the machine shop, these men were neither marginal farmers, unskilled workers, local residents, nor recipients of Long's benevolence. It took them less than a year to conclude that plant expansion and Dunlitz's managerial policies had to be countered with organized activity. In 1960 they forced Long to recognize a union we will call the International Metal Workers, an organization already familiar to many of them. Rather than forming a separate local, the men at Electric Inc. joined a Metal Workers' local in Lakeside. According to Long, the foundry workers were "men who had always known a union and who wouldn't work without one. They were tough cats."

Three years after the foundry went union, the NLRB certified the Metal Workers to represent production and maintenance workers in the machine shop. Of the 63 eligible voters, 45 voted for the Metal Workers and 12 against them. There was no other union on the ballot, although five or six employees already belonged to the Pattern Makers Union. Everyone I interviewed remembered that Dunlitz and Long were the most ardent supporters the union had, with the one exception of Oscar Mucker, the union district representative. Mary Ellen Paulson, for example, remembered that "Long went around and asked his oldest workers, who didn't want a union, to support the Metal Workers in the machine shop because he wanted them to." Harriet Johnston had not forgotten how "they kept preaching to us 'union, union.'" Long asked her "to support the Metal Workers union coming into the machine shop," though before "he had always talked against it." Thomas Kyper explained that:

> When the Lakeside company decided that there had to be a union in the Town shop, Long was instructed to send his foremen around to tell the workers that they had to have the Metal Workers.

After the union election, Long "left the company." The details of his resignation are not known to me, but there were many rumors on the subject, and Long's own vagueness about it lends them support. Harriet Johnston thought that "things just got too big for Clarence to handle. He didn't have the education to run a big company," she explained. Others thought that Long was involved in some shady deals. Still others said that Long had just mismanaged the shop and when Dunlitz realized this, he reluctantly asked him to resign. A year after Long resigned, Dunlitz closed the Lakeside factory and moved the entire business to Electric Inc.

Subsequent managements have been unable to imitate Long's informal managerial style. From the beginning Dunlitz had the "wrong attitude" towards the workers, best summed up in his remark that they were "dumb farmers." The most obvious consequence of Dunlitz's managerial policies were turnover rates which during the 1960s increased from "one or two workers every eight or nine months" to "sixty to eighty workers every month." According to Thomas Kyper, "many of these people would quit and be hired back. The company had some kind of unwritten rule that they would rehire at least four times." Either unwilling or unable to treat workers as individuals with unique personalities, problems and needs, Dunlitz tried to rule the shop through the union. Though the union officials were willing to co-operate, the workers were not.

THE UNION

Mary Ellen Paulson recalled that "it took about a year for people in the machine shop to discover that the Metal Workers was a company union." To earn this reputation, the union participated in management's efforts to formalize work practices and to establish a strict code of shop regulations. Everyone in the shop has a favorite union story. With bitterness disguised as cynicism, these stories reveal the callousness of the trade unionism practiced by the Metal Workers and the corruption intrinsic to the union's bureaucratic structure. Union officers at Electric Inc. acted as "hatchet men" for the company. They "looked the other way" when the company ignored the union contract. They talked down to the membership, without trying either to understand their grievances or to fight for their interests.

A typical incident involved Arthur Hooke, until recently a powerful union officer, and Doris Blake a woman with 21 years seniority who was forced to retire. Doris was old and the company considered her a safety risk. Hook and other union officers remained silent while the company ignored seniority rules and demoted her from punch press to grinding, the worst department in the shop. At one point in this campaign, Hooke told Doris Blake that she was "too old to work." Though this was undoubtedly true, she could not afford to retire. Nevertheless, Doris Blake lost her job in 1973 and died two years later, a broken and bitter woman.

Until recently irresponsible men and women held union office because few workers bothered to vote in union elections. In the 1974 election for chief steward, less than 60 of the 400 workers eligible to vote cast a ballot. Union offices have been used as stepping stones to managerial posts. Four foremen, a personnel manager, a plant supervisor, and several other managerial employees formerly served as union officers. Although this union to management mobility represents a well-worn pattern, the problem is not one of personal weakness alone. The union's hierarchical structure and constricted conception of change have waylaid even the best-intentioned union officer.

The union's eagerness to do the company's dirty work, and the ease with which the company snatched union officers to fill managerial positions, discouraged the rank and file. What little support the union had in the beginning quickly dissipated. Less than 30 of the 63 workers eligible to join the union after the NLRB election joined willingly, while initiation fees were automatically deducted from the wages of the others. Within a year after the NLRB election, the rank and file stopped voting in union elections or attending union meetings. Workers who tried at different times to reform the union and to make it responsible to the rank and file either ran up against brick walls or accepted managerial positions offered by the company. The union came into the shop from the top, and it never developed more than a perfunctory interest in the rank and file and their grievances.

Although wages were half the national average for machine-shop workers, the Metal Workers never called a strike. Workers walked out in 1971 and 1974 over the objections of both company and union. In November 1971, workers struck Electric Inc. for the first time in shop history. Wages and the length of the new contract were the central issues. During the strike, which lasted three weeks, union officers negotiated with the company but ignored the strikers. The rank and file, however, remained solid behind their demand for a 26-month contract, ten months short of the usual contract length. Though both company and union opposed this demand, they were forced to concede before workers would agree to return to work.

Two days before Christmas, workers ratified the latest union-company offer by a slim margin. The wage increase, which was the highest in the company's history, amounted to 18 cents per hour effective December 17, 1971, and 43 cents over the next two years. By 1974 this settlement brought the average wage for a machine-shop worker to $2.93 per hour, plus incentive and overtime. At that rate annual income was approximately $6,500, an inadequate amount even in 1972, when a moderate annual income for a family of four was $11,000, according to United States Government calculations.

After a bitter and discouraging struggle, workers had won a wage increase and a 26-month contract. Unsatisfied, "a few workers" expressed anti-union and anti-company sentiments by refusing to pick up advanced paychecks the company issued on December 23 to brighten the Christmas season. According to one woman worker, it was "like a slap in the face. We were serious about the strike, and wanted to stay out. Could have stayed out. We didn't need [the company's] help."

Wages, extended benefits, and a company-proposed Job Evaluation Plan were issues in 1974, when once again workers walked out over the objections of both company and union. Job Evaluation quickly became the key issue in this strike, which lasted a week. The incentive system at Electric Inc., a remnant of the Long era, had to be overhauled because workers were "beating it." Even though job operations had changed, workers ran production at the old rates and made sure that new workers did too. In order to beef up their ability to control workers' time and productivity, the company offered to buy the incentive system from the union for an increase in wages of 10 cents per hour. Without access to company books, it is impossible to determine the fairness of this offer. But in my own case it meant a loss of $20 to $50 per week in incentive pay.

In exchange, the company gained the right to revise, add, or eliminate "any job classifications" warranted by new conditions, "including but not limited to changes in methods, equipment, speeds and feeds, material, new equipment, processes or techniques." Although no one supported the company's right to "evaluate" jobs in this manner, there were mixed feelings about the sale of the incentive system. In a referendum election held during the strike, assembly workers voted against selling the incentive system while the majority of machine-shop workers supported the sale. The women in assembly felt they could "beat" any incentive system while many machine-shop workers stated that there "was too much partiality and favoritism involved with the distribution of incentive work." Under the system at Electric Inc. the group leaders, who were union members in managerial positions at the production level, had the authority to assign incentive work. Intentionally or not, incentive work could be used to intimidate or harass

300

workers who had lost favor with the group leader. Often it caused arguments among workers in a department, especially if it was not rotated so that everyone got a chance to "make some money." Although machine-shop workers endorsed the sale of the incentive system, they did not support the company's Job Evaluation scheme. Just about everyone saw that for what it was.

During the 1974 strike, the Metal Workers surpassed even their 1971 performance. They asked the more militant workers to betray the rank and file and promote the union's proposals. The negotiating team worked behind closed doors and maintained an informational screen. In fact, at the union meeting ostensibly called to discuss the contract, Oscar Mucker said he would throw out anyone who asked questions. One woman then asked about the sagacity of selling the incentive system for a dime, and was thrown out. During this meeting, workers began to circulate a petition calling for the dismissal of Oscar Mucker. Over 100 workers signed it, even though success would have left them without a liaison between the International and the local in the middle of a strike. Just before the balloting began, members of the union negotiating team stood before the rank and file and repeated company threats to close the shop if the contract was not ratified. Faced with this mess, workers agreed to go back to work, but only after the company agreed to a two-year contract and promised that Job Evaluation would not mean speed-up.

BYPASSING THE UNION

Workers at Electric Inc. have defended themselves against company-union collusion and irresponsible trade-union practices by relying only on themselves and the network of friendships they developed. The actions they have taken range from simply demanding on the spot that a dull and therefore hazardous shaffering tool be sharpened, to secretly writing a letter to OSHA begging Federal inspectors to take action on a malfunctioning punch press that had already cost several fingers. Some have organized to throw out the old union officials or to throw out the union altogether and replace it with the UE. Many workers have heard from friends and relatives that the UE is a stronger and fairer union than the Metal Workers. While incumbent officers have been replaced, it is much harder to replace the union itself because of NLRB regulations that bar such an action except during the last 30 days of the contract.

These and other actions against the company have been carried out by an informal resistance network of workers, headed by a middle-aged woman who operates a turret lathe in the machine shop. Whatever the grievance, workers go first to the union; and if they fail to get results, which is usually the case, they next see Esther Szabo. Although she claims to "have a poor memory," she knows three-fourth of the workers by their first names.

Esther Szabo began to work at Electric Inc. in 1966. Since turning 17, she had worked in small, non-union shops in Cleveland and Lakeside. When she came to Electric Inc., she expected to earn higher wages and to find relaxed working conditions similar to those she had known in her former jobs. From her brother and brother-in-law she had heard that Electric Inc. "was a nice place to work," a rumor contradicted by the fact that "they were always hiring." She recalled that the two most frequently heard comments about the union were "they just take your money" and "they never do anything."

An early confrontation with the Metal Workers involved the rescheduling of union meetings. In 1966 the union held its monthly meeting at the City Hall on Tuesday evening, making it impossible for second-shift workers to attend. When Esther Szabo suggested that the meetings be held on Sunday afternoons instead, other workers supported her, and the union president rescheduled the meetings. But attendance, usually confined to stewards and officers, did not improve. A few meetings convinced Esther that exasperation with the union, not apathy, accounted for the lack of rank-and-file participation.

A detached observer would probably have found those union meetings entertaining. Minutes were improperly recorded and gave little if any indication of what had transpired. Formality and Robert's Rules were invoked only to cut off a disgruntled speaker or a discussion in which real grievances were expressed. Officers used three-fourths of the meeting time to wade through administrative material. Meetings ended with a sigh of relief, a salute to the stamina of those who had endured the entire two hours. Esther Szabo remained silent when the Tuesday-evening meeting time was restored.

Less than a year after winning this hollow victory, she began a campaign to have a pay phone installed in the shop cafeteria. The seriousness of having no convenient means with which to communicate with the outside world was underscored when a second-shift worker was stranded at the plant because her car would not start. The woman had to walk half a mile to Town at 2:30 A.M. to telephone for help. The women workers were especially concerned. They feared being stranded, and they also wanted to be able to "call home during breaks and lunch times to check if everything was okay with their children." After this incident, Esther Szabo went to Waltz, the union president, and requested that a phone be installed for the workers. "Waltz wasn't interested," so she went to a foreman, but he too "wasn't interested." Finally Esther Szabo wrote a petition demanding that the company install a public phone, and "everyone signed it." After taking it around to second-shift workers during breaks and lunchtime, she came in early the next day to ask first-shift workers to sign also. Pressure from below forced the union to take up the issue, and the workers got a phone. Two months later the same procedure was used to get a dollar changer in the cafeteria.

In 1970, when the company ordered foremen to stop workers from practicing their usual routine of quitting five minutes before the end of the shift to wash their hands, workers went to Esther Szabo. They had just assumed their right to wash off company dirt on company time, even though the union contract did not mention it. As far as the union officers were concerned, this attempt to alter established routine was outside the union's jurisdiction because "nothing was said about it in the contract." At the request of fellow workers, Esther launched a harassment and intimidation campaign against Waltz, the perennial union president. She took every opportunity to convince him that they "deserved" the five minutes to clean up. She argued that the company had no right to change established work practices unilaterally. To silence this woman, Waltz agreed to do what he could. Meanwhile, workers supported Esther Szabo's actions by continuing to quit five minutes early. In the face of such strong resistance, Waltz had to go to the company and tell them their plan would not go down with the workers. And the company backed down.

In March 1974, just one month before the union contract expired, the Metal Workers supported a company plan to fire several workers who had accumulated many years of seniority. "There was a rumor going around the shop that the company had made a list of twenty workers who were too slow and they were going to fire them." Furthermore, it was rumored that Bill Stewart, a handicapped worker with five years in the milling department, was at the top of the list. Although Stewart filed a grievance, the union hierarchy ruled there was "no case" and his grievance never went to arbitration. From the union, Stewart went to Esther Szabo, who was both fellow worker and neighbor.

As word got around the shop, a variety of responses contributed to a general sense of outrage. In addition to a genuine concern for Stewart's welfare, there was anger, because the company's plan defied established seniority policies, and fear, because no one knew for sure they weren't "next on the list." After discussing the problem informally with several trusted friends, Esther Szabo started a petition supporting Stewart's right to his job. She explained that "people signed it because they weren't sure if they were on the list, and they realized that even if they weren't on this list, they had to stop this sort of company heavy-handedness or they could be next on some future list." Strong opposition defeated the company once again, and no one was fired. Workers interpreted the company's action on two levels. Taken at face value, it was an understandable, though unacceptable, plan "to get rid of the deadheads." More disturbing, however, it was a way of testing workers' reactions to unilateral changes in work regulations, especially those affecting productivity. Rumors about the company's Job Evaluation Plan were already widespread, and workers thought this incident substantiated them.

Informal resistance networks at Electric Inc. are not exclusively crisis-oriented. In every department, workers restrict production, collectively or individually, while co-workers "look the other way," becoming accomplices in an ongoing assault on the clock. Tools disappear or inexplicably break. Machines "act up" or stop functioning altogether. Sympathetic set-up operators "take their time" preparing machines for new assignments. Job orders "disappear" or become so illegible that office copies have to be consulted. In the traffic of shift changes and interdepartmental flow, barrels, boxes, and trays of parts and materials simply "get lost." Ignoring the protests and threats of foremen, time-study men, and group leaders, workers cooperate to stint the work, inadvertently asserting their right to control production.

Until recently, workers also cooperated on a daily basis "to beat the incentive system," now replaced by Job Evaluation. The fact that the company wanted to abandon the incentive system is an indication of how successful the workers had been. Under the old system, as the union contract expressed it, time-study men used "MTM, time study, standard data, or other recognized tools of industrial engineering" to assign jobs a parts-per-hour rate. Workers were expected "to make" these rates, and were paid incentives of 1 percent above the base rate "for each percent of production increase above the normal rate." Since the company reserved the right to retime any job consistently run over 150 percent of the "normal rate," workers seldom produced more.

Workers modified most jobs to slow the pace, taking the risk that the company would "catch on" and order the rate men to retime the job. If there was no "better way" to do the job, workers could either forego quality or falsify documents on which they recorded daily totals. According to Esther Szabo many workers think they "can't gain anything" by doing their best, so "they cover themselves" by finding "happy mediums" of production, somewhere between their "good days" and "bad days" output. She explained that "most people feel they should produce something" but they are careful not to exceed "their bad days' production" by too much, lest the company demand it all the time. Another tactic was to complain formally about "unreasonable rates" to anyone who would listen, while informally cooperating with others to stint production below the set rate. In 1974 this practice was becoming increasingly widespread in response to the company's systematic effort to reevaluate jobs and assign new rates.

When production could not be stinted, nor the rate "made," workers not on piecework assisted those who were, "to make it." Finding opportunities to do this depended largely upon the department's structure. It was easiest for women in assembly where workers on piecework labored alongside those on straight time at narrow wooden benches. Machine operators, on the other hand, standing alone at individual machines, had a more difficult time getting away from their non-rated tasks and assisting a worker on piecework at another machine. When the company began to crack down in 1974, it became even harder for machine-shop workers to practice mutual aid, and they were among the first workers in the shop to conclude that incentive pay was no longer worth the time and effort it took to earn it. They did not, however, vote to replace incentive with Job Evaluation, the company's latest scheme to increase productivity.

Fighting back through an informal network demands both awareness and participation from the majority of workers. Esther Szabo explained her activities by saying that she "wants to help people," as long as "the problem is legitimate." She doesn't "fight lost causes." People come to her because she has spoken out in the past and continued to fight for a justice that she doesn't articulate. She "starts something" and expects people to back her up with whatever it takes to win. Petitions have been effective, and they are not taken lightly. To sign a piece of paper that could "get lost" as it travels through the shop, eventually falling into company hands, is a very serious and risky business. Protective labor legislation still leaves the company plenty of room to find grounds for dismissing a worker.

One pay phone, a dollar changer, and a Sunday union meeting, five minutes to wash up, a two-year contract, and stinting production cannot be construed into an impressive list of victories. Th realities of the wage system, with its long hours, low wages, hazardous working conditions, speed-up, monotony, meaningless work, and squandered talent, continue to diminish the workers at Electric Inc. Yet these realities should not obscure the lesson of their resistance. The informal network reasserts the very lines of confrontation that the union has obscured through its cooperative relationship with the company. Informal resistance has done more to threaten the authority of the boss than has the institutionalized negotiating of the Metal Workers. Because the network is called forth, not by a "contract," but rather by an unarticulated understanding of what is fair play in the context of an adverserial relationship with the boss, their actions have gone beyond legality. It is in this ability to transcend the formal constraints of both the union and the company that one sees the roots of even greater challenges to the boss.

THE SOCIAL NETWORK

Clarence Long understood how socializing with his employees could mitigate the resentment he incurred for paying low wages and expecting long hours and maximum output. According to him, "workers should be made to feel important. Even the lowest-paid worker is a human being." For their own reasons, workers at Electric Inc. have formed an elaborate social network which operates both inside and outside the shop. This social network is the backbone of their informal resistance, as well as a means to counteract the numbing effects of tending machines and assembling parts eight or more hours a day, five days a week, fifty weeks a year for a lifetime.

In the many opportunities workers find to interact outside the shop, people become friends and, occasionally, lovers. Men, and an increasing number of women, frequently socialize over a glass of beer at the local working-class taverns before, during, or after work. Second-shift workers regularly begin their weekend on Friday night by meeting spouses and friends from other factories at a favorite bar. More formally organized parties occur at workers' houses on Saturday evenings. At these get-togethers men and women from different ethnic and cultural backgrounds drink, talk, sing, and dance. While most workers enjoy singing and listening to the country and western music that can be heard even in the factory, they tolerate the more modern stuff generally favored and occasionally performed by younger workers.

There are also camping trips and shopping sprees, Sunday dinners shared with friends and relatives, and weekday visits to people's homes for coffee, conversation, counseling, and moral support. Fellow workers act as surrogate analysts, marriage counselors, child specialists, educators, and other professional people who are too expensive or too removed by the lines of class to be consulted directly. On a lighter scale there are occasions to bake bread, distribute surplus garden produce, exchange old clothes, especially those of children, swap mechanical and other expertise, and "just plain help out."

Since the amount of time spent in these off-the-job encounters and activities is limited by the 40-to-60-hour work week, socializing continues on the job. Workers in assembly, for example, try to arrange their jobs so that they can talk, control the pace of work, assist other workers, and restrict production. Often workers make something special out of their lunch breaks, either by organizing a pot-luck shop dinner or, during the summer months, by picnicking behind the factory. The company has tried to institutionalize this practice, and has offered to build a "picnic area" near the shop.

During working hours, people take time to discuss families, homes, news events, politics, working conditions, and themselves. These discussions have a built-in momentum, grounded in the need to humanize the workplace and punctuated by the whistles of the shift. They offer a chance to regain some control over the time already forfeited to the boss.

In these discussions workers find strength and support to make small but important adjustments in their lives. Faith left a husband who beat her. Dorothy took a job on first shift so that she could spend more time with her huband and children. Others began to fight for improved safety conditions. Still others discovered in these conversations the courage to resist endless assaults by group leaders who tell them to work faster, or foremen who keep track of how many times they go to the bathroom, or personnel managers who order them to come to work 15 minutes early without pay.

The effects of these social encounters are evident throughout the shop. Young countercultural women, for example, introduced the older women workers to the latest information about vitamins, health foods, wholesome living, primal scream therapy, yoga, and human sexuality. As one women explained, the older women "got hooked." They began to fix their hair differently. Some of them donned blue jeans for the first time. Everywhere, women could be heard talking about how good they felt now that they were eating better, doing exercises, and taking vitamins. As a few women shared their personal experiences, other people seemed to open up, joining in discussions which occasionally centered on supposedly "private matters" such as abortion, birth control, "free" relationships, and family troubles. In this two way exchange of information older workers taught their younger counterparts how to restrict production. These workers also had much to share about shop etiquette, survival, and "the good old days," when management seemed less intrusive.

Interacting in yet another way, a few people formed study groups to read and discuss Jack London's *The Iron Heel*, John Steinbeck's *In Dubious Battle*, Studs Terkel's *Hard Times*, and Alix Kates Shulman's *Memoirs of an Ex-Prom Queen*. More popular reading material includes farming magazines and "futures" farm reports, *Popular Mechanics*, astrology magazines, and do-it-yourself engineering and electrical publications. This, like all reading material, is prohibited in the shop. Of course people ignore this rule. Miscellaneous reading material I passed around the shop and discussed with friends included articles in *Economic Notes* and *Monthly Review*, War Resisters League literature, and David Montgomery's "What's Happening to the American Worker?" Often these pieces pertained to a particular shop discussion, issue, or argument.

Apparently sensitized through some heated discussions about women's rights on the job, in December 1973 men in the second-shift automatics department walked off their jobs when they learned that the company had denied Muriel Pawlowski's bid for a job in their department. Their understanding of her rights had been shaped for the most part by what they saw on television and experienced in the shop. From this introduction to sexual politics, they determined that an equal right to a job for which a woman was qualified was "women's liberation and it was okay." Within an hour after the men walked into the personnel manager's office to protest the company's decision, Muriel was awarded the bid. To date only the maintenance and tool-and-die departments are all-male.

In addition to the interactions of small groups of workers, there are also social encounters which involve the entire shop. For second-shift workers the most common of these are birthday celebrations and going-away parties. Preparations for the latter begin about a week in advance of the worker's last day. Food lists circulate around the shop during working hours, and workers sign up to bring a dish or some other necessary item. Usually the women prepare something at home and with few exceptions, each man contributes a dollar towards a ham or roast. George Binns, a tool-and-die-maker keeps an electric frying pan in the tool room just to prepare special dishes for such occasions. On the night of the party, workers drop off their contributions in the assembly department, where half a dozen women "get things ready."

When the eight-o'clock whistle blows, 80 workers line-up behind the guest of honor and the feast begins, resulting in a festive scene carried out at a pace that would have delighted Frederick Winslow Taylor.

When the 8:30 whistle signals the end of the dinner break, people mosey back to their departments and resume work. Foremen make a habit of leaving assembly a few minutes before 8:30 to avoid confrontations with those workers who linger past the last whistle. Women in assembly clean up the mess on company time, and everyone returns at the ten-o'clock break to finish the leftovers and to have cake and coffee. Birthday celebrations follow a similar pattern, but usually on a smaller scale unless the person being honored is especially well known and liked.

Though the factory continues to be an inhospitable place over which workers have very little control, they have not deferred completely either to the noise and grime or to the boss. Interacting on and off the job they have instead integrated their personal and political lives to form a resistance network that extends from shop to home. Within this unrecognized and unofficial structure, workers at Electric Inc. have personalized their battles with the boss and politicized their personal struggles with themselves and with each other, often just trying to get through another working day.

THE CONGLOMERATE ERA

As the economy began to wind down in 1974, the company began to crack down. Tightened discipline strained the resources of the informal resistance network because "it was becoming more difficult to get to the bathroom to pee," let alone to discuss problems in the shop. Esther Szabo explained that the network had been most effective when working conditions remained sufficiently relaxed to give workers an opportunity "to meet in the restrooms" or to gather around their machines to discuss problems, make plans, and sign petitions. By 1975, only one shift with a skeleton crew of fewer than 100 workers operated the shop. When workers realized that these lay-offs undermined their ability to affect shop conditions, they decided to take over the union. Although Esther Szabo had often been asked to run for union office, she refused until 1976, when cutbacks had defeated the informal network approach, and the other "right people," workers who had also exercised informal leadership, stepped forward to run with her. In the election, the largest turnout in shop history defeated incumbent officers, including those who had held office since 1963. Of the 200 workers eligible to vote, 144 cast ballots, while the union officers denied another 200 workers the right to vote because they were laid off. Esther Szabo lost the presidency by two votes to the candidate she supported, winning instead the office of corresponding secretary, where she feels she can most effectively use her skills. This latest turn of events belongs to the conglomerate era, and it needs to be connected to the relevant changes in management practices at Electric Inc.

Dynamo Inc. purchased Electric in April 1967 for an undisclosed amount of cash. Although Dynamo had been incorporated only in 1960, by 1967 it was one of the "major growth companies in the world." As a conglomerate engaged in "research and manufacturing of electronic systems, components and controls, tool and die steels, aircraft and guided missile systems, material technology, geophysics, and oceanography . . . ," Dynamo received government contracts, exceeding 70 million dollars in 1972. Between 1960 and 1973, when their military contracts began to decline, Dynamo acquired controlling interest in hundreds of small businesses, including insurance and finance companies, and purchased others outright, as was the case with Electric Inc. Prior to 1973, the management of the Dynamo conglomerate showed little interest in Electric Inc. But without the guaranteed profits from government contracts and war production, Dynamo was forced to pay more attention to its non-military sector. To achieve a competitive market position with factories such as Electric Inc., Dynamo introduced new managerial policies and made structural changes in the production process.

To everyone's surprise, Dynamo fired the old Electric Inc. managers. Young men who had gotten their managerial training in slick, gigantic, "growth" companies where the workforce was organized by "big labor" unions such as the United Auto Workers, Steel Workers, or Machinists replaced them. Even Lawrence Dunlitz got the ax. At the bottom, Dynamo managers launched an efficiency drive aimed at increasing productivity. Evidence of this could be seen in the institutionalization of foremen/worker relations, the replacement of incentive by Job Evaluation, and an unprecedented concern for absenteeism, "goofing off," and the volume of scrap metal being produced.

Along with structural changes, Dynamo introduced the latest fashion in paternalism. Its theme was the familiar one of "one big happy family," but the family had become a "TEAM." In a July 18, 1974, letter to "fellow employees," Richard Kraft, president of Dynamo Electric Inc., exposed the company's new approach to worker/management relations. He wrote:

Dear Fellow Employees,
    One of my first objectives as your new President is to try to create for each of you the feeling that your job at Dynamo Electric is the best, most challenging and most exciting you have ever had. To accomplish this, we are working hard to improve conditions, to supply the needed tools and to further develop the friendly, businesslike atmosphere of the Company.
    A Team Effort—all of us working together—is required to accomplish the job we have to do. There are many things we in management work on which *we* think are good ideas, or we feel *you* think are good ideas, but I would like to have a better feel of what is on your mind. For this purpose, I am having a personal mailbox placed in the cafeterias where you can write

me a note directly, telling me your thoughts on how we are doing the job and what we can do to improve.

We need to work together, and we need to listen to each other. I hope this mailbox will help to accomplish part of this communication.

Workers realized that Kraft was trying to take advantage of their experience and expertise without undermining basic assumptions about the role of workers and the distribution of power in the factory. To a lesser extent, so had Clarence Long, and though both men employed paternalism, there were important differences. In contrast to Long's owner-operator paternalism, in which he recognized workers as individual farmers or housewives with special needs to be given special consideration, Dynamo introduced a paternalism in which workers are treated as fools who can be manipulated with the proper mixture of psychology, intimidation, and style. Beneath management's new suit of understanding, consideration, confidence, and good-will, workers detect the odor of dirty underwear.

One feature of the new paternalism has been the creation of a recreation fund to promote sports teams and annual company-worker picnics. Kraft explained that "during working hours we work hard to produce quality products at the lowest possible cost. When the working day is over, we deserve some recreation!" Additional efforts to personalize the factory experience have included open-house parties for the workers and their families, a plant beautification program, a President's Suggestion Box that workers stuff with complaints, and a shop newspaper that has issued some very entertaining blurbs from the "President's Corner." Inspired by the 1975 Christmas season, Kraft composed a commentary on "Electric Inc. Spirit," that "esprit de corps, others might think of—as dedication to a common goal or perhaps pride in accomplishment."

He claimed to "see it in the eyes of the people as" he walked "through the plant in the morning." Wherever he looked he saw "pride on the faces and a joy in the eyes of everyone. . . ." Thinking it was "a matter of pride in the work being done and the knowledge that important work is being accomplished with skill and craftsmanship," he declared how "proud and grateful" he was "to be part of this . . . family and to be swept up in this spirit," emanating from this "truly . . . great place to work." No one need take but one walk through this shop to conclude that Kraft perceived things incorrectly.

As an instructor, he fared no better. In another message, for example, Kraft revealed how workers could help "underprice our competition." He implored each worker to ask:

Is my machine producing good parts every minute that it could during the day, or are there times when it could be producing more? Am I getting the most production out of my equipment? Am I using my time wisely or is there wasted motion? Are there some additional few minutes during every hour that I could use more productively?

310

Equally concerned about waste, he suggested that workers ask themselves two more simple questions: "Are we wasting material? and, Are we wasting time?"

Workers, according to Esther Szabo, realize that Kraft is wasting his time. They have ignored his lesson, and in general, "are suspicious of the new treatment." "They think it probably foreshadows something bad." The new paternalism has produced "lots of uneasiness," and helped to generate "lots of rumors in the plant" as to what all this means. Workers have also acted through the union to counter the company's new approach to industrial management. According to Esther, "We're trying to do something from here [the union], just like we did something from inside the shop. If we're not successful, we'll try something else."

CHAPTER SIXTEEN

Where Is the Teamster Rebellion Going?

by Staughton Lynd

Every occupation has its own ambience. We are familiar with the particular mystiques of farm workers, coal miners, secretaries. At this moment, perhaps no occupational group has more vividly impressed itself on the public mind than the truckdriver, or, to use the archaic term which denominates the union, "teamster."

Dan E. Moldea's *The Hoffa Wars: Teamsters, Rebels, Politicians, and the Mob* (New York and London, 1978) and Steven Brill's *The Teamsters* (New York, 1978) by and large feed the romanticized notion of teamster exceptionalism. And in truth, the history of truckdriving in this country since the 1930s leaves one gasping. Consider, for instance:

- The leading organizer of teamster industrial unionism in the 1930s was not Hoffa, but Farrell Dobbs, a member of the Socialist Workers Party. Dobbs preached the need for regional union organization and a national collective bargaining agreement. "I realized," Hoffa later stated on television, "how right he was" (Moldea, p. 28). Yet it was also Hoffa who, as a personal favor to Dan Tobin, then president of the International Brotherhood of Teamsters, took a hundred or so goons into Dobbs's Minneapolis stronghold at the beginning of World War II and, in Hoffa's phrase, "had the war" (Moldea, p. 32). As Dobbs points out,

Reprinted from Vol. 13, No. 2 (March-April 1979).

Hoffa was helped in winning it by the Minneapolis Police Department, the courts, the mayor, the governor, state anti-labor legislation, and the Government of the United States, which jailed Dobbs and 17 others as the first victims of the Smith Act.

• Hoffa appears first to have been introduced to organized crime by his mistress, Sylvia Pagano (Moldea, p. 25). Then, in 1941, when John L. Lewis's brother Denny sought to organize Michigan teamsters for the CIO, a raid which the UAW declined to support, "Perrone, Angelo Meli, Frank Coppola, and other crime figures gave Hoffa the support he needed to drive the CIO raiders out of Detroit" (Moldea, p. 37).

• Hoffa was sent to prison for jury tampering by the testimony of Edward Partin, who, it seems, was offended when Hoffa threatened in 1962 to assassinate Robert Kennedy. One of the many Teamster fellow travellers who pressured Partin to recant his testimony so that Hoffa might be released from prison was Audie Murphy, most decorated GI of World War II (Moldea, p. 279).

• Harold Gibbons, Socialist, boss of the St. Louis teamsters, womanizer, and eligible heir to Hoffa's power, broke with Hoffa when, as both Moldea and Brill recount, Gibbons (then helping Hoffa to administer the national organization) ordered the flags at Teamster headquarters in Washington lowered to half-mast after John F. Kennedy's assassination.

• The exhausted National Guardsmen who fired on students at Kent State University on May 4, 1970, had been transferred from policing a wildcat strike of teamsters (Moldea, p. 265).

• The CIA, through, among others, its deputy director of plans Richard Bissell (a Yale man), and evidently with Hoffa's help, offered the Mafia $1,000,000 to kill Castro. This was more than letting out a contract. Under Batista the American mob had substantial business investments in Cuban organized vice. Part of the deal between the CIA and the mob was that American gangsters use "their old contracts on the island to set up a small network of spies" so as "to pinpoint the roads that Castro might use to deploy troops and tanks in meeting the attacking forces" (Moldea, p. 130, quoting *Time* magazine. See, in general, his chap. 7, "Teaming Up Against Castro," based in good part on the Church Committee investigation).

• During the month prior to John F. Kennedy's assassination, Jack Ruby talked on the phone with Irwin Weiner, chief Teamster bondsman (October 26); Barney Baker, a Teamster enforcer (November 7, 8, 11); Murray Willer, head of the Southern Conference of Teamsters (November 8). Ruby also called Nofio

Pecora, a prominent member of the Marcello "family" (October 30), and Baker was in contact with David Yaras, a brutal man who had helped to organize Local 390 in Miami, and was a recognized go-between for Marcello and Santos Trafficante, with whom Ruby was jailed in Cuba in 1959. Government investigators allege that on November 21 Ruby was in the offices of oil millionaire H. L. Hunt at about the same time as Jim Braden, a criminal and Teamster afficionado who was also near and in the Texas School Book depository the next day, November 22, when John F. Kennedy was killed (Moldea, chap. 8, "Coincidence or Conspiracy").

During the early Teamster organizing, Dobbs, but not Hoffa, tried to improve the working conditions of owner-operators. When Hoffa was imprisoned in the 1960s his underworld supporters were bought off and thereby won over by Frank Fitzsimmons. Accordingly, Hoffa, when he was released from prison by Nixon, perforce turned to rebellious owner-operators and other dissidents in an effort to build a base for his return to Teamster office. Thus Hoffa supported the 1974 wildcat of the Fraternal Association of Steel Haulers against high gasoline prices.

Clearly incidents such as the above are the stuff of Teamster romance. They foster the image of macho, country-and-western truckdrivers, a little bit different from all others, "thinking and talking about their cowboylike pasts, presents, and futures" (Moldea, pp. 326–327).

However, truckdrivers are employees like other workers and face essentially the same problems. This is true even of owner-operators, whose essential contention in the work stoppage underway is that they are *not* small businessmen, subject to the anti-trust laws, but employees protected by the National Labor Relations Act. Truckdrivers own their own tools (if owner-operators) or (even if company drivers) have more control over their conditions of work than the assembly-line worker. These circumstances contribute to the elan of teamster rebels, just as underground work, danger, and the cultural isolation of Appalachia no doubt have something to do with the remarkable spirit and solidarity of miners. Still it is a dangerous error, which offers no real help to the dogged men and women seeking to change the Teamsters union, to suppose that the problems faced by truckdrivers are fundamentally unlike the problems confronting miners, autoworkers, steelworkers, and the rest of us.

All major American unions remain in need of a thoroughgoing democratic revolution. Autoworkers cannot vote directly for their national union officers. Steelworkers cannot vote directly on the Basic Steel Contract. In these unions, filing a grievance is a good deal like dropping a stone into a very deep well. In none of these unions do members possess elementary rights of due process, such as the right to be present at proceedings where one's grievance (say, a grievance protesting a discharge) is discussed; the right to be represented by one's own attorney; the right to have a written record made of the proceeding; the right to continue on the job until finally shown to be "guilty"; and so on.

The International Brotherhood of Teamsters is simply a little more so. In Teamsters' organizing, the employer is often pressed to contribute for the right *not* to be unionized. Among teamsters, dissidents get their houses bombed (Tom Gwilt, William "Red" Anderson, Jim Leavitt) or, at least in New Jersey, get killed (Anthony Castellito). And as everyone knows, Teamster honchos invest their members' pension funds in casinos, phony real estate developments, the drug trade, et cetera, more brazenly than their counterparts elsewhere.

Hence the special pathos of rebellion among teamsters, as, in a similar although by no means identical context, among farm workers or Southern pulpwood workers. Evil is so dramatic. The simplest democratic decencies, such as the right to elect shop stewards, appear almost revolutionary. To listen even casually to the rhetoric of Teamster rebels is to appreciate how bourgeois democracy, and Christianity, have functioned historically as revolutionary credos. At the 1977 convention of Teamsters for a Democratic Union a keynote speaker invoked Magna Charta, Milton's "Areopagitica" (which he struggled to pronounce but understood perfectly), and the Bill of Rights. At the 1978 TDU convention Peter Camarata, the organization's candidate for Teamster president, described himself as a born-again Christian. There was nothing at all funny about either speech. These are the beliefs which enabled these courageous rank-and-file leaders to believe that they can, indeed, overcome some day.

Accordingly, Marxists who organize within the Teamsters union face a familiar dilemma. Only with their energetic aid, seemingly, can the bourgeois revolution in the union be effected. Yet the fruits of successful democratic business unionism are all too evident. The mainline CIO unions—UAW, Steelworkers, and so on—offer one set of examples. Arnold Miller's election to the presidency of the United Mine Workers and its sequel is another. One need go no further than the history of the Teamsters themselves to prove the point still again. The IBT Bad Guys—Hoffa, Fitzsimmons, Rolland McMaster, Dave Johnson—were one and all rank-and-file reformers in the 1930s. Dan Moldea, scathingly impatient with the so-called reformation of Hoffa's last years, nonetheless affirms that in the 1930s Hoffa showed "unparalleled enthusiasm for . . . union democracy, rank-and-file control of officials and union policies" (Moldea, p. 27). Moreover, "he was willing to make tremendous personal sacrifices . . ." (Moldea, p. 28). What happens to such individuals? Can it be prevented? Must union organization endlessly reproduce dull and corrupt bureaucracy as a result? Why should TDU, or PROD, or FASH, avoid the same fate, much less move on from union reform to socialist transformation?

Critical reading in this connection are Steven Brill's painstaking and brilliant chapters on the typical Teamster member, Al Barkett (Brill, pp. 25 ff., chap. 7), the typical honest local union officer, Ron Carey (chap. 5), and the atypical, tragic Harold Gibbons (chap. 10). Barkett, in the last analysis, supports the existing leadership because it has paid off materially for him. Carey, in the last analysis, opposes the existing leadership because it prevents him from advancing in the union without total sacrifice of principle. Gibbons, in the last analysis, compromised so long that when the time came to take his life in his hands and challenge Fitzsimmons for the Hoffa legacy, he was silent.

Brill and Moldea differ somewhat about the early Gibbons. Brill tells of his conversion to socialism at a University of Wisconsin summer school for workers in the Depression. Moldea, citing the McClellan Committee hearings, states that Gibbons "literally purchased" St. Louis Local 688. But I have no reason to doubt Brill's account (pp. 356–357) of what Gibbons did with Local 688 in the late 1940s and early 1950s as the Cold War set in.

"Gibbons' workers got free, unlimited hospitalization and medical care for themselves and their spouses and children—a benefit virtually unheard of in 1951. 'Other workers, if they had any health protection at all,' Gibbons explained, 'had insurance. But that had limitations. If you had to have an appendectomy the insurance gave you $75. But the doctor charged you $150, so you were stuck. That was no good. Some of the guys I was organizing were making 35 cents an hour, and they couldn't afford that. So we built our own Labor Health Institute with its own doctors [57 of them working part-time by 1951] that handled everything. It was the first prepaid health plan as far as I know, and the employers paid for all of it.' Gibbons' members also got free dental care (except for bridgework and dentures, which they got at cost.) They got free home nursing services, drugs and eyeglasses at cost, and free legal advice. By 1951 they also had pension benefits—at least four years earlier than other Teamsters locals won them.

"When food prices rose rapidly that year, the union opened a non-profit grocery for its members. A few years later, Gibbons persuaded the employers to pay for a recreation center as part of the employee health program. Wholly financed by employers, it had become, by the early '60s, an unparalleled complex that included an indoor swimming pool and gymnasium center for winter recreation and a 300-acre outdoor swimming, camping, tennis and golfcourse complex in suburban St. Louis. In short, the workers had the same kind of country-club facilities that their bosses had. 'Many of our members were from the slums,' Gibbons said. 'I saw the health-and-recreation camp as the only way to get their kids some fresh air and a decent place to play in. It was the first time recreational facilities were ever defined as part of a legitimate union health plan that the employers could pay for. For the members and children who were black, it was the only decent place they could go, because everything was segregated in those days.'

"Gibbons fought segregation in St. Louis. 'We used the union as a social force.' In January of 1952, two years before the Supreme Court's decision striking down school segregation, Gibbons published a union plan for the desegregation of St. Louis's public schools. At the time, public schools were required by the Missouri constitution to be divided by race. 'It was just plain common sense. But what a reaction the fuckin' thing got,' Gibbons recalled. One St. Louis resident called it 'a Russian booby trap,' in a letter to a local newspaper. When the civil-rights struggle in the South opened on other fronts in the middle '50s, Gibbons thrust 688 into the battle headlong: 'If you were black you couldn't get into a theater anywhere in the city of St. Louis except in the black community,' he recalled. 'And you couldn't find anywhere outside the black community for a black woman to eat or go to the john when she was shopping. Our Local 688 led that whole goddamn fight. We picketed the theaters. We broke 'em down. We went down and sat in restaurants while we were in drug stores. We raised hell. We busted the city wide open.'

"Civil rights was not the only social and political front into which Gibbons threw his union's muscle. A system of 'community stewards' was established to put Teamsters power to work in the neighborhoods. In each ward with more than twenty-five Local 688 members, a community steward organized meetings where members expressed themselves about garbage collection, street lights and other local services, and pressured officials to take action. As Gibbons explained it, 'If, let's say, we needed a playground in that neighborhood, we'd have the steward get all our members in that neighborhood together and start raising hell. We'd call a meeting, and you know when you're talking about a playground it isn't just for Teamsters members. So our guys would get every goddamn neighbor to go to the meeting, too. In the 24th Ward, which was our best ward, we'd have 1,500 or 2,000 people, when the ward committee man might get 150 to *his* meetings. He'd die. And you know he'd listen to us.'

"The union tackled citywide issues as aggressively as it did neighborhood service problems: 'The streetcar companies were raising their fares and cutting back on service. Well, we have an initiative deal in Missouri where you can get up petitions and put something on the ballot. I mobilized the membership to sign petitions, and we got enough to put it on the ballot. The result is we socialized the goddamn transit system. . . . We now have a bistate agency that runs all the busses. . . . When a private company fucked up the sewerage system in the county, we went out and got all the signatures necessary and got a metropolitan sewer district—established strictly on the basis of 688's activities. . . .' "

This picture of Local 688 in the early years of Gibbons's ascendancy provides a glimpse of what a union might be which insisted on facing community as well as workplace issues, which explicitly organized the class as opposed to this or that segment of workers, and which, in so doing, began to transcend the apparent limitations of unionism and to function as a political party.

Something like this is envisioned by the Marxist organizers within the Teamsters who speak of returning the union to class struggle militancy. The objective tendency relied on to bring that change about is "the employers' offensive." Now, it makes good sense to follow Marx in supposing that as industries (truckdriving included) become more capital-intensive, and as the world economy gradually tilts toward publicly owned, centrally planned economies, employers in the United States will demand more surplus value, more productivity. What is much less clear is that this tendency is likely to radicalize the union as an institution. Surely, we will increasingly see unions roused to battle to defend gains of the past which they had supposed secure. But this is militancy, not radicalism. To suppose that "the employers' offensive" in itself will make unions something other than the cumbersome, parochial, bureaucratized entities they so obviously are, is like the vision that fascism would bring about socialism.

I should like to speak from my own experience about a somewhat different scenario whereby the struggle for democracy in unions might transform itself into a struggle for democracy in the society at large.

Whatever else it produces, the struggle for democracy, decency, and elementary rights in unions is likely to yield:

1. A network of friends, that is, persons who will respond more readily and effectively to the next crisis than if their common struggle within the union had not occurred.

2. Local bases of power, such as control of a number of local unions, which tend to legitimize a next effort because erstwhile rank and filers now speak from the president's chair and on official stationery.

Even these modest achievements may come at a great price. The more oppressive the union, the greater the temptation to forget that the employer is the main oppressor. American labor law offers the extraordinary worker far more tools and freedoms with which to combat his or her union, than to engage the company. Union politics can become a sandlot wherein workers vent frustrated energy against one another. Too, even local union office makes one part of the system. The reformer who becomes local union president is expected to deliver for the rank and file to a degree which the power of both the company and the international union over the local make impossible. These contradictions place strain on the very comradeship which it is the principal purpose of all this blood and tears to bring into being. Let two close friends in a rank-and-file movement decide by lot which of them will run for the local union presidency and which will remain on the shop floor; they can count themselves lucky if a year hence the latter, whoever it turns out to be, is not denouncing the former as a sellout.

But suppose, nonetheless, that the principal product of the struggle within the union is a group, with some small victories to its credit, some local union offices to legitimize its existence, and the beginnings of a point of view. What next?

For what it is worth, in my own experience the only objective situations in which I have seen working-class Americans naturally and organically begin to consider essentially Socialist ideas is when an industry decides to leave town. No doubt it is a localized version of the Depression of the 1930s. The authority to rule of local businessmen and politicians comes into question. Questions are asked: Who gave the X company the right, suddenly and unilaterally, to decide to leave? Why don't we buy the damn place? Slogans emerge (I am quoting the signs at the picket line December 29 against closing the Brier Hill mill in Youngstown): "People not profit." "Save Our Valley."

The existing union structures cannot handle a crisis of this kind. Bargaining about investment decisions is beyond their experience, and seems faintly un-American. For the big international union even the loss of 5,000 members is a relatively minor setback, readily made up by recruiting another 5,000 elsewhere. The official union, in a situation of this kind, attends to orderly funeral arrangements: who will get what kinds of benefits when.

Therefore "the group," ensconced in the local union offices which it took over in its union reform phase, begins to function as the actual union leadership of the area. The benefit approach is rejected. "First we try to save our jobs. Then, if we fail, it'll be time to talk about benefits." Community activists recognize in this newfound rank-and-file muscle the only practical hope of getting the corporation to change its mind. Thus the union reformers assume de facto direction of a broader coalition including church groups, some of the political leadership, and other local unions and local rank-and-file groups. Meantime internal union politics loses some of its glamor, for the question is whether there will be any union at all next year. And the most pragmatic member will be found agitating, not for a change in the department's incentive pay rate, but to "Keep Our Mill Open."

I am suggesting that rank-and-file rebellion moves on to radicalism when, by one route or another, it comes up against the control of investment decisions. Every industry presents this issue in some form. Thus truckdriving, phenomenologically so different from making steel, has its own version of investment decisions. Weak companies force drivers to stay on the road longer, drive faster, and if they fail, are merged by means opaque to the ordinary employee. Indeed, the perspective of "the employers' offensive" has in mind just such practices as seeking ever greater productivity.

There is thus no deep divide between the perspective of the Marxists working within the Teamsters, and the outlook I have been trying to suggest. Yet there is a difference. I believe groups like Miners For Democracy or Teamsters for a Democratic Union drift into an expectation that their ultimate objective is to take over and clean up the international union. I believe this perspective to be in error. For this great expectation, union reformers are repaid in broken hopes and inactive co-workers. It would be better, I think, to project much more modest goals. Yes, there can be a "combined development" whereby the impetus of bourgeois revolution carries over into further struggle, but this comes, perhaps, more by the creation of networks of trust and local bases than by illusory takeovers of national institutions. Yes, union struggle can produce its centers of "dual power," but likely these will be local.

The organizing model I am proposing to Teamster rebels and others is a middle way between the labor strategy of the Old Left and the labor strategy of the New. The Old Left sought to take leadership in national unions. To Old Leftists, like those in District 31 of the Steelworkers union, once you take power in a local the next thing to think about is how to do the same thing in the region, and no sooner is regional office won than the national campaign begins. The New Left, on the other hand, has often disdained even the office of steward, let alone a position on the local union executive board. In a nutshell, I suggest that it is right to run for the offices of steward and local union president, despite the very real compromises involved, and wrong to seek higher position or to control the union on a broader scale. Radicals in local office, according to the view urged here, should think horizontally: they should reach out to their counterparts in other locals of the same international union, and other locals and rank-and-file groups in different unions in the community. Their aspiration, in substance, should be a "parallel central labor union," or, in rare situations, control of the official central labor body to which all unions in a locality send delegates. Such institutions should be seen as places where rebels in various work settings can meet one another, and educate each other into a consciousness which, because sensitive to the circumstances of all involved, is perforce a class consciousness. Local labor parties or some functional equivalent would be a natural next step.

The foregoing perspective appears to be workable. Since it is not superhumanly demanding in the manner of national campaigns, it permits participants to remain human beings and therefore, to stay involved. I should think any one could make real progress in this direction in any community over a period of, say, five years. Perhaps this middle way offers an opportunity, as the song suggests, to take it easy but take it.

320

CHAPTER SEVENTEEN

Holding the Line: Miners' Militancy and the Strike of 1978

by James Green

The significance of the recent miners' strike—one of the longest in recent history—seemed to fade when the United Mine Workers accepted an unpopular contract on March 24, 1978, and returned to work, complaining bitterly about how little they had won as a result of their long strike. How important was the miners' strike of 1977–1978? Should it be viewed as a total defeat for the miners? Or was it a strike in which the rank and file minimized its losses through a long and militant industrial action? What does the strike mean for the tarnished "reform" administration of Arnold Miller, for the rank-and-file movements within the UMW? Finally, what are the implications of the strike for the Left?

Some of the most important questions raised by the strike have to do with the particular militancy and tenacity coal miners display in strike situations. What are the sources of combativity among this group of workers? Are coal miners a uniquely rebellious group within the working class because of their work situation and their "cultural isolation"? Or does the miners' militancy—which has been expressed in a remarkable wave of wildcat strikes leading up to this national walkout—come from sources common to other groups of workers? It is too soon to answer these questions with certainty, but they can be approached by examining the recent history of miners' militancy and by exploring its deeper roots in the past.

Reprinted from Vol. 12, No. 3 (May-June 1978).

The 1977–1978 coal miners strike must be viewed in the context of an overall offensive by the capitalist class. The first target was the social wage (education, health and welfare benefits, etc.) paid to non-unionized workers, consumers, and welfare recipients, especially in the cities. During the urban fiscal crises unionized public-sector workers also suffered serious setbacks. But now the capitalists have shifted to the more difficult terrain of a strongly unionized basic industry. According to a lead article in *The New York Times*, following the March 24 contract ratification: "For thirty years bargaining has focused on union demands: seniority rights, pay, pensions, layoff protection, time off, and medical care. But in recent months the spark points in contract talks have been management demands for givebacks or 'takeaways'—the cancellation of some of labor's old gains."[1] Finding it difficult to wring more productivity out of workers (this is especially true in coal), capital is attacking the wage increases demanded by workers to keep up with inflation. But more important, employers are attacking the social wage workers have won, particularly in the form of health and pension benefits. These two issues were main points of attack in the recent contract strike between the UMW and the Bituminous Coal Operators Association (BCOA).

The coal companies have made enormous profits in the 1970s. Between 1970 and 1974, profits doubled. Nonetheless they still forced concessions from the miners in the 1974 contract—which caused widespread rank-and-file dissatisfaction with the Miller administration. With coal stockpiles high and the demand for steel down in 1977, the corporations who control the mines (mainly larger steel and oil companies) decided to take back even more from the miners in this contract. Plagued with wildcat strikes that limited productivity under the last contract, the BCOA wanted to bring the miners under control this year. If they could enforce "labor stability" by disciplining wildcat strikers and instituting incentive schemes, the coal operators could take even greater advantage of the increasing demand for coal that will develop under Carter's energy policy. As Tom Bethel wrote in *Coal Patrol*: "With the UMW leadership in obvious disarray, the coal operators went to the bargaining table last October armed with a long shopping list of humiliating demands. In the wake of three years of chaotic labor relations, they wanted nothing less than total control of the UMW work force."[2] To get it they were willing to take a long strike, confident that the miners would be on their knees by the end of January.

THE 1978 CONTRACT

The BCOA did not confine its attack to limiting hourly wage increases or to eliminating the right to strike. They also wanted to take away some of the gains the UMW had achieved through its Health and Retirement Funds. Won in the great strike after World War II, these funds provide health care and pension benefits to over 820,000 active and retired miners and their families. Although the funds are jointly administered by industry and union, the UMW has traditionally controlled them. Conceived and implemented by some of America's most radical medical people, the miners' health fund developed a consumer-controlled system of free clinics designed to deliver preventive medical care.[3] Although the funds were in constant jeopardy because they were tied to the tonnage of coal produced, they nonetheless represented the most advanced form of "socialized" medicine available to working people in the U.S.

The initial BCOA demands amounted to nothing less than a dismantling of the UMW Health and Retirement Funds. Free health benefits were abolished, and miners would be forced to pay deductibles ranging up to $700 per year. From a pooled health fund administered largely by the UMW, the benefits would revert to a company-by-company system, which would provide coverage through private insurance companies. This would allow individual coal companies to use health benefits as a weapon against troublesome workers. The new system also meant death to the miners' free clinics and their concept of preventive medicine. So just at the time when public support was beginning to crystalize for some kind of socialized medicine, the capitalists have moved to destroy the most progressive health care plan serving working people.

After the rank-and-file miners rejected a contract offer with these provisions on March 5 (largely around the health benefits issue), the public began to see that this was no ordinary strike, that the miners were holding the line for the whole working class in struggle to save the collective gains they had achieved in the social sector.

The pension issue was tied closely to the health benefits issue. Initially the BCOA retained the distinction between the pensioners who retired before 1976 and those who retired after that date and receive much higher benefits. But neither group, including victims of black lung, would have had increases sufficient to keep up with the cost of living. Many working miners have fathers and uncles, as well as widowed mothers and aunts on pensions, and they were outraged by the BCOA offer to increase monthly pension benefits to only $275 per month and to add the burden of paying some health care costs under the deductible system. The operators added insult to injury by agreeing to guarantee some health benefits to pensioners only if the UMW agreed to fine wildcat strikers $20 a day, with the fines going to the retired miners' health fund. Another kind of social wage—the UMW pension fund—was under attack.

Finally, in its notorious "labor stability" clause, the BCOA demanded a contract provision to punish wildcat strikers and ensure industrial discipline generally. The first proposed contract gave the operators the right to fire any miner who "picketed, threatened, coerced or fomented or otherwise" became involved "in the cause of an unauthorized work stoppage." This is dangerously broad language—very similar to the kind used in court injunctions. Furthermore, the employers demanded the right to fire "some but not all" of the miners engaged in an unofficial strike, giving management new powers to victimize certain militants.[4]

While the BCOA demanded broad rights to discipline wildcat strikers, it also bargained for an incentive scheme to increase production—a form of scientific management miners have always opposed, fearing that this would be an "incentive" to disregard safety procedures, endangering all miners.

Finally, the operators took aim specifically at the wildcat strikes waged over health and safety issues at the point of production by demanding that members of the mine safety committees be subject to discipline "for closing down an area of a mine or attempting such a closing." This demand made it blatantly obvious that the BCOA drive for "labor stability" and increased productivity would come at the expense of safety.

Shaken by the cuts in the Health and Retirement Funds and the fear that more wildcats would bust the funds completely, Arnold Miller prepared to make major concessions to the BCOA. Labor stability was also necessary for the solvency of the union benefits program. With coal stockpiles high and the BCOA obviously taking a hard line in negotiations, Miller apparently believed the rank and file would settle for wage increases after a short strike. However, rank-and-file opposition quickly surfaced against the plan to use fines against wildcat strikers to compensate for lost revenues to the health and pension funds. When Miller heard from local and district officials that this provision would lead to certain rejection of the contract, he dropped the "payback" scheme. On March 5, he presented—and the Bargaining Council approved for rank-and-file ratification—a contract that differed little from the one already rejected. After more than three months on strike and with the threat of a Taft-Hartley injunction facing them, the miners were expected to bite the bullet and accept the contract. Though many pundits predicted a close vote, the UMW membership rejected the offer by a resounding 2 to 1 margin.

Up to this point, the operators had imposed their will on the miners, making dictatorial demands which they backed up with big stockpiles and the assumption that the weakly led, highly divided UMW could not take a long strike. They accurately assessed the weakness of the leadership but they underestimated the strength and determination of the rank and file. Though militants did close down some non-union mines and disrupt the flow of scab coal, they found it difficult to spread the strike. They were aided, however, by an unusually severe winter which depleted stockpiles quickly and literally froze the movement of non-union coal along many waterways. The BCOA did not understand that the miners' solidarity and tenacity had actually increased as a result of the long strike, that their cumulative sacrifices made them more determined than ever to hold out. The Federal Government also ignored the miners' grim determination to "take no backward step" and to refuse to work without a contract. Presidents had invoked the hated Taft-Hartley Act before only to have the miners defy it, but the defiance of the anti-strike law in March was particularly widespread. The strike had now become a rank-and-file struggle, and it was still holding solid. It was also beginning to receive much more support from other unions around the country, even though most of the big contributions, like the UAW's $2 million grant, went directly into the International's coffers.

After the contract rejection on March 5, intense rank-and-file opposition emerged to the new BCOA contract. The offer made some concessions to the workers, but it retained the clauses dismantling the health care system and preserving the inadequate pension system. While traveling in West Virginia during this period, we observed the anxiety of the UMW officials assigned to sell this new contract with its takeaway provisions, the activity of the Left, especially the Miners Right to Strike Committee (MRTSC) and the Miners Support Committee in opposing the contract, and the hostility of rank-and-file miners who felt cheated and betrayed. At a March 18 rally sponsored by the two Committees in Beckley, West Virginia, we heard Mike Branch of the MRTSC cheered by a crowd of about 200, including many miners, when he said "I'm tired of being pushed around, shoved around and sold out." Commenting on the shifting tide of the strike, an eloquent young miner named Doug Riston likened the struggle to the Ali-Spinks heavyweight title fight. The operators won the early rounds of the strike, but the miners came back in the late rounds and landed some serious blows on the owners. On March 24, the bell would ring for the final round. If the UMW lacked the stamina to carry on the fight the BCOA would win the decision, by a technical knockout. And that's what happened.

Discouraged by a sell-out leadership and strained by over 100 days without pay, the miners gave in and voted to accept the contract by a margin of 56 percent with much closer margins in West Virginia, the center of a strong movement to recall Arnold Miller from the presidency.

A New York Times columnist remarked on the contempt expressed for the UMW president in the coal country, which "is all the more poignant because he has, quite literally, set his people free."[5] It is wrong to suggest that Miller did this single-handedly, but he did lead the Miners for Democracy movement which restored the rank-and-file right to vote on the contract and to elect district officials, two reforms that were sources of Miller's difficulties in getting this contract ratified. Although Miller's weak leadership and increasing paranoia (which led him to dismiss most of his reform-oriented staff for "insubordination") are clearly related to the intensity of the rank-and-file agitation in recent years, the press is propagandizing for union oligarchy when it blames Miller for the so-called "anarchy" in the UMW.[6]

In selling this contract to the membership, Miller has sold his union down the river and assured an even more determined opposition movement to his leadership. What then is the balance sheet for this strike? Was the contract accepted on March 24 an unmitigated defeat for the miners?

The answer is no, because the resounding rejection of the earlier contract on March 5, and the miners' clear determination to carry the strike on longer, forced some concessions from the BCOA. The result was certainly not a victory for the miners, but through their militancy and tenacity the union's rank and file minimized defeat in a strike which started out with the deck totally stacked against them. Furthermore, the rank-and-file miners again demonstrated their ability to conduct a national strike from the bottom up—in opposition to top leaders and the government.

In the contract ratified on March 24 the BCOA granted an increase in wages of roughly 25 cents an hour more per worker. This will amount to a 37 percent increase in labor costs during the life of the contract, during which time profits are expected to increase at many times that rate. Naturally, the operators were willing to give most on the wage front; they admitted this even before the strike started. The idea was to take away the social wage in the benefit area, to make everything dependent upon hourly wages, especially medical care. The BCOA made some concessions on pensions (the pension increase, such as it is, went into effect in 1978), but the inadequate monthly pension of $275 remains as does the great inequity in pensions between miners who retired before and after January 11, 1976. Health coverage for miners' widows, which would have been available for only *one month* after death in the rejected contract, will be extended to five years after death in the new contract. This is an important gain, but it is small consolation to the miners and their families for the dismantling of the health fund (and the free clinics) and the establishment of private health insurance plans with deductibles. The latter is clearly the biggest corporate "takeaway" in the contract.

The most important result of the March 5 contract rejection came when the BCOA dropped its threatening "labor stability" clause. The "right to strike" forces succeeded in removing the contract provision disciplining wildcat strikers. However, the operators still have the power to do this under an arbitration ruling handed down on October 10, 1977, by the Arbitration Review Board, a body created under the 1974 contract to act as an appeals board in grievance cases. "ARB 108" became a subject of great controversy in the coal fields after the March 5 contract rejection and the withdrawal of the "labor stability" clause. This memorandum, in which the Board upheld a coal company's right to fire miners for setting up an unauthorized picket, does contain some very frightening language:

> The case at hand involved picketing. In terms of what is understood in other industries, it is seen as a willful and defiant act on the very fabric woven by both parties for their mutual benefit, and it is thus created as a capital offense.

326

The BCOA is now forced to rely on this ARB memorandum 108 (which was, amazingly enough, signed by the UMW member of the Board), instead of a contractual provision. So the miners gained an important point. Still, the very existence of ARB 108 is threatening, as is the union leadership's apparent willingness to sacrifice the right to strike and the right to free speech in order to gain labor stability.

In short, the BCOA, though it was forced to drop its labor stability clause, got most of what it wanted in this contract. This included the dismantling of the Health Funds, the right to remove members of the mine safety committees for leading wildcats, and a somewhat different form of the incentive pay system. However, the incentive scheme's likelihood of success is limited by the fact that a majority of miners in each local have to vote to accept the plan. Given the coal diggers' widespread fear that incentive schemes will cause more violations of safety standards, it is doubtful that the BCOA can use this scheme to gain the productivity it wants. It is also unlikely that the employers' power to fire mine safety committeemen will stop wildcats over unsafe conditions. It is one thing to put something into a contract; it is quite another to enforce it, especially in the coal industry. Both the incentive scheme and the attack on the mine safety committees' autonomy conflict with the coal workers' growing concern over safety and with their traditional ability to defend their "work rules" at the point of production, a tradition discussed in more detail later.

THE RECENT SOURCES OF COAL MINERS' MILITANCY

The militancy and solidarity displayed by the rank and file in this long strike comes primarily from the life-and-death nature of the issues and, secondarily, from the union bureaucracy's apparent willingness to accept big "takeaways" by the companies.

In order to fully understand the rank-and-file militancy in the recent strike, we have to go back to 1969. In January of that year regular miners formed the Black Lung Association in West Virginia to push for a state law compensating victims of the disease which struck most veteran miners. In February and March of the same year rank-and-file miners in West Virginia conducted one of the most important "political" strikes in modern labor history to protest the need for a black lung law. The awakening within the ranks prompted Joseph "Jock" Yablonski, a Pennsylvania miner, to run against John L. Lewis's corrupt successor, W. A. "Tony" Boyle. Yablonski ran a strong race against Boyle, charging that Boyle was "in bed with the coal operators." But the insurgent campaign lost out to the bureaucracy amid charges that the Boyle machine had stolen votes in the December elections. On New Year's Eve 1969 "Jock" Yablonski, his wife, and his daughter were murdered by gunmen directed by Tony Boyle. At the Yablonski funeral the Miners for Democracy (MFD) was formed to carry out the fight against Boyle's obnoxious regime.

The MFD was not at the outset an organization of rank-and-file miners; it was led primarily by attorneys, notably Jock's sons, who launched a legal attack on the Boyle machine, and by a group of reformers in Charlestown, West Virginia, around the *Miner's Voice*, edited by Don Stillman. However, later in 1970 another political wildcat strike in southern West Virginia brought forth another rank-and-file organization, the Disabled Miners and Widows of Southern West Virginia. At the end of the year an MFD slate in Pennsylvania District 5, led by Lou Antal, defeated the Boyle machine. Then a strike at the end of the BCOA-UMWA contract in 1971 led to a confrontation between the rank and file and the leadership for more strike benefits and a stronger set of contract demands; this scenario would be repeated again over the next two contracts.[7]

Meanwhile the MFD legal strategy, which involved considerable fund raising among Eastern liberal donors, began to pay off. A number of court cases were brought forth attempting, among other things, to throw out the results of the 1969 election and to prosecute the Boyle leadership for corruption in using funds. In May of 1972 the courts not only brought down two major decisions awarding district autonomy, but on May Day 1972 Judge Bryant overturned the 1969 election. Later in May, the MFD convention in Wheeling, West Virginia, united the MFD, the Black Lung Association (headed by a retired Cabin Creek miner named Arnold Miller), and the Disabled Miners and Widows Association.

The campaign leading up to the December 1972 election was hard-fought and extremely dangerous, but despite intense Red-baiting and threats by the Boyle machine (who used their control over pensions to gain votes from retired miners) the MFD slate headed by Arnold Miller won an inspiring victory with 56 percent of the vote. Shortly after his election, which Miller claimed as a victory for the rank and file, the MFD was disbanded. More importantly, the Black Lung Association lost some of its independence and was brought under the control of the union leadership. This seemed reasonable at the time since the same man was president of the union and the Black Lung Association. As a result, the rank-and-file militancy in the coal fields dissipated for several years, until the Miller administration negotiated the 1974 contract. Rank-and-file miners in West Virginia actually struck to obtain copies of the contract which they believed to contain "sell-out" provisions. The coal companies were making unprecedented profits and the miners wanted to dig in for a strong fight; they felt betrayed by Miller, as we saw in the last part of Barbara Kopple's film, *Harlan County, U.S.A.* In the winter of 1975 thousands of miners wildcatted against the contract the Miller administration had negotiated. A massive rank-and-file opposition movement against the UMW leadership had surfaced.

In the summer of 1976 came the most important explosion of militancy within the ranks. Protesting the use of federal court injunctions, arrests, and fines against wildcat strikers from the Cedar Coal Company in Kanwaha County, West Virginia, 150,000 miners went out on strike—almost every union member east of the Mississippi. This remarkable nationwide political strike, which elicited cries of "industrial anarchy" from the BCOA, forced the federal judges in Charleston (who did not like to be totally defied) to withdraw their fines and injunctions. It was a great victory for the rank and file.[8]

Arnold Miller, of course, came out against the strike, and blamed its prolongation on a "handful of radicals," presumably the members of the Revolutionary Communist Party who led the Miners Right to Strike Committee. But when Miller came to West Virginia to speak against the strike, he was jeered in Charleston and forced to withdraw from his speaking date at UMW Local 1759 where this amazing walkout began. In fact, when on August 10, 1976, Miller told a tumultuous meeting at a Charleston hotel that he could not allow the miners to defy the courts and that they would face certain defeat, he played into the hands of the militants. The strikers not only defied the courts, they forced the federal judges to lift the injunctions and withdraw the fines.[9] According to a Morgantown newspaper the big 1976 wildcat strike ended "only after Miller pledged to seek right to strike provisions" in the 1977–1978 contract negotiations.[10]

THE MINERS RIGHT TO STRIKE COMMITTEE
AND THE ROLE OF THE LEFT

As the right to strike sentiment grew stronger in the coal fields the left has played a greater role in politicizing the issue. The main left formation has been the Miners Right to Strike Committee (MRTSC). In the recent strike however, other leftists have been active in miners' support work, especially in the two West Virginia strike support committees at Beckley and Morgantown.

The Miners Right to Strike Committee emerged from a wildcat in West Virginia during the winter of 1974 when Governor Arch Moore imposed a gas limit during the fuel crisis, a limit that prevented miners from getting back and forth between home and work. During this strike a young miner from the Beckley area named Mike Branch joined with some disgruntled local officials in southern West Virginia (a hotbed of wildcat strike activity since 1969) and formed the MRTSC. Branch, along with several other young miners who moved into the coal fields from other areas, belonged to the Revolutionary Union (RU), which became the Revolutionary Communist Party (RCP) in October of 1975. Though RU and later RCP members formed the leadership of the Right to Strike Committee, they had support from other militants in the West Virginia coal fields. In November of 1975 members of the Committee joined the march to support the Brookside strikers in Harlan County, where they circulated "right to strike" petitions while organizing some support in eastern Kentucky. (This march is documented, along with an interview with Right to Strike activists toward the end of the film *Harlan County, U.S.A.*)

By this time the MRTSC had already begun to draw fire from the International. In the summer of 1975, when Miller was faced with yet another massive West Virginia wildcat (this one to protest injunctions forcing Logan County miners back to work), the UMW president attacked the Right to Strike Committee after a newspaper story "exposed" RCP leadership of the Committee. Although the Committee did apparently suffer from Red-baiting in Kentucky, it remained active in West Virginia. RCP members admitted that they were Communists and insisted that there were non-Communist members in the Committee as well, hoping to undercut the conspiracy theories put forth by the press and the bureaucracy. The MRTSC reportedly made some enemies in the rank and file by insisting that the 1975 wildcat continue until the right to strike was granted, but according to one Committee member, the group maintained enough importance in West Virginia to play an important role in a March 1976 wildcat strike protesting White House delay in signing an amended black lung law. By the summer of 1976, when the massive national wildcat strike occurred against the Cedar Creek injunctions, Miller was even less effective in Red-baiting the Committee and blaming the strike on a "handful of radicals." The point is that by this time the MRTSC had been articulating for four years a demand for the right to strike that masses of rank-and-file miners had already *asserted* in many places, and particularly in West Virginia where the Committee was active.

During the recent strike the MRTSC aimed its attack squarely on the labor stability clause in the first two contract offers. When that clause was dropped, it zeroed in on the effects of the ARB 108 decision. The two Miners' Support Committees, which contain some representation from the MRTSC, placed some very effective advertisements in the West Virginia newspapers emphasizing the "takeaways" by comparing the proposed contract provisions with the "rank-and-file demands" expressed by delegates at the 1976 UMW district and national conventions. The activities of the two West Virginia support committees, which include the establishment of a remarkable "free clinic" in Beckley, deserve a separate discussion because the organizational activities in question could serve as models for future left strike support work. The relationship of the MRTSC to the Support Committees was problematic throughout the strike, because the red-baiting of the former spread to the latter.

The Revolutionary Communist Party members in the MRTSC have been the object of most of this Red-baiting. Their trade-union work in West Virginia has been unusually successful because of the key issue they have chosen to develop—the right to strike—and because they have learned from their mistakes (e.g., they are trying to correct an earlier impression they created that the main problem was Arnold Miller and the other "hacks" in the bureaucracy.) The RCP people in the Committee have tried to raise broader demands, but they have resolutely stuck to trade-union issues, refusing to dilute their appeal for the right to strike by calls for party-building. In many ways RCP politics in West Virginia resemble the early syndicalist phase of the CPUSA during the 1920s when the Party attempted to build a rank-and-file movement within the AFL through the Trade Union Educational League.

An RCP article entitled *Miners Struggle at the Crossroads* (based on an article in the December 1977 issue of *Revolution*) argues that the rank-and-file movement of miners has grown up "spontaneously" and states the classic Leninist criticism of the limitations therein. It then calls, not for building a party, but for "rank-and-file organization." The RCP's analysis of the massive wildcats is that they are not "clean-cut" affairs, the implication being that they need to be organized. In any case, they are certainly not "spontaneous" actions. The pamphlet merely mentions the fact that these strikes move from mine to mine with the "stronger locals" becoming "storm centers" that draw "neighboring mines into the struggle." This leaves the development of wildcat strikes at a very abstract level, and suggests a vacuum of local leadership that Communists must fill. Until we know more about the history of militant locals in states like West Virginia—the locals that have initiated wildcats, spread them to other states in 1976, and acted as vanguards in the recent strike—our knowledge of the rank-and-file movement will remain somewhat abstract. We know that strikers in the mine fields take advantage of the traditional antipathy to crossing picket lines, that they can use "stranger" picketing more effectively than other workers, and that the use of CB radios and phone chains has been effective in spreading wildcats, but there is much more to know before any "lessons" can be drawn for rank-and-file movements in other industries. The RCP's Leninist analysis of the miners' movement exaggerates its spontaneous origins and dwells on the politicization of that movement in the period since the MRTSC has been involved. It is important to note that the movement *began* with a remarkable *political* strike for a black lung law in West Virginia almost ten years ago. However, the RCP does not grossly exaggerate its role or even the role of the Right to Strike Committee (which probably includes about 30 to 40 members with a few hundred supporters mainly in West Virginia). The influence of the Committee is, in fact, directly dependent upon the massive, nationwide concern among miners to retain the right to strike.

MINERS AND THE WILDCAT STRIKE

The Miners Right to Strike Committee's attempt to politicize wildcat strikes and to use them as a flashpoint for organizing a rank-and-file movement is based on the rising level of unauthorized strike activity since the ratification of the 1974 contract. Of course, the pattern of unofficial strike activity goes back much further in the history of the industry. Ever since the UMW started engaging in nationwide collective bargaining, its officers have pledged to discipline wildcat strikers, but local strikes still occurred frequently over issues not covered in the contract. Before 1943, many of these strikes went unrecorded, but in that year, when the miners defied the Federal Government in four national strikes (each time violating the wartime "no strike" pledge), the number of newly recorded unauthorized work stoppages increased to 400, including many over local grievances. In 1944 there were 792 stoppages mostly of a local nature, and for the next decade between 400 and 600 such stoppages occurred each year. During this time there were also seven "official" industrywide strikes, including the 59-day walkout in 1946 that established the Health and Pension Funds, and the 1949 strike in defiance of the Taft-Hartley injunction.[11]

Between 1952 and 1964, when hundreds of thousands of miners lost their jobs as a result of mechanization and competition from other fuels, Lewis—who accepted the need for mechanization—authorized only two national work stoppages. Unauthorized work stoppages averaged less than 200 per year during this period, though the coal miners still struck at three times the national average despite heavy layoffs in the industry. This differential grew even wider in the 1960s as the number of work stoppages in soft coal shot up from 160 in 1966 to 266 in 1968 and then to 457 in 1969, the same year that West Virginia coal miners launched their famous "political" strike to force the state legislature to pass a black lung law.[12] With the rank-and-file agitation around black lung, the assassination of reform candidate Jock Yablonski and the organization of the Miners for Democracy, work stoppages increased even more dramatically. Five hundred work stoppages took place in 1970, when the mines were shut down following the Yablonski murders in January and through the efforts of the independent Disabled Miners and Widows organization protesting inadequate compensation from the UMW's welfare and retirement fund. "Both of these strikes might be classified as political strikes," according to a report of the Labor Studies Institute of the University of West Virginia, "although they were directed more at the internal affairs of the union than toward broader political goals."[13] Of course these strikes *against the union* were of great importance, as was the 1969 black lung strike, because they signaled the politicization of the rank-and-file miners struggle.

An unusually high number of the mine work stoppages since World War II have been local wildcat strikes. Between 1966 and 1970 most strikes in U.S. industry took place during renegotiation of the contract with a third or less occurring during the term of the agreement, but Appalachian miners struck 93 percent of the time during the term of the contract. In addition to the health and benefit strike protests, miners struck increasingly over safety issues, alarmed no doubt by the 1968 explosion at the CONSOL mine in Farmington, West Virginia that killed 78 miners.[14]

In addition to the growing concern over safety in the mines (which still have the highest fatality rates in U.S. industry), a number of other issues have contributed to the rising level of wildcat strikes.

A new generation of workers has entered the mines. The average age of the mine worker has decreased from 49 in 1968 to around 31 today. In fact, there is a gap between the generations with many middle-aged miners in one group and many miners in their early twenties in another. There is no hard evidence to support this but it does seem that the younger miners who have entered the pits in the 1970s (instead of leaving for the city as their older brothers did in the 1950s and 1960s) are more heavily involved in wildcat strike activity, especially in the larger mines where young miners compose most of the midnight to 8 A.M. "hoot owl shift." Along with this very young group are miners in their early thirties who are Viet Nam vets (West Virginia had the highest per capita fatality rate during the Indo-China war). Like the well-publicized long-haired workers who revolted against GM at Lordstown in 1972, these workers are willing and able to buck the authority of mine foremen and managers whose corporations are pushing for more and more productivity in time of high profitability. Coal company profits increased 100 percent between 1970 and 1974 while miners wages gained by only 7 percent. The operators' reckless drive for productivity and profitability has all but sabotaged grievance procedure.

After nearly 30 years of working through the same grievance procedure, the 1971 contract introduced some reforms. Serious problems result because miners (a) could not have representation at the first stage of the procedure, (b) only had three grievers on the mine committee, an inadequate number to ensure work-place representation in today's large-scale, multiple-shift mines, (c) were prohibited from discussing grievances on company time, and (d) experienced long delays in the grievance procedure, which forced miners to substitute the wildcat strike for the grievance procedure. There has been a tendency, according to the West Virginia University study of work stoppages, to "view the grievance procedure, not as a flexible tool through which bargaining over issues which arise on a day-to-day basis takes place, but as a formal, almost judicial procedure for settling conflicts. . . . It may well be that that emphasis on procedure rather than on problem solving is so entrenched in the labor relations of this industry that no changes are possible. If this is so, the grievance procedure will continue to fail as substitute for the wildcat strike."[15] Since 1971 that failure has been manifested in an increasing level of wildcat strike activity that cost the industry 2.5 million "man-days" of labor in 1977. A union official who defends members in grievance procedures at the arbitration level told us: "The companies are still using the grievance procedure the wrong way; they use it to delay issues. These corporation lawyers just don't look into the human factors in a grievance."

Work relations in the coal industry have never been good. This sector has been a nightmare to industrial relations experts since the turn of the century. Various craft traditions and work rules established a form of job control at the pit face which protected the miners' rights until the 1930s when mechanization radically altered work relations in the mines. Miners now work under factory-like supervision with a higher ratio of foremen to workers than in most manufacturing industries. Under these circumstances miners have preserved few of their traditional "freedoms"—like the right to stop working when a foreman entered the "room" and the right to establish their own quitting times—but some of the old work rules have been preserved in union contracts.[16] The three-man mine committee is now inadequate for handling grievances (for the reasons mentioned above), but it, along with the safety committees established more recently, retained more power at the workplace than most shop stewards in other industries who have stopped working full-time to become paid troubleshooters. The BCOA contract demand to make mine committeemen subject to discharge for "bad conduct" is the most recent, and most blatant corporation attempt to gain full control over miners at the point of production.

The entry of younger, less "disciplined" miners has not only exacerbated the troubles caused by the deterioration of work relations and the destruction of the grievance machinery; it has clearly contributed to a continued weakening of the work discipline that forced miners to work even when they were exhausted, injured, undernourished, and fearful for their safety. The abolition of the piece-rate system and the introduction of mechanized day work undercut the miners' traditional freedom to control the pace and length of the working day free from company supervision. But the system of measured day work—combined with the hourly wage increases the UMW has won from a booming coal industry—now gives the miners more choice about whether or not to work for a full week's time. Rising absenteeism and wildcat striking have hurt the U.S. coal industry productivity (though it is still five times higher in the U.S. than in other countries where the safer "long wall" mining method is used).[17] As a result the BCOA's initial contract demands in 1978 included severe measures designed to reduce work irregularity and increase productivity.[18]

MINERS' CULTURE

Here cultural traditions come into play. Relatively isolated in rural sections of Appalachia and other poor states, the coal miners have not been immersed as completely in the consumer culture as have other workers. They are still closer to their rural roots than the Appalachians who have migrated to Detroit, Cleveland, and Chicago. Living in the hollows is cheaper and simpler than it is in the cities and suburbs. This may be related to the difficulty the corporations have experienced in forcing miners to accept the "wage trick" (i.e., individualized wage increases instead of collectivized benefits). The isolation of miners' communities may also be connected with their seeming imperviousness to public opinion, press coverage, and government pressure during strike situations. While the isolation of the coal miners in one-industry towns may in fact be connected to their ability to hold out in long strikes, it is wrong to accept the academic sociological theory that cultural isolation in itself is the reason for the miners' "high propensity to strike." This theory conveniently assigns miners, along with lumber workers, sailors and other groups of isolated workers, to a marginal status, so that their class-conscious behavior appears as a "deviant" form of behavior.[19] Ben A. Franklin, who covered the strike for the *New York Times*, bought this theory. In an article headlined: "Coal Strikers: Mountain Men are Clannish, Combative," he emphasizes the miners' backwardness and the "Celtic ethnicity" of the Appalachian miners. "In the Anglo-Saxon—not to say Druid—heritage of the southern mountain coal towns, there is still xenophobic uneasiness about 'furriners' who work in other fields." Franklin deemphasizes the class consciousness in the miners' militancy by reducing that militancy to an expression of clannish, mountaineer hostility to outsiders.[20]

The theory of strike propensity based upon isolation, ethnicity, and backwardness is an inadequate explanation of miners' militancy today. First of all, the coal towns are not nearly as isolated now as they were even two decades ago. More to the point, many miners have worked in other parts of the country, notably Midwestern industrial cities, and have returned to the mines since production increased in the 1970s. They are not clannish backwoodsmen. Secondly, the emphasis on the miners' combative Celtic ethnicity is misplaced. As coal industry historian Keith Dix pointed out to us, the tradition of the local strike, and the combativity that went with it, came more from the ethnically mixed Pennsylvania and Illinois fields than from the Southern mountain mining areas. Furthermore, even in Appalachia many blacks and Eastern Europeans joined the Anglo-Saxon natives in the mines. Finally, these native-born white miners showed an unusual willingness to cooperate with black and foreign-born miners in order to fight the companies and to form industrial unions. Indeed, the isolated, clannish miners of rural Alabama and Appalachia showed much more willingness to work in common with Afro-Americans than did the white workers in modernized, cosmopolitan areas.[21]

This is not to say that the miners' culture is irrelevant to their strong traditions of resistance. There is a proud mountaineer culture which even outsiders absorb after a few generations: West Virginia and Kentucky have a particularly vital mountain musical tradition to which the many fighting miners' songs are deeply indebted. This is also a gun culture where hunting is a favorite pastime. Of course the fact that miners are able and, if necessary, willing to use firearms means that West Virginians and Kentuckians have been more likely to resort to armed struggle against gun thugs, police, and strikebreakers than other workers.

Political traditions are also important. West Virginia, for example, was unionized much later than some of the other coal fields. Because the UMW came so late to West Virginia, it presented itself to miners as an institutionalized collective-bargaining organization which would bring the benefits of a national contract to the hollows, but would allow for little self-organization or local autonomy. Since the International was so unresponsive to the serious local grievances of West Virginia miners, these workers held on to the right to strike during the term of a national contract. The bitterness of the conflict in this state, which actually involved large-scale armed struggle after World War I, made miners more outraged than most when UMW leaders, like President John P. White (1912–1917), took jobs with the coal companies. West Virginia UMW districts also opposed the growing dictatorship of John L. Lewis in the 1920s. In short, to explain the militancy of miners in West Virginia or elsewhere, we must look beyond "variables" like cultural isolation put forth by sociologists who hope that "modernization" will finally bring "labor stability" to the coal fields.

TRADITIONS OF SOLIDARITY

Unlike other craftsmen who used the job control they exercised to form exclusionary craft unions, the skilled miners allied with unskilled helpers and surface workers to form their industrial union in 1890. And from that point the United Mine Workers of America was one of the country's most militant unions when it came to organizing the unorganized. The rising level of miners' strike activity in the 1880s resulted from violations of accepted rules and practices, and payment systems during a period of vast productive expansion. Strikes were not motivated simply by economic wage demands nor were they regulated according to the business cycle, as most academics believed. Miners engaged in an increasing number of "control strikes"— issues of union recognition, work rules, and conditions. In order to defend their traditional freedoms against mechanization and rationalization, skilled miners allied with other workers, like helpers and drivers. In other words, by the time the UMWA was founded miners had already seen the necessity of solidarity among all grades of workers around "general and inclusive demands" as distinct from the narrow, exclusive craft union demands.[22]

As the mining industry was further consolidated under the aegis of the rail and steel corporations, miners saw the need for strike unity among workers who labored in different mines and in different regions. The formation of a national industrial coal miners union in 1890 was a necessity for workers pitted against the country's biggest corporations. For example, in 1902 all of the anthracite miners in the country walked out in one of the most important national strikes of the era, forcing President Theodore Roosevelt to threaten seizure of the mines if the corporations did not make some concessions to the union. The unusual nationwide unity displayed by miners from Alabama to Pennsylvania in this current strike testifies to the survival of industrial union traditions of solidarity.

Industrial unionism also opened the miners' organization to black and immigrant miners. And it helped to make UMW members receptive to the appeals of the Socialist Party in the 1910s. The Debsian Socialists, who successfully introduced a resolution at the 1911 UMW convention favoring the "collective ownership and democratic management of the means of production," believed that the miners' brand of industrial unionism was "socialism with its working clothes on."[23] John L. Lewis's iron-handed control over the union in the 1920s and his purging of Socialists did a lot to subvert this vision of industrial unionism; but the UMW's vision was restored in the 1930s, as Lewis did an about face, and helped make the Miners' Union the champion of the unorganized and the foundation of the new CIO unions. Since World War II and the drop in UMW membership from 600,000 in 1946 to about one-third that number today, the pioneer industrial union has lost much of its power and prestige.

Furthermore, with the emergence of collective bargaining for national contracts, locals and even district bodies lost their voice in deciding union policies. "Within a very narrow context," writes one historian, "the centralization of decision-making within the union can be justified—most industries are themselves concentrated and corporate labor policies are rarely determined by local plant management. It takes large centralized power on the part of unions to deal with large aggregatres of industrial capital. . . ."[24] Further, industrial unions have often been led by "strong men" who justified their power as a necessity in dealing more effectively with big business: they were the Hillmans, Dubinskys, Reuthers, and John L. Lewises. Indeed, there is no better example of how the contradiction between national collective bargaining and union democracy was played out than Lewis's nearly 40 years as UMW president. During the 1920s Lewis shrewdly and ruthlessly purged his enemies in the various districts, including socialists like Alex Howatt, and his main rival, John Brophy of Pennsylvania. During a reorganization drive in 1933, Lewis brought two-thirds of all UMWA district offices under control of the International: Lewis argued that administrative efficiency and collective bargaining power conflicted with district autonomy. In 1936, when discussing the direct election of district officials, Lewis stated: "It is a question of whether you desire your organization to be the most effective instrumentality within the realm of possibility . . . , or whether you prefer to sacrifice the efficiency of your organization . . . for a little more academic freedom in the selection of some local representatives in a number of districts."[25]

Many UMW members today believe that Lewis was right—that he had to assume nearly dictatorial powers in order to reorganize the union and help launch the CIO against some of the most brutal corporations in the country. Of course, Lewis's legacy to industrial unionism remains a contradictory one. Today President Arnold Miller attempts to maintain the contradictory position of pursuing the nationwide pattern of collective bargaining as well as continuing to push himself as the reformer who ousted Tony Boyle and helped the rank and file regain the right to ratify the contract, to enjoy district autonomy, and to elect their district officials. Of course Miller is a much weaker leader than John L. Lewis. Who isn't? In any case, Miller's troubles flow from the fact that he is trying to pursue the traditional pattern of nationwide collective bargaining while allowing for a level of union democracy and district autonomy Lewis would have found inconceivable.

So the miners' current militancy can hardly be tied directly to the legacy of Lewis, though the UMW "godfather" is still remembered for his "no backward step" policy and his defiance of federal government power. Therefore the legacy of the national industrial union—so thoroughly shaped by Lewis's 40-year reign—is also of dubious significance, even though traditions of industrial union solidarity remain alive.

In the hand-loading piecework era which lasted up to the 1930s the isolated, irregular work of the skilled miner allowed for an amazing degree of control at the point of production where "company men" were few and far between. When it signed its first national contract, the UMW was required to penalize members for lack of discipline and irregularity, but the union refused to enforce contractural rules and allowed the customary work rules to prevail. In 1921 the journal *Industrial Management* advised factory owners not to hire miners because of their lack of discipline. In the mines, "the possibility of constant supervision or of surprise tests do not exist. The coal miner is accordingly trained to do as he pleases. . . . Transplant such a man into a factory where production is speeded and no imagination is required to picture what will happen."

"There are many other things also in the daily life of miners that make for their solidarity," Goodrich wrote, referring to the amount of time miners had to socialize while not working or when traveling to and from work on the "man trip."[26] By the late 1920s mechanized production was extending into the union fields and undermining the sources of miners' job control by making mine work more factory-like and more subject to close supervision. However, scientific management has never been very successful in the mines. Mining is still such a varied, difficult task that it has been impossible for management to take all of the decision-making power away from miners on the job.

Though mechanized production has taken away some of the skilled miners' traditional freedoms, social solidarity has remained as part of the job. It still takes miners a long time to get to and from the pitface; work is still somewhat less regular than assembly-line production, and still somewhat difficult to supervise. And of course mining is still extremely dangerous. The hazardous nature of the work continues to unite workers on the same shift and in the same mine. In many smaller union locals, like the famous Brookside local in Harlan County, this unity is reflected in strike solidarity.

It would be romantic to suggest however that unity in coal strikes comes easily and naturally because of the collective danger miners face. Miners are also a very individualistic bunch whose unity has to be obtained through organization. In the nineteenth century coal mining was one of the trades in which workers were especially proud of their "manliness," often engaging in bloody fights against the operators' gunmen. "The craftsmen's ethical code demanded a 'manly' bearing toward the boss," writes one historian. "Few words enjoyed any more popularity in the nineteenth century than this honorific, with all its connotations of dignity, respectability, defiant egalitarianism, and patriarchal male supremacy." Displaying "manliness" in dealing with one's fellow workers was as important as it was in confronting the bosses. "Undermining or conniving" at another man's job was considered "hoggish behavior." For example in the early work rules of the UMW was imbedded the "principle of the square turn, or equal distribution of mine cars" expressing the traditional miners' feeling that each man "ought to get a fair share of the work that is going." Stealing another man's car or his coal, or endangering other brothers with dangerous work habits was not only considered "unmanly" behavior; it constituted grounds for expulsion from the union. In this sense the quality of "manliness" was associated not only with male supremacy but with the rights and freedoms a "freeborn" American workingman ought to defend.[27] Of course, the traits of bravado and macho were also involved, and indeed they still are, because many miners still feel the need to prove themselves as "men" before the bosses, their fellow workers, and their families.

Needless to say, these traits have negative effects, especially in personal lives. When these "manly" qualities are combined with the strong individualism of many miners, there can be disastrous results ranging from ignorance of safety rules to performance of lone acts of terrorism. Only a few women are now working in the mines, but maybe they will bring some changes, because mining is one of the jobs most clearly stereotyped as "man's work." The male culture of the miner helps explain a sense of solidarity and combativity at the workplace level and the local union level, but the wider support culture created by mining families and communities is far more important in this regard.

The role played by women in this strike and in mining strikes down through the years deserves special treatment in and of itself. Suffice it to say in this context that the unusual militancy of women in mining communities has made a critical difference in many struggles. The historical record shows these women playing far more than a supportive role; they have been a vanguard in violent confrontations with scabs, police, and gun thugs. This was certainly the case in the Brookside strike, as depicted in *Harlan County, U.S.A.* The music of Aunt Molly Jackson, Sarah Ogan Gunning, and Hazel Dickens expresses a cumulative sense of class hatred that has built up in union families for generations, but the music also shows that the women are fighting for themselves as well as their men and their children. No one expressed this sensibility more clearly than Florence Reece when she wrote "Which Side Are You On?" during the Harlan County mine wars of the 1930s.

Finally, the kind of community support the miners often achieve not only helps them hold out in long strikes but also increases their militancy. There was strong community solidarity within late nineteenth-century mining towns against the actions of the alien, absentee-owned corporations, often controlled by railroads. Farmers and merchants, as well as doctors, lawyers, preachers, and even law officers, took the side of the miners against the bosses, because they too were threatened by the company-controlled town in which independent proprietors would be restricted or eliminated.[28] The petty bourgeoisie in the mining camps was also closely connected to the mining families through commercial ties (the miners were their only clients or customers) and through kinship ties (many saloon keepers, etc. were retired miners). So these people often extended the miners credit, and even joined them in battle against the company's forces. This tradition seems to have held up as well. As the *New York Times* reported, the "miners' ability to weather a long strike is aided by merchants' support and credit." A grocer on Cabin Creek in West Virginia said the miners there "were good, honest people, but they've had to fight for everything they've got. They're our people and we have to help them anyway we can. Nobody's going hungry in this valley if I can help it."[29] During the great mining strikes of this century and the last the middle class in mining communities has frequently faced a polarized situation, a violent situation of class conflict in which they chose to stand with the miners when asked: "Which Side Are You On?"

CONCLUSION

To return then to the questions raised at the outset: it seems that the long strike of 1977–1978 was not an unmitigated defeat, but rather a bitter rank-and-file struggle in which the miners minimized the defeats the operators tried to inflict upon them.

What will the future bring? Many UMW members fear that the union itself is in danger not because of internal "anarchy" as the press would have it, but because the "takeaways" in this context will make it even more difficult to organize non-union mines. At the moment only about one-half the coal mined in the U.S. is union coal.

The miners' defiance of Taft-Hartley has again shown in their refusal to give up the right to strike in the face of government repression; this might serve as an important lesson to other workers. Furthermore, the strike prevented the BCOA from establishing a routine contractual process for firing wildcat strikers. However, under the protective umbrella of the ARB 108 decision, operators will be able to move against the "instigators" of unofficial work stoppages. The wildcat strike trend will probably ebb as the miners recover from their long strike. But the guerilla warfare at the point of production may actually increase as companies try to enforce industrial discipline to gain the productivity increase they were denied under the last contract.

Arnold Miller's leadership, badly shaken as a result of the last contract ratification, is now the subject of scorn and hostility in many of the coal fields.[30] If Miller himself is to retain any credibility, he will have to move radically in the next few years, perhaps in the direction of organizing the unorganized. In any case, whatever happens to the UMW leadership and whatever happens to company policy vis-a-vis wildcats, the rank-and-file coal miners are in an unusually strong position to make their own history. Though great losses were sustained in this strike, one does not get the sense that the miners returned to work defeated. Frustrated and angry, yes, but not defeated.

NOTES

The author thanks all of the people in West Virginia who took the time and effort to discuss the current strike and the political work connected with it, especially Rich Diehl, Keith Dix, Betty Justice, Bruce Miller, Fred Barkey, Howard Green, and the members of the Miners Support Committee in Beckley. Thanks also to Margery Davies and Priscilla Long for good advice, and to Frank Brodhead for his vital help with interviewing, researching, and editing.

1. *New York Times*, March 26, 1978, p. 1.

2. *Coal Patrol*, no. 35, Feb. 15, 1978, p. 1.

3. Curtis Seltzer, "Health Care by the Ton," *Health PAC Bulletin*, no. 79 (1977), pp. 1–8, 25–32.

4. Linda and Paul Nyden, "Showdown in Coal: A Miner's Report Pamphlet" (Pittsburgh, 1978), p. 17. It seems likely that the big steel companies who own the captive mines and are so dependent upon coal as a fuel source are behind this new effort to bring totalitarian control to the workplace. After the defeat of Sadlowski's right-to-strike forces in the recent United Steel Workers election, the companies now enjoy a no-strike contract with the union under the Experimental Negotiating Agreement. The steel corporations, who ran their captive mining towns like concentration camps until the early thirties, would clearly like to impose this pattern on the coal mining industry. What's more, they are especially dependent upon the high-quality bituminous coal mined only in Appalachia and southern Illinois, the most militant and wildcat-prone of all the coal fields.

5. *New York Times*, March 26, 1978.

6. See "The U.M.W.: In Near Anarchy," *Time*, March 20, 1978, p. 10.

7. Rick Diehl, "UMWA Reform Insurgency: A Recent History," *People's Appalachia*, Winter 1972–1973, pp. 4–5.

8. Charleston (W.Va.) *Post-Gazette*, July 27, Aug. 29, 1976. Thanks to Keith Dix for sending copies of the newspaper stories on the 1976 wildcat.

9. Ibid., Aug. 9, 11, 1976.

10. Morgantown *Dominion-Post*, Sept. 1, 1976.

11. Keith Dix, Carol Fuller, Judy Linsky, and Craig Robinson, *Work Stoppages and Grievance Procedure in the Appalachian Coal Industry*, West Virginia University Institute for Labor Studies (Morgantown, W.Va., 1970), pp. 6, 9.

12. *The Institute for Labor Studies* report concludes the following after studying the statistics from 1953 to 1970: "The percentage of all workers involved in work stoppages in the coal industry was fifteen times greater than the percentage of workers involved in all U.S. (non-coal) strikes."

During this same period 3.3 percent of workers in industries other than coal were involved in work stoppages on an average, increased from a low point of 1.6 percent in 1963 to 4.4 percent in 1970. In bituminous coal an average of 49.5 percent of all workers engaged in strikes over the same period, increasing from a low point of 15.2 in 1961 to an amazing 170.9 percent in 1969. The reason that the percentage could exceed 100 is that some miners engaged in more than one work stoppage in a given year. Ohio, Pennsylvania, and West Virginia, the most unionized states, had the biggest percentage of miners involved in work stoppages, while Tennessee, still an open-shop state, had the lowest. Keith Dix et al., *Work Stoppages*, pp. 16–22.

13. Ibid., pp. 5, 10, 13.

14. Ibid., p. 9. It is difficult to measure the incidence of strikes over safety questions, because they are often listed under other causes. In fact, what the Bureau of Labor Statistics reports as the "issue in a work stoppage may not, in fact, be the basic cause of that stoppage. For example, a local strike may occur and the reported issue might be the company's discharging of a mine worker. The facts behind the situation might show that the employee was discharged because he refused to obey working orders from his foreman. The facts might show further that the reason the particular worker refused to follow orders was that he believed that if he did so he would jeopardize his own safety." A safety strike might therefore be listed as a work stoppage caused by a discipline problem. Ibid., p. 27.

15. Ibid., p. 71. Also see Keith Dix on miners' wildcats in *People's Appalachia*, Winter 1972–1973, pp. 22–24.

16. Keith Dix, *Work Relations in the Appalachian Coal Industry: The Hand-loading Era, 1880–1930*, West Virginia University Bulletin No. 7–2 (1978).

17. Ibid.; Nyden and Nyden, "Showdown in Coal," p. 2.

18. *Coal Patrol*, no. 35, Feb. 2, 1978, pp. 9–10.

19. Clark Kerr and Abraham Seigel, "The Inter-industry Propensity to Strike," in Kerr, *Labor and Management in Industrial Society* (Garden City, N.Y., 1964), pp. 105–147. I am indebted to Steve Brier for insightful criticisms of this theory in an unpublished paper entitled "Ethnicity and Class Consciousness in the Colorado Coal Mines."

20. *New York Times*, March 5, 1978.

21. On the importance of industrial unionism in general and the UMW in particular with respect to interracial organizing, see Paul B. Worthman and James R. Green, "Black Workers in the New South, 1865–1915," in Nathan I. Huggins et al., eds., *Key Issues in the Afro-American Experience* (New York, 1971), vol. 2, pp. 47–69.

22. Jon Amsden and Steven Brier, "Coal Miners on Strike: The Transformation of Strike Demands and the Formation of a National Union," *Journal of Inter-Disciplinary History* 7 (Spring 1977): 583–616.

23. On the Socialist Party influence in the UMW during the 1910s see John H. M. Laslett, *Labor and the Left* (New York, 1970), chap. 6. In the Southwest where the Socialists controlled two UMW districts in this period the Socialist Party established its earliest and strongest locals in the mine union locals where UMW struggles had already established some solidarity across lines of race, nationality and skill. See James R. Green, *Grass-Roots Socialism: Radical Movements in the Southwest, 1895–1943* (Baton Rouge, 1978), chap. 5.

24. Keith Dix, "The Point of Production," *People's Appalachia*, Winter, 1972–1973, p. 25.

25. Ibid.

26. Carter Goodrich, *The Miner's Freedom* (Boston, 1925), pp. 57–66.

27. David Montgomery, "Workers' Control and Machine Production in the Nineteenth Century," *Labor History* 18 (Fall, 1976): 491. For an excellent first-hand account of the miners' pit face control and their informal work rules, see John Brophy, *A Miner's Life* (Madison, Wisc., 1964), chap. 4.

28. Herbert Gutman, "The Worker's Search for Power," in H. W. Morgan, ed., *The Gilded Age: A Reappraisal* (Syracuse, 1963), pp. 38–68.

29. *New York Times*, March 10, 1978.

30. Editor's note: Following the 1978 strike Arnold Miller suffered a heart attack and was replaced by his more conservative vice president, Sam Church. In December of 1982, Church lost his bid to be elected UMW president to Rich Trumka, an insurgent candidate, who tried to revive some of the aims of the Miners for Democracy.

CHAPTER EIGHTEEN

Shop-Floor Politics at Fleetwood

by John Lippert

I work at the Fleetwood Fisher Body plant in Detroit. A lot of you have probably seen or heard of it—it's that big old factory over on Fort St. where we make bodies for Cadillacs.

I want to talk to you today about what it's like to work at Fleetwood. But instead of describing my individual experience at Fleetwood, I want to try something a lot more ambitious: I want to analyze the collective experience of *all* the workers at Fleetwood. But this is not just analysis for the sake of analysis. I want to use my analysis of Fleetwood to uncover ways in which not only myself but a lot of workers can assume more control over our working lives.

Let me outline my argument so that you can see what I'm driving at:

In terms of economics, the main struggle going on at Fleetwood is between the workers and management over the amount of labor that will go into the Cadillacs. In terms of politics, the main struggle is between two groups of workers who are competing with each other over how that struggle with management will be carried out. One group of workers (who are usually but not always old) are trying to force management to bargain more equitably around a labor/money exchange which is itself not fundamentally questioned by these workers. The other group of workers (who are usually

Reprinted from Vol. 12, No. 4 (July-August 1978). Based on a talk presented to Wayne State University's Weekend College.

but not always young) have yet to accept the validity of that labor/money exchange and are in constant rebellion against it.

I call this struggle political for the simple reason that many of the participants in it are quite aware of what's going on. The workers are constantly thinking about the economic necessity and the structure of authority that forces them into the plant in the first place. And they are constantly trying to figure out what to do about it.

The struggle between these two groups of workers gives rise to what I'll call an advanced set of political issues and a conservative set of political issues, both of which are expressed quite clearly in the plant. On the basis of the advanced issues, some workers are questioning the very nature of their role as producer in the society. On the basis of the conservative issues, other workers are trying to use their role as producer as leverage to get what they can get.

My goal today is not just to analyze these political currents in the plant. I want also to analyze as precisely as I can the theoretical and organizational dilemmas which confront people who are pursuing the advanced issues. And I want to analyze ways in which these dilemmas can be broken down.

So now I want to begin my description of shopfloor politics at Fleetwood:

The first thing I have to point out, unfortunately, is that competition forms the initial basis for all our social interaction in the plant. This is true by definition: we're at Fleetwood to sell our labor, and so we compete in a tight market with others who have the same commodity to sell. We compete primarily with people outside the plant who are looking for work. But we also compete with other workers in ways which have great impact on the terms of our employment. Some jobs are better than others. Some pay more than others. A lot of times we need favors from the foremen, so we compete with each other over them. For instance, it's always easier for some people than others to get a pass to go home early.

It's important to start with this notion of competition because this provides the framework within which all our other collective efforts must develop. Strictly speaking, our collective identity is not one that's defined by unity and common interests. Our collective identity is defined by disunity and competing interests.

I'm glad to say that competition doesn't form the totality of our interactions in the plant. There's cooperation inherent in any mass industrial enterprise (although as it stands now this cooperation is advantageous mainly to the management). But outside of the work itself, groups of workers do associate on the basis of coherent group identities. And strong individual friendships do emerge among a lot of people.

Now in a situation as complex as Fleetwood, you have a lot of different groups doing a lot of different things. When I talk about how advanced and conservative issues arise in the plant, I'm obviously referring to what people do and think in relation to their work itself. Work at Fleetwood has a certain homogeneous character—it's an assembly plant. And so there are a certain range of possibilities of what people can think and do about their work.

My main goal today is to demonstrate to you the existence of a group of workers who I will call the vanguard group. I define the vanguard group in this way: they are a coherent group of people who are consistently trying to push through on the most advanced possibilities and most advanced political issues in the plant. I want to make it clear that this vanguard defines *itself* by what it does, by its own *practice* in the plant. They're not fulfilling some prophecy that was laid down a couple hundred years ago.

Now what are the advanced issues that the vanguard group attempts to act on? I define those issues in this way: the vanguard group is composed of those people in the plant who resist the reduction of their needs, personalities, and individualities to fit the needs of assembly line discipline. The vanguard group is composed of those people who refuse to think of themselves as only auto workers, who refuse to act as if they are mere appendages to this giant mechanical monster.

But I have to give you some facts so that you have a better idea of what I'm talking about. Let me say first that 20 percent of the workforce belong to this vanguard group. Not all the people in the plant are trying to resist assembly line discipline. Here are six other coherent groups who identify themselves by their *practice* in the plant:

1. There are a lot of old people in the plant who are just hanging on until they retire.
2. There are a lot of recent immigrants who are still pretty confused by their new environment.
3. There are a lot of people who lack self-confidence to such an extent that they actually need the identity which is supplied for them by the line.
4. There are a lot of small businessmen who are delighted to have a captive audience on which to operate: you've got all kinds of loan sharks, dope peddlers, numbers men, and so on.
5. There are a lot of brown-nosers who openly collaborate with the foremen to such an extent that they actually *benefit* from the structure of authority.
6. And there are a great mass of people who are dissatisfied with their work environment but who are not actively trying to change it: their main goal during the working day is to just "get by."

So here are six groups of workers whose practice in the plant can be called conservative. I want to return later on to describe these conservative workers in more detail. I'm just pointing them out here to give a better idea of who the vanguard workers are.

But now I want to make some descriptive generalizations about the people in the vanguard group. Within the group, blacks and whites are equally represented and there are a small number of women between the ages of 25 and 32. The people might have come from other areas of the country, but they are now comfortable within a complex urban environment. A lot of them have fought in Vietnam. Most have families. Most have high school diplomas. And some have taken courses at local colleges.

But as I said before, a vanguard defines itself by what it *does*, and in order to fully describe what I mean by vanguard, I have to describe what these people *do* to actively resist factory discipline. In order to do this, I want to focus for a few minutes on one section in the plant, the Kotan section. This is generally believed to be the most militant section in the plant.

The most obvious activity of the vanguard group in the Kotan section is that they lead the yearly slowdown over manning levels in the department.

The Kotan job is a unique job at Fleetwood in that it requires a lot of skill on the part of the workers. Their job is to install the vinyl tops. They have to place the top on the car, stretch it to get all the wrinkles out, cut it to precise length and so on. All of this can take 20 minutes or more, and so they have about 40 teams of two people each working in rotation while the line is moving. That means there's a lot of people working on the job—with reliefmen and extras the total comes to about 110. This is another unique aspect of the Kotan job: there's so many of them that when they act in unison they have a lot of power.

Every year there's a model change at Fleetwood, and every year work is added to the Kotan job and workers are eliminated. So every year the Kotan people take the job in the hole. This is a fairly common event at Fleetwood. But when the Kotan people do it it's extraordinary. They don't just take the job in the hole 50 or 60 feet. They take it down 500 or 600 feet. And they cause a lot of disruption.

But I want to focus on the activity of the vanguard group in this struggle. First of all, they are the ones who initiate the slowdown and who articulate the demands. There are always a lot of rumors and threats that fly around before the slowdown begins. The foremen go around and say that everyone will be fired or that the corporation is so sick of having trouble at Fleetwood that they want to shut it down entirely. The union comes around and says the slowdown won't be necessary since progress is being made in the negotiations. A lot of workers will be swayed by these rumours, since they're hoping to avoid a drawn-out struggle anyway.

So it's up to the vanguard to take the lead. They have to say first of all that it's not impossible for workers to take the company on and win. They have to say also that it's not impossible for workers to act as a group. And they have to say that it's only on the basis of pressure from the shop floor that the union will be able to do anything in the negotiations anyway. So off they go down into the hole.

Most workers in the Kotan section would never initiate the slowdown. But they will follow the lead of the vanguards. There are plenty of brown-nosers who don't want to go along. And so it's up to the vanguards to convince them, something which might require physical harassment. There are certain forms of sabotage which can go along with the slowdown. And the vanguards have to keep a close eye on the union, to see what kind of deals are being made.

But another responsibility of the vanguards is to keep the slowdown going once it's begun. The battle often lasts for weeks, and the pressure is intense. The vanguards have to keep people's spirits up, to see that they avoid unnecessary mistakes and so on. Once a speed-up grievance has been filed by the union, it's impossible for the company to discipline people for simply being in the hole. But they can throw people out for mistakes of workmanship or for coming back late from break. The company is clearly most interested in nailing the vanguards for this kind of thing: sometimes they just make up lies about what a certain person did. And so from the first day of the slowdown, the company begins throwing people out into the street. One of the most thrilling things for me as I watch this is to see new leaders step forward as the old ones get thrown out.

But the most exciting thing about the slowdowns is that you can actually see workers winning victories. This happened in 1976. The battle lasted for weeks, and more and more people were thrown out. But finally, on a certain Friday night, the company couldn't replace all the people they had thrown out and still cover for normal Friday night absenteeism. That meant they had to let one out of six cars go down the line without a vinyl top. The repair costs were staggering, and so on that night the company gave in. Manning levels were increased in the department and everyone who had been thrown out was brought back with full pay.

Now this was only a short-term victory in the sense that several months later the company cut back on the manning levels, and because the whole battle began again with the next model change. But through the year, the vanguards had preserved the camaraderie that had developed during the slowdown. And so when the next battle came, they were ready. How did these workers preserve their identities through the year?

One of the big prizes the Kotan people get by winning these slowdowns is that they get a little extra time between their jobs. They tend to congregate then in coherent groups in specific areas on the department. The identities of the groups are defined mainly by what people *do* in relation to factory discipline. The old men huddle along the line between the stock area and the area where the glue is sprayed on. The brown-nosers hang out over by the foremen's desk. The bible readers hang out in the back, where they discuss philosophy and stuff. There are a group of black moderates and a group of white moderates who hang out at the picnic tables by the foremen's desk. And the black and the white vanguards hang out over by the windows.

The main thing that goes on over by the windows is that people are self-conscious about maintaining the community and the camaraderie which was formed during the slowdowns. If the slowdowns were just sporadic events, maybe participation in them wouldn't be sufficient to justify calling a certain group vanguard. But if the slowdowns happen every year, if the same people lead them, and if those people try to preserve their community year in and year out, then the concept of vanguard becomes much deeper. But what are the daily sort of events which keep the community going?

In the first place, there's always some sort of specifically collective event going on by the windows. Maybe it's a group dinner a few guys are preparing. Maybe people are collectively reading and discussing the newspaper. Maybe they're getting together a softball game or a picnic outside the plant. And people are always just standing around and talking. There's an information network for militants that extends throughout the plant, and people are always discussing the latest rumor, the latest move by the union and so on. But they also talk about anything else that comes up: they might talk about religion, about marriage, about bringing up kids, about fixing up their houses, about keeping their cars running and so on. These are not superficial discussion. People talk about their values, their beliefs, their fundamental perceptions of the universe in which they find themselves.

The funniest thing that goes on by the windows is that there's a constant rowdiness back there. People are always up to something. The big thing last fall was pitching quarters. It was initiated by some of the white vanguards, and pretty soon the games grew into big events—people would gather around and cheer and so on. Eventually the foreman came over and told people to stop, and then it became a game of hide and seek—people would sneak in a few games while the foreman wasn't looking. Pretty soon some of the black vanguards started playing, then some of the white moderates. Pretty soon people all over the department were playing, partly for the fun of it and partly for the joy of outfoxing the foreman. The game even caught on in the back corner where I work, but only after it had died down in the Kotan area.

After the pitching quarters game faded out, the new game became basketball. People would carve hoops out of packing material and shape balls out of tape and cardboard. And then they'd have really dynamite games of two on two or three on three. This lasted for a couple weeks, and then the foreman started tearing down the hoops.

The big event at Christmas (besides the party) was that the whole group participated in making a Christmas tree. They cut the tree out of some cardboard, stapled it to some wood from a packing crate, and then painted and decorated it with anything they could find in the plant. It was really elaborate. It was eight feet tall; it had Christmas balls and candy canes on it; it even had a chimney with stockings and logs burning in the fireplace. It was a work of art. But then, lo and behold, the foreman came and tore down the tree. It wasn't that there was anything so destructive about the tree. It's just that the foreman had been trying all year to break the identity of that group—these were the same people who lead the slowdowns. I should say for the record that the general foreman later ordered the foreman to put the tree back up. But it didn't matter much then. The Christmas spirit had been ruined.

Now this, I think, constitutes a good description of the vanguard group in Kotan. But Kotan is a unique section: it's unique in ways which make the vanguard activity much easier to see. But there are a lot of vanguard people in the plant who are isolated, and so what they do is much harder to see. How do these vanguard people express themselves in isolation?

Well I'm going to take myself as an example of this. I work in the back, about 50 yards from the Kotan area. It's a pretty quiet corner. The group interaction is nowhere near as intense as in Kotan. And most of the people are committed to what I'll describe later as conservative courses of action.

The job I do is also different from Kotan in that there's no skill involved: I don't do any one coherent operation. I do a lot of different things on each job. This is the typical kind of job we have at Fleetwood.

On the Eldorados I have to shoot a retainer inside the quarter glass window. A retainer is a short strip of metal: I'm not sure what its purpose is. On the Sedans and Broughams I have to shoot a bumper inside the front door. A bumper is this small piece of plastic that goes "bump" when you close the door. And on these cars and the Coupes and the Sevilles I have to put masking tape on the surfaces near where the vinyl top will go. My tape is to prevent glue from getting all over when they spray the cars before installing the vinyl tops. I put yards and yards of masking tape on each car. The tape has to be in precise position and it has to be slicked down.

There's nothing hard about the individual components of the job. My work is light and fast. It might take several weeks to learn to coordinate the various tasks. And it might take months to get really good. But eventually the main problem is *time*: you have to come to grips with the necessity of actually having to *do* that shit. You have to come up with some way of making sure your identity doesn't get destroyed by your work.

The main way I try to do this is to minimize the thought and labor which are required to do the job. I don't have to think too much about what I do: I just start running and let the momentum carry me. But I have to be careful not to get into a bad mood, not to let my morale slip, not to be aware of the passage of time. As far as the work goes, I'm always cutting little corners, finding little shortcuts. I don't want to describe too much of this publicly since they might start watching me, but let me say that most people at Fleetwood are surprised at how many shortcuts you can take and still not get caught. I want to be clear here that I'm not the only worker playing this game: almost everybody does it. The assembly line gives very little incentive to do otherwise. And I should say also that the foremen and the general foremen and the superintendents and the plant managers are also playing the game: they're all trying to see what they can put over on higher levels of management. If you think all this has an impact on the quality of the final product, you're right. Poor quality is not an accident these days: it's built into the very essence of the system.

But what do I do as an individual worker with the time I save by taking these shortcuts? I'm good enough at my job now that I can do two or three cars in a row fast and then have maybe 15 or 20 seconds for myself in between. The main thing I do with these interludes is read. I read the paper every day and I read books. Some of the books are quite complex. The main thing I've had to learn in order to read under these conditions is to remember what I've read and to be able to quickly find where I've left off. Reading is very important to me. It takes my mind somewhere else. I'm not the only one who reads; a lot of people do it, except that they might read magazines or do crossword puzzles; some people might knit or sew, but people can generally keep busy during the little gaps between their jobs.

And like most people, I do a lot of talking when I'm working. I talk to people next to me or to people who are passing through. And in the same way as a lot of people, I consciously try to circulate around the plant during my break time. There's a whole network of these vanguard people who seek each other out and visit. The discussions are not always political. People are just trying to make the day go by a little faster. They're trying to make the day more interesting.

Another major social event is at lunchtime. A lot of people go out to the bar across the street or they sit in their cars and talk. I go out every day. I usually have a beer or two. It's a chance to relax a bit, to enjoy a change of scenery. Pretty soon there's a coherent group of people in the plant who have come to know each other through their interactions in the parking lot.

Another major way that people resist the discipline of the factory is through absenteeism. Most people in the plant work every day, but that's just because they need the money. There's a certain percentage of people in the plant who aren't so pressed for cash and so they don't feel the need to come in every day. The company has been trying for years and years to get these people to come in, but there's really not much the company can do about it.

Another major event which defines this vanguard group in the plant is the wildcat strike we had at Fleetwood in the summer of 1976. The shop committee of the local called the strike, but they got their signals crossed badly. So at the time of the walkout there was a lot of confusion as to who was going and why. A lot of people turned back or waited at the door to see what would happen. Six hundred people walked out, but it was only because they felt it was time for a walkout regardless of the union's ability or inability to lead it. There were a lot of positive and negative consequences of the wildcat; some people got fired and all the rest. But one thing I do want to say is that that group of 600 people survived the walkout relatively intact, and they have continued to participate heavily in the other kinds of vanguard activity I've been describing today (*RA* vol. 11, no. 5).

So this, I think, is a fair description of the vanguard activity in the plant: you have periodic slowdowns; a lot of day to day interactions which keep the militant community in the plant alive; a lot of people struggling in isolation to not let their identities be totally overwhelmed by their work; chronic absenteeism and occasional explosive events like a wildcat. People are always pushing, always moving, always looking for some kind of change. People are always thinking and talking, too. I want to ask now a very important question in trying to assess the political importance of this activity: I want to see what kind of consciousness is being expressed by what people are doing. What do people believe about themselves and society to make them act this way?

I think there are several generalizations which can be made about what these people think. The first thing to point out is that their shop floor militancy is from their own point of view a reflection on what they think of the entire society, not just what they think of Fleetwood. Their experience throughout society has taught them that they have to fight for anything they're going to get. A lot of them have fought in Viet Nam; both blacks and whites have had to contend with state authority in the streets and in the welfare office. If they perceive a bottleneck in the production process, if they perceive that a slowdown in Kotan can be a very powerful thing, then they're ready, willing and able to take advantage of it.

Another primary belief among this vanguard is that there is no equality of opportunity in the society and that they themselves are working far below their capacity. This is felt particularly among blacks. Most people talk about getting out of the plant. But few people ever make it.

It's a common belief among these people that basically you have to hustle just to survive at Fleetwood, that you have to work hard to maintain your morale and your self-image. This is the main purpose of the small groups that people are a part of on the shop floor. It's also the main purpose of the shop floor militancy itself.

These workers have long since given up any hope of satisfaction from their work. They try to have a good time with people around them. But they seek their main satisfaction at home. People have hobbies that they're into. And they have great hopes for their marriages and their relationships with their kids. But there's a lot of tension and hard work that go along with having a family. So for many people it seems like real satisfaction is more the exception than the rule.

These workers have some sense about how the work is affecting their health in the long run. They worry about stress, about drinking, about popping too many pills. But they have very few alternatives in the short run, so they figure, "What the hell can you do?"

These vanguard workers generally feel that Fleetwood is going downhill. The dominant outlook in the plant is that "all you can do is hang on and make as much money as you can before the bottom falls out." People basically feel that you have to have twenty years in the plant now in order to have a decent shot at getting a full pension.

This perception of instability and decline contributes to a general cynicism about their own ability to act as a group. They understand correctly that they are powerful only insofar as they can impede production. And so they sense how they are undermined if they are based in a declining industry. This also dampens their enthusiasm for traditional liberal rhetoric about "Saving our Jobs." People know intuitively that this has very little basis in political economy.

This is similar to the long range outlook of people in the Kotan area. People are convinced that eventually the company will eliminate the section, either by installing the tops automatically or by having two-tone painted tops and so on. The Kotan people don't respond to this by staying out of the hole now. But they are not very hopeful about the future.

The best of these people, the real vanguard, are also very cynical about the general prospects for change in the society. They've already tried, through these slowdowns and things, to challenge portions of the power structure, and so they know how well entrenched it is. And they're also very cynical about the ability of workers to act collectively. How can it be otherwise, when they've literally had to fight to organize something as seemingly fundamental as a slowdown in the department over speed-up? What does this say about the possibility of broader actions?

This vanguard group at Fleetwood has been exposed to Socialist or Communist movements in this country for many years, and have a pretty sophisticated opinion of where the left is at. One guy put it to me this way: "Revolution is a nice idea. But it's one of those things that you can talk all day about and never quite get anywhere." People aren't unsympathetic to the Left. It just doesn't mean much to them.

Most people don't think the union is any kind of long term solution to their problems. And they have little faith in what it can do in the short run. But they tend to defend the union from company attack. And they don't like it when people attack the union when there's nothing available by way of short-term alternatives.

Part of their lack of faith in the union is that they perceive it as tied to wage and benefit packages. They'll take the money and the benefits. But they say quite clearly that these alone will never add up to a solution to their problems.

So in general, I'd sum up the outlook of this vanguard in this way: They're extremely alienated from their role as producer in the society. They have an ability to organize to get what they can in the short run. They have a perception that long run change will require broad collective effort on the part of the workers. And they're generally cynical about the prospects for these changes to come about.

So then, why are these vanguard groups important? I would say first that the collective identity of these vanguard groups is in essence the composite of many individual efforts to not let our individual identities get wiped out by the work we do. We take part in a collective identity which is entirely of our own making. We've already overcome the competition which lies at the bottom of initial interactions. We've rejected the notion that what we get from the society comes through exchanging our labor. What we get now comes through our own ability to organize and fight for it. In fact, we've organized now to fight for something which the company can't give us anyway, which is our dignity and integrity as human beings.

I think the activity of these vanguard groups is important also because it embodies a vivid condemnation of how society is organized today. In fact it's hard to imagine how any society could be organized such that the demands of these vanguard groups could be met. The activity of these groups, in fact, give me the best clues I've ever had as to what a truly revolutionary society would look like. These workers would never accept a society that called itself revolutionary if the unskilled workers were simply ordered to do arbitrary, repetitive labor. Any technologically advanced society is going to require a division of labor between mental and manual laborers. But these vanguard workers of today would never accept a division of labor in which they were not fully active, fully conscious participants in the decision-making process. If unskilled labor is required by a revolutionary society, it won't be arbitrarily imposed on the workers. They will have a lot to say about the terms and the conditions under which they will work.

But beyond that, the existence of these vanguard groups in the plant is important because it proves that people's identities *can't* be stamped out by this system of production. These vanguard groups make it possible to imagine conscious mass participation in a movement to change this society. And these vanguard groups throw out hope that a society characterized by conscious mass decision-making can indeed emerge.

But I don't want to get too carried away when I say this. I don't want to say that the revolution is occurring down at Fleetwood. In fact, these vanguard groups would be the first to say that they're not organized to achieve anything more than they've got, which is a slightly more humanized existence at Fleetwood.

And furthermore, people have a deep understanding of how dangerous the powers-that-be are. They're not about to take any chances, any more general steps unless the goals are pretty clear and unless they have some reasonable chance to succeed. It's like what a lot of people have discovered when they take their jobs down into the hole: it's a very unpleasant experience to have nine or ten foremen standing in your face.

And so fear, fear itself, is a very important part of the outlook of people at Fleetwood. A lot of people look at what happened to John Kennedy or Martin Luther King and say, "If people like that can get killed, we don't stand a chance." People may not know who killed these men or why. And they may not be trying to analyze the dangers that would actually be faced by a movement of workers. But the subjective implications of this fear are still very important. People say, "The hell with it. I'll just get along as best as I can."

And people are still basically cynical about the ability of workers to act collectively as a group; this is the single most concrete expression of how people perceive their powerlessness today. They feel like even if they did create some worker organization to fight for their interests, pretty soon somebody from the rank and file would rise up and sell it out. Workers talk almost wistfully about how different it was 10 or 15 years ago, when things were different, when people did stick together. The union was a much bigger part of people's lives then, so I ask people if the union has changed. People shake their heads and say, "No, it's the people. The people have changed." Nobody can be more specific. People just lower their heads and walk away.

So even though the vanguard exists at Fleetwood, even though they're a very powerful force on the shop floor, I'd still have to call the atmosphere at Fleetwood a generally conservative one. I don't mean that people believe in George Wallace or anything like that. I just mean that people aren't into taking too many chances. They're apprehensive about the future, and they believe they'd be doing well to just maintain the life they've carved out for themselves at this point.

Now I want to describe more fully these conservative currents that run through the plant. I've spent all this time talking about the vanguard group but I don't want to distort their importance. The vanguard group compromises no more than 20 percent of the workforce, and they are not the dominant group in the plant. I want to talk now about what the rest of the people, these 80 percent are doing.

The main conservative current is expressed when people simply don't challenge their work environment. They accept it as given and then try to find little nooks and crannies within which they can express themselves comfortably. Very few people actually like their work or take pride in it. Very few people believe that there's an equitable exchange going on between workers and management. But for a lot of different reasons, a lot of people don't challenge what goes on around them.

A lot of people who fall into this category are just timid; they're people who are not accustomed to leaving an imprint on the people around them. Most workers have been told from the day they were born that their perceptions of the world are not important to anybody. A lot of people actually believe they don't have anything important to say. A lot of people don't circulate too much in the plant: they may never talk to people 30 or 40 feet down the line from them. Maybe they lack self-confidence. Maybe they are recent immigrants and are still confused by the language and customs around them. And there are a lot of old people in the plant who have seen shop floor struggles come and go in the plant for years, and who have long since given up the hope of seeing any fundamental change. All they want to do is get out.

Most of the people in the plant are just into getting by. They maintain a low profile in the plant. They interact with a small group of friends. They do their job and go home. That's it.

A lot of people, maybe 20 percent, are into making individual deals with the foremen. These deals can be quite extensive and can radically alter their working experience. Maybe they'll get out a little early. Maybe their job won't get any more work put on it. Maybe they'll get extra overtime or a specific date for a vacation. And these people will do lots of things for the foreman in return. Maybe they'll cover a certain job if somebody doesn't show up. Maybe they'll come in early to stock the line before it starts. These people obviously contribute to the conservativeness of the situation: they're not about to rock the boat because they don't have to. We have two women in our area who have hot coffee and doughnuts ready for the plant superintendent each morning. This superintendent is a particularly devilish man— he's the one responsible for setting up all the jobs; he personally implements the speed-up in the plant. Now I have nothing against personal friendship. But of all the people in our section, these two women were the only ones who got work taken off their jobs by writing a speed-up grievance with the union. So there is definitely something fishy going on.

Conservatism is also built into the hiring policies in the plant. 90 percent of the people hired there in the last five years have had a brother or a mother or a cousin working there. Anybody else who got hired was just plain lucky. This practice doesn't totally co-opt the workforce, but it helps. It helps create a situation where people are trying to get ahead by flowing with the system instead of against it.

Something else contributes to the conservatism of the plant: lots of people concede so much to management before they begin to fight that it's hard for them to win anything. This is the basic weakness of people caught within the labor/money exchange.

I had a fight once with my partner Frank that illustrates this. He wanted me to stop reading my books because he was afraid the bosses would use it as an excuse to give us more work. Frank is the kind of guy who can never think of anything else but work in the first place, so at first I wasn't sure what to make of what he was saying. But he insisted so finally I went along. But after several hours I started up reading again. Part of it was that I was going crazy. And part of it was that I felt like not reading was putting us in a position of weakness vis-a-vis the foreman anyway. I don't want to always be worrying and posturing toward what they *might* do. If they're going to do something, let them go ahead and do it. And until that time comes, I'm going to worry about what *I* want to do. I knew I was taking a chance by reading. But part of what I was telling the foreman by reading was that he would sure as hell have a fight on his hands if he came around messing with us. That seemed to me to be a much stronger position to be in.

This bargaining-from-weakness is also clearly characteristic of the union. The union is not an offensive organization in that it attempts to advance the interests of the workers even if that means fundamental changes in the society. The union is a defensive organization. It's trying hard now to maintain a certain terrain on which it and the company can bargain to their mutual advantage. It is possible for the union to win concessions from management. But management can win concessions from the union—primarily it wants the union to guarantee labor stability. So the union is required by definition to try and force the workers to funnel all their discontent into the grievance procedure.

Now I hope it's clear from what I've said so far that the union is not at all successful in doing this. Workers have a lot of other ways of fighting back. There are a lot of good strong militants who refuse on principle to call the union. Most people will call the union because it is one option open to them and because it does complicate the life of a foreman. But it's not their main tactic: people know that if all they can do is write a grievance about something then they are in a lot of trouble. One of the most telling indications of the state of the union today is that the best militants, the leaders of this vanguard for instance, don't run for union positions. Instead what you get in the union are the politicians, the people who feel some personal motivation to play that kind of role. The decision about who would be a good rep is almost never a collective decision in a department.

The basic weakness of the union is that it's tied directly to the labor/money exchange and it can't move away from it. The union tries to alter that exchange so that the balance is more in favor of the workers. But it's constantly on the defensive. A good example of this is that the company has in the last year fired several people for collecting unemployment or welfare at the same time they were on the company payroll. Some of these people got their jobs back, but the company obviously extracted a price. By being forced to deal with those kinds of issues, the union is continually sacrificing it's ability to push for more offensive gains. Another example of this at Fleetwood is the paralysis of the local union. We haven't had a local contract in about 18 months. For much of that time the local union has been begging the International to let them go on strike. But the International constantly jams them up. So now, all of a sudden we've got a soft market for Cadillacs and we've got the threat of layoffs because of the coal strike. So now, lo and behold, the International is supposedly ready to let us go out on strike. It's ridiculous.

Probably the saddest statement about the union today is that in many ways it actually works against the development of a collective identity among the workers. They don't settle grievances on their merit; they trade groups of grievances off one against the other. That means almost by definition that the interests of the younger workers are sacrificed for the interests of the older workers. Workers are not allowed to comment on any grievances but their own. Departmental meetings to discuss union affairs are avoided like the plague. And the only real cooperation between different locals is over the wage and benefit packages in the national agreement. On matters of health and safety and so on, each local is left to slug it out alone.

Now I'm not suggesting doing away with the union or anything like that. Sometimes that's all you've got. I myself was fired at Fleetwood once, and I spent the next four months on the telephone. I was almost begging those union guys to take up my case. The weakness of the union is built into the very essence of the institution. It's not dependent on the personalities of certain "bureaucrats" or anything like that.

This is especially true when the union is rapidly deteriorating into a simple interest group mechanism. The union today is clearly moving toward protectionism. It's not moving toward more militant pursuit of the workers' interests.

The auto industry is not in very good shape today. It's in a short term slump which they didn't anticipate and which they are *hoping* won't be too severe. And the long-term stagnation the industry faces is obvious: the industry is on an international level too big. They have the capacity to build more cars than the market can bear, but they have to run the system at near or full capacity in order to be profitable. We'll be seeing cutbacks in the next few years as some of the older plants get phased out. And we'll be seeing a series of classic business cycles in which the market is periodically flooded and then drained of cars. And in an atmosphere already characterized by high unemployment, auto workers will be increasingly on the defensive. And the auto companies will use their plight to extract concessions from the workers, the unions and anyone else they can get their hands on.

Of all the issues that come up in the plant, the issue of layoffs is one of the most difficult for me to relate to politically. It cuts the guts right out of workers struggles in the plant. Most workers see the handwriting on the wall and regard it with resignation, because they see clearly how the layoffs cut into their own ability to fight. How do you fight something that big, especially when all the options are lousy? A lot of politicians are into throwing around the slogan of "Save our Jobs." But all these ideas are variations on the same theme: the government steps in to either prop the industry up or else to cut off foreign imports. Neither of these suggestions could fundamentally change the economy to the long-term advantage of the workers. Both these suggestions leave the workers in a totally defenseless position in the plant, and leave auto workers pitted against other groups in the society: either other displaced groups who could also use the government money or else auto workers in other countries who could also use the work. And so all of these scenarios set up tremendously volatile political pressures in the society.

The union, of course, will fight to hang on to its present base of power. It's simple: the less members it has, the less clout it has. And so they'll get sucked right into the protectionist tide. This has already happened in such industries as steel and clothing, where the companies and the unions march hand in hand down to Washington to plead for relief. A good thing to watch will be if the UAW abandons its traditional policy against import controls on foreign cars. I would go so far as to predict it'll happen soon, and when it does, you know they're running scared.

I've been listing all these conservative trends in the plant, and I can't finish up without listing the most conservative trend of all, and that is the government itself. It's not just conservative; it's downright repressive. And it's the ultimate obstacle that auto workers face today.

There's no better example of this than what happened down at the Trenton Engine plant. They have a problem with heat down there; the temperature can go up to 130 degrees in the summer. After many years of struggle about this the company finally agreed in writing to give people passes to go home early if it got too hot. But during a heatwave last summer the company suddenly stopped giving people passes. A lot of bitterness resulted and then a walkout. But after a few days of this, the company called in the government, and the government was more than happy to oblige. They issued an injunction against picketing, and then they hauled seven people at random out of a crowd and charged them with contempt of court. These people actually went to jail. The strike ended and a lot of people were disciplined. And by then the only thing the union could do was to try to get some of the penalties removed. All but one of the people who were fired were eventually brought back. But the plant is still hot. The union is still pretty helpless in trying to do anything about it. And the workers now know that if they take matters into their own hands again they'll have to take the government all over again to get anywhere.

Now I don't want to sound like a pessimist or anything. I think that what the workers did at Trenton was fantastic and I think they deserve all the support we can give them. But we have to be clear what the dangers are: the stronger the workers got at Trenton the more heat they brought down on themselves. And if it happened at Trenton it'll happen at Fleetwood or anywhere else workers get too strong. If we're talking about any fundamental changes taking place on the shop floor, the government is the ultimate obstacle we'll have to contend with. The same thing is pointed out very clearly by the coal strike. (See Chapter 17.)

CONCLUSION

The advanced currents in the plant do contain the potential for changes in the society. But people committed to them face a lot of problems. The most immediate dilemma faced by these vanguard workers is that they have to continually reaffirm their short-term interests as workers in the society even though they're rebelling against that very role in the long run. Each day for them is a continuing, painful purgatory. They make compromises which are even more painful for them because they are acutely aware of their powerlessness. The vanguard people know they need to work in order to survive, even though they hate that work from the start. They know they need the union, even though it's clearly an expression of their weakness more than their strength. They know a layoff would make them weak, even though their presence in the plant has been the focus of their rebellion for years.

Another basic problem of the vanguard workers is that they are frozen into place now because so many workers around them are committed to conservative courses of action. And they are frozen into place by their isolation in one plant: it's very difficult for these vanguard groups to link up between plants. It's very difficult for them to link up with other sectors of the population who share their basic alienation from the present organization of society.

Now I don't have the answers to these dilemmas in the classic sense. I can't roll out a magic formula that will solve the problems overnight. All I can do is point out one or two things that can be done to move the situation ahead from where it is now.

The main thing I'd like to see in the short run is for the vanguard groups at Fleetwood and elsewhere to get more articulate and outspoken about what they do. Their activity provides not only a vivid condemnation of how the society is presently organized. It also provides a lot of clues about how the society can be transcended. I'd like to see these groups have public meetings to actually express their views to the rest of society. An immediate advantage of this is that the vanguard groups could fill a tremendous void in the society. Politicians from Jimmy Carter on down justify what they do at least rhetorically by claiming to speak for "the common man." If workers themselves said what they think, particularly if these vanguard groups said what they *don't like* about the society, the entire political complexion of the country would change. If these vanguard groups could coordinate their activity on a multiplant basis, they'd be an incredibly powerful force in the society.

Now maybe I can be accused of putting the best possible light on the subject, but I am convinced that these vanguard groups are becoming more articulate these days. I think the fact that I've been able to make this kind of speech to this kind of group is evidence of this fact. This articulation is a very slow process of course, and there are a lot of problems.

I think one of the main problems is the language itself. Workers are not trained to think that their perceptions of the world are important. And so many workers are not skilled in the arts of communication. A lot of workers don't read. Very few write. Our language is the language of domination of the people at the bottom of society, not the language of their self-expression.

Another linguistic problem is political: what would you call a meeting in which vanguard groups of several plants got together? Would it be a "Socialist" meeting? Would it be forming a "party"? I don't know. I've had more exposure to these words than most people in the room, and it's still hard for me to say what they mean. And most of what they ordinarily mean is bad. But what words would you use to describe what you'd be doing?

Another problem is time: workers are generally so busy just trying to survive that they can't be running around to meetings all the time. This is particularly true if the premises of the meeting aren't all that clear.

But in general, I'd say the main problem facing these vanguard groups is *theoretical* in nature. Right now, they're organized in a negative way, around what they *don't like*. In order to switch over to a positive organization, in order to fight for what they *do like*, they'd have to completely transform their outlook. They'd have to begin to try and *create* something that they thought was important.

This is a very cynical age we're living through. And workers have more reason to be cynical than most people. To create a *positive* organization in such an age is a difficult thing: it's time consuming; there's lots of unclarity about what you'd be doing; and the forces of repression are never far behind.

But if these vanguard groups did opt for a positive organization, they'd have a lot to gain. Their activity already embodies a serious alternative to this society. Any further articulation and coordination of that activity would allow them to swing a lot of weight.

The initial step is for these vanguard groups to begin seriously communicating their views to the rest of society. In so doing, they've already rejected the dominant notion in the society that workers have nothing important to say. They've already rejected the cynicism and self-contempt which are part of being a worker today; these attitudes are nothing but a reflection of powerlessness. In trying to build these positive organizations, these workers would actually have to achieve the age-old dream of becoming "actors on the stage of history." They'd be completely transcending the role of worker as we know it today.

The potential for these developments is clearly present at Fleetwood and elsewhere today. How far it can go, what obstacles remain: there's still a lot we don't know yet. But one thing we can say for sure. The situation in the plant is such that we are not starting from scratch.

CHAPTER NINETEEN

Tanning Leather, Tanning Hides: Health and Safety Struggles in a Leather Factory

by Andrew Rowland

The organization of industry around profits and industrial efficiency necessitates a constant conflict with workers' health and safety. Industry is dangerous, not because of some series of technological decisions that were made long ago, but because of day-to-day decisions that determine the organization of the labor process. Workers' lives are threatened by a thousand and one small decisions that put industry profits and efficiency above worker health.

As workers become increasingly aware of corporate mismanagement in this area, health and safety is becoming a more and more prominent issue in the American workplace. It has also emerged as a powerful organizing tool. It is an issue on which activists can win concrete victories and, at the same time, raise crucial questions about the human rationality of the capitalist labor process. In this sense, health and safety victories can act as "non-reformist reforms."[1]

This article is based on my experience working in a leather tannery as a safety researcher over a six-month period. I was hired to rewrite safety codes at the plant and to develop a questionnaire that would convince the Occupational Safety and Health Administration that the tannery workers had been trained in safety procedures.[2]

Reprinted from Vol. 14, No. 6 (November-December 1980).

THE TANNERY

The place where I worked (I will just call it the Tannery) is located along a river in a small California town. It is a leather factory, indistinguishable from any other factory to the outside observer except for the strange and sickening smell that permeates the plant and surrounding neighborhood. The smell is a by-product of the series of chemical processes through which cow hides are stripped of their hair and transformed into different grades of leather. These hides are, in turn, cut, polished, and dyed to the specifications set by the shoe factories and craft people who buy leather from the Tannery.

The leather-tanning industry is in the process of concentration and modernization.[3] Many of the smallest tanneries that cannot keep up with the pace of change are being bought up or closed down. Although the Tannery is still under one-person ownership, it is not the same small-craft operation it was in the 1860s. In line with the general trend in the industry, the Tannery has expanded rapidly in the past eight or nine years. It now employs 420 workers, considerably more than the industry average.

Production never stops at the Tannery. Three shifts of workers keep the process moving 24 hours a day. In response to pressures for modernization within the industry, the Tannery management is constantly experimenting with new ways to make a better grade of leather or to process the leather faster and gain on their competitors.

As the tanning industry matures, it moves closer in many ways to the chemical industry and away from the leather-tanning craft it once was. Like the chemical industry, it has become a dangerous place to work. According to a government booklet, its accident and illness rate is "five times higher than the average for all other industries."[4]

THE MYTH OF THE SAFE WORKPLACE

When I first began working at the Tannery I was struck by how dangerous it looked. The ground was constantly slick and wet with pools of chemical wastes. Warning signs about dangerous chemicals were posted everywhere. Forklifts loaded with hides were going in every direction, and a lot of the machinery looked unbelievably old and in a poor state of repair. I was therefore shocked when the insurance investigator assigned to the Tannery told me it was "an exceptionally clean shop." John Woods, the plant safety engineer, said, "This tannery has the lowest accident rate of any tannery in the country and most of the accidents that do occur are only minor cuts and back injuries." Despite their assurances I soon found that their comments did not reflect the objective reality of working in the Tannery.

In 1977 there were 318 accidents in the Tannery according to management's safety log. Since there are about 420 employees working there at any one time, this means there were approximately three accidents per four employees working that year. Of these accidents, 114, or about one third of all reported accidents, were serious enough to require a physician's care *and* days off from work. These statistics do not include unreported accidents or "near misses." Nor do they give any indication of the long-range effects of the many dangerous chemicals used at the Tannery that contribute to occupational disease.

The reason such a clear discrepancy exists between the actual working conditions in the Tannery and the way they are reported by some of the principal people involved in safety surveillance is the main topic of the rest of this paper.

THE ACCIDENT

Despite the fact that the accident statistics reported for the Tannery in 1977 are unusually high for any manufacturing establishment, the plant engineer told me that "last year, 1977, was our best year for safety— probably because people were more cautious after the accident."

"The accident," as everyone in the Tannery refers to it, shook up everyone involved and affected many more. For many workers it was a turning point in their consciousness about health and safety.

According to a Tannery foreman who was working nearby, it happened this way:

> The tannery had just instituted a new procedure. I can't remember whether the procedure was two or three days old when the accident happened. The new procedure called for a doubling of the sulfahydrate in the hides in the Beamhouse but they weren't supposed to be treated with acid in chrometan [the next department in the process]. On the first day the employee who was later killed was supervised and didn't add the acid [the way he did in the normal operation]. On the second or third day of the experiment the employee did not hang the new procedure on his clipboard. Instead he followed the old procedure—adding acid, which created enormous quantities of the poison gas and he was killed. The foreman in chrometan had told the worker the new procedure, *so if you're going to blame anyone you'd have to blame the [dead] employee himself for not following procedures* [emphasis added].

A mechanic who was twenty yards away from the accident when it happened gave this description:

> It never should have happened! The company didn't tag the operation as experimental and didn't post the new recipe. Furthermore, the worker who always adds the chemicals simply threw in the chemicals that were lined up for him to throw in—someone had lined up the chemicals wrong and included acid among the chemicals to be added. The worker who died simply added a chemical that was lined up for him. He died when he opened the trap door on the vat in order to add the next round of chemicals like he was supposed to.

I saw him open the door and saw him instantly collapse face down. Me and a guy I was working with began to run toward him. We smelled the rotten egg smell and recognized it as Hydrogen Sulfide gas. As maintenance men we had gotten a memo that explained the properties of Hydrogen Sulfide gas and sulfahydrate liquid. The memo was only written in five or six copies. Workers who weren't in maintenance didn't get it. We ran to the oxygen equipment. Meanwhile two other workers ran to help the guy who fell. One of them was heavy-set and panting hard when he got there—he collapsed instantly. We dragged two men away and gave them mouth-to-mouth but their skin was turning purple and they both had died.

Altogether five people were hospitalized from exposure to hydrogen sulfide fumes; two died and the other three recovered a few days later, apparently with no long-term side effects.

The local newspaper coverage of the accident reported that the Tannery management had given the following statement to the press:

The accident was not an error in formulation. It was the result of a "human being" dumping the wrong material in the huge drum used for removing hair from the hides.

The California Occupational Safety and Health Administration was called in to investigate the accident. It fined the company $915 for not giving the workers information about possible hazards and for not training workers in the use of emergency rescue equipment.

The incident shook up many people around the Tannery. The newspaper reported that some tannery workers were not satisfied with the safety measures at the plant. It quoted one worker who said: "They tell you to add this and to add that—they don't tell you what can happen or whether it's dangerous."

In response to the new uneasiness many workers were beginning to express after the accident, Tannery management acted swiftly. They had a special hydrogen sulfide gas alarm system installed in the chrometan area that would issue a warning siren when dangerous amounts of the gas were present. They also bought a portable gas tester that could check levels of hydrogen sulfide at any specific worksite. This had the effect of making most people at the Tannery believe that management was doing all it could to protect employees from a similar tragedy ever occurring again.

I was extremely surprised, therefore, when I found out (eighteen months after "the accident" occurred) that the hydrogen sulfide warning system in the Tannery had never been calibrated. This meant that the "safety equipment," which every person working in that area depended on, would go off in the presence of the gas—but no one could say at what level. When the assistant foreman in the area requested that the system be properly calibrated, management refused, claiming the $800 calibration tube required was too expensive. To make matters worse, the portable hydrogen sulfide gas tester, which was the backup protection for the larger system, proved to be an unreliable and inaccurate piece of equipment. Nothing was done to replace it even after the foreman working in that area issued formal complaints on several occasions.

Tannery management also cut corners with the emergency rescue equipment. One maintenance worker told me that the air supply equipment was so flimsy that the fire department representative who came out to train workers in its use said he "would never use it in a million years." The maintenance worker who had formerly been in charge of rescue operations in the Tannery told me he no longer had anything to do with the emergency air supply equipment because "I got in a hassle with John [the plant engineer] about not following OSHA regulations on them." When he had pointed out that there were many areas of the plant where an explosion or fire would prevent people from being able to reach an air pack (as the tanks were called), the company refused to buy any more equipment because the tanks cost a couple of hundred dollars apiece.

The "accident," and management's response to it represent three characteristic patterns in the way Tannery management routinely deals with health and safety issues. The patterns are (1) *blaming the victim for accidents*, (2) *cutting costs, often ruthlessly, in the installation and use of safety equipment*, and (3) *trying to make the workplace appear safe, without necessarily being safe*. In this way, management's response to health and safety can be interpreted as a conscious manipulation of the workforce and as a mechanism of social control meant to insure that workers continue to produce even under the most dangerous conditions.

These responses on the part of Tannery management are not unique. In fact, they are totally consistent with the industrial vision of safety that began to develop at the turn of the century and which continues to guide industrial safety practices in many industrial plants today.

MANAGEMENT CONTROL VERSUS WORKER HEALTH: SOME HISTORY

In 1906 serious work accidents reached a peak in the steel, railroading, and mining industries which were in the forefront of American economic expansion. One study of work accidents documented 526 work-related *fatalities*, more than one a day, for the year 1906–1907 in Allegheny County, Pennsylvania, alone.[5] At the time, industry and government sources agreed that the new class of immigrant workers were responsible for the high accident rate. This excerpt from a government report on mining accidents was typical:

> The responsibility for accidents rests in most cases with the men injured.
> . . . They know little or nothing of rock formations, of fire damp, of the
> properties of coal dust, and of the handling of explosives—matters about
> which every coal miner should be thoroughly informed. To determine
> whether a piece of slate or roof is or is not likely to fall often requires a

considerable degree of experience, and the majority of Slavs, Magyars, and Italians have not this experience. . . .[6]

Another way of interpreting this information would be to say that the deskilling of craft workers that took place in this industry in the late 1800s created a situation where the new mass-production workers no longer had the knowledge to protect themselves.

The impact of this deskilling process on worker health can still be seen today. In most modern work settings, the individual worker has little knowledge of, or control over, the total work process—not even enough to take the kind of precautions that he or she would normally take if placed in a potentially dangerous situation outside the workplace. The less knowledge and control workers have over the labor process, the more certain one can be that accidents will occur. In another sense these are not accidents at all but an inherent part of the capitalist labor process where workers no longer have the basic protection of controlling their own environment.

In this way the fatal accident that occurred at the Tannery can be viewed as historically specific. It could not have occured if it had not been for the deskilling that had taken place in the leather industry.

THE ROOTS OF MANAGEMENT SAFETY PRACTICES

At the turn of the century there was a growing anti-corporate sentiment in this country and labor was moving to organize in basic industry. Management, first in steel, then in other industries, began to experiment with new ways to simultaneously improve its public image, undermine worker resistance, and increase its control of the labor process. Aggressive public-relations campaigns, pension plans, stock subscription programs, as well as Taylorism and scientific management programs, were all part of this process.[7] So were the safety programs that began to proliferate at this time.

Facing organizing drives, an extremely high accident rate, and a negative public image, the United States Steel Corporation began a safety drive in 1906 that soon developed into a national movement. Judge Elbert Gary, chief executive of U.S. Steel promised his board of directors, "If you will back us in it, we'll make it pay."[8] Gary established safety committees to inspect each plant and make recommendations on possible improvements. In a move that anticipated the development of company unions several years later, Gary selected small numbers of workers to participate on those committees in many plants.[9] Several of the largest corporations in the country soon developed safety programs based on the model developed at U.S. Steel. Anticipating the introduction of state workmen's compensation laws, U.S. Steel then introduced its own compensation plan in 1910 with the provision that injured employees or their families received payment for job injuries, *irrespective of liability, unless they sued the corporation*. By 1915 every industrial state in the country had some type of workmen's compensation law along the lines of the U.S. Steel plan.[10]

As soon as the workers' compensation laws transferred the financial burden of industrial accidents from workers to management, industrial safety programs blossomed into a nationwide "Safety First" movement.[11] The focus was on warning against carelessness on the part of workers. Despite the fact that the large corporations were now ready to pay for industrial accidents (in exchange for not getting sued), they were not ready to assume moral responsibility for those accidents. In 1920 the Bureau of Safety of U.S. Steel claimed that 90 percent of the work accidents it had studied were caused by the inefficiency of the workers.[12] The insurance industry helped to create and develop the National Safety Council during this period. It quickly became industry's spokesperson on issues of industrial safety and remains so today.

During this period, the insurance industry laid the ideological groundwork for present-day management attitudes toward safety. (The ideology that workers cause accidents only began to develop *after* skilled workers had lost their control over the labor process.) In 1931, H. W. Heinrich of Travelers Insurance Company published what was to become a standard textbook of industrial safety.[13] First conceived in the early 1920s, *Industrial Accident Prevention: A Scientific Approach* has been reprinted in five editions, the latest in 1980.

Heinrich's contribution was to recognize that industrial safety is inextricably tied to control of the labor process. "Accident prevention," he wrote, "is both science and art. It represents above all other things, *control* of man performance, machine performance, and physical environment."[14]

Heinrich spent his whole career developing the argument that workers, not machines, are the main cause of accidents, with the corollary that management is also at fault for not controlling the actions of workers more closely. This is the basis for his four basic theorems that make up the "domino sequence of industrial accidents."

> These theorems show that (1) industrial injuries result only from accidents [note here that Heinrich completely ignores the whole issue of occupational diseases thay may be built into the labor process]; (2) accidents are invariably caused by unsafe acts of persons or by exposure to unsafe mechanical conditions; (3) unsafe actions and conditions are caused only by *fault of persons*; and (4) faults of persons are created by environment or acquired by inheritance.
>
> From this sequence of steps in the occurrence of accidental injury it is apparent that man failure is the heart of the problem. Equally apparent is the conclusion that methods of *control* must be directed toward man failure.[15]

Heinrich's theories became popular with industry because they provided another argument for consolidating management of the labor process, at a time when workers were actively resisting that control. His theories came on the heels of Fredrick Taylor's theories of scientific management and were received by management in much the same spirit. Taylor himself recognized safety as an essential aspect of industrial planning.[16] Heinrich's approach played down the acquisition of expensive equipment and the need to redesign the labor process to make it safe. Like Taylor, Heinrich emphasized instead that gains would come out of closer and closer control of every movement that workers make. He wrote:

> The causes of accidents are identical with the causes of inefficient production [and] the remedies are similar and may be applied by the same persons. Thus in the work of identifying and eliminating the causes of accidents, we are simultaneously improving industrial productivity.[17]

In other words, it is the capitalist's job to extract labor from workers; if the capitalist is at all lax in this process, workers will resist and cause production to be inefficient and accidents to occur.

Heinrich's theories were important for the insurance industry as well, because they provided a basis for intervening into the manufacturing process without pitting safety against profits. The focus was workers, not equipment.

Heinrich also aided the insurance industry immensely by establishing a clear demarcation between worker *safety*, which industry was prepared to assume the financial risk for, and worker *health*, which it was not. Chronic health problems caused by exposure to industrial toxins clearly do not fit into Heinrich's theorems, and it is on this basis that the insurance industry has actively fought compensation for occupational disease from exposure to silica, asbestos, and cotton dust. The theoretical demarcation between health and safety was so widely accepted that even today, all government OSHA offices are broken down into separate divisions for safety and health. Similarly, health and safety professionals are trained in either health or in safety, but almost never in both.

THE LIMITATIONS OF SAFETY IDEOLOGY

Today Heinrich's theories still form the theoretical basis for many of management (and insurance company) responses to occupational health and safety issues.[18] Heinrich's theories have survived, essentially intact, far longer than the principles of scientific management on which they were at least partially based. Nevertheless, workers' expanded conception of their basic rights as well as the rapid changes that have occurred in the labor process since World War II, now threaten management's ability to keep the lid on health and safety issues. As the split widens between the managers who plan work, and the workers who execute it, workers find it more and more difficult to accept the notion that management should organize and control the labor process but that labor should take responsibility for accidents.

In addition, the same technological breakthroughs that have been at the heart of American industrial expansion since World War II now threaten to explode the already delicate legitimation crisis that management is facing. The introduction of thousands of toxic chemicals like kepone, DBCP, and vinyl chloride into the lives of American workers without effective safeguards has created an epidemic of occupational and environmental disease. No one can predict the full impact of that epidemic; each new set of epidemiologic studies seems to identify new high-risk groups. The chronic diseases caused by toxic chemicals do not readily fit into the safety ideology that management has operated under for the past 50 years. In contrast to work accidents, it is extremely difficult to make workers accept the blame for chronic diseases caused by chemicals that they watched *management* introduce into the labor process.

In many ways the rigidity of the safety ideology created by the insurance companies accounts for the multiplying problems that industry faces in responding to health and safety challenges. The rest of this paper will focus on the contradictions and limits of management response to health and safety in the Tannery.

THE BREAKDOWN OF SAFETY IDEOLOGY
WITHIN THE TANNERY

Once a month the Tannery management, foremen, and the insurance company representatives meet in a nearby country club for lunch and a safety meeting. The insurance company reduces the Tannery's workers' compensation premiums for holding these meetings. During one of these meetings, the owner of the Tannery stood up and revealed management's real orientation to health issues:

> This safety thing can be exaggerated. There are always some people who are going to have bad reactions to a condition—for example, a rash. But if it's the condition and not the person, why doesn't everyone exposed get the rash? When people get scared about health and safety they start to run like a bunch of turkeys—and then they do something really stupid—and back themselves into a corner and get themselves in real trouble unrelated to the hazard they panicked over in the first place.
>
> Everyone assumes the Tannery is going to be dangerous so at the slightest thing they get hysterical. Every time I take a group of high school students around, at least two or three girls get hysterical and faint. And this health and safety thing is the same for the employees.

The Tannery spends a lot of money on workers' compensation insurance: over $400,000 a year. For this money the insurance company provides technical expertise in setting up a safety program and pays out all successful workers' compensation claims.

In one sense both the Tannery management and the insurance company have a financial stake in reducing occupational hazards so that compensation costs—either in premiums or as reimbursement—are minimized. Yet both management and the insurance carrier have distinct limits on how far they are willing to go in order to minimize those hazards. As I have tried to point out, management's goal is to minimize the amount of money spent on safety. The insurance company has to be very careful not to suggest "impractical" changes like purchasing or replacing major pieces of equipment or machinery that would be viewed as unnecessarily expensive. It also has to be careful not to suggest changes in the way work is done that might threaten management's prerogative of controlling the labor process. Ironically these constraints also prevent the insurance company from effectively spotting or challenging the most significant workplace hazards. This is one of the reasons why the Tannery has switched its insurance carrier several times during the last few years. Two different insurance companies represented the Tannery in the short period of time I worked there.

The first company had a three-pronged approach. Each month it presented management with a list of the previous month's accidents to review. It also gave management a 10 percent discount on the premium for holding monthly safety meetings among top management personnel and setting up a "workmen's committee" that submits monthly recommendations. (As far as I could tell, this second committee just existed on paper.) The insurance company also posted safety posters throughout the plant. These posters had the same clear message: workers—in particular, careless workers—cause accidents. Each major area of the shop had posters prominently displayed that admonished the people working there with slogans like "The Best Safety Device Is a Careful Man" or "Tools Don't Cause Accidents. It's How They Are Used." None of these approaches were particularly effective in reducing accidents, however.

The second company promised the Tannery a more aggressive approach in reducing accidents that was "especially designed to help reduce insurance and production costs and improve employee morale at the same time." This did not mean reorganizing the work to make it more safe. Instead (as the promotional literature proudly explained) it meant taking steps such as insisting that injured workers see an insurance-company doctor before seeing their own doctor, pressuring injured workers to return to work early, and making sure that disabled workers were immediately visited by an insurance company representative because "if we show that we are concerned about his welfare and answer any questions he might have, the injured employee is much less likely to turn to an attorney for advice, advice which ultimately costs management money."

In an attempt to control the rising accident rate the insurance company set up a process where foremen were held responsible for accidents in their department, on the theory that the foremen were in a position to control the labor process and reduce accidents. They weren't. The program did not cut the accident rate but did stir up a lot of resentment among foremen who saw themselves caught between management's constant production push on the one hand, and its lip service to safety on the other.

Unable to reduce accidents with any of these measures, the insurance company and the Tannery management initiated an employee "safety contest" with great fanfare. Every worker was rewarded with $5 worth of Safeway grocery coupons if his or her department had less than the usual number of lost-time accidents in a month. This had the effect of encouraging workers not to report "minor" injuries and pitting the injured workers against the people they were working with. (Someone with a slight back injury or cut might get pressured into ignoring the injury in order to have his or her department qualify for the coupons.) Although the number of actual accidents was not reduced, the contest did reduce the number of *reported* accidents each month. Yet in order to accomplish this, both management and the insurance company also exposed how shallow their commitment to improving health and safety conditions really is. As Woods, the Tannery plant engineer, stated, "No one at the Tannery has ever changed a procedure simply because of health and safety."

The huge discrepancy between the lofty way safety is discussed by management and the lowly place it really occupies in industrial planning creates a deep ambivalence in the people responsible for it. As Woods told me:

> The issue of health and safety is an emotional issue. The impact of seeing someone you work with lose a finger really can't be measured. . . . Ideally you'd want to spend as much time and money as was necessary on health and safety but if you did maybe you couldn't run a business.

Typical of the small decisions that affect worker health in the long run was the decision by Tannery management to start using sulfahydrate in liquid rather than dust form. The liquid form was cheaper and better suited for a semi-automated system that management had installed. Yet the liquid is much more dangerous because it always gives off small amounts of hydrogen sulfide gas, which has been shown to cause chronic lung disease.

The problem here, from management's point of view, is that workers begin to stop believing that management has their best interests at heart once the negative consequences of this type of decision ever become obvious.

Several different Tannery workers seemed to enjoy telling the story of the run-in with management over the new silicone treatment process. The Tannery was trying out a new way to treat and waterproof the hides with silicone and with perchloroethylene, which is the solvent dry cleaners use. Perchloroethylene is now suspected of being a cancer-causing substance.[19] The workers who were told to do the operation started to complain of headaches and dizziness, but Woods, the plant engineer, insisted the operation was completely safe. A few days later, Woods had the trailer which serves as his office moved further away from the operation because he was getting headaches. When the workers confronted him about moving the office, he again insisted the operation was completely safe. Then one worker asked: "If it is so safe, why does it say *Danger—Prolonged Exposure May Cause Death* on the drum it came in?" The company still refused to make changes in the operation, so the workers called OSHA in. OSHA measured the levels of perchloroethylene which were five times the highest allowable limit and made the company install some big fans. Soon after, the company discontinued the operation because it hadn't been worth it.

This incident and several other cases where the Tannery management skimped on safety equipment caused one of the union representatives to say, "When you tell me Woods says it is safe, I don't know what that means—sometimes it just means it's too expensive to fix it."

In order for control to be effective, workers have to believe in management's desire and ability to act in the worker's best interests. Yet, in a place like the Tannery, workers have to wonder whether managment is even *capable* of organizing the labor process in any way that does not put short-term cost-cutting as its immediate goal.

WORKERS' RESPONSE

Despite the dangerous working conditions at the Tannery and management's callous stance toward health and safety problems, the Tannery workers have not developed a collective way to fight for a safer workplace.

In part this is because many workers have—to a certain extent—accepted management's safety ideology. On several different occasions workers told me that the biggest hazard on their job was "people making stupid mistakes." When I would ask questions about whether production pressures or other management shortcuts ever forced mistakes Tannery workers often told me they didn't. One maintenance worker told me, "Sure, Lester [the owner of the company] cuts corners here and there—but then again, he is in business and doesn't do anything I wouldn't do if I were in his position." While discussing the "accident" and the hydrogen sulfide gas hazard at the Tannery, one worker told me: "The good thing about this Tannery is the ventilation," referring to the fact that the mixing area and parts of chrometan are outside. "If the mill had not been exposed, eight men instead of two might have died last year."

For some workers the dangers were so omnipresent that they became just part of the job. "There's no two ways about it, factory work is dangerous and factory work is boring," the union president told me philosophically after explaining how he had recently lost the end of his finger in a machine.

In addition to the many psychological factors that played into the situation, there were also several important structural reasons why Tannery workers had not collectively pushed for better health and safety conditions in the plant.

Management repression played a role in undercutting resistance. As one worker told me, "The company always tells you about all your benefits and medical coverage [for work-related injuries] but if you try to use it you won't get advanced. Most of the Mexican workers who work here have learned that if you are quiet, you rise quickly." Referring to Tannery workers' reluctance to push for better health and safety conditions, one militant worker in the union told me, "People working here know that there's only one other place in town—the Cement Company—that pays as well as the Tannery and they don't want to risk losing their job."

In most industries, having a union is a crucial protection for workers who want to improve their health and safety conditions. Yet as recently as last year the Tannery union was so weak that no union representative accompanied the OSHA people on their inspection of the plant after "the accident," or participated in the closing conference where the results of OSHA's investigation were reviewed.

According to Bob, the president of the union, the main reason for the weakness of the union even though it had been in the Tannery a long time was that "it was a company union. It's kind of a carrot and stick situation where they really have you by the balls—hanging all these rewards in front of you. Many of the union presidents (in the past) ended up being foremen. . . . I've been trying to make this a *real* union."

Yet in the area of health and safety, the union was doing very little. Bob told me that he thought that "health and safety really isn't an issue at the Tannery because the Company is quite safety-conscious and John is quite flexible about those issues." For the most part the union allowed the management safety committee and John Woods to set policy on health and safety issues. The parallel worker safety committee was entirely inactive as far as I could tell, simply a device for the company to get a discount on workers' compensation insurance. Bob explained to me that he was on the plant's safety committee but couldn't really say that he knew what was going on. He had not read OSHA's report on the silicone operation several weeks after it had been issued.

Racism played an important role in keeping the union weak. Attendance at union meetings was extremely poor. Nearly all those who came were white workers from the "dry-end departments." The union contract divides the workforce into three parts: the wet end, the dry end, and maintenance. The wet end of the plant includes the mixing and chrometan departments where the hides are first converted into leather. The dry-end departments involve finishing operations where the leather is cut, polished, and coated. Everyone in the Tannery acknowledges that the most tiring and dangerous work in the Tannery is performed in the wet end.[20] It is also the area of the plant where minority workers—predominantly Chicano, but also black, Vietnamese, and Portuguese—are concentrated.

The department (as opposed to plantwide) seniority system set up in the union contract greatly contributes to the racial division within the plant. As one Chicano worker in chrometan explained it to me, this occurs as a three-step process: (1) Because the work in the wet end is so hard and so dangerous, there is a high turnover rate there and a much lower turnover rate in the dry end. (2) Glad to be working in an area with other workers from the same ethnic group who speak their language, many of the minority workers initially assigned to the wet end do not want to move when their 90-day initiation periods ends. In contrast, at least half of the white workers initially assigned to chrometan apply to be transferred to the dry end at this time. (3) Minority workers who feel more comfortable after a period of time like a year, can only transfer to the dry end by forfeiting the seniority time they have accumulated.

The sharp division in the workforce, created in part by the seniority system, undercuts the union's strength in a cyclical fashion. The union fought for the issues most pressing to their primary constituents—workers in the dry end. For example, because the dry end was mostly a piecework system, the union fought hard to prevent the rates from being slashed or the piecework system abolished as management repeatedly threatened to do. For many dry-end workers, health and safety was a problem viewed as facing workers in the other end of the plant, and consequently health and safety issues were not pushed by the union. Yet the union's neglect of those same issues meant that wet-end workers had little incentive to join the union.

Despite the serious weaknesses that plagued the union, a rather remarkable understanding exists among some Tannery workers. One maintenance worker told me, "There are times when I think a condition is unsafe and I simply refuse to work in the area—I don't care what anybody tells me because it's not worth it."

Another production worker told me, "At the Tannery you don't have to do something if you don't want to." "What happens?" I asked. "Nothing, you just don't do it. Sure you get some pressure put on you but the union will step up for you." Another worker standing there said, "I remember when I refused to drive a heister [forklift] when the company said I had to even though it zig-zagged because the steering was all fucked up. You'd have to be pretty stupid to work with something you thought was dangerous."

In other words, some workers have individually established the right to refuse work they consider unsafe. Given management's insistence on controlling the labor process, this represents a considerable degree of resistance.[21] Despite the obvious weakness of the union, some workers feel confident in their ability to assert this right and get whatever backing they need from the union.

These acts of individual resistance are tolerated by the Tannery management for two reasons. First of all, if workers have the right to refuse unsafe work, they have to assume more responsibility if they get hurt doing work they agreed to do. For example, after Tannery management put in a fleshing machine that could handle a whole hide rather than half of a hide, there was a large jump in the number of back injuries because, rather than automatically station two people to handle the hides where before there had been one, it was left up to the individual worker's judgment whether he wanted more help with a particular hide (the hides vary from 50 to 150 pounds).

The one reason this refusal of unsafe work is acceptable to management is because it is an individual act. This was most graphically represented to men when the union president told me that he himself wouldn't operate the machine the black man working next to him was using. He explained that it had a chipped rotor and was therefore very dangerous. Missing was a sense of the union's collective responsibility for determining whether working conditions are safe. Nevertheless, management is walking on a dangerous tight rope when it tolerates individual worker resistance. Invariably the day will come when several workers will decide to walk off the job together.

After a longstanding dispute about the safety of the brakes on the mills that mix the chemicals (which half a dozen people work on at a time), the workers in that department, backed by the union, shut the operation down. One worker, particularly excited, told me:

> We locked the Mill out last week [and the owner] Lester, he went apeshit."

CONCLUSION

Health and safety issues are important because they constantly threaten to raise the issue of who controls the organization of the labor process.

Industrial safety has been used as a force to co-opt workers' concerns about the way their work is organized. Safety has been also used to focus attention on individual workers' responsibilities for accidents and to divert attention away from management's role in planning and directing the labor process.

At the same time management's refusal to take real responsibility for protecting workers' health—particularly for chronic health conditions—has opened the issue of whether worker control of the labor process is the only way workers can be assured that their health will be protected. This is particularly true because many of the technological advances industry has made since World War II have also carried new potential dangers for the people who work with them.

Occupational health issues have a tendency to affect large numbers of workers over long periods of time and therefore are potentially powerful issues to organize around. In contrast, occupational-safety issues are more often (though not always) focused on an individual worker, on an individual machine, for a brief moment. By battling out occupational health issues on the terrain of safety, management has been able to keep worker resistance individuated. Yet ironically, at the same time, management's refusal to take worker health seriously has left open the possibility that workers may collectively demand the knowledge and the power to design the labor process with their own needs in mind.

That possibility remains far in the future. In the meantime, current struggles to create active union safety committees[22] with the right to shut down dangerous work, and the right to know every chemical that is being used in the labor process, are small but significant steps in the long journey toward a democratic workplace.

NOTES

An earlier version of this paper was presented at a conference on the "Labor Process" at the University of California, Santa Cruz, in March 1980. I would like to thank Nancy Shaw and Jim O'Connor for their encouragement for doing this study and Hannah Creighton, Fred Block, Jim O'Connor, and the editors of *Radical America* for their helpful comments on earlier drafts. I also would like to specially thank Wendy Luttrell for her encouragement and critical comments throughout the project.

1. Andre Gorz, *Strategy for Labor: A Radical Proposal* (Boston, 1967), pp. 7–8.

2. Typical questions were: "What is a warning sign that an area where you work is so noisy you might be losing your hearing?"; "If you start to develop a skin rash, what should you do?"; "If you discover an unsafe condition while doing your job, what should you do?"

3. Tripactite Technical Meeting for the Leather and Footwear Industry. See *Report 1: General Examination of Social Problems in the Leather and Footwear Industry* and *Report 2: Effects of Technological Developments on the Occupational Structure and Level of Employment in the Leather and Footwear Industry* (Geneva, 1969).

4. U.S. Department of Health, Education and Welfare, *Good Work Practices for Tannery Workers*, DHEW Pub. (NIOSH) 76-157, (Washington, D.C., 1976).

5. Cited in Joseph Page and Mary O'Brien, *Bitter Wages* (New York, 1973), pp. 46–47.

6. Cited in Issac A. Hourwich, *Immigration and Labor* (New York, 1912).

7. Richard Edwards, *Contested Terrain: The Transformation of the Workplace in the Twentieth Century* (New York, 1979), pp. 90–111.

8. Page and O'Brien, *Bitter Wages*, p. 57.

9. David Brody, *Steelworkers in America: The Non-Union Era* (New York and San Francisco, 1969), p. 166.

10. Brody, *Steelworkers*, p. 167.

11. Ibid., p. 167.

12. Ludwig Teleky, *History of Factory and Mine Hygiene* (New York, 1948), p. 148.

13. H.W. Heinrich, *Industrial Accident Prevention: A Scientific Approach* (New York, Toronto, and London, 1950), p. 48.

14. Ibid., p. 1.

15. Ibid., pp. 1–2.

16. Ann and Herman Somers, *Workmen's Compensation: Prevention, Insurance, and Rehabilitation of Occupational Disability* (New York, 1954), p. 201.

17. Heinrich, *Industrial Accident Prevention*, p. 3.

18. In the preface of the 5th (1980) edition of Heinrich's book, Dan Peterson, a safety management consultant, and Nestor Roos, professor of insurance and director of safety management for the University of Arizona's Center for Occupational Safety and Health, write: "Few of us perhaps realize just how influential this book was. *It was and still is the basis for almost everything that has been done in industrial safety programming from the date it was written until today. Industrial Accident Prevention* was the only text in industrial safety that laid down principles: and those principles still guide practitioners today" (italics added).

19. "Causes of Death among Laundry and Dry Cleaning Workers," *American Journal of Public Health* 69 (1979): 508–510.

20. Work in the wet end involves continuous heavy lifting as the hides are loaded and unloaded in and out of huge mills where they are chemically treated. It also involves frequent exposure to various solutions of caustic chemicals, ammonia fumes, low levels (and potentially high levels) of hydrogen sulfide gas. It also involves continuous exposures to various chromate solutions that may very well be cancer-causing. See W.M. Gafafer, *Health of Workers in Chromate Producing Industry: A Study*, Public Health Service Pub. No. 192 (Washington D.C., n.d. [1950s]).

21. Although the Supreme Court ruled in favor of workers' right to refuse unsafe work in their Whirlpool decision last year, the impact of that ruling remains unclear on the shop floor. The issue is—what is considered an imminent danger that justifies workers refusal to work as opposed to an everyday hazard that can be worked out in normal management-labor negotiation. Every day these issues are raised in different types of workplaces all over the country and resolved according to the level of worker organization and strength in a particular workplace. Given the general weakness of the Tannery union, these incidents of refusing to work unsafe jobs seemed very bold.

22. Two key objectives of the COSH movement have been to give workers the right to know the substance that they are working with and to establish strong worker health and safety committees in every workplace. (COSH groups are coalitions of workers, unions, and professionals that now exist in some 15 or 16 geographic areas of the United States. Some of the largest COSH groups have over 50 local union sponsors.)

CHAPTER TWENTY

Workers' Control and the News: The Madison, Wisconsin, *Press Connection*

by Dave Wagner
interviewed by Paul Buhle

EDITOR'S INTRODUCTION

The Madison, Wisconsin, Press Connection *(1977–1980) was a worker-run newspaper started by striking employees of Madison's two dailies. Published at first as a weekly striking paper, in which editorial and production workers pooled their skills, the* Press Connection *evolved into a cooperatively owned daily which long outlived the strike. Shares were held by unions, other organizations, and individual supporters. Its peak circulation was 13,600, reached early in 1979. Always short on advertising and cash, the PC became an early victim of the current recession as it suspended publication in January 1980.*

THE *PRESS CONNECTION'S* ORIGINS

The leadership of the *PC* in its origins was provided by two groups. There were the leaders of the production unions under whose banner the newspaper strike (which led to the founding of the *PC* as a strike paper) was called; they were, for the most part, printers, pressmen, and mailers, men, white, mostly in their forties and fifties, union members from way back who were going through their first big strike. There were also the leaders of the editorial unions (one a local of the Newspaper Guild, the other an independent) who had come to union activism from a background in other struggles,

Revised version of an interview that appeared in Vol. 14, No. 4 (July-August 1980).

notably from the gay rights, feminist, and anti-war movements. Some of this group had been Vietnam veterans with anti-war sentiments (that was also true, by the way, of some of the leaders of the production unions) and others were just plain pissed off at the bosses' provocations.

Needless to say, there was tension between these two groups, at least on a few key issues. For the most part, however, for reasons I'll get into later, there was a remarkably strong feeling and practice of solidarity throughout the strike.

As for "community attitude," it is precisely the kind of phrase overindulged in by the *PC*; we never defined the "community," though we wanted to use the phrase to our advantage—usually it meant "the otherwise unspoken for" and referred to people in the inner city. It's a worthless euphemism, much like the use of the term "progressive" to mean "socialist." We used it despite the constant awareness that within the Madison "community" there were many thousands who supported former mayor Bill Dyke, who later became Lester Maddox' vice-presidential running mate. Madison is a bit schizoid.

Our practical reasons for trying to "organize the community" were, first, that many of us knew that our chances of stopping production at the struck plant were next to nil; and second, that we faced a tremendously difficult, always uphill battle to persuade many people who abhor racism, sexism, and imperial adventures that working people *as workers* have an equally universal cause. It's remarkable how some liberals can go into a St. Vitus dance of anxiety on this point when "liberal" union busters appear on the scene.

(It's also true that women and minorities, sometimes with the ready sneer that "unions never did anything for me," were among the first to cross the picket lines. We tried, sometimes with great difficulty, to explain to our own members that the long years of racial and sexual discrimination in the union were coming home to our roost. Not everyone understood. But we had to hammer away, even at one point printing in the strike paper a statement that the union leaders would not tolerate anti-Semitic, racial, or sexist epithets on the picket line. Some of the production craft people had enormous difficulty understanding why scabs could not be called by any epithet at hand. But they tried. One incident I will never forget occurred late one night when a particularly good-hearted but outraged pressman, who had been struggling for days to bite his tongue when a black security guard sailed through the line, finally could take it no longer. He stepped in front of the guard's car, leaned toward the windshield, and yelled, "You . . . Polak!" It was our turn to be bewildered. I hope someday to be able to write a short piece on "picket line culture," the stage on which workers put on masks to become themselves.)

As for labor struggles of the seventies, ours was the first definitive one in Madison with the exception of a brief but important teachers' strike in 1976;

our main job, through the *PC*, was to explain our own story and to give as much support as we could to the many other unions that began to hit the pavement soon after we did. Because we had defined ourselves, fitfully at first but with more and more clarity, as a feminist paper, we were able to play a rather more active role than usual in supporting nurses in a threatened citywide strike. When the cab companies conspired to boot out their union (for the third time in a decade), we were in a unique position to support the unions, expose the often illegal finagling of their former bosses, and encourage their effort to found a worker-run cab company of their own. We were able, in our opinion columns and in our news pages, to give unique coverage to the teachers' contract battles; they not only trusted us, their locals bought a great many shares in our cooperative, and of all the unions were most sympathetic to our insistence that labor struggles were part and parcel of sexual, racial and political issues. Our biggest failure was with the meatcutters' strike. Well over 2,000 workers at a local meatpacking plant walked out for the first time in Madison history (they too were provoked by layoffs), but their leadership was dominated by the members of the old guard at the central labor council with whom the *PC* regularly crossed swords. Though we gave the meatcutters as much supportive coverage as we could, we had a sense that it was not entirely welcome. More than anything except the dramatic mayoral election—which found the new and old guards bitterly split—this strike showed the extent to which our political notions about unionism were not universally shared by Madison unionists.

Like many other folks around the country in the seventies, we cast about to find whatever *local* history and tradition of resistance might be useful. In Madison that tradition was the Progressivism of Old Bob La Follette. One of the papers we had struck (my old employer, the *Capital Times*) had once been the organ of the Progressive Party; our line was that the paper had drifted far away from its founding principles and that our own paper would try to refresh that honored Wisconsin tradition.

We were certainly not unaware of the contradictions within the history of the Progressive movement, and indeed they were pointed out to us often by our socialist readers. (Madison has, judging from certain election returns and subscription lists, about 6,000 Socialists.) But it was the only foundation at hand; in Milwaukee, we could have conceivably plugged into the old Socialist Party tradition, but there was no history of that—no ethnic base, for that matter—in Madison. Since our strike was fundamentally a strike against a larger corporate newspaper chain, namely Lee Enterprises out of Iowa, it made sense to fight along anti-corporate lines. For one thing, like all newspapers we had to rely on display advertising, and the old Progressive inclusion of small businesses within the anti-corporate struggle made sense for us financially. We never denied the *PC*'s self-interest here, but by the end it became evident that the line we had established at the beginning for economic reasons was politically justified. We became acutely aware of the difficulties small businesses have in finding credit, competing with the huge cash reserves of corporations, and otherwise finding a niche in an economy dominated by only 500 corporations. Those small businesspersons who understood our position gave us extraordinary support—in part, of course, because our rates were extraordinarily low. The larger businesses boycotted us consistently; since the 1940s, newspapers have been unable to survive on the small-business trade alone.

We tried, then, to forge together labor activists, feminists, small businesspeople, community organizers (the latter on issues such as school closings and property speculation), the poor, the Left (from the electoral to the cultural activists), students, and blacks (though the last two were most indifferent to our efforts) into a broad-based front against the reactionaries who were putting their own quiet agenda back on the table in Madison. While the *PC* was fresh and kept its quality up, the coalition held. Later, because of certain mistakes on our part, including the occasionally necessary abrupt criticism of elements in one's own coalition, and because of a decline in quality derived from staff attrition and economic realities—not to mention a string of serious political defeats for the Left in general—the coalition wavered.

It is a vastly different undertaking to attempt to build a "counter-economy" in a city rather than a "counterculture" on a campus. In printing defenses of the small businesses' struggle on the one hand and occasional teeth-gritting screeds from Left sectarians on the other, we tried to open up our pages as a wide-open forum. At the same time, we tried to encourage the notion that, as the economy continued to decline, a broad national coalition (based in local struggles) would have to emerge at some point, and that activists would eventually have to accept economic, job-oriented analyses as a common starting point for everyone.

It was this kind of thinking that led us to embrace with such enthusiasm the founding of the Progressive Alliance in Detroit, to which we gave extensive on-the-spot coverage. In retrospect, it seems clear that the cautions given in *Radical America* about that organization (which, by the way, were useful in our editorial meetings) were correct. But at the time it was the only game in town—and one we desperately needed in our constant search for national tendencies we could plug our readers into. (I'm convinced, by the way, that at some point there will be a wave of leftist dailies in the U.S.—but not until there is a movement that will provide the core of the news; a newspaper, especially a daily with its constant need for copy, becomes shrill in isolation, tries to create as much as to interpret the news, and runs the risk of simply becoming a "better" liberal paper than the liberals put out. We were a few years too early.)

In the meantime we found that cooperative ownership of a newspaper can create unusual pressures both editorially and politically. We were self-managed to a remarkable degree, but we had owners as well. Each single-issue group had its own idea of what the *PC* should become and which issues it should feature; many of them bought membership in the co-op, not only to demonstrate support but to have a say in our policies. So the editors were often called on the carpet in an office meeting when the paper deviated a jot or a tittle from the established line. It was not like a traditional newspaper where the editors condescend to deal with a small group the paper doesn't really need; these were most often comrades as anxious to keep *their* paper from embarrassing itself as they were determined to keep it pointed resolutely in the right direction.

If we tried to keep the labor orientation as editorial ballast, we were still pulled in many different directions by the coalition members who were also owners. For that matter, political divisions emerged within the staff toward the end. Two incidents occurred in the fall of 1979 that seemed to sum up the experience of the *PC* at its best and worst, things we continue to chew on in this strangely reflective time that follows several years of manic activity.

The first was our decision to publish a letter, banned elsewhere by the Justice Department, purporting to describe the "secrets" of the H-bomb. The day after we published the letter the government dropped its case against the *Progressive* magazine. It was a big moment for the *PC* as a newspaper, and there was a sense of victory. It was the vindication of co-op ownership and workers' control in the sense that all the privately-owned papers had refused to defy the government even in the name of First Amendment rights—rights which we of course harped on at symphonic length, and rights which for once were deposited in the hands of editors unhampered by a corporate board. (We were sometimes criticized by Leninists and others for thumping for the First Amendment, which they felt was a bourgeois civil liberty; our attitude was that bourgeois civil liberties were only the beginning of what will someday be demanded. . . .)

The second incident, which occurred only two weeks later, was grimmer. It began when a Milwaukee-based anti-abortion group plastered Madison with billboards that carried a photo of a three-month-old baby and the bizzare slogan, "Kill her now, its murder; six months ago, abortion." It was, to say the least, provocative. A reporter and a photographer were assigned to do a story. The reporter was thorough enough to find and write that defacements of the billboards were covered by the owners' insurance. Within days a spontaneous, systematic defacement began.

Then came a key move from the anti-abortion group. "If you're so high and mighty on the First Amendment," they said to the *PC*, "you will print a full-page ad of ours that reproduces the billboard and argues for our right not to have them defaced." The ad read, "Their bomb and our baby."

Question: should we print a full-page ad which we found nauseating? If we did, the pro-abortion groups in our coalition would, they told us, be upset enough to picket the *PC*. The ad would be an insult to women, in particular those women who had had abortions (by implication they were being called murderers) and we would be putting an opportunist interpretation on the First Amendment by claiming that anyone had the right to buy space in the paper. That's the way the straight press does it, they pointed out, but the PC shouldn't be like the straight press.

If we refused to run the ad, it would kick out from under the paper one of its editorial pillars; once we set ourselves up as arbiters of free speech (by denying access to the public prints) we would more or less be conceding to the Justice Department's case that "in some cases" these rights should be abridged. We had exposed ourselves to $10,000 in fines and ten years in prison each to deny that. If we backed down when the issue was reversed we would, some staff members felt, be victims of "ideological blackmail."

The dilemma, as it turned out, was resolved, or rather unresolved, in the worst and most destructive way possible. The decision to run the ad was in the jurisdiction of the general manager, who was determined to run it. Meanwhile, the editor and editorial board (whose authority was then in doubt because of a missed election) decided to run a same-day editorial attacking the ad. The general manager opposed the editorial on the grounds that same-day opinionating was "unprofessional" and reported the matter to the board of directors on the evening of publication. The board decided in favor of simultaneous publication of the ad and the editorial, but when that decision was reported to the general manager he refused to go along with it. As a result the ad ran alone, pickets appeared in front of the *PC* offices, and the editorial belatedly ran the following day.

It was a stalemate. Something cracked inside the paper at that moment. The board could not fire the general manager without inviting serious turmoil inside the staff, where he had the strategic support of some people who felt that the paper was failing economically because it was "too far to the left." The issue was never resolved to anyone's satisfaction, the lines of authority were never reestablished, and the tension between self-managment and cooperative ownership intensified without there being time to make it a productive conflict. By the time the annual shareholder's meeting rolled around, at which 500 people were present and voting, the only serious issue that remained was the financial crisis that made it necessary to close down the paper.

PC's political direction was formed by the new and sometimes strange combinations of forces at work on it. I think it will be some time before we draw the right lessons from the mistakes or from the victories.

WORKERS' CONTROL IN ACTION

There is absolutely no doubt that without the twin principles of workers' control and pay parity the *PC* would never have lasted the 27 months from October 1977 to January 1980.

But first let me give you a picture of how it worked. When we began as a strike weekly, the presidents of the five unions appointed workers in each of their ranks who had the widest respect as skilled and diligent craftspersons (as opposed to political officers in the leadership who were often better talkers than workers). These production leaders were pulled together into a Production Council which I was asked to chair (because of experience in the sixties in production problems when I worked in the underground press). Once a week, sometimes twice, we met and hammered out logistical problems. For the most part no one in the council had the slightest idea of the mysteries of the other crafts, and so democratic decision-making was absolutely unavoidable—it was the only process that could possibly have worked under the circumstances. These weekly meetings, for me, were the most exciting part of the strike. The mutual respect, the rounds of congratulation to individual workers and crafts for difficult jobs well done under impossible circumstances, the unquestioning trust in each other as skilled workers— here was the culmination of years of dreams and theories. Hell yes, it worked, and it continued to work all through the paper's history. Over the months the walls of mystery were gradually battered down until workers in each department had fairly clear ideas of the problems and work tempos of adjacent departments; this was invaluable for the larger meetings involving all the workers, where political discussions were not allowed to become abstracted too much from the practical limitations of production.

Pay parity was the complement to workers' control. All through the paper's history the weekly paycheck (except, later on, those of the advertising reps who worked on commission) remained the same for each worker. It avoided the resentments that could have torn the paper apart within six months. (Of course, the size of the paycheck was so small that it more or less guaranteed equality in self-exploitation. As the old strikers left us one by one, we became more familiar with the *external demands of the labor market* on the pay scales. I doubt that the principle could have held forever. Yet without it, we never could have lasted 27 months).

These two principles worked soundly for the internal politics of the paper. The only alternative would have been massive infusions of money at the very start—enough showing up in our paychecks that we should forgo participation, that is, business as usual. But there were two unresolved problems.

Toward the end we found that the pay was too low to hold skilled workers, despite the fact that the majority held on as long as they could. They were replaced, at first, by people with little experience but with a strong political commitment to the experiment. But some people also showed up who were completely unskilled, who had little work experience of any sort, no understanding of union rules (which were the cornerstone of workers' control from the beginning), and little experience in large organizations. They worked in the circulation and advertising departments, and what we had was a kind of lumpenization of the workforce on those departments. Never has that class distinction been made clearer to me, or with more pain. These new people lacked discipline, performed erratically, refused to analyze financial information, and would not respect collective decision-making. The youth culture of the sixties (ah, roots!) has become, no doubt because of its classless and utopian spirit, a nostalgic refuge for those who not only will not but cannot hold a job, or, rather, cannot *do* work. The Black Panthers' paper in the sixties and Madison's *Take Over* in the seventies glorified the "lumpen" consciously, with arguable points. No one but the sectarians has bothered to dispute these points, because discretion has become the better part of politics.

The other problem was that neither the financial leaders (including me) nor the other workers made an effort to democratize financial skills. Workers' control will, I am convinced, be impossible until schools carry mandatory courses on the basic categories of the balance sheet. Workers simply must be able to distinguish between balance sheets, financial statements, pro forma budgets, and cash budgets—and be able to interpret them. For me the process of decipherment was difficult enough (I spent two years on the *PC* board of directors); we never should have democratized that process without spending many long hours of catch-up at the expense of production (which, in a daily paper, has its own fierce schedules).

Finally, while workers' control and pay parity worked for a long time, the losses in the business end forced the paper over time to tie itself more and more dependently to credit institutions and contractors, until the space for financial maneuvering shrank to a narrow corridor indeed. In that situation workers sometimes had difficulty understanding the priorities assigned to incoming revenues.

Our effort to build a "countereconomy" in Madison got nowhere (except in our help to the worker-owned cab company); many more building blocks will have to be in place for that to appear on the scale we imagined. Even then we will have to be particularly careful that we are not simply creating an economy of the poor and for the poor, relieving in the process a considerable social burden from the corporations and the government.

I am satisfied that the actual work and the production schedules remained firmly in the hands of workers in each department, though the direction of that work was usually in the hands of the Production Council. That body, after the paper was sold by the unions to the workers and then to cooperative shareholders, (eventually about 800 of them), came to be made up of the elected heads of each department. They in turn were supervised by three assistant managers, who were elected by the workforce at large. The only member of management who was not elected was the general manager, who was appointed by the board of directors (they, of course, were elected by the co-op members, or shareholders). It was a balance between workers' control and community control; some of the ideas of Gar Alperovitz went into the board's discussions about achieving that balance.

In an essay, historian David Montgomery refers to a *PC* worker who said, with regard to a seminar he attended on workers' sharing in decision-making, that he found the seminar irrelevant because people at the *PC* saw no need for "management participation." That remark came comparatively early in the experience. At that point "management" referred to the old bosses at the struck plant. Eventually we did develop a management of our own. By the end only one of the three elected managers remained; they were replaced by "acting" managers who, under the pressure of business, were clearly perceived as the only persons with the required specialized skills—particularly in the business office. We folded the paper shortly before the next round of elections, so the problem of succession was never met in practice.

Some workers felt that workers' control had become something of a charade. That feeling ranged from a few disciplined workers who saw no need for department heads, elected or not, to the group of marginal workers that continually lost political struggles because of naivete or lack of organizing experience.

Similarly, among the old guard of original strikers, particularly in the production crafts, workers' control was felt to be too "ideological" and unnecessary; the printers (International Typographical Union) clung to their union control of production to the end.

Each department had a Workers' Council for matters of discipline, hiring and firing. In the craft departments they remained largely unused because union committees had identical functions; some departments were too small to need them. Only the editorial department really made use of it, and it proved to be particularly valuable; we found that elected workers took their tasks very seriously and had a moral authority, particularly in matters of discipline, that often allowed them to be more stringent in their decisions than the elected management could afford to be.

It's true that workers' control is not always efficient, at least in the short run. Internal political questions seemed to erupt from time to time into a crisis in which the various elected bodies and leaders would redefine their roles and authority to achieve every imaginable parliamentary advantage. Periodically resentments and latent struggles, often around a symbolic issue, would come to a real boil. For days production efficiency would be compromised by caucuses, organizing, and lobbying as the lines of the various splits formed. But once the issue was resolved there was a general feeling that the unspoken had been uttered and that deep-seated wounds which in other work circumstances would have been allowed to fester had been revealed in what some of us came to call "labor theater"—and production would then return to a higher level of efficiency than before. In the long run, I am convinced, these political passion plays—in which everyone had lines to deliver, poses to strike, and quite often sound arguments to make—are inextricable parts of the way workers' control will look in the future. Once these rain storms passed, the air in the office was usually remarkably invigorating. I only wish we had had many more years to see how the process developed. If the form was theatrical, the content, until the end, remained rational; I was never disappointed by it, anxieties of the moment aside.

THE *PRESS CONNECTION* AND THE UNIONS

When our strike hit the city in October 1977, the Madison Federation of Labor was a moribund organization, dominated by the building trades and run by an out-and-out business unionist. The first electoral challenge to his leadership, organized by the public employees two years earlier, had been crushed outright. A month after the *PC* went down the tubes the same man was reelected, after a challenge by the same group, by a margin of only about 55 to 45 percent. The failure of the building trades and the business unionists to support *any* strike effort in the preceding two years, along with steady hammering by the *PC*, changed the atmosphere. I have no doubt that the old guard will be thrown out next year. Unfortunately, the Federation has precious little power in any case; it will be largely a symbolic victory, I think.

But this same strain between business-unionist and insurgent tendencies seems to exist all around the country. Clearly something will have to give within the next decade.

I fully expect that, once the insurgents consolidate their gains by the middle eighties, the building trades hereabouts will withdraw, either formally or informally, from the Federation. I also expect to see new kinds of associative bodies spring up in which the CIO-oriented unions from the AFL-CIO will sit down with insurgent Teamsters and UAW members.

Who knows what may lie beyond that? Getting that far will be the fruit of 15 years of struggle. But I do know from my experience at the *PC* that there are many, many articulate and committed veterans of the sixties and seventies who are only awaiting an opening. It could all happen very rapidly, depending on how the issues develop and at what tempo. Time is on the side of the insurgents.

CHAPTER TWENTY-ONE

The Past
and Future
of Workers' Control

by David Montgomery

To speak of workers' control in America is difficult, because little of the theory of the workers' control movement came out of this country. American experience forces us to begin with the world of practice, and then to probe some of the ideological implications of that practice. In fact, American workers have waged a running battle over the ways in which their daily work and the human relations at work were organized over the last century, and in the process they have raised issues which go far beyond the confines of "wage and job consciousness" or "bread and butter" unionism, into which historians have long tried to compress the experiences and aspirations of American workers.

What does "workers' control" mean? Perhaps the best way to answer the question is to begin with consideration of its opposite: the separation caused by industrial capitalism between those who direct the work to be done and those who carry out the directions. This separation is rooted in two of the most fundamental characteristics of our economic order. The first is that the historical evolution of capitalism involved a concentration of productive power in collective forms on a scale never before dreamed of. Production became a group activity, and the groups involved have typically become larger and larger over the last century and a half. Moreover, as production has become more collective in form, the technical knowledge

Reprinted from Vol. 13, No. 6 (November-December 1979).

which guides that activity has correspondingly become separated from the actual carrying out of the work. It has increasingly become codified in the form of engineering of scientific knowledge, which is in the heads of specialists hired by the owners to manage the works, rather than in the heads of the workers themselves. This process appeared in manufacturing even before the development of high level machine technology, and it has continued on ever rising levels since the emergence of factories, reaching its highest peak in today's automated firm. Science and technology themselves have been appropriated by capital and confront ordinary working people as alien, inanimate, hostile forces.

The second fundamental characteristic of our economic life is that the bottom line in determining what production methods are to be used and what is to be produced is neither the quality of working life nor the utility of the articles created, but rather the profitability of the enterprise. What is quintessential in capitalism is not simply its historically unique manner of turning out unprecedented quantities of goods, but also that the production of goods is not the basic motive of those who own and direct the factories. The production of profit is their basic motive. Thus how we work and what we are producing are both determined by standards of profitability, accumulation, and cash flow—not by the standard of making life more satisfying during our brief stint on this earth. This distinction was neatly identified by Carter Goodrich, when he wrote in his classic study of coal miners' control struggles in 1926:

> It is often said that modern society has chosen efficiency in production rather than richness of working life. [In actual fact,] society makes no choices as such, and the countless individual decisions out of which have come mass production as efficient as that at Ford's and jobs as dull as those at Ford's have most of them been made without the slightest reference to the quality of working life that would result. . . . They are made on the basis of figures of output and cost and profit for the immediate business in the immediate future.[1]

Goodrich's book appeared at a moment in history when the struggle for workers' control over the methods and purposes of industrial production was more explicit, articulate and widespread throughout the capitalist world than at any other time in history, the period around the end of World War I. That period in the United States deserves close attention, but first it is necessary to examine its historical background. For half a century before that epoch there had been much in the daily practice of American workers to challenge the notion, which we encounter everywhere today, that no modern industrial society could possibly function *without* the two attributes of capitalism I have identified: the separation of direction from production and the dominance of profit accumulation over the creation of useful goods and services.

In the late nineteenth century American industry contained pockets of extensive control over productive processes exercised by groups of skilled workers. It is important to speak precisely here, so as not to give the impression that in some "good old days" the two basic attributes of industrial capitalism did not apply. That is not the point. The point is that even within that system numerous and important groups of skilled workers were able to assert their collective control over those portions of the production process that fell within their domain.

Skilled craftsmen then brought into the workplace characteristics which enabled them to challenge their employers, often successfully, for control over the direction of their own work and that of their helpers, and to some extent over what was being made. The first of these characteristics was simply their knowledge of the production processes. The puddling of iron, the blowing of window glass, the cutting of garments, or the rolling of steel was not learned in school or taught to the workers by their employers. It was rather learned on the job in ways which gave the craftsmen a knowledge of what they were doing that was far superior to that of their employers. No one was more keenly aware of this relationship than the "father of scientific management," Frederick Winslow Taylor. He believed that the first step in systematizing management was for the employers to learn what their skilled workers knew and did, in other words, to study the skilled tradesmen and expropriate their knowledge.

But the control struggles of the late nineteenth century cannot be explained by craft workers' knowledge alone. That technical knowledge was embedded in a moral code governing behavior on the job, a code which was not individualistic, but one of mutuality, of the collective good. Part of this code on all but the most highly seasonal jobs was a clearly determined stint, or level of output, that any decent member of the trade would not exceed. The violator of that code was condemned as a hog, a runner, a chaser, a job wrecker, or some other such choice epithet. To go flat out for oneself was simply dishonorable behavior. So was any action by which one worker connived against or "undermined" a fellow worker on the job. This code of mutuality was as important to the collective direction of the job as was the craftsman's knowledge, and it was often embodied in the work rules of unions. In fact, it is in those union rules that the most explicit formulations of the craftmen's ethic are to be found.

One of the most elaborate sets of work rules from the period was by the window glass blowers, gatherers, cutters, and flatteners, who belonged to Local Assembly 300 of the Knights of Labor. They provided, among other things, that blowers should not work at all from June 15 to September 15, when the heat of the glass furnace was hard to bear. Only after the union was defeated by mechanization did summer glass-making become routine. The rules also specified that "no blower or gatherer shall work faster than at the rate of nine rollers per hour, excepting in the case of rollers falling off, or pipes breaking." The "standard size of single strength rollers" was fixed at "45 × 58 to cut 38 × 56." In other words, it was the union that standardized the size of windows in late nineteenth-century America. Poor glass, absenteeism, and drinking which interfered with production were punished by union fines. To help secure obedience to union rules and to decisions of the shop committees, the foremen were obliged to belong to the union and submit to its discipline.[2]

The important point is not just that these rules were elaborate, but that they embodied a moral code for which glass workers were prepared to fight. Consider this description from *John Swinton's Paper* in 1884 of the strike which ensued when the employers tried to compel blowers to produce more than the 48 boxes of glass per week prescribed by their union. The language of the report reveals clearly what glass blowers thought of themselves and of their rules.

> The last fight of the manufacturers was made on the "forty-eight box limit." The reduction of wages was only the excuse. This is no secret. How the high-rolling manufacturer did splutter over this! His gouty limbs stumbled across it, and he broke his grip. He knew that if the limit was taken off, the men could work ten or twelve hours every day in the week; that in their thirst for the mighty dollar they would kill themselves with labor; they would "black sheep" their fellows by doing the labor of two men; they would employ apprentices innumerable to help them through; in their individual reach for that which governs the country [the dollar], they would ruin their association. The men said no. They thundered out no. They even offered to take a reduction that would average 10 per cent all around, but they said, "We will keep the forty-eight box limit." Threats and curses would not move them to make more than forty-eight boxes of window glass a week, and finally, in despair, the grasping dollar-lover gave way and said, "Keep it and be d____d." They have it still and they won't be damned by any but their employers.[3]

Two aspects of this late nineteenth-century experience should be emphasized. First, even in the setting of modern technology and large-scale production it was possible to have collective direction of the way in which jobs were performed. Moreover, such direction required not only a struggle against management's efforts to control the work, but also a rejection of individualistic, acquisitive behavior. The practical and ideological aspects of this contest were inseparable from each other.

Second, this control by the crafts was the primary target of attack for managerial reformers in the early twentieth century. Scientific management—which might properly be described by paraphrasing today's language, as a systematic job impoverization program—emerged out of a drive, evident in every advanced industrial country as corporate enterprise waxed larger and international competition grew more intense at the turn of the century, to increase labor productivity. In England, France, Germany, and this country there were innumerable experiments with incentive pay schemes, designed to entice workers into going flat out for the almighty dollar, or mark, or franc. Frederick Winslow Taylor entered the debate at precisely that level with his paper, "A Piecework System." Taylor's message, however, was that tinkering with pay systems would not solve the problem. It was necessary, he argued, to go to the root of the problem: to expropriate the workers' knowledge and to subvert his moral code. Only then could pay schemes serve as incentives to higher output. The instrument which he and his fellow engineers devised for acquiring mastery over the craftsmen's skills was time and motion study. Through such studies, methods of working could be standardized and presented to the workers as orders from the engineering and planning departments.

Nobody carried these developments farther than Henry Ford, who was in the unique position, when he opened his Highland Park plant in 1914, of being able to produce some thousand cars a day without a storage yard. Virtually all of them were sold to dealers the day they came off the line. Ford's engineers were able to devise not only thoroughly standardized production tasks for each of the plant's 15,000 employees, but also extraordinarily specialized machine tools, each of which did just one operation in the fabrication of a single part for the eventual Model T. The plant was also filled with assembly lines, big and small, where components were fashioned, all leading to the final assembly line. In their thorough study of the Ford works, Arnold and Faurote reported that the company had no use for experienced workers. It preferred machine tool operators who had nothing to unlearn, "who have no theories of correct surface speeds for metal finishing, [but] will simply do what they are told, over and over again, from bell-time to bell-time."[4] To run a factory with such operatives Ford also had to have a splendidly equipped tool room, where 270 skilled workers, for whom nothing was "scamped or hurried," created the tools, jigs, and equipment needed by the production hands to carry out their work. Last but hardly least, the company employed an enormous supervisory staff. Everywhere scientific management was introduced, it required a vast proliferation of supervisors. In Ford's machine shops alone 510 overseers of one type or another had the authority to fire any operative. Arnold and Faurote's figures suggest that in early 1914 they averaged almost a firing a day apiece.[5]

The pioneers of scientific management attacked the ideology of the craftsmen, as well as their knowledge. The workers' moral code was contemptuously labelled "soldiering," and their pretentions to directing their own daily tasks were denounced as dangerous folly. The "man who is fit to work at any particular trade," wrote Taylor, "is unable to understand the science of that trade without the kindly help and cooperation of a man of a totally different type of education."[6]

Conversely, craftsmen resisted Taylor's innovations on both the practical and the ethical level. The introduction of time study, standardized work procedures, and incentive pay encountered dogged resistance, especially among metal workers. That resistance cannot be discounted as simple conservatism or "Luddism." A machinist at the Rock Island arsenal, Hugo Lueders, was asked if he objected to the planning of production. He replied: "The men would very readily welcome any system. They want it bad." Like so many workers today, Lueders saw nothing desirable in slipshod management. But he added quickly, "As far as having a man stand back of you and taking all the various operations you go through, that is one thing they do not care for."[7]

Lueders's hostility to time study and standardization was evidently shared by many other workers. When someone in his arsenal was seen measuring a planer in a way that suspiciously suggested that he was making measurements for standardized clamps and bolts, he was ostracized, and other machinists demanded his instant discharge. At the Watertown arsenal the molders agreed among themselves that, if a stopwatch showed up in their department, all of them would cease working. When time-study men did appear at the American Locomotive works in Pittsburgh, the company had been careful to negotiate a prior agreement with the unions, but the workers assaulted the time-study men and drove them from the plant. The same workers also scornfully rejected incentive pay. American Locomotive had followed a common practice of Taylor's disciples, designed to circumvent workers' animosity toward incentive pay: they divided their employees' pay into two envelopes, one containing the standard hourly rate and the other any premium which a worker had earned. This device was designed to make any individual's acceptance of the new pay plan "voluntary." At American Locomotive, however, workers made a bonfire of the incentive pay envelopes, and the reforming manager left Pittsburgh to try his hand elsewhere. Meanwhile at the Norfolk Navy Yard the mere appearance of time clocks had provoked a general walkout and a union rally in protest, and at Starrett Tool in Athol, Massachusetts, workers passed a whimsical resolution to treat time clocks simply as part of the furniture.[8]

Terms like "Sodom and Gomorrah" and "Pandora's Box," which numerous letters to the editor of the *Machinists' Monthly Journal* applied to Taylorized workshops, revealed the depth and pervasiveness of the feeling in the craft that scientific management was not only a threat to workers' livelihoods, but also morally outrageous. And the machinists' contempt for "the kindly help and cooperation" being offered them by men "of a totally different type of education" was captured in a poem, which Dennis O'Shea wrote for his union's journal in 1908. O'Shea was inspired by the often repeated statement of Carl Barth, designer of the twelve-variable slide rule for calculating machine speeds and feeds, that he dreamed "sometimes in between work and sometimes at night . . . that the time will come when every drill press will be speeded just so and every planer, every lathe, the world over, will be harmonized, just like the musical pitches are the same all over the world."[9] O'Shea depicted Barth's dream this way:

> The demonstrator sat in his easy chair,
> And as he smoked his cigar dreamed a dream so fair,
> In the haze of the rings of smoke he blew,
> A picture he saw of which I'll tell you:
> In fancy he saw a building grand
> Of which he was in supreme command;
> There were lathes and planers and milling machines, too;
> Of wheel presses and bolt cutters there were quite a few;
> Horizontal and vertical mills by the score;
> Of slotters and shapers a great many more.
> While the shop—my, what a marvelous place!
> Men moved like as though they were running a race.
> And he thought of what a great change he'd wrought
> Since he the other machinists had taught
> To do their work so quick and fast
> And not to be loafing over their task,
> But make all the money for the company, then
> They'll be treated like cattle instead of like men.

O'Shea continues by contrasting the new lust for speed with his trade's traditions of quality production.

> And he smiled as he thought of the old slow way
> When a man would turn up one axle a day.
> First he'd center it up so good and true,
> Then take a roughing cut or two,
> And a finishing cut so nice and fine,
> And then roll the bearings to make them shine,
> Square up the ends, then make the fits,
> Take it out of the lathe, and that was it.
> But just look how he had changed this way—
> A man had to do twelve of them now a day.
> They simply wheel them into the lathe,
> Turn the whole thing up in one might shave,
> Throw it out again and then it was done,
> And the lathe man would say, well, that's going some.

The same contrast is repeated through different departments of the plant. But the poem ends in a delightfully unexpected way, by portraying the "demonstrator" as an offender against working-class morality and as hopelessly outclassed in technical knowledge by those to who he is issuing commands.

So his thoughts ran along in this beautiful way,
And in fancy he could hear the directors say,
You're such a good man to keep down the pay
We have decided to raise yours twenty dollars a day . . .
Alas at this point the telephone rang,
And as he took the receiver a voice through it sang,
Hello! Is this you dear? I am glad you're so near,
I've just been told something awful I want you to hear,
The boys say you're a welcher, a piker at heart,
In a good honest bet you wouldn't take part;
That you hold your job because of your drags,
When you ought to be out with a sack gathering rags,
In a cobbler's shop you would surely shine,
Or a pulling the candy you could do just fine.
As for teaching machinists why let the thing pass,
Public opinion decides you're an incompetent Ass.[10]

Of course, the attitudes and values evident in O'Shea's poem can be found in American machine shops to this day. One consequence of the modern style of management is the sense of rivalry and mutual contempt which pervades the relations between production workers and engineers. Nevertheless, that animosity was especially explicit during the years around World War I, and it was also then that the struggle against the systematized management was most successful.

Historians have been somewhat misled on this score by Milton Nadworny's study, *Scientific Management and the Unions*.[11] Nadworny correctly argues that during the war years union officials increasingly came to reconcile their views with those of Taylor's followers. But what was happening on the shop floor was quite the opposite. The insatiable demand for labor gave workers a feeling of self-confidence, which produced among other things more strikes during 1917 and 1918 than any previous year in American history, in spite of the no-strike pledges of the unions. The records of the National War Labor Board and other agencies which attempted to cool down these disputes reveal that they often involved time studies, incentive pay, and work standardization. The quickest way workers could be convinced to return to the job was to get rid of these innovations.

Many struggles of the World War I epoch, however, involved more than just resistance to management's new techniques. As union strength grew and workers became more aware of their ability to manipulate government war agencies, workers began advancing their own plans for reorganization of work relations. These plans differed significantly from the familiar craft techniques of the late nineteenth century. Because the erosion of the position of skilled workers was clearly irreversible, workers had to come to grips with the *new* way in which factories operated. To be sure, some crafts in the building trades and many tool and die makers could simply demand standard craft rates and craft rules of the old form. But others, among whom scientific management had already wrought extensive changes, developed novel sets of demands and new forms of self-organization.

Consider the machinists, helpers, and tool makers at the vast Mesta Machine Company near Pittsburgh. They struck in 1917 and again in 1918 for the abolition of the time-study and premium pay schemes, the establishment of three or four standard wage rates, the eight-hour day, and recognition by the company of a shop committee to deal with all grievances from the plant. This pattern of demands was commonplace by the end of the war, and it deserves attention. First of all, a demand for standardization was arising in this instance not from the managers, but from the workers. The new payment plans had generated a proliferation of individual wage rates, and employers openly defended having "as many hourly rates as there are human beings"[12] in the factory as necessary for the efficient operation of the works. The workers realized that the old standard craft rate was now hopelessly obsolete, but they did try to create a determinate set of classifications to cover everyone, and one with a narrow spread between the highest and the lowest rates.

Second, strikers virtually everywhere demanded the standard work day of eight hours, and they enjoyed considerable success on this front. The struggle for a shorter work week made more headway between 1910 and 1920 than in any other decade of this century, despite adamant employer resistance. Third, new forms for organizing the collective power of workers were developed. Sometimes craft unions were coordinated through metal trades councils, and many unions opened their doors to unskilled workers, but virtually everywhere some form of shop committee or stewards' body assumed the task of directly representing the rank and file. Workers of this epoch were keenly aware that to speak of "workers' control" without effectively organizing workers' power is to drift into fantasy land.

Finally, as these struggles became more intense, they were increasingly often linked to far-reaching political demands. The munitions workers of Bridgeport, who had been seasoned by four years of chronic industrial battle by 1919, for example, held huge rallies to protest post-war layoffs. From these rallies they petitioned the president of the United States for the "creation of National Labor Agencies to assure in all industries a living wage and every right to union organization; collective bargaining and collective participation of the workers in control of industry;" a reduction of hours; "extensive necessary public works" to create jobs; and finally, the "abolition of competition, criminal waste and profiteering in industry and substituting co-operative ownership and democratic management of industry and the securing to each of the full product of his toil."[13]

This was the age of the Plumb Plan on the railroads, the miners' pamphlet *How to Run Coal*, and the convention of delegates from 30,000 striking miners in Illinois who voted to make as a condition of returning to work the collectivization of the mines. Themes of public ownership, workers' education, and political action played a constant counterpoint to shop floor demands between 1918 and 1922. Needless to say, the employers fought tooth and nail against all such proposals. Their mood was summed up by President Loyall A. Osborne of Westinghouse Electric, who wrote as a member of the National War Labor Board to its chairman, William Howard Taft, warning against concessions to labor and against "our Board being used as an instrument of propaganda by the labor unions." Said Osborne:

> It is quite natural that you should approach these questions in a different frame of mind than do we, for you have not for years, as we have been, fighting the battle for industrial independence. You have not had constantly before you as a part of your daily life evidences of bad faith, restriction of output, violence, disregard of obligations and irresponsibility that has ever been the characteristics of their organizations.[14]

Osborne's statement reflected the determined posture which his fellow employers assumed before the Board. Representatives of Bridgeport's manufacturers, for example, insisted on four principles in their personal relations: total and exclusive control over production by the employers; remuneration of each employee according to his or her individual merits; evaluation of those merits by the employer alone; and the resolution of all conflicts between employers and employees without "outside" interference, from unions or government.

By the end of the depression of 1920–1922 the resistance of unions to these pretensions of management had been decisively crushed in most basic industries. All that remained of the formerly overt struggle for workers' control were its faint echoes in the Baltimore and Ohio Plan and a few similar "workers' participation" schemes on one side, and the programs of small, isolated revolutionary parties on the other. Nevertheless, unorganized workers carried on the battle in covert forms. Among other things, the regulation of output which nineteenth-century craft unions had embodied in the stint did not disappear from American industrial life: it went underground. Instead of beng openly proclaimed as union "legislation," restriction took the form of secretive defiance by small groups of workers to management's authority. In a word, the stint had become sabotage.

Moreover, it became something of an obsession with workers, as is evidenced by a document liberated from the Chevrolet company's files during the Flint sit-down strike of 1937. This was a report of a spy on workers' conversations during the first shift. Surely one sign of management's scientific character was the fact that workers were now known by number, rarely by name. A few excerpts from this report suggest the tenor of the workers' discussion of output:

Employee 7556046 . . . in conversation, was heard to say that he had completed his production by 2:45 P.M., and that he loafed for forty-five minutes before he quit work at 3:30 P.M.

At lunch time [on the second shift] the majority of the men had completed from 68 to 70 camshafts and in checking the sheet, it was evident that the other men had the same number. The check-up was made after the final pick-up had been made by 556594 (Leon D. Witham, transferred 10-30-35). When one of the employees had ten completed shafts, and when 594 (Witham) took only two of them, he asked the reason, to which 7594 replied,

"You have turned in 62 and that's enough."

The other was heard to ask, "Why, what difference does it make as long as I only get 124 in the nine hours?" and 7594 answered, "Well, last night they picked the sheet up on me at supper time and if a man has 66 to 70 shafts turned in for the first half of the shift they will expect you to turn in the same amount for the second half so we leave the shafts until after supper, just in case somebody should check the sheet and find out what the men are really doing."

There was considerable discussion among the employees of the plant about production, which conversation started before work this morning and continued throughout the entire day. The discussion was interrupted by the foreman during the lunch period, but was resumed in another location in Plant 5. . . .[15]

This covert style of struggle from the 1920s and 1930s is still very much with us today, but the rapid spread of union contracts during the late 1930s brought some significant changes, and a new challenge to management. With union protection came both a resurgence of the audacity and self-confidence among workers that had been evident during the war years and an eagerness among the rank and file to settle old scores and to change the conditions under which they worked forthwith. Consequently both management and governmental agencies sought to limit the influence which the new unions would have over work relations and production processes and to develop machinery for dealing with grievances which would leave the initiative in production and personnel questions with management. The task was not an easy one, as employers' laments from the late 1930s about their "unmanageable" workers make clear. But the goals toward which sophisticated managers were striving were neatly summed up by Sumner Slichter in a study published by the Brookings Institution in 1941, *Union Policies and Industrial Management.*

Convinced that unionism had become too securely established in American industry to be uprooted once agian, Slichter set out to study in detail the practices and arrangements which affected the ability of workers and of managers to control what happened in their plants. He concluded that from management's vantage point, the ideal form of union would be industrial in form and bureaucratic in structure. Industrial unions were to be preferred to craft, because the latter not only generated chronic jurisdictional disputes, but were also wedded to the vested interests of particular groups of workers within the existing technology of the firm, and thus posed more formidable obstacles to change than a union whose constituency is diffused throughout the whole plant. On the other hand, he warned, an industrial union whose leadership shared the daily experiences of members on the shop floor and sought to solve problems where and when they arose could make a mockery of scientific management. Only officers with secure tenure and a secure contractual relationship with the firm could develop an understanding of management's needs and problems.

Industrial relations did not take the shape proposed by Slichter just because he said so, but they were reshaped in that direction by a lengthy process, which involved the thorough regulation of industrial disputes by "tripartite" bodies during World War II, business' postwar crusade for "management's prerogatives," and the Taft-Hartley Law. That act of 1947 virtually outlawed any union activity other than bargaining over wages and conditions with their members' immediate employers and made unions liable for damages in case of strikes in violation of contacts. As early as the 1950s it was evident that the widespread incorporation of management's rights clauses into union contracts and the increasing rigidity of grievance procedures meant that conflicts over the pace or arrangement of work had reverted to the subterranean, sabotage forms of preunion days. Strikes about such questions were more often than not unofficial, and in this connection court decisions restricting such strikes on the basis of the Taft-Hartley Act have become increasingly important. In 1975 the district Federal court covering western Pennsylvania ruled in the Eazor Trucking Company case that any union was liable to damage suits in case of a wildcat strike by its members if the union did not do everything in its power to get the members back to work.[16]

Moreover, what contractual defenses of workers' control over work relations unions have maintained—largely through "past practices" clauses and through the defense of members against disciplinary sanctions—find themselves today under vigorous attack from management's side at the bargaining table. "Take-back" bargaining is the current vogue in management strategy, and its advocates make no bones about the fact that their primary objective is the elimination of whatever obstacles remain in union contracts to their authority over the workplace. "We pay good money," they argue, "and we want output in return."

Of all workers' control issues, the one which has assumed special prominence in our own times is that of preventing plant closings. Here the problem is not how the job is performed, but whether there will be a job at all. Since the workers of American Safety Razor sat down in its Brooklyn plant in 1954, American workers have often declared that they have a right to a voice in corporate decisions about where work is to be carried on. Most such struggles since that time have employed political strategies: the workers have mobilized their communities to demand that their Congressional representatives or the Department of Defense force the company to continue operating at the old site. A few have used the pressure of strikes and boycotts. In every case the objective has been to force management to bargain over what it always claimed as its exclusive and ultimate authority under "free enterprise," to decide what it wanted to produce where.

In some recent instances workers have sought ways to reopen a plant which has been abandoned by a multiplant corporation under their own management, or some sort of community ownership. For example, when Youngstown Sheet and Tube announced that it would close its Campbell Works, local union members enlisted the aid of a ministers' council to promote a movement for acquisition of the plant by the community. The implications of this effort are profound. As the project's economic consultant, Gar Alperowitz, has made clear, community ownership of the mill cannot succeed without new governmental purchasing policies for steel wares that are directed primarily at the needs of urban America, in mass transit, housing development, et cetera. In other words, if a community-operated plant with any degree of workers' control is going to function, it must have its output determined by the nation's need for use values—by the real and sorely neglected needs of the American people—not by the rule of maximum profitability in the marketplace.[17]

The Youngstown idea has not been carried to fruition, but it has caught on elsewhere. In Buffalo, when the Heat Transfer Division of American Standard threatened to close down, the Buffalo AFL-CIO Council voted to take over the plant, if necessary, and operate it under union direction. Several plants in Jamestown and Dunkirk, New York, have already been kept alive by their workers' assuming ownership.

This is the setting of the most important discussions of workers' control today. And outstanding example of what is now possible has been provided by the birth and survival of Wisconsin's worker-controlled newspaper, the Madison *Press Connection*. Its origins lie in a long strike of the employees of Madison's major newspapers, provoked when their owners undertook to cripple or destroy their craft unions. Having gone out on strike and realizing that all the skills needed to put out a newspaper were to be found among the people walking the picket line, these workers decided to start their own newspaper as a rival to their scab-operated former employers. The *Press Connection* soon developed a network of readers such as few papers could boast, because in order to get subscriptions and operating funds, newspaper workers had to solicit support from union and farmers' organizations all over Wisconsin. As they did so, the people with whom they talked told them that they thought of and wanted from the newspaper. Responding to readers' suggestions and criticisms (that is, creating something useful for the people of Wisconsin) became essential to the survival of the paper.

Moreover, on my own first visit to the *Press Connection*'s offices and composing room, I saw a workplace that looked more businesslike—in the true sense of the term—than anything I had seen before in my life. Each department had been physically designed by the people who worked in it, to make their work as efficient, easy, and accurate as they could make it, while it was also equipped with the flowers, pictures, et cetera necessary to make the setting congenial. These journalists, bookkeepers, layout artists and printers were not socializing: they were putting out a newspaper of value to the local residents. And they were running it by their own collective decisions. (See Chapter 20.)

A group of these workers told me that they had gone to a seminar held by industrial relations experts on the question of workers' participation in management. They had listened to all the projects and experiments described there, saying nothing until close to the end of the day, when one of them put up his hand. He said: "I'm sorry. We can't quite relate to this discussion. You see, we found in the *Press Connection* that we don't need management's participation."

The control struggles which involve nothing but the immediate participation of those involved are those which emerge out of small groups of workers in direct relationship with each other. An example is the decision of cam shaft turners among themselves as to how many shafts they will produce. Nobody from outside the group is needed for that sort of control—though we must remember that the parameters within which workers make such a decision are decisively fixed by the boss.

When we think in terms of operating a plant, however, two aspects of the question must be clearly confronted. First, it is not possible to build a fully participatory management within the existing economic framework. One cannot make socialism in one factory. Even if The People's Campbell Works was opened in Youngstown, it would still be enmeshed in an economy governed by market rules and oriented in financial and sales practices, as well as in known management techniques, toward the logic or profit. Those who are thinking of producing use values under collective direction within that system are facing an uphill battle every day.

The significance of that uphill battle depends on other developments connected with it, and this is where the political side of the struggle comes in. One factory by itself will sink or—if it survives—will not be self-managed very long. In Jamestown, New York, where six factories boast their "self-management," I found that three of them were impossible to distinguish from any other factory, except that the managerial group may have included as many as a dozen members.

The second point follows from the first. What matters is the connection we make (in thought and deed) between struggles to change work relations and struggles to change the purpose for which we work. In recent years our fascination with the challenge of participatory democracy to hierarchy and bureaucracy has sometimes obscured the related, and more fundamental, challenge of popular economic needs to production for profit. A movement which aims to link collectively directed production to collectively determined economic needs cannot be confined to the workplace alone.

Will we then end up with nothing but another ruling bureaucracy? The crucial point is not to pose this question in either-or terms. Our thinking on this matter may be helped by the study, recently published by Andrew Zimbalist and Juan Espinoza, of 420 publicly operated factories in Chile during the Popular Unity government. They found that the actual level of participation of workers in plant management varied greatly from one factory to another. Where the plant had been nationalized by government decree and a governing structure introduced from the outside, the workers assumed actual collective direction very slowly, if they did so at all. On the other hand, where the plant had a long history of organized struggle and the workers themselves were active in its nationalization, their level of involvement was impressive. Their official representatives in those instances reflected an active base among the rank and file, which made "self-management" a living reality—in determining the product line, as well as in work relations. In other words, the dynamics of real political struggle do not allow us to treat action "from below" and "from above" as mutually exclusive.

There are two important differences between the early kind of worker control and today's experiments in worker participation and worker management. First, the struggle for workers' control in the nineteenth century began with the production process—or rather, with discrete elements of the production process. Molders, for example, collectively regulated the technique and the relations among themselves and between themselves and their helpers in the foundries of many different enterprises. At the high point of their craft struggle, they fought for a single set of rules regulating molding in many competing enterprises at once. But those molders did not contest their owners' ownership and direction of the enterprise as a whole. Even when they were socialists, they envisaged the transfer of the industry to their complete control as an ultimate objective, not as the immediate goal of direct action. Like the legendary British machinist, they drew a chalk line around "their" territory within the boss's factory, and they demanded that the boss deal with them from the other side of that line.

Today's struggles around plant closings begin with the front office, rather than with the foundry or some other segment of the production process. They aim first and foremost at financial control of the enterprise, to keep it in business. Although some accounts from plywood or asbestos firms indicate that the advent of workers' self-management made personal relations between workers and supervisors less authoritarian and more relaxed, very seldom has the basic pattern of decision-making and supervision inherited from private ownership been quickly and drastically modified. The John Brown Shipyard, occupied by its workers, the Madison *Press Connection*, set up by strikers, and the British and Irish Steam Packet Company of Dublin, where an imaginative works council "advised" the new managers after nationalization so effectively as actually to take command, are three instances in which control of the shop floor and control of the front office were inseparably connected. Nevertheless, the different starting points of the two forms of struggle are crucial. The primary objective of struggles against plant closings is to keep a job, not to change it.

The second difference is closely related to the first. The point of departure for workers' control struggles in the nineteenth century was the superior knowledge of production processes possessed by some workers. Today's struggles begin with the scientifically managed factory. That means that battles against plant closings, or against take-back bargaining, must embrace much, or even all, of the plant's workforce. They must also devise new styles of organization, just as their predecessors in the epoch of World War I had to do. Today the problem is to cross the lines of the "bargaining units" defined by the NLRB, so as to mobilize technical and clerical employees (and possibly even portions of the local management facing conglomerate owners), along with the production workers. Also like their predecessors of sixty years ago, they must undertake, through self-education, to learn the whole business, so as to overcome the gulf between mental and manual labor, which scientific management has spawned.

But finally, there is an important similarity between the earlier and the present struggles. Craftsmen battling for control of their trades were keenly aware, as I have pointed out, that to formulate and enforce their own rules meant to repudiate and do battle with the ethic of acquisitive individualism. The more far-sighted workers of that epoch also knew that to achieve workers' control meant to uproot the jungle of capitalism itself, along with its ethical code. It is equally evident today that corporations milk branch-plants dry and abandon them, heap "take-back" demands on the bargaining table in the name of productivity, and—ironically—even experiment with "job enrichment" schemes, not to create more of the goods people need, but to maximize their cash flow and their accumulation of still more capital. The struggles of workers and of communities for control over their own destinies in this setting becomes a battle to change the rules of the economic game itself.

NOTES

1. Carter L. Goodrich, *The Miner's Freedom: A Study of the Working Life in a Changing Industry* (Boston, 1925), pp. 5–6.

2. *By-Laws of the Window Glass Workers, L.A. 300, Knights of Labor* (Pittsburgh, 1899), pp. 26–36.

3. *John Swinton's Paper*, March 23, 1884.

4. Horace L. Arnold and Fay L. Faurote, *Ford Methods and Ford Shops* (New York, 1919), p. 42.

5. Ibid., pp. 45–46.

6. F.W. Taylor, "Testimony Before the Special House Committee," in *Scientific Management, Comprising Shop Management, Principles of Scientific Management, Testimony Before the Special House Committee* (New York, 1947), p. 49.

7. U.S. Congress, *Hearings before the Special Committee of the House of Representatives to Investigate the Taylor and Other Systems of Shop Management* (Washington, D.C., 1912), p. 1000.

8. For discussion, of these incidents, see D. Montgomery, "Quel Standards? Les Ouvriers et la Reorganisation de la Production aux Etats Unis, 1900–1920" *Le Mouvement Social*, 102 (Jan.-March 1978), pp. 101–127.

9. U.S. Commission on Industrial Relations, *Final Report and Testimony* (Washington, D.C., 1916), vol. 1, p. 889.

10. *Machinists' Monthly Journal* 20 (July 1908): 609.

11. Milton J. Nadworny, *Scientific Management and the Unions, 1900–1932* (Cambridge, Mass., 1955).

12. Attorney for the Bridgeport manufacturers, quoted in Alexander M. Bing, *War-Time Strikes and Their Adjustment* (New York, 1921), p. 200 n.

13. "Petition for the Creation of National Labor Agencies," National War Labor Board, Case File 132, Box 22, R.G. 2, National Archives.

14. Loyall A. Osborne to William H. Taft, May 31, 1918, in Records of the National War Labor Board, E 15 Administrative Files, R.G. 2, National Archives.

15. F. F. Corcoran to M.K. Hovey, "Suggestions and Information," Henry Kraus Papers, Box 9, Archives of Labor History and Urban Affairs, Wayne State University. I am grateful to Steven Sapolsky for bringing this document to my attention.

16. Editor's note: As this article was going to press, the courts seemed to have overruled the Eazor case, declaring in *Carbon Fuel Co.* v. *UMW* (1979) that unions were not "vicariously liable" for the independent actions of wildcat strikers.

17. Editor's note: See Staughton Lynd, *The Fight Against Shutdowns* (San Pedro, 1982).

Contributors

ERNEST ALLEN, JR. was an active member of the League of Revolutionary Black Workers. He is now acting Chairman of the W. E. B. Du Bois Department of Afro-American Studies, University of Massachusetts, Amherst.

ALLIANCE AGAINST SEXUAL COERCION based in Cambridge, Massachusetts, was founded by three women active in the movement against rape. It then began working against sexual harassment at work in the ways described in this article. The principle authors of that essay were AASC members, Freada Klein, Lynn Rubinett, Denise Wells, and Nancy Wilber with help from Alice Friedman. The Alliance address is P.O. Box 1, Cambridge, MA. 02139.

HAROLD M. BARON is currently working full time to complete two books on racism under advanced capitalism. He has served as the Director of the Research Department for the Chicago Urban League and on the staff of the Associated Colleges of the Midwest. His article on "The Demand for Black Labor" was reprinted as a pamphlet and went through numerous printings.

SUSAN PORTER BENSON teaches women's history at Bristol Community College in Fall River, Massachusetts. She has worked for the New England Joint Board of the Amalgamated Clothing and Textile Workers

Union as a labor educator and has completed a dissertation at Boston University on women department store workers. And she was the co-editor of the *Radical History Review* issue on public history.

PAUL BUHLE founded *Radical America* in 1967 and served as an editor until 1973. He is now an associate editor. He also edited the journal *Cultural Correspondence*, and has written widely on the history of radicalism and popular culture. He lives in Providence and is Director of the Oral History of the American Left project at Tamiment Institute in New York.

MARY BULARZIK is a historian and the author of a Ph.D. dissertation at Brandeis University entitled "Sex, Crime and Justice: Women in the Criminal Justice System of Massachusetts, 1900–1950." She works with the Alliance Against Sexual Coercion.

MIKE DAVIS was active in the Students for a Democratic Society and in a rank-and-file Teamsters group in Los Angeles. He lives in London and is an editor of *New Left Review*.

ROSLYN L. FELDBERG teaches sociology and womens' studies at Boston University. She has written several articles on clerical work and is currently co-authoring a book on clerical work, the family work connection, and the class consciousness of women clerical workers.

DOROTHY FENNELL wrote a dissertation at the University of Pittsburgh on the crowd in the Whiskey Rebellion and worked in the factory she writes about here. She has also taught labor history to prisoners enrolled in B.A. programs at Beacon College and Boston University and is now on the staff of the American Working Class History Project in New York.

MARY FREDERICKSON teaches history at the University of Alabama, Birmingham. She was Assistant Director, the Southern Oral History Program at the University of North Carolina, Chapel Hill, where she completed her dissertation on the Southern Summer School for Women Workers. She has co-edited the collection on *Workers' Education for Women*.

JAMES GREEN has been a *Radical America* editor since 1972. He now teaches history and directs the Labor Studies Program at University of Massachusetts, Boston. He is a founding member of the Massachusetts History Workshop and the Massachusetts Labor History Society. He is also co-author of *Boston's Workers: A Labor History* and author of *Grass-Roots Socialism: Radical Movements in the Southwest, 1895–1943* and *The World of the Worker: Labor in Twentieth Century America*.

NELSON LICHTENSTEIN teaches history at the Catholic University of America. He is the author of *Labor's War at Home: The C.I.O. in World War II* and is now writing a social history of work at Ford's River Rouge complex.

Contributors

JOHN LIPPERT has worked as an assembler in Detroit auto factories since 1973, including the General Motors Fleetwood and Willow Run plants. He has written about labor for various publications including the *New York Times, Der Speigel*, and the *Detroit Free Press*.

STAUGHTON LYND is an associate editor of *Radical America* who was active in the civil-rights and anti-war movements in the 1960s. He is the author of several historical studies including *The Intellectual Origins of American Radicalism* and is co-editor with Alice Lynd of *Rank and File: Personal Histories by Working-Class Organizers*. He practiced labor law in a Youngstown, Ohio, firm until he was fired for the publication of his booklet *Labor Law for the Rank and File*. He now works for Northeast Ohio Legal Services. He was been active in the movement against plant shutdowns in Youngstown and Pittsburgh and is the author of *The Fight Against Shutdowns* (Singlejack Books, Box 1906, San Pedro, CA., 90733, $9.95).

MANNING MARABLE teaches history and political economy at Fisk University and is Director of the Race Relations Institute in Nashville. He is the author of *From the Grassroots* and writes a regular political column by that title that appears in 28 black and/or socialist newspapers.

DAVID MONTGOMERY worked as a machinist and a union activist before he became a historian. He is the author of *Beyond Equality: Labor and the Radical Republicans, 1862–1872* and *Workers' Control in America*. He now teaches history at Yale University and edits the journal *International Labor and Working Class History*.

GEORGE RAWICK is a historian who lives and works in St. Louis. He is the author of *From Sundown to Sunup: The Making of the Black Community* and editor of the 19-volume collection of Works Progress Administration interviews with former slaves, *The American-Slave: A Composite Autobiography*.

ROY ROSENZWEIG teaches history and directs the oral history program at George Mason University. He is the author of *"Eight Hours for What We Will": Workers and Leisure in an Industrial City, 1870–1920*. He is also an editor of the *Radical History Review*.

ANDREW ROWLAND is an occupational health educator and researcher who has been active in the occupational health movement in California and Pennsylvania. He is currently a member of the health technical committee for PHILAPOSH, a coalition of professionals and unionists fighting for better occupational health conditions in the Philadelphia area. He has written an annotated bibliography on occupational disease among black workers and co-authored a chapter on that subject for a forthcoming occupational health text book.

Contributors

DAVE WAGNER was an editor and is now an associate editor of *Radical America*. As a reporter for the Madison, Wisconsin, *Capital Times* he was an active member of the Newspaper Guild. During the strike he describes here Dave became the production coordinator for the worker-controlled strike newspaper, the *Madison Press Connection*. He was also elected to the Board of Directors.

STAN WEIR is a co-founder, with Robert Miles, of Singlejack Books in San Pedro, California, which publishes books about work by workers and how-to books for a labor-force audience. He is also an associate editor of *Radical America*. During the first 23 years of his worklife he was a merchant seaman, auto worker, truckdriver, longshoreman, and union organizer. He was fired from his job on the San Francisco waterfront along with 81 others in 1963. Since that time, in addition to publishing, he has been teaching grievance and collective bargaining skills to practicing unionists.